COMPUTER
BOOK SERIES
FROM IDG

The Internet For Dummies® Starter Kit™ Edition

Cheat Sheet

S0-BAK-336

Fill in Your Important Internet Information Here

Your e-mail address:

_____

@_____

Your Internet provider's data phone number (the number your software dials):

_____

Your Internet provider's technical-support phone number (if you want to talk to a human being):

_____

Your Internet provider's technical-support department's e-mail address:

_____

For SLIP and PPP accounts:

Your Internet hostname (you may not have one assigned):

_____

Your IP address (you may not have one assigned):

_____._____._____._____

Your Internet provider's DNS (domain name server):

_____._____._____._____

Your Internet provider's mail gateway (for outgoing mail):

_____

Your Internet provider's POP mail server (for incoming mail):

_____

Your Internet provider's news server (for Usenet newsgroups):

_____

Hostname Zones

(Three-letter last word of Internet hostnames; for two-letter country codes, go to http://net.dummies.net/countries.)

com	Company or individual
edu	Educational institution
gov	Government
mil	Military
net	Network organization
int	International organization
org	Nonprofit or other noncommercial organization

Acronyms to Know

BTW	By the way
RTFM	Read the manual
IMHO	In my humble opinion
ROFL	Rolling on floor, laughing
TIA	Thanks in advance
YMMV	Your mileage may vary

IDG
BOOKS
WORLDWIDE

...For Dummies: #1 Computer Book Series for Beginners

The Internet For Dummies® Starter Kit™ Edition

Cheat Sheet

E-Mail Addresses

To Send To	With This Address	Type This:
AOL	SteveCase	stevecase@aol.com
AT&T Mail	agbell	agbell@attmail.com
AT&T WorldNet	TedVail	tedvail@worldnet.att.net
BITNET	*user@node*	*user@node*.bitnet or *user%node*.bitnet @cunyvm.cuny.edu
CompuServe	77777,7777	77777.7777@compuserve.com
Delphi	jsmith	jsmith@delphi.com
Easylink	1234567	1234567@eln.attmail.com
FIDONET	MarySmith 1:2/3.4	mary.smith@p4.f3.n2.z1.fidonet.org
GEnie	J.SMITH7	J.SMITH7@genie.geis.com
MCI Mail	555-2468	5552468@mcimail.com
MSN	BillGates	billgates@msn.com
Prodigy Classic	ABCD123A	abcd123a@prodigy.com

Useful Web Pages

http://www.yahoo.com/	Yahoo! index to the Web
http://www.infoseek.com	
http://www.stroud.com/	Stroud's Consummate Winsock Applications
http://www.unitedmedia. com/comics/dilbert	Dilbert
http://att.net/dir800	AT&T 800-number directory
http://www.usps.gov/ncsc	U.S. Postal Service ZIP codes
http://www.scout.cs.wisc. edu/scout/report	InterNIC Scout Report
http://net.dummies.net	Updates to this book
http://www.four11.com	Four11 phone and e-mail directory
http://www.altavista. digital.com/	AltaVista Web search page
http://www.us.imdb.com/	Internet Movie Database

Usenet News Hierarchies

alt	Alternative newsgroups
comp	Computer-related topics
misc	Miscellaneous topics
news	Usenet-related topics
rec	Recreational topics
sci	Scientific topics
soc	Social and societal topics
talk	Discussions and arguments

Types of URLs

file://*pathname*	File stored on local computer
ftp://*hostname*/*pathname*	File on FTP server
http://*hostname*/*pathname*	World Wide Web page
gopher://*hostname*/*pathname*	Gopher menu
mailto:*address*	E-mail
telnet:*hostname*	Telnet to log in to system

. . .For Dummies: #1 Computer Book Series for Beginners

COMPUTER BOOK SERIES FROM IDG

References for the Rest of Us!®

Are you intimidated and confused by computers? Do you find that traditional manuals are overloaded with technical details you'll never use? Do your friends and family always call you to fix simple problems on their PCs? Then the *...For Dummies*® computer book series from IDG Books Worldwide is for you.

...For Dummies books are written for those frustrated computer users who know they aren't really dumb but find that PC hardware, software, and indeed the unique vocabulary of computing make them feel helpless. *...For Dummies* books use a lighthearted approach, a down-to-earth style, and even cartoons and humorous icons to diffuse computer novices' fears and build their confidence. Lighthearted but not lightweight, these books are a perfect survival guide for anyone forced to use a computer.

> *"I like my copy so much I told friends; now they bought copies."*
>
> **Irene C., Orwell, Ohio**

> *"Quick, concise, nontechnical, and humorous."*
>
> **Jay A., Elburn, Illinois**

> *"Thanks, I needed this book. Now I can sleep at night."*
>
> **Robin F., British Columbia, Canada**

Already, hundreds of thousands of satisfied readers agree. They have made *...For Dummies* books the #1 introductory level computer book series and have written asking for more. So, if you're looking for the most fun and easy way to learn about computers, look to *...For Dummies* books to give you a helping hand.

IDG BOOKS WORLDWIDE

7/96r

THE INTERNET FOR DUMMIES®

STARTER KIT EDITION

by John R. Levine, Carol Baroudi,
Margaret Levine Young, and Hy Bender

Foreword by Paul McCloskey,
Executive Editor, *Federal Computer Week*

IDG Books Worldwide, Inc.
An International Data Group Company

Foster City, CA ♦ Chicago, IL ♦ Indianapolis, IN ♦ Southlake, TX

The Internet For Dummies®, Starter Kit Edition

Published by
IDG Books Worldwide, Inc.
An International Data Group Company
919 E. Hillsdale Blvd.
Suite 400
Foster City, CA 94404
http://www.idgbooks.com (IDG Books World Wide Web site)
http://www.dummies.com (Dummies Press Web site)

Library of Congress Catalog Card No.: 96-80290

ISBN: 0-7645-0107-0

Printed in the United States of America

10 9 8 7 6 5 4 3 2 1

4E/SV/QS/ZX/IN

Distributed in the United States by IDG Books Worldwide, Inc.

Distributed by Macmillan Canada for Canada; by Transworld Publishers Limited in the United Kingdom and Europe; by WoodsLane Pty. Ltd. for Australia; by WoodsLane Enterprises Ltd. for New Zealand; by Longman Singapore Publishers Ltd. for Singapore, Malaysia, Thailand, and Indonesia; by Simron Pty. Ltd. for South Africa; by Toppan Company Ltd. for Japan; by Distribuidora Cuspide for Argentina; by Livraria Cultura for Brazil; by Ediciencia S.A. for Ecuador; by Addison-Wesley Publishing Company for Korea; by Ediciones ZETA S.C.R. Ltda. for Peru; by WS Computer Publishing Company, Inc., for the Philippines; by Unalis Corporation for Taiwan; by Contemporanea de Ediciones for Venezuela. Authorized Sales Agent: Anthony Rudkin Associates for the Middle East and North Africa.

For general information on IDG Books Worldwide's books in the U.S., please call our Consumer Customer Service department at 800-762-2974. For reseller information, including discounts and premium sales, please call our Reseller Customer Service department at 800-434-3422.

For information on where to purchase IDG Books Worldwide's books outside the U.S., please contact our International Sales department at 415-655-3023 or fax 415-655-3299.

For information on foreign language translations, please contact our Foreign & Subsidiary Rights department at 415-655-3021 or fax 415-655-3281.

For sales inquiries and special prices for bulk quantities, please contact our Sales department at 415-655-3200 or write to the address above.

For information on using IDG Books Worldwide's books in the classroom or for ordering examination copies, please contact our Educational Sales department at 800-434-2086 or fax 817-251-8174.

For press review copies, author interviews, or other publicity information, please contact our Public Relations department at 415-655-3000 or fax 415-655-3299.

For authorization to photocopy items for corporate, personal, or educational use, please contact Copyright Clearance Center, 222 Rosewood Drive, Danvers, MA 01923, or fax 508-750-4470.

is a trademark under exclusive license to IDG Books Worldwide, Inc., from International Data Group, Inc.

About the Authors

John R. Levine was a member of a computer club in high school — before high school students, or even high schools, had computers, where he met Theodor H. Nelson, the author of *Computer Lib/Dream Machines* and the inventor of hypertext, who reminded us that computers should not be taken seriously and that everyone can and should understand and use computers.

John wrote his first program in 1967 on an IBM 1130 (a computer roughly as powerful as your typical modern digital wristwatch, only more difficult to use). He became an official system administrator of a networked computer at Yale in 1975. He began working part-time, for a computer company, of course, in 1977 and has been in and out of the computer and network biz ever since. He got his company on to Usenet (see Chapter 11) early enough that it appears in a 1982 *Byte* magazine article in a map of Usenet, which then was so small that the map fit on half a page.

He used to spend most of his time writing software, but now he mostly writes books (including *UNIX For Dummies* and *Internet Secrets,* both published by IDG Books Worldwide, Inc.) because it's more fun and he can do so at home in the tiny village of Trumansburg, New York, and play with his baby daughter when he's supposed to be writing. He also co-hosts a weekly radio call-in show on the Internet (visit `http://iecc.com/radio` for local times) and does a fair amount of public speaking. (To see where, see his home page, at `http://iecc.com/johnl`.) He holds a B.A. and a Ph.D. in computer science from Yale University, but please don't hold that against him.

Carol Baroudi first began playing with computers in 1971 at Colgate University, where two things were new: the PDP-10 and women. She was lucky to have unlimited access to the state-of-the-art PDP-10, on which she learned to program, operate the machine, and talk to Eliza. She taught Algol and helped to design the curricula for computer science and women's studies. She majored in Spanish and studied French, which, thanks to the Internet, she can now use every day.

In 1975 Carol took a job doing compiler support and development, a perfect use for her background in languages. For six years she developed software and managed software development. For a while she had a small business doing high-tech recruiting (she was a headhunter). Though she wrote her first software manuals in 1975, her *job* since 1984 has been writing. Carol has described all kinds of software, from the memory-management system of the Wang VS operating system to e-mail products for the PC and Mac. For the past several years, she has been writing books for ordinary people who want to use computers. She enjoys speaking to academic, business, and general audiences about the impact of technology on society and other related topics.

The mother of a fantastic six-year-old, Carol loves acting and singing and will fly to France on any excuse. She believes that we are living in a very interesting time when technology is changing faster than people can imagine. Carol hopes that as we learn to use the new technologies, we don't lose sight of our humanity and feels that that computers can be useful and fun but are no substitute for real life.

Unlike her peers in that 40-something bracket, **Margaret Levine Young** (`www.gurus.com/margy`) was exposed to computers at an early age. In high school, she got into a computer club known as the R.E.S.I.S.T.O.R.S., a group of kids who spent Saturdays in a barn fooling around with three antiquated computers. She stayed in the field throughout college against her better judgment and despite her brother John's presence as a graduate student in the computer science department. Margy graduated from Yale and went on to become one of the first microcomputer managers in the early 1980s at Columbia Pictures, where she rode the elevator with big stars whose names she wouldn't dream of dropping here.

Since then Margy has co-authored more than 16 computer books on the topics of the Internet, UNIX, WordPerfect, Microsoft Access, and (stab from the past) PC-File and Javelin, including *Dummies 101: The Internet for Windows 95, Dummies 101: Netscape Navigator, Internet FAQs: Answers to Frequently Asked Questions, UNIX For Dummies,* and *WordPerfect 7 For Windows 95 For Dummies* (all published by IDG Books Worldwide, Inc.). She met her future husband, Jordan, in the R.E.S.I.S.T.O.R.S., and her other passion is her children, Meg and Zac. She loves gardening, chickens, reading, and anything to do with eating and lives near Middlebury, Vermont.

Hy Bender has written humor articles for such fun publications as *Mad* magazine, *Spy, American Film,* and *Advertising Age.* He has also written dozens of classroom software-training manuals and computer video-training scripts and eight books to-date, including the critically acclaimed *Essential Software for Writers* and *PC Tools: The Complete Reference.* For IDG Books Worldwide, Inc., Hy and Margaret Levine Young have co-written *Dummies 101: The Internet for Windows 95, Dummies 101: Netscape Navigator,* and the upcoming *Dummies 101: Netscape Communicator.* In his spare time, Hy runs a New York reading group for writers, works on drafts of a novel and a screenplay, and pursues way too many interests for his own good.

Dedication

John dedicates his part of the book (the pages with the particularly dumb jokes) to Sarah Willow, who doesn't sleep, and to Tonia, who stays up with her, showing the dedication only a mother could have.

Carol dedicates her part of the book to Joshua, with all her love, to her friends, who remind her that there's more to life than writing books, and to Coleman Barks, whose translations of the great poet Jeladdin Rumi inspire, enliven, and ignite.

Margy dedicates this book to Jordan, Meg, and Zac, who make life worth living.

Hy dedicates this book, with love, to Tracey M. Siesser and Morris Bender.

Author's Acknowledgments

Many of the tables in *The Internet For Dummies,* Starter Kit Edition, were adapted from material provided *gratis* by people on the Internet. Many thanks to the Internet community for its support.

All four authors particularly thank our editors at IDG Books Worldwide, Inc., Rebecca Whitney and Diane Steele, for believing us when we said that we were finishing this revision, despite all evidence to the contrary. We also want to thank all the folks listed on the Publisher's Acknowledgments page for their hard work in making this book happen.

Margy would like to thank Jordan, as ever, for his support while I did this revision, and Meg and Zac for being such extraordinary people. She would also like to thank her cousins Susan, Jim, and Don Arnold, for providing housing with such a superb view.

Thanks also to Anne Bonnet, Sarah W.'s sitter, for summarizing the reader comment cards.

The entire contents of this book were submitted by the authors to the publisher over the Internet. Edited chapters were returned for review the same way. We thank EPIX (Trumansburg, New York), Centnet (Cambridge, Mass.), LightLink (Ithaca, New York), and SoVerNet (Bellows Falls, Vermont), our Internet providers.

ABOUT IDG BOOKS WORLDWIDE

Welcome to the world of IDG Books Worldwide.

IDG Books Worldwide, Inc., is a subsidiary of International Data Group, the world's largest publisher of computer-related information and the leading global provider of information services on information technology. IDG was founded more than 25 years ago and now employs more than 8,500 people worldwide. IDG publishes more than 275 computer publications in over 75 countries (see listing below). More than 60 million people read one or more IDG publications each month.

Launched in 1990, IDG Books Worldwide is today the #1 publisher of best-selling computer books in the United States. We are proud to have received eight awards from the Computer Press Association in recognition of editorial excellence and three from *Computer Currents'* First Annual Readers' Choice Awards. Our best-selling *...For Dummies*® series has more than 30 million copies in print with translations in 30 languages. IDG Books Worldwide, through a joint venture with IDG's Hi-Tech Beijing, became the first U.S. publisher to publish a computer book in the People's Republic of China. In record time, IDG Books Worldwide has become the first choice for millions of readers around the world who want to learn how to better manage their businesses.

Our mission is simple: Every one of our books is designed to bring extra value and skill-building instructions to the reader. Our books are written by experts who understand and care about our readers. The knowledge base of our editorial staff comes from years of experience in publishing, education, and journalism — experience we use to produce books for the '90s. In short, we care about books, so we attract the best people. We devote special attention to details such as audience, interior design, use of icons, and illustrations. And because we use an efficient process of authoring, editing, and desktop publishing our books electronically, we can spend more time ensuring superior content and spend less time on the technicalities of making books.

You can count on our commitment to deliver high-quality books at competitive prices on topics you want to read about. At IDG Books Worldwide, we continue in the IDG tradition of delivering quality for more than 25 years. You'll find no better book on a subject than one from IDG Books Worldwide.

John J. Kilcullen

John Kilcullen
CEO
IDG Books Worldwide, Inc.

*Eighth Annual
Computer Press
Awards ≥1992*

*Ninth Annual
Computer Press
Awards ≥1993*

*Tenth Annual
Computer Press
Awards ≥1994*

*Eleventh Annual
Computer Press
Awards ≥1995*

IDG Books Worldwide, Inc., is a subsidiary of International Data Group, the world's largest publisher of computer-related information and the leading global provider of information services on information technology. International Data Group publishes over 275 computer publications in over 75 countries. Sixty million people read one or more International Data Group's publications each month. International Data Group's publications include: **ARGENTINA:** Buyer's Guide, Computerworld Argentina, PC World Argentina; **AUSTRALIA:** Australian Macworld, Australian PC World, Australian Reseller News, Computerworld, IT Casebook, Network World, Publish, Webmaster; **AUSTRIA:** Computerwelt Osterreich, Networks Austria, PC Tip Austria; **BANGLADESH:** PC World Bangladesh; **BELARUS:** PC World Belarus; **BELGIUM:** Data News; **BRAZIL:** Annuario de Informática, Computerworld, Connections, Macworld, PC Player, PC World, Publish, Reseller News, Supergamepower; **BULGARIA:** Computerworld Bulgaria, Network World Bulgaria, PC & MacWorld Bulgaria; **CANADA:** CIO Canada, Client/Server World, ComputerWorld Canada, InfoWorld Canada, NetworkWorld Canada, WebWorld; **CHILE:** Computerworld Chile, PC World Chile; **COLOMBIA:** Computerworld Colombia, PC World Colombia; **COSTA RICA:** PC World Centro America; **THE CZECH AND SLOVAK REPUBLICS:** Computerworld Czechoslovakia, Macworld Czech Republic, PC World Czechoslovakia; **DENMARK:** Communications World Danmark, Computerworld Danmark, Macworld Danmark, PC World Danmark, Techworld Danmark; **DOMINICAN REPUBLIC:** PC World Republica Dominicana; **ECUADOR:** PC World Ecuador; **EGYPT:** Computerworld Middle East, PC World Middle East; **EL SALVADOR:** PC World Centro America; **FINLAND:** MikroPC, Tietoverkko, Tietoviikko; **FRANCE:** Distributique, Hebdo, Info PC, Le Monde Informatique, Macworld, Reseaux & Telecoms, WebMaster France; **GERMANY:** Computer Partner, Computerwoche, Computerwoche Extra, Computerwoche FOCUS, Global Online, Macwelt, PC Welt; **GREECE:** Amiga Computing, GamePro Greece, Multimedia World; **GUATEMALA:** PC World Centro America; **HONDURAS:** PC World Centro America; **HONG KONG:** Computerworld Hong Kong, PC World Hong Kong, Publish in Asia; **HUNGARY:** ABCD CD-ROM, Computerworld Szamitastechnika, Internetto online Magazine, PC World Hungary, PC-X Magazin Hungary; **ICELAND:** Tolvuheimur PC World Island; **INDIA:** Information Communications World, Information Systems Computerworld, PC World India, Publish in Asia; **INDONESIA:** InfoKomputer PC World, Komputek Computerworld, Publish in Asia; **IRELAND:** ComputerScope, PC Live!; **ISRAEL:** Macworld Israel, People & Computers/Computerworld; **ITALY:** Computerworld Italia, Macworld Italia, Networking Italia, PC World Italia; **JAPAN:** DTP World, Macworld Japan, Nikkei Personal Computing, OS/2 World Japan, SunWorld Japan, Windows NT World, Windows World Japan; **KENYA:** PC World East African; **KOREA:** Hi-Tech Information, Macworld Korea, PC World Korea; **MACEDONIA:** PC World Macedonia; **MALAYSIA:** Computerworld Malaysia, PC World Malaysia, Publish in Asia; **MALTA:** PC World Malta; **MEXICO:** Computerworld Mexico, PC World Mexico; **MYANMAR:** PC World Myanmar; **NETHERLANDS:** Computer! Totaal, LAN Internetworking Magazine, LAN World Buyers Guide, Macworld Netherlands, Net, WebWereld; **NEW ZEALAND:** Absolute Beginners Guide and Plain & Simple Series, Computer Buyer, Computer Industry Directory, Computerworld New Zealand, MTB, Network World, PC World New Zealand; **NICARAGUA:** PC World Centro America; **NORWAY:** Computerworld Norge, CW Rapport, Datamagasinet, Financial Rapport, Kursguide Norge, Macworld Norge, Multimediaworld Norge, PC World Ekspress Norge, PC World Nettverk, PC World Norge, PC World ProduktGuide Norge; **PAKISTAN:** Computerworld Pakistan; **PANAMA:** PC World Panama; **PEOPLE'S REPUBLIC OF CHINA:** China Computer Users, China Computerworld, China InfoWorld, China Telecom World Weekly, Computer & Communication, Electronic Design China, Electronics Today, Electronics Weekly, Game Software, PC World China, Popular Computer Week, Software Weekly, Software World, Telecom World; **PERU:** Computerworld Peru, PC World Profesional Peru, PC World SoHo Peru; **PHILIPPINES:** Click!, Computerworld Philippines, PC World Philippines, Publish in Asia; **POLAND:** Computerworld Poland, Computerworld Special Report Poland, Cyber, Macworld Poland, Networld Poland, PC World Komputer; **PORTUGAL:** Cerebro/PC World, Computerworld/Correio Informático, Dealer World Portugal, Mac*In/PC*In Portugal, Multimedia World; **PUERTO RICO:** PC World Puerto Rico; **ROMANIA:** Computerworld Romania, PC World Romania, Telecom Romania; **RUSSIA:** Computerworld Russia, Mir PK, Publish, Seti; **SINGAPORE:** Computerworld Singapore, PC World Singapore, Publish in Asia; **SLOVENIA:** Monitor; **SOUTH AFRICA:** Computing SA, Network World SA, Software World SA; **SPAIN:** Communicaciones World España, Computerworld España, Dealer World España, Macworld España, PC World España; **SRI LANKA:** Infolink PC World; **SWEDEN:** CAP&Design, Computer Sweden, Corporate Computing Sweden, Internetworld Sweden, it.branschen, Macworld Sweden, MaxiData Sweden, MikroDatorn, Nätverk & Kommunikation, PC World Sweden, PCaktiv, Windows World Sweden; **SWITZERLAND:** Computerworld Schweiz, Macworld Schweiz, PCtip; **TAIWAN:** Computerworld Taiwan, Macworld Taiwan, NEW ViSiON/Publish, PC World Taiwan, Windows World Taiwan; **THAILAND:** Publish in Asia, Thai Computerworld; **TURKEY:** Computerworld Turkiye, Macworld Turkiye, Network World Turkiye, PC World Turkiye; **UKRAINE:** Computerworld Kiev, Multimedia World Ukraine, PC World Ukraine; **UNITED KINGDOM:** Acorn User UK, Amiga Action UK, Amiga Computing UK, Apple Talk UK, Computing, Macworld, Parents and Computers UK, PC Advisor, PC Home, PSX Pro, The WEB; **UNITED STATES:** Cable in the Classroom, CIO Magazine, Computerworld, DOS World, Federal Computer Week, GamePro Magazine, InfoWorld, I-Way, Macworld, Network World, PC Games, PC World, Publish, Video Event, THE WEB Magazine, and WebMaster; online webzines: JavaWorld, NetscapeWorld, and SunWorld Online; **URUGUAY:** InfoWorld Uruguay; **VENEZUELA:** Computerworld Venezuela, PC World Venezuela; and **VIETNAM:** PC World Vietnam.   1/24/97

Publisher's Acknowledgments

We're proud of this book; please send us your comments about it by using the Reader Response Card at the back of the book or by e-mailing us at feedback/dummies@idgbooks.com. Some of the people who helped bring this book to market include the following:

Acquisitions, Development, and Editorial

Project Editor: Rebecca Whitney

Acquisitions Editor: Michael Kelly, Quality Control Manager

Product Development Director: Mary Bednarek

Media Development Manager: Joyce Pepple

Associate Permissions Editor: Heather H. Dismore

Technical Editor: Bill Karow

Editorial Manager: Mary C. Corder

Editorial Assistant: Chris H. Collins

Production

Project Coordinator: Valery Bourke

Layout and Graphics: Brett Black, Cameron Booker, Elizabeth Cárdenas-Nelson, Angela F. Hunckler, Todd Klemme, Brent Savage, Michael Sullivan

Proofreaders: Joseph C. Landrock, Rachel Garvey, Karen York

Indexer: Ty Koontz

Special Help: Suzanne Packer, Kevin Spencer

General and Administrative

IDG Books Worldwide, Inc.: John Kilcullen, CEO; Steven Berkowitz, President and Publisher

IDG Books Technology Publishing: Brenda McLaughlin, Senior Vice President and Group Publisher

Dummies Technology Press and Dummies Editorial: Diane Graves Steele, Vice President and Associate Publisher; Judith A. Taylor, Brand Manager; Kristin A. Cocks, Editorial Director

Dummies Trade Press: Kathleen A. Welton, Vice President and Publisher; Stacy S. Collins, Brand Manager

IDG Books Production for Dummies Press: Beth Jenkins, Production Director; Cindy L. Phipps, Supervisor of Project Coordination, Production Proofreading and Indexing; Kathie S. Schutte, Supervisor of Page Layout; Shelley Lea, Supervisor of Graphics and Design; Debbie J. Gates, Production Systems Specialist; Tony Augsburger, Supervisor of Reprints and Bluelines; Leslie Popplewell, Media Archive Coordinator

Dummies Packaging and Book Design: Patti Sandez, Packaging Specialist; Kavish+Kavish, Cover Design

◆

The publisher would like to give special thanks to Patrick J. McGovern, without whom this book would not have been possible.

◆

Contents at a Glance

Cartoons at a Glance

By Rich Tennant • Fax: 508-546-7747 • E-mail: the5wave@tiac.net

page 271

page 61

page 315

page 213

Table of Contents

Foreword

A couple of years ago I was the original Internet Dummy. Although I had been covering technology in one form or another for ten years as a journalist, I considered most computers to be typewriters on steroids. I just needed a good text editor, about 15 megabytes of storage, and a push-button phone.

Also, I thought most of my office mates who actually did bury their heads in their personal computers were the newsroom equivalents of heating and air conditioning engineers. I had better things to do than marvel about "personal productivity tools" or "spreadsheet performance." Computing in a bubble, I thought.

Then while I was on vacation, a colleague ran some telephone wire into the back of my computer, loaded a communications package, and left me a note about how to launch the operation.

Readers, that note is now framed in my office. Eventually that telephone wire led to the Internet and the single most amazing, entertaining, and educational experience of my career.

Quite simply, the Internet has revolutionized the way I interact with the outside world, altered my work habits, and burst the bubble around my PC. It has also challenged my thinking about the future of personal communications technology. And I believe that sooner — rather than later — those changes will be mapped onto society as a whole.

Consider this: My $1,000 PC is now a personal broadcasting station that reaches more people than the CBS affiliate in Washington, D.C. I can get more local viewers with a single e-mail posting to the Internet than Sally Jessy Raphael can get in a sweeps month.

Or this: I'm going to send this piece to my editor for about a sixtieth of a cent — it will take roughly a sixth of a second. (Memo to the Letter Carriers Union: Invest in night schools, *now.*)

Or this: When Vice President Al Gore released his proposal for the National Information Infrastructure, his personal vision for the information superhighway, it was zapped to my e-mail box that very morning, courtesy of an Internet group I belong to that is interested in such matters. (Hey, *Washington Post!* Poof! You're a newsletter!)

I've also had some amazing interactions on the Internet, the implications of which I am still trying to figure out. For instance, a few months ago I was logged on to the Internet equivalent of a live online forum in which two other people were present. Now that's not so unusual, considering the popularity of similar forums running on the dressier, private online services. But then one of them handed me a photograph. Actually, it was a little more complicated than that — download the file and stomp on it a few times — but that is essentially what happened. Rather than exchange text messages, we swapped graphics.

Although it was a simple transaction, given that I was in Washington, D.C., and the other two people possibly in Wheaton, Illinois, and Durban, South Africa, it was an amazing interaction. Wait until baseball card collectors get hold of that one.

But that is one of the joys of the Internet. Its constantly evolving set of applications is being driven not so much by software developers but by its users, all crowding around, talking, and trying out new things.

And while the Internet has turned around the way I interact with the outside world, it has also made me more keen about the technology on my end of the wall jack. Those little pieces of software that make my personal computer more of a convenience have a whole new power and meaning when attached to the two million computers on the Internet.

I now run short digital motion pictures on my PC. The software and the graphics are tucked away in their proper places on the Internet. My PC is humming with software — Indiana Jones never saw more icons. My home and office are now wired together. And I no longer discredit the office PC tinkerers; I just urge them to get on the Internet.

I therefore urge you to read *The Internet For Dummies Starter Kit* Edition. It will guide you with patience and a refreshing sense of humor through the sometimes daunting job of getting going on the Net. But you will be rewarded. And the rest is up to your imagination.

Paul McCloskey
Executive Editor
Federal Computer Week

Introduction

● ●

*W*elcome to *The Internet For Dummies,* Starter Kit Edition. Lots of books are available about the Internet, but most of them assume that you have a degree in computer science, would love to learn every strange and useless wart of the Internet, and enjoy memorizing unpronounceable commands and options. We hope that this book is different.

Instead, this book describes what you actually do to become an *internaut* (someone who navigates the Internet with skill) — how to get started, what you really need to know, and where to go for help. And we describe it in plain old English.

We have made many changes for this new edition. When we first wrote *The Internet For Dummies,* a typical Net user was a student who connected from school or a technical worker who had access through work. Now, three years later, the Net has grown like crazy to include millions of (dare we say it?) normal people, connecting on their own nickel from computers at home, along with students ranging from elementary school to adult education. Now we focus on the parts of the Net that are of the most interest to typical users — the World Wide Web and how to find things there, including how to use Netscape Navigator and Microsoft Internet Explorer (the most popular Web programs), how to send and receive electronic mail (e-mail) for person-to-person communications, and how to download interesting things from the Net.

This CD-ROM edition is new too. For the first time, we have gathered our favorite shareware and freeware programs for the Internet and included them in the back of the book, along with complete installation instructions. The CD-ROM has programs to connect your computer to the Internet, e-mail programs, Web-browsing programs, newsgroup-reading programs, file-transfer programs, online chat programs — you'll find out what we're talking about as you read the book.

About This Book

We don't flatter ourselves that you're interested enough in the Internet to sit down and read the entire book (although it should be a fine book for the bathroom). When you run into a problem using the Internet ("Hmm, I *thought* I knew how to find somebody on the Net, but I don't seem to remember now"), just dip in to the book long enough to solve your problem.

Pertinent sections include

- ✓ What the Internet is
- ✓ How to get connected to the Net
- ✓ Climbing around the World Wide Web
- ✓ Finding people, places, and things
- ✓ Communicating with e-mail (electronic mail)
- ✓ Getting stuff off the Net
- ✓ Where to find services and software

How to Use This Book

To begin, please read the first four chapters. They give you an overview of the Net and some important tips and terminology. Besides, we think that they're interesting.

If you're brand-new to the Net, we suggest that you continue reading through Part II to get a sense of what you can do on the Net. Part II will become more like reference material over time, but it's useful to get a sense of what you'll be doing.

When you're ready to get yourself on the Internet, turn to Part III and pick the option that best suits you and your circumstances.

Parts IV and V are there to egg you on and provide extra support.

We try hard not to introduce a technical term without defining it, but sometimes we slip. Sometimes too, you might read a section out of order and find a term we defined a few chapters back. To fill in the gaps, we include a glossary.

Because the Internet is ever-changing, we have expanded our book to include an online area to help keep it up-to-date. Whenever you see our special Whoosh icon, it means that we have more up-to-the-minute information available on our Web site:

```
http://net.dummies.net
```

When you have to type something, it appears in the book like this:

```
cryptic command to type
```

Type it just as it appears. Use the same capitalization we do — many systems care very deeply about CAPITAL and small letters. Then press the Enter or Return key. The book tells you what should happen when you give each command and what your options are.

Who Are You?

In writing the book, we assumed that

- ✔ You have or would like to have access to the Internet.
- ✔ You want to get some work done with it. (We consider the term "work" to include the concept "play.")
- ✔ You are not interested in becoming the world's next great Internet expert, at least not this week.

How This Book Is Organized

This book has five parts plus an appendix. The parts stand on their own — you can begin reading wherever you like, but you should at least skim Parts I and II first to get acquainted with some unavoidable Net jargon and learn how to get your computer on the Net.

Here are the parts of the book and what they contain:

In Part I, "Welcome to the Internet," you learn what the Net is and why it's interesting (at least why we think it's interesting). Also, this part has stuff about vital Internet terminology and concepts that will help you as you move through the later parts of the book. It discusses how you get on the Net, gives some thoughts about children's use of the Net, and talks about the latest rage in corporate intranet technology.

Part II, "Using Your Internet Account," looks at the most important and useful Net services: the World Wide Web, electronic mail, Usenet, and getting stuff off the Net. You learn how to navigate the Web and search for all kinds of things, how to exchange electronic mail with people down the hall or on other continents, and how to use electronic mailing lists and newsgroups to keep in touch with people of similar interests. You also learn how to *download* things from the Net.

When you're ready to get yourself online, you have to pick a service provider. In Part III, "Getting an Internet Account: Some Popular Entrance Ramps," we describe the three most popular routes: Internet service providers that provide PPP and SLIP accounts, America Online (AOL), and CompuServe.

Part IV, "The Part of Tens," is a compendium of ready references and useful facts (which, we suppose, suggests that the rest of the book is full of useless facts).

In Part V, "Resource Reference," you learn about where to find Internet providers, Net software, and more sources of information about the Net.

The appendix provides all the information you need to install the programs on the CD-ROM.

What's on the CD-ROM

Here's what you can do with some of the programs on the CD-ROM, with the chapters that describe them (to find out how to install the programs, see the appendix):

- ✔ **AT&T WorldNet Service software (for Windows 95, Windows 3.1, and the Mac):** Sign up for an Internet PPP account with AT&T WorldNet, which has local phone numbers throughout the urban and suburban United States. Each software kit includes either Netscape Navigator or Microsoft Internet Explorer. Installation instructions are in the Appendix.

- ✔ **Trumpet Winsock (for Windows 3.1) and FreePPP (for the Mac):** Connect to almost any Internet SLIP or PPP account, as described in Chapter 13. Folks with Windows 95 can use the Windows 95 built-in dial-up networking feature.

- ✔ **Eudora Light (for Windows 95, Windows 3.1, and the Mac):** Our favorite freeware e-mail program; Chapters 7 and 8 tell you how to use it.

- ✔ **Free Agent (for Windows 95 and Windows 3.1) and InterNews (for the Mac):** These newsreaders let you participate in Usenet newsgroups (discussion groups). Chapter 11 explains how to use them.

✔ **WS_FTP (for Windows 95 and Windows 3.1) and Anarchie (for the Mac):** Download programs, graphics, and other files from the Net, as discussed in Chapter 12.

✔ **mIRC (for Windows 95 and Windows 3.1) and Ircle (for the Mac):** Participate in Internet Relay Chat (IRC), a bunch of real-time worldwide conversations. Although we don't describe IRC much in this book, you should take a look at this Web page for the details:

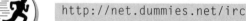

    http://net.dummies.net/irc

✔ **NetTerm (for Windows 95 and Windows 3.1) and NCSA Telnet (for the Mac):** Log in to other computers on the Net. See this Web page for more info:

    http://net.dummies.net/telnet

✔ **Hot Dog (for Windows 95 and Windows 3.1) and BBEdit Lite (for the Mac):** Create your own Web pages, as described in Chapter 6.

✔ **WinZip (for Windows 95 and Windows 3.1) and StuffIt Expander and DropStuff with Expander Enhancer (for the Mac):** Expand the zillions of compressed files you find on the Net (see Chapter 18).

✔ **Paint Shop Pro (for Windows 95 and Windows 3.1) and Graphic Converter (for the Mac):** Create pictures for your Web site or look at pictures you download from the Net.

✔ **ThunderByte Anti-Virus (for Windows 95 and Windows 3.1) and Disinfectant (for the Mac):** Protect your computer from viruses, as described in Chapter 12.

✔ **Adobe Acrobat Reader (for Windows 95, Windows 3.1, and the Mac):** Read and print documents formatted as Acrobat files; the appendix tells you how to both install and use the Acrobat Reader.

Icons Used in This Book

Lets you know that some particularly nerdy, technoid information is coming up so that you can skip it if you want. (On the other hand, you might want to read it.)

Indicates that a nifty little shortcut or time-saver is explained.

Arrrghhhh! Don't let this happen to you!

Points out a resource on the World Wide Web that you can use with Netscape Navigator, Microsoft Internet Explorer, or other Web software.

Points you to more up-to-the-minute information on our very own Web site. Hey, this book is *alive.*

Alerts you to one of the software programs on the CD-ROM in the back of this book.

What Now?

That's all you need to know to get started. Whenever you hit a snag using the Net, just look up the problem in the table of contents or index in this book. You'll either have the problem solved in a flash, or you'll know where you need to go to find some expert help.

Because the Internet has been evolving for close to 30 years, largely under the influence of some extremely nerdy people, it was not designed to be particularly easy for normal people to use. Don't feel bad if you have to look up a number of topics before you feel comfortable using the Net. After all, most computer users never have to face anything as complex as the Internet.

Feedback, Please

We love to hear from our readers. If you want to contact us, please feel free to do so, in care of IDG Books Worldwide, Inc., 7260 Shadeland Station, Suite 100, Indianapolis, IN 46256.

Better yet, send us Internet electronic mail at internetcd@dummies.net, or visit this book's Web home page, at http://net.dummies.net. These electronic addresses put you in contact only with the authors of this book; to contact the publisher or authors of other *...For Dummies* books, visit the publisher's Web site, at http://www.dummies.com, or send e-mail to info@idgbooks.com, or send paper mail to the address just listed.

Part I
Welcome to the Internet

The 5th Wave · By Rich Tennant

"SINCE WE GOT IT, HE HASN'T MOVED FROM THAT SPOT FOR ELEVEN STRAIGHT DAYS. ODDLY ENOUGH THEY CALL THIS 'GETTING UP AND RUNNING' ON THE INTERNET."

In this part . . .

The Internet is an amazing place. Because it's full of computers, though, nothing is quite as simple as it should be. First we look at what the Internet is, how it got that way, and how to figure out how to get your computer in touch with the Net. We tell you what's happening, what people are doing, and why you should care. We give special attention to family concerns and resources and take a quick look at *intranets,* which is Internet technology gone corporate.

Chapter 1

What Is the Net?

What Is the Internet?

It depends on whom you ask. The Internet and the technologies that make it work are changing faster than anyone can keep track of. In this chapter we begin with the basics and tell you what the Internet is and, just as important, what has changed during the past couple of years so that you can begin to have an understanding of what it's all about.

If you are completely new to the Internet, and especially if you don't have much computer experience, *be patient with yourself.* Many of the ideas here are completely new. Allow yourself some time to read and reread. It's a brand-new world with its own language, and it takes some getting used to. Many people find it helpful to read through the entire book quickly one time to get a broader perspective of what we're talking about. Others plow through a page at a time. Whatever your style, remember that it's *new* stuff — you're not *supposed* to understand it already. Even for many experienced Internet users, it's a new world.

Even if you're an experienced computer user, you may find the Internet unlike anything you have ever tackled. The Internet is not a software package and doesn't easily lend itself to the kind of step-by-step instruction we can provide for a single, fixed program. Although we are as step-by-step as we can be, the Internet resembles a living organism that's mutating at an astonishing rate more than it resembles Microsoft Word or Excel, which sit quietly on your computer and mind their own business. After you get set up and get a little practice, using the Internet seems like second nature; in the beginning, however, it can be daunting.

The *Internet* — also known as the *Net* — is the world's largest computer network. "And what is a network?" you might ask. Even if you already know, you might want to read the next couple of paragraphs to make sure that we're speaking the same language.

A computer *network* is basically a bunch of computers hooked together somehow. In concept, it's sort of like a radio or TV network that connects a bunch of radio or TV stations so that they can share the latest episode of "The X-Files."

Don't take the analogy too far. TV networks send the same information to all the stations at the same time (it's called *broadcast* networking); in computer networks, each particular message is usually routed to a particular computer. Unlike TV networks, computer networks are invariably two-way, so that when computer A sends a message to computer B, B can send a reply back to A.

Some computer networks consist of a central computer and a bunch of remote stations that report to it (a central airline-reservation computer, for example, with thousands of screens and keyboards in airports and travel agencies). Others, including the Internet, are more egalitarian and permit any computer on the network to communicate with any other.

The Internet isn't really a network — it's a network of networks, all freely exchanging information. The networks range from the big and formal (such as the corporate networks at AT&T, Digital Equipment, and Hewlett-Packard) to the small and informal (such as the one in John's back bedroom, with a couple of old PCs bought through the *Want Advertiser*) and everything in between. College and university networks have long been part of the Net, and now high schools and elementary schools are joining up. In the past year or two, Internet usage has been increasing at a pace equivalent to that of television in the early '50s; the Net now has an estimated 60 million users, with a projected 500 million by the turn of the millennium.

So What's All the Hoopla?

Everywhere you turn, you hear people talking about the Net — like they're on a first-name basis. Radio shows give you their e-mail address, and strangers ask whether you have a home page. People are "going online and getting connected." Are they really talking about this same "network of networks?" Yes, *and* there's more.

With networks, size counts for a great deal because the larger a network is, the more stuff it has to offer. Because the Internet is the world's largest computer network, it has an amazing array of information to offer.

The Internet is new communications technology that is affecting our lives on a scale as significant as the telephone and television. Some people believe that when it comes to disseminating information, the Internet is the most significant invention since the printing press. If you use a telephone, write letters, read a newspaper or magazine, or do business or any kind of research, the Internet can radically alter your entire world view.

When people talk about the Internet today, they're usually talking about what they can do and whom they have met. The Internet's capabilities are so expansive that we don't have room to give a complete list here (indeed, it would fill several books larger than this one), but here's a quick summary:

- ✔ **Electronic mail (e-mail):** This service is certainly the most widely used — you can exchange e-mail with millions of people all over the world. People use e-mail for anything they might use paper mail or the telephone for: gossip, recipes, rumors, love letters — you name it. (We hear that some people even use it for stuff related to work.) Electronic *mailing lists* enable you to join in group discussions with people who have similar interests and meet people over the Net. *Mail servers* (programs that respond to e-mail messages automatically) let you retrieve all sorts of information. (See Chapters 8, 9, and 10 for details.)

- ✔ **The World Wide Web:** When people talk these days about surfing the Net, they often mean checking out sites on this (buzzword alert) multimedia hyperlinked database that spans the globe. The Web, unlike earlier Net services, combines text, pictures, sound, and even animation, and it lets you move around with a click of your computer mouse. New *Web sites* are growing faster than you can say "Big Mac with cheese," with new sites appearing every minute. In 1993 when we wrote the first edition of this book, the Internet had 130 Web sites. Today it has more than 600,000, and statistics indicate that the number is doubling every two months.

    The software used to navigate the Web is known as a *browser.* The most popular browsers today are Netscape Navigator and Microsoft Internet Explorer. We tell you all about them in Chapters 5 and 6.

- ✔ **Information retrieval:** Many computers have files of information that are free for the taking. The files range from U.S. Supreme Court decisions and library card catalogs to the text of old books, digitized pictures (nearly all of them suitable for family audiences), and an enormous variety of software, from games to operating systems.

    Special tools known as *search engines, directories,* and *indices* help you find information on the Net. Lots of people are trying to make the fastest, smartest search engine and the most complete Net index. We tell you about two of the most useful, AltaVista and Yahoo!, so that you get the picture. As mentioned in the introduction to this book, you see a Web icon here and there; it points to resources you can retrieve from the Net yourself (see Chapter 7).

✔ **Electronic commerce:** This term is just a fancy word for buying and selling stuff over the Net. It seems that everybody's doing it, and now the software is available to make sending your credit card number over the Net safe and secure. You can buy anything from books to stock in microbreweries. We talk about the relevant issues later in this chapter.

✔ **Newsgroups:** A system called *Usenet* is an enormous, distributed, online *bulletin board* with about 700 million characters of messages in more than 20,000 different topic groups flowing daily. Online bulletin boards date from the 1970s — they're systems set up for people of like interests for discussion via e-mail, message areas, and real-time chat. Although most independent, non-Internet-connected bulletin board systems have been replaced by the Internet, the boffo bulletin board of all time, Usenet, is alive and well and is integral to the Internet. Topics range from nerdy computer stuff to hobbies such as cycling and knitting to endless political arguments to just plain silliness. The most widely read Usenet newsgroup is one that features selected jokes, most of which *are* pretty funny (see Chapter 11).

✔ **Intranets:** Wouldn't ya know? Businesses have figured out that this Internet stuff is really useful. They're using e-mail and Web technologies on their own internal networks and calling them *intranets*. We talk about intranet specifics in Chapter 3.

✔ **Games and gossip:** A game called *MUD (Multi-User Dimension* or *Multi-User Dungeon)* can easily absorb all your waking hours. In it, you can challenge other players who can be anywhere in the world. *Internet Relay Chat (IRC)* is a party line over which you can have more or less interesting conversations with other people all over the place. Although IRC seems to be frequented primarily by bored college students, you never know whom you will encounter. Many Internet providers (the folks who are gonna get you connected to the Internet — see Chapter 2) have facilities for "chatting" that enable you to have online conversations with a bunch of people at the same time. Although we don't cover IRC in this book, you can read about it on our Web pages; see Chapter 22 to find out where.

A Few Real-Life Stories

Seventh-grade students in San Diego use the Internet to exchange letters and stories with kids in Israel. Partly it's just for fun and to make friends in a foreign country, but a sober academic study reported that when kids have a real audience for their stuff, they write better. (Big surprise.)

In some parts of the world, the Internet is the fastest and most reliable way to move information. During the 1991 Soviet coup, a tiny Internet provider called RELCOM, which had a link to Finland and through there to the rest of the Internet world, found itself as the only reliable path to get reports in and out of Moscow because telephones were shut off and newspapers weren't being published. RELCOM members sent out stories that would have been in newspapers, statements from Boris Yeltsin (hand-delivered by friends), and their personal observations from downtown Moscow.

Medical researchers around the world use the Internet to maintain databases of rapidly changing data. People with medical conditions use the Internet to communicate with each other in support groups and to compare experiences.

The Internet has more prosaic uses too. Here are some from our personal experience:

When we began our megabook, *Internet Secrets,* we posted notices on the Net asking for contributions. We got responses from all over the world. Many of these contributors became our friends. Now we have people to visit all over the world. It could happen to *you.*

We get mail every day from all over the world from readers of our *...For Dummies* books and are often the happy recipients of readers' first-ever e-mail messages.

The Internet is its own best source of software. Whenever we hear about a new service, it usually takes only a few minutes to find software for our computers (various computers running various versions of Windows and a Macintosh Power PC), download it, and start it up. Nearly all the software available on the Internet is free.

The Internet has local and regional parts as well. When John wanted to sell a trusty but tired minivan, a note on the Internet in a local for-sale area found a buyer within two days. Margy's husband sold his used computer within half an hour of posting a message on the relevant Usenet newsgroup.

Why Is This Medium Different from Any Other Medium?

The Internet is unlike all the other communications media we have ever encountered. People of all ages, colors, creeds, and countries freely share ideas, stories, data, opinions and products.

Anybody can access it

One great thing about the Internet is that it's probably the most open network in the world. Thousands of computers provide facilities that are available to anyone who has Net access. This situation is unusual — most networks are very restrictive in what they allow users to do and require specific arrangements and passwords for each service. Although pay services exist (and more are added every day), many Internet services are free for the taking. If you don't already have access to the Internet through your company, your school, or a friend's attic, you probably have to pay for access by using one of the Internet access providers. We talk about them in Chapter 2.

It's politically, socially, and religiously correct

Another great thing about the Internet is that it is what one might call "socially unstratified." That is, one computer is no better than any other, and no person is any better than any other. Who you are on the Internet depends solely on how you present yourself through your keyboard. If what you say makes you sound like an intelligent, interesting person, that's who you are. It doesn't matter how old you are or what you look like or whether you're a student, a business executive, or a construction worker. Physical disabilities don't matter — we correspond with people who are blind or deaf. If they hadn't felt like telling us, we never would have known. People become famous in the Net community, some favorably and some unfavorably, but they get that way through their own efforts.

Every continent?

Some skeptical readers, after reading the claim that the Internet spans every continent, may point out that Antarctica is a continent, even though its population consists largely of penguins, who (as far as we know) are not interested in computer networks. Does the Internet go there? It does. A few machines at the Scott Base on McMurdo Sound in Antarctica are on the Net, connected by radio link to New Zealand. The base at the South Pole is supposed to have a link to the United States, but it doesn't publish its electronic address.

At the time this book was written, the largest Internet-free land mass in the world is apparently New Guinea. (Bali got on the Internet in 1994.)

The Net advantage

Maybe it's obvious to you that Internet technology is changing so quickly that you have barely had time to crack the spine of *The Internet For Dummies,* 3rd Edition, and here you are holding the fourth edition. "Could it possibly be all that different?," you ask yourself. Trust us — we asked ourselves the same thing. The answer, by the way, is a resounding "Yes." It's *that* different again this year. Though the technology has gotten somewhat better, faster, and easier to use, what has changed the most this past year is who's using it to do what. The big shift is from "Oh, that's interesting" to "Hmm, I wonder whether I can find something on the Web about that." More and more people are turning to the Net for information before they pick up the phone or go to the library.

Here are some of the things people use the Internet for:

- ✔ **Finding people:** If you have lost track of your childhood sweetheart, now's your chance to find him or her anywhere in the country. You can use one of the directory services to search the phone books of the entire United States. We tell you more about this in Chapter 7.

- ✔ **Finding businesses, products, and services:** New Yellow Page directory services enable you to search by the type of company you're looking for. You can indicate area code or zip code to help specify the location. People are shopping for that hard-to-find special gift item. A friend told us of her search for a bear pendant that took her to a company in Alaska that had just what she was looking for.

- ✔ **Research:** Law firms are finding that a great deal of information they formerly paid $600 an hour to find from commercial services can be found for close to nothing when they go directly to the Net. Real estate appraisers use demographic data available on the Net, including unemployment statistics, to help assess property values. Genetics researchers and other scientists download up-to-date research results from around the world. Businesses and potential businesses research their competition over the Net.

- ✔ **Education:** School teachers coordinate projects with classrooms all over the globe. College students and their families exchange e-mail to facilitate letter writing and keep the cost of phone calls down. Students do research from their home computer. The latest encyclopedias are online.

- ✔ **Travel:** Cities, towns, states, and countries are using the Web to put up tourist and event information. Travelers find weather information, maps, transportation schedules, and museum hours online.

- ✔ **Marketing and sales:** Software companies are selling software and providing updates via the Net. (The folks making money from the manufacture of floppy disks are looking for new products. Aside from the large pile of AOL disks we now use as coasters, most software distribution is migrating to the Net.) Companies are selling products over the Net. Online bookstores and music stores allow people to browse online, choose titles, and pay for stuff over the Net.

- ✔ **Love:** People are finding romance on the Net. Singles ads and match-making sites vie for users. Contrary to Internet lore, the Net community is no longer just a bunch of socially challenged white men under 25.

- ✔ **Healing:** Patients and doctors keep up-to-date with the latest medical findings, share treatment experience, and give one another support around medical problems. We even know of some exceptional practitioners who exchange e-mail directly with their patients.

- ✔ **Investing:** People buy stock and invest money. Some companies are online and trade their own shares. Investors are finding new ventures, and new ventures are finding capital.

- ✔ **Organizing events:** Conference and trade-show organizers are finding that the best way to disseminate information, call for papers, and do registration is to do it on the Web. Information can be updated regularly, and paper and shipping costs are dramatically reduced. Registering online saves on-site registration staff and on-site registration lines.

- ✔ **Nonprofits:** Churches, synagogues, and other community organizations put up pages telling about themselves and inviting new people.

Electronic Commerce

We hear many new buzzwords and phrases aimed at confounding the innocent and filling the pockets of would-be consultants. We hear about "digital commerce," "electronic commerce," "digi-cash," "virtual checks," and "smart cards." If you care, entire books are being written about this subject. The one topic in this area that you need to know about is buying stuff over the Net. (If you plan to set up your own business and sell stuff over the Net, you need more info than we have pages in this book to cover it.)

The earth-shattering, startling new idea of how to buy things over the Net lies buried in the inner meaning of the following phrase: "Enter your credit card number." We're not saying that you shouldn't exercise caution, but our experience of buying stuff over the Net in the past year tells us that you have no great cause for alarm. What have we bought? Books, CDs, clothing, encyclopedia subscriptions, and matchmaking subscriptions. Here's what you need to know.

Security in general

Some folks seem particularly wary of sending their credit card number over the Net. If you use a credit card at all, remember that the credit card companies are even more concerned than you are about the idea of any kind of credit card fraud, on or off the Net. All cards have a limit on the amount of fraudulent use for which you're liable — with many credit cards, you're not responsible for any charges resulting from your card or card number being stolen — and the most they can hold you responsible for, if you're a U.S. resident, is $50. Any fraud higher than that amount is the card company's problem, not yours.

Despite all the foofaraw (a technical term) about the risks of online credit card use, we haven't found one single case of a card number being stolen in transit over the Internet. On the other hand, every day we hand our actual physical cards with our handwritten signature to gas station attendants wearing distinctive outfits in bright colors not found in nature, to servers at restaurants, and to clerks at all sorts of stores. Do you know what they do with the card before they give it back to you? Do you worry about it? We don't.

The point is, if you're comfortable using a credit card at all, you needn't get really scared about using it over the Net just because it seems new.

Security in specific

To avoid the possibility of bad guys or gals electronically listening to the bits of your private information whirring across the Net, stripping them off, and redirecting them to purchase their dream vacations, schemes have been invented to encode info sent over the Net so that even if the villains intercept the info, it won't do them any good — it gets all mixed up and hidden in such a way that only the legitimate recipient can decode it. The software that processes this information safely, hiding everything from possible perverse perusal, is known as a *secure server*. Many Web browsers (read more about them in Chapter 5) have secure servers built right in. If you're the least bit antsy about sending your card number over the Net, stick to secure servers.

Software that takes your credit card number (or any other information) over the Net without encoding it is known as an insecure server. Insecure servers are perfectly adequate for many transactions and shouldn't be shunned automatically. Think about the information that's being requested and whether you think that the risk of fraud is a problem. If you do, hold out for a secure server or find another way (such as using the phone) to carry out the business you need to do.

Some Thoughts about Safety and Privacy

The Internet's a funny place. In some ways it's completely anonymous and in others not at all. In the good olde days, people usually had Internet usernames that bore some resemblance to their true identity — their name or initials or some combination in conjunction with their university or corporation gave a fairly traceable route to an actual person. Today, with the phenomenon of screen names (courtesy of America Online) and lengthy strings of numbers (courtesy of CompuServe), revealing your identity is, at best, optional.

Depending on who you are and what you want to do on the Net, you might, in fact, want different names and different accounts. Here are some legitimate reasons for wanting them:

- ✔ You're a professional — a physician, for example — and you want to participate in a mailing list or newsgroup without being asked for your professional opinion.

- ✔ You want help with an area of concern that you feel is private and would not want your problem known to people close to you who might find out if your name were associated with it.

- ✔ You do business on the Net, and you socialize on the Net as well. You might want to keep those activities separate.

Safety first

The whole anonymous nature of the Internet has its downside as well. Although it's relatively rare, horrible things have happened to a few people who have taken their Internet encounters into real life. Many wonderful things have happened too. We have met some of our best friends over the Net, and some people have met and gotten married — no kidding!

We just want to encourage you to use common sense when you set up a meeting with a Net friend. Here are a few tips:

- ✔ Talk to the person on the phone before you agree to meet. If you don't like the sound of the person's voice or something makes you feel nervous, don't do it.

- ✔ Depending on the context, try to check the person out a little. If you have met in a newsgroup or chat room, ask someone else you know whether they know this person. (Women, ask another woman before meeting a man.)

- ✔ Meet in a well-lit public place. Let someone else know where you're going.

- ✔ If you're a kid, take a parent with you. If you're not a kid but you're a little nervous, bring along a friend.

The Net is a wonderful place, and meeting new people and making new friends is one of its big attractions. We just want to make sure that you're being careful.

Protect your privacy

Here in the United States, we have grown up with certain attitudes about freedom and privacy, many of which we take for granted. We tend to feel that who we are, where we go, and what we do is our own business as long as we don't bother anyone else. Well, it would seem that a whole bunch of people are very interested in who we are, where we go (on the Net, at least), and, most especially, what we buy. All this interest is being sanctioned in the name of that ever-so-altruistic-keeping-only-our-best-interests-in-mind holy being Marketing. We tell you this in case you're sensitive about data being collected about your personal Net habits. The next two sections tell you what's happening.

Please pass the cookies

To enhance your online experience, the makers of Web browsers, such as Navigator and Internet Explorer, have invented a type of special message that lets a Web site keep track of when you have visited that site. They thoughtfully store this info, called a *cookie,* on your very own machine to make your next visit to the same site smoother.

This info can in fact make your next transaction smoother, but it can also cause you some problems. Many cookies are quite handy. When you're using an airline-reservation site, for example, the site uses cookies to keep the flights you're reserving separate from the ones other users might be reserving at the same time. On the other hand, suppose that you use your credit card to purchase something on a Web site and the site uses a cookie to remember your credit card number. Suppose that you did this from a computer at work and the next person to visit that site used the same computer. They could, possibly, make purchases on your credit card. Oops.

It may be true that cookies can make your life more convenient. You have to be the judge of that. Every Web server can offer you cookies. You need to know that this kind of software exists so that if you are concerned about your privacy, you can take steps to protect it.

Cookie files usually have the name *cookie* associated with them —cookies.txt and MagicCookie, for example. You can delete your cookie files — your browser will create a new, empty one. Modern browsers can tell you about cookies and ask you whether to accept them as servers offer them to you. When Carol checked her Macintosh, she found two cookie files — one from Navigator and one from Internet Explorer. If she hadn't been looking for them, she never would have known that they were there.

Cookie files cannot get other information from your hard disk. They only collect information that the browser tells them about. As a general rule, we all need to be on the lookout for programs we install that do a little more than advertised.

Internet Explorer keeps, in addition to the cookie file, a history file of where you have been on the Web. (Look in your Internet Explorer folder for something called History.html.) If anyone other than you uses your computer, you might want to delete this file after your use, unless you don't care who sees it. Courts have ruled, by the way, that companies own their computers and their contents. You have no "right to privacy" at work, even though most of us find the idea creepy. Companies can eavesdrop on phone calls, read your e-mail (going and coming,) and read anything that's on your computer, including a history file detailing where you have searched. We find this tasteless and disturbing, so we think we ought to warn you.

Encryption and pretty good privacy

The Internet is not so private a place as you might think. While we're sitting in our homes typing on a keyboard, we hardly get the sense that someone could be watching our every move. Yet information gets relayed from machine to machine, and along the way, if someone really cares, she or he might be able to take a look at what comes across the wire. Whether you're sending your credit card number or sending e-mail, you might feel more comfortable if the absolute secure nature of the transmission were guaranteed.

You can guarantee security using encryption. *Encryption* is high-tech-ese for encoding — just like with a secret decoder ring. You know — codes, spies, secret messages. Software exists that helps you package up your message and send it in a way that nobody can read it except the intended recipient. Some folks say that sending e-mail that's not encrypted is equivalent to sending your message on a postcard. Encryption is the virtual envelope that defies prying eyes. In practice, we rarely encrypt e-mail, though we're happy to know that the option exists. One reason we don't is that at this point it's too darned cumbersome. When e-mail software comes with encryption built-in, many more people will choose to use it. In the meantime, if you feel that you need it, you can learn about PGP, which stands for Pretty Good Privacy. Because it's complicated enough to require pages of explanation, we don't have room in this book to go into the details, but check Chapter 22 for pointers to where you can find out more. New, easier-to-use versions of PGP come out every month or two, so by the time you read this chapter, a PGP add-in may well be available for your favorite mail program.

Where Did the Internet Come From?

If you're not interested in Net history, just skip to the beginning of Chapter 2.

The ancestor of the Internet was the *ARPANET*, a project funded by the Department of Defense (DOD) in 1969, both as an experiment in reliable networking and to link DOD and military research contractors, including the large number of universities doing military-funded research. (*ARPA* stands for Advanced Research Projects Administration, the branch of Defense in charge of handing out grant money. For enhanced confusion, the agency is now known as *DARPA* — the added *D* is for *Defense*, in case there was any doubt where the money was coming from.) The ARPANET started small, connecting three computers in California with one in Utah, but it quickly grew to span the continent.

The reliable networking part involved *dynamic routing*. If one of the network links became disrupted by enemy attack, the traffic on it could be rerouted automatically to other links. Fortunately, the Net rarely has come under enemy attack. Cutting a cable during road construction (known in the biz as *backhoe fade*) is just as much of a threat, however, so it's important for the Net to be backhoe-resistant.

Because the ARPANET was wildly successful, every university in the country wanted to sign up. This success meant that the ARPANET began getting difficult to manage, particularly with the large and growing number of university sites on it. It was broken into two parts:

- ✔ MILNET, which had the military sites
- ✔ The new, smaller ARPANET, which had the nonmilitary sites

The two networks remained connected, however, thanks to a technical scheme called *IP (Internet Protocol)*, which enabled traffic to be routed from one network to another as necessary. Because all the networks connected in the Internet speak IP, they all can exchange messages.

Can the Internet really resist enemy attack?

It looks that way. During the Gulf War in 1991, the U.S. military had considerable trouble knocking out the Iraqi command network. It turned out that the Iraqis were using commercially available network routers with standard Internet routing and recovery technology. In other words, dynamic routing really worked. It's nice to know that dynamic routing works, although perhaps this was not the most opportune way to find out.

Although there were only two networks at that time, IP was designed to allow for tens of thousands of networks. An unusual fact about the IP design is that every computer on an IP network is, in principle, just as capable as any other, so any machine can communicate with any other machine. (This communication scheme may seem obvious, but at the time most networks consisted of a small number of enormous central computers and a large number of remote *terminals,* which could communicate only with the central systems, not with other terminals.)

Meanwhile, back at the classroom

Beginning around 1980, university computing was moving from a small number of large *time-sharing* machines, each of which served hundreds of simultaneous users, to a large number of smaller desktop *workstations* for individual users. Because users had gotten used to the advantages of time-sharing systems, such as shared directories of files and e-mail, they wanted to keep those same facilities on their workstations. (They were perfectly happy to leave behind the disadvantages of time-shared systems. A sage once said, "The best thing about a workstation is that it's no faster in the middle of the night.")

Most of the new workstations ran a variety of *UNIX,* a popular (and, for many versions, free or close to it) type of operating software that had been developed at AT&T and the University of California at Berkeley. The people at Berkeley had a government contract to improve computer networking, so their version of UNIX included all the software necessary to hook up to a network. Because workstation manufacturers also began to include the necessary network hardware, all you had to do to get a working network was to string the cable to connect the workstations, something that universities could do for cheap because they usually could get students to do it.

Then, rather than have one or two computers to attach to the ARPANET, a site would have hundreds. What's more, because each workstation was considerably faster than an entire 1970s multiuser system, one workstation could generate enough network traffic to swamp the ARPANET, which was getting creakier by the minute. Something had to give.

The national network

In 1991, then-Senator Al Gore decided that, for the United States to continue to be a competitive, with-it, first-world kind of country, we should have really great computing and networks. He sponsored the High-Performance Computing Act of 1991, which is supposed to hook up all researchers, universities, primary schools, government agencies — you name it — into one big, happy, and very fast (100 times faster than the primary Internet links are now) network called the National Research and Education Network, or NREN, though there's been little perceptible progress toward actually building anything.

What this means for you is debatable. Many people find the prospect of a network brought to them by the same people who run the post office and Amtrak to be underwhelming, and it is certainly true that fast commercial networks, which are already under construction, will appear long before the NREN arrives. On the other hand, if you are in an impoverished part of the educational establishment, such as a public elementary school, the NREN is supposed to hook you up to the same resources as the big guys — and the reports trickling in from the field say that getting Internet access in the K-12 world is pretty exciting.

In mid-1996, the Congress passed an enormous telecommunications reform bill that offers, among other things, the dubious pleasure of getting your Internet access, local phone, long-distance phone, mobile phone, pager, cable TV, and probably laundry and dry cleaning all on one bill. (Imagine what fun it will be when they screw up.) One of its provisions affects the *Universal Service Fund,* a long-standing system that equalizes phone rates between urban and rural areas and lets USF money be used for putting schools on the Net as well as for the traditional rural telephone subsidies. Because this is a potentially very large source of money for wiring up schools, you might even start to see some action soon.

Enter the National Science Foundation

The next event was that the National Science Foundation (NSF) decided to set up five supercomputer centers for research use. (A supercomputer is a really fast computer with a hefty price, like $10 million apiece.) The NSF figured that it would fund a few supercomputers, let researchers from all over the country use the ARPANET to send their programs to be "super-computed," and then send back the results.

The plan to use the ARPANET didn't work out for a variety of reasons — some technical, some political. So the NSF, never shy about establishing a new political empire, built its own, much faster network to connect the supercomputing centers: the *NSFNET.* Then it arranged to set up a bunch of regional networks to connect the users in each region, with the NSFNET connecting all the regional networks.

The NSFNET worked like a charm. By 1990, in fact, so much business had moved from the ARPANET to the NSFNET that, after nearly 20 years, the ARPANET had outlived its usefulness and was shut down. The super-computer centers the NSFNET was supposed to support turned out to be a fizzle: Some of the supercomputers didn't work, and the ones that did were so expensive to use that most potential customers decided that a few high-performance workstations would do just as well. Fortunately, by the time the supercomputers were on their way out, the NSFNET had become so entrenched in the Internet that it lived on without its original purpose. By 1994, several large, commercial Internet networks had grown up within the Internet, some run by large, familiar organizations such as IBM and Sprint and others run by such specialist Internet companies as PSI and Alternet. The NSFNET has been wound down, with its traffic taken over by commercial networks.

Although the NSFNET permitted traffic related only to research and education, the independent, commercial IP network services can be used for any legal purpose. The commercial networks connect to the regional networks just as the NSFNET did, and they provide direct connections for customers. Chapter 20 lists some commercial IP providers.

Outside the United States, IP networks have appeared in many countries, either sponsored by the local telephone company (which is usually also the local post office) or run by independent national or regional providers. The first international connections were in 1973 with England and Norway. Nearly all countries are connected directly or indirectly to some U.S. network, meaning that they all can exchange traffic with each other.

The term *Internet* first appeared in 1982 with the DARPA launch of the Internet Protocol (IP).

Chapter 2

Internet, Here I Come

- -

In This Chapter
▶ Connecting to the Net
▶ Determining whether you're on the Net already
▶ Learning about connection strategies

- -

Which Way to the Internet?

"Great," you say, "How do I get to the Internet?" The answer is "It depends." The Internet isn't one network — it's 100,000 separate networks hooked together, each with its own rules and procedures, and you can get to the Net from any one of them. Readers of previous editions of this book pleaded (they did other things too, but this is a family-oriented book) for step-by-step directions on how to get on, so we get as step-by-step as we can.

Here are the basic steps:

1. Figure out what type of computer you have or can use.

2. Figure out which types of Internet connection are available where you are.

3. Figure out how much you're willing to pay.

4. Set up your connection and decide whether you like it.

Do You Have a Computer?

There's really no way around this one. Because the Internet is a computer network, the only way to hook to it is by using a computer.

Nope!

If you don't have a computer, you still have some options. If you have a computer at work, particularly if it's already set up to handle electronic mail, you may already have an Internet connection (see the following sidebar, "Are you already on the Internet?").

If you don't have the work option, the next most likely place to find Net access is in your public library, particularly if your local cable-TV company thinks it wants to get into the Internet business: Because hooking up to the Internet over a TV cable turns out to be a technical nightmare, cable companies often set up one free connection at the library first to get the bugs out. (Because it's free, it's hard to complain when it doesn't work.)

Many communities are setting up local access clubs with volunteers setting up shop in church basements. The Internet has become so popular that organizations are springing up all over the place just to teach you all about it. In Boston, Virtually Wired Educational Foundation offers courses and connect-time for modest fees — $3 for an entire day of surfing and $10 for a calendar month. Two-hour introductory courses are $40.

Many cities also have *freenets,* a type of local community computer system that usually has a link to the Internet. Except in Los Angeles, freenets are indeed free (although they won't turn down a contribution if you want to support them.) If you know anyone who already has access to the Web, maybe you can coax them into checking out the following location, which provides a current list of freenets around the world:

```
http://www.genealogy.org/NGS/netguide/freenets.html
```

Another possibility is a local community college or continuing-education center. They often have short and inexpensive Introduction to the Internet courses. You may be wondering at this point, "What kind of loser book tells people to go out and take a course?" You can get two things from a course that you can't possibly get from any book: A live demonstration of what the Internet is like and, more important, someone to talk to who knows the local Internet situation. Although you can certainly get on the Net without a class (we did, after all), if an inexpensive class is available, take it.

Popping up with surprising speed are cybercafés. You can now surf the Net while sipping your favorite beverage and sharing your cyberexperience. If you want to check out the Internet, cybercafés are a great place to try before you buy. If you end up going the cybercafé route, check out the cybercafé section in Chapter 19.

Are you already on the Internet?

If you have access to a computer or a computer terminal, you may already be on the Internet. Here are some ways to check.

If you have an account on an online service, such as CompuServe, America Online (AOL), Prodigy, Microsoft Network (MSN), or MCI Mail, you already have a connection to the Internet. At the least, you can send mail, and some online services provide relatively complete Internet connections.

If you use a bulletin board system (BBS) that exchanges messages with other BBSs, again you can exchange e-mail with the Internet.

If your company or school has an internal e-mail system, it may also be connected to the Internet. Ask a local mail expert.

If your company or school has a local computer network, it may be connected directly or indirectly to the Internet, either just for mail or for a wider variety of services. Networks of workstations usually use the same type of networking the Internet does, so connection is technically easy. Because networks of PCs or Macs often use different types of network setups (most commonly Novell Netware or AppleTalk), it's more difficult, but still possible, for the people who run the network to hook it to the Internet.

Yup!

Ah, you do have a computer. (Or maybe you're thinking about buying one.)

One approach (let's call it the geek, or deranged, approach) is to run network cables — held in place by duct tape, of course — all over your house, climb up on the roof, put up radio antennas, and fill up the attic with humming boxes full of routers and subnets and channel service units and heaven knows what else. Although this approach can be made to work (John has done it, in fact, more than once), if you were the kind of geek who liked to do that sort of thing, you probably wouldn't be reading this book.

The other approach, the normal approach, is to use a computer and a phone line to dial in to an Internet service in which the geeks have already set things up for you. Carol and Margy favor this approach.

Let's Be Normal

To make the normal approach work, you need four pieces:

- A computer
- A modem to hook your computer to the phone line

✔ An account with an Internet provider, to give your modem somewhere to call

✔ Software to run on your computer

We look at each of these items in turn.

Any Computer Will Do

People argue at great length about the advantages and disadvantages of various types of computers. We don't do that here (although, if you buy the beer, we're happy to argue about it after work). Pretty much any personal computer made since 1980 is adequate for at least some type of connection to the Internet, although some computers make it easier than others.

The leading contenders are, fortunately, the most popular: IBM-compatible computers running Windows and Macintoshes. On either of those computers, you can get the spiffiest type of Internet connection (known as a PPP or SLIP connection, but we worry about that later), which makes it possible to use the nicest point-and-click programs to get pictures, sounds, and even movies from the Net.

On any other type of computer, you can still have a text-only Internet connection that isn't as cool as the fancy ones but is still adequate for a great deal of both Net surfing and useful work.

Modems, Ho!

A *modem* is the thing that hooks your computer to the phone line. Because the usual way to hook up to the Internet is over the phone, you need a modem. Modems come in all sorts of shapes and sizes. Some are separate boxes, known as *external* modems, with cables that plug in to the computer and the phone line with power cords. Others are inside the computer, with just a cable for the phone, and some of the newest ones are tiny credit-card-size things you stuff into the side of your computer. (They still have a cable for the phone — some things never change.)

Matching the variety of physical sizes is an equally wide variety of internal features. The speed at which the modem operates (or the rate at which it can stuff computer data into the phone line) ranges from a low of 2400 bits per second (bps, commonly but erroneously called baud) to 33,000 and even 56,000 bps. Some modems can act as fax machines, and some can't. Some have even more exotic features, such as built-in answering machines.

Pretty much any modem made in the past ten years is adequate for an initial foray on the Net, and most computers sold in the past couple of years come with built-in modems, so if you already have a modem, use it.

If you don't have a modem, here's our suggestion about what you should buy: Get an inexpensive 28,800 bps external modem that's intended for use with your type of computer.

We suggest 28,800 bps because anything slower isn't much cheaper. We prefer external modems because you can install them without opening up your computer and because external modems have indicator lights that can be useful when you're trying to get things going. Although there are differences between inexpensive modems and expensive ones (try throwing them up in the air and see what happens when they hit the floor), they aren't of much importance unless you plan to be online 24 hours a day, you're an unusually violent computer user, or (the serious reason) you're on a noisy phone line way out in the country.

Most 28,800 bps modems are also fax modems, which means that with a suitable program, usually included with the modem, you can send and receive faxes with your computer. We find that feature moderately useful, but not so much that we would pay extra for a fax feature.

Be sure to get a cable to connect the modem to your computer, and be sure that it has connectors which match the computer — three different types of plugs may be on the back of the computer.

Note to laptop computer owners: If your computer has credit-card-size PC Card slots but no built-in modem, get a PC Card modem that fits in a slot so that you don't have to carry around a separate modem when you take your computer on the road. Although it costs more, it's worth it.

To find out where you can get more information about modems, turn to Chapter 22.

Normal Terminal Program:
Is That Contagious?

To be able to use other people's computers, you need some software to go along with your modem. Most online services and many Internet providers give or sell you software for Windows and the Mac; if you have some other type of computer or want something simple, however, you can use simpler software that usually comes with the computer or with the modem.

This simpler software is called *terminal-emulation software* because it makes your computer look like just another terminal (that is, a keyboard and a text-only screen) on that remote computer.

Windows users can use Windows Terminal, a rudimentary but usable terminal emulator that is a standard part of Windows 3.1.

For Mac and Windows users who plan to use something fancier than a terminal emulator, we come back and talk some more about software after we discuss the possible Internet providers, because the software and the provider have to match.

Providing That . . .

You have to pay to subscribe to a provider to give you your Internet connection. You use your computer and modem to call in to the provider's system, and the provider handles the rest of the details of connecting to the Net.

There are (wait — no, how did you guess?) many different types of Internet providers, with a trade-off among ease of use, range of features, and price.

Big ol' commercial providers

You can choose one of the big, commercial online services, such as America Online, CompuServe, or Microsoft Network. Each has its own software package that you run on your computer and that connects you to the service. The online services have versions of the packages for Windows, Mac, and, in most cases, DOS. Although you can still use CompuServe with a terminal emulator if you have some other type of computer, AOL requires that you use its software, and MSN requires that you have Windows 95. Even the services you can use via a terminal emulator look much nicer if you use the software package.

Most of the commercial providers started in business as "information utilities"; that is, they originally provided service to just their own users, without connecting to the outside. Although they all eventually connected to the Internet, a large part of what each of the commercial providers offers is proprietary material specific to that provider.

How much does this all cost?

You can spend a great deal of money on your Internet connection. Or you can spend practically none. Here are a few things to look out for.

Provider charges

Pricing schemes vary all over the lot. Some providers charge you by the hour, and others have a flat rate per month. Many have "blended" schemes: For a monthly charge you get a set number of hours, and you pay by the hour if you use more than that. Most providers have a flat rate of $20 per month or less, which we recommend even if they also have a lower blended rate. If you do pick one with limited free hours, studies have shown that the average Internet use is about 18 hours per month.

A few providers charge more for daytime use than for nights and weekends, although that's much less common than it used to be.

If you or your kids become regular online users, you will find that time stands still while you're online and that you use much more online time than you think you do. Even if you think that you will be on for only a few minutes a day, if you don't have a flat-rate plan, you may be surprised when the bill comes at the end of the month.

Phone charges

If you're not careful, you can end up paying more for the phone call than you do for your Internet service. One of the things you do when you sign up for an online service is to determine the phone number to call. *If at all possible, use a provider whose number is a free or untimed local call.* If you use a local or regional Internet service provider, that provider will have a short list of phone numbers you can use. Of the national providers, AOL,

IBM, AT&T, and CompuServe have their own national networks of dial-in numbers; the rest piggyback on other networks, such as Sprintnet (from Sprint) and Tymnet (from MCI). (To add to the confusion, many providers other than CompuServe also use the CompuServe network.) If one national provider has a local number, therefore, they probably all do because it's a Sprintnet, Tymnet, or CompuServe number that will work for any of them.

If you cannot find a provider that's a local call for you, your options are limited. Although some providers have 800-number access, that's rarely a good deal because you pay extra by the hour for using the 800 number. (Someone has to pay for that 800-number call, and that someone is you.) If you have a long-distance plan, such as Sprint Sense (Sprint) or Friends and Family (MCI), you can put your provider's phone number on your list of frequently called numbers and get a low rate that should be less than 10 cents per minute for nights and weekends. (That's still more than $5 per hour.) Be sure to compare rates for in-state and out-of-state calls because in many cases an out-of-state call is cheaper even though it's farther away.

Here's a real-life story that happened to one of our readers, who wrote to ask us to warn other people. She bought a new computer with Internet software already installed. When she started it up, the software said that it would find a local access number for her. She entered her area-code and the first three digits of her phone number to aid the search. The software found a number and configured her program to dial it automatically. She believed it, not unreasonably, when it said that it had found a local access number. She found out differently, however, when her $500 phone bill

(continued)

(continued)

arrived. To be sure that this situation doesn't happen to you, if you let your Internet provider's software find a local access number for you, check that number before you let your computer dial it. If the number has a 1 and an area code in front of it, it's probably not a local number. Check for the availability of a truly local provider, as explained in Chapter 20. At minimum, call your local long-distance carrier and find out your charge per minute.

If you're a long, expensive toll call from anywhere, take a look at Juno Online and MCI Mail, described later in this chapter, which offer only one service (electronic mail) but have 800-number access from anywhere in the country at no hourly charge.

Here are some good things about the big commercial services:

- ✔ They're relatively easy to get connected to and use.
- ✔ They claim to have lots of helpful people you can call when you get stuck. (Our first-hand experience doesn't necessarily substantiate these claims.)
- ✔ They offer flashy screen- and mouse-oriented programs to help you use them.
- ✔ They offer proprietary services and information not available elsewhere on the Net (although much of the material that used to be available solely via these services has now moved to public areas on the Net).
- ✔ Many give you a way to limit what your kids can access.

Here are some bad things about the big commercial services:

- ✔ They limit you to whatever specific set of Internet services they choose to offer; if you want something else, you're out of luck.
- ✔ They make it more difficult or in some cases impossible to get to parts of the Net considered controversial. (Some people consider this restriction to be an advantage, of course.)
- ✔ They can be relatively expensive if you spend more than a few hours a month online. AOL has restructured its pricing, however, to a monthly flat rate.

Figures 2-1 and 2-2 show typical screens from two of the major commercial services.

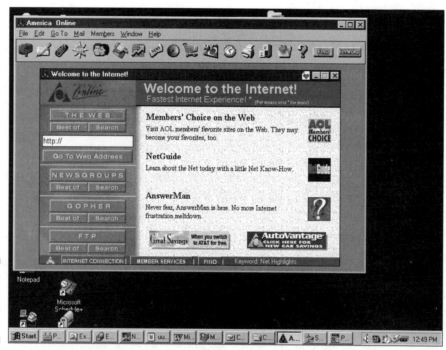

Figure 2-1:
America
Online is
on-screen.

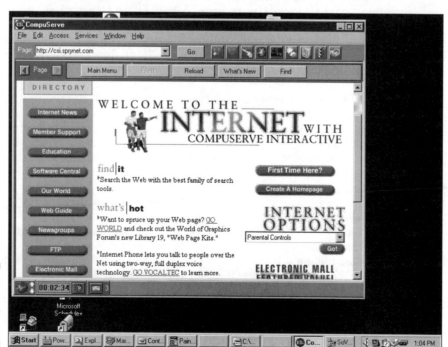

Figure 2-2:
CompuServe
at your
service.

The Internet, the whole Internet, and nothing but the Internet, so help us. . . .

The next type of provider to look at is an *Internet service provider,* often abbreviated *ISP.* (We computer types just love TLAs — three-letter acronyms.) An ISP is similar to a commercial service, but with the important difference that its primary business is hooking people to the Internet. It turns out that nearly all ISPs buy their equipment and software from a handful of manufacturers, so the features and services one ISP offers are much like those of another, with such important differences as price, service, and reliability. Think of it as the difference between a Ford and a Buick, with the differences between your local dealers being at least as important in the purchase decision as the differences between the cars.

ISPs provide two different types of access: PPP/SLIP and shell. Most ISPs offer both types, though shell access is a dying breed. Some offer both with a single account, and others require that you choose one or the other.

SLIPping up

The newer type of connection to the Internet is known as *PPP,* or *SLIP,* access. (PPP and SLIP have technical differences, but because they're not important to normal users, we say PPP/SLIP to mean either.) When you connect to your provider with PPP/SLIP, your computer becomes part of the Internet. You type stuff directly to programs running on your computer, and those programs communicate over the Net to do whatever it is they do for you.

The biggest advantage of this type of access is that the programs running on your computer can take full advantage of your computer's facilities so that they can draw graphics, display windows, play sounds, receive mouse clicks, and otherwise do all the fancy stuff that modern computer programs do. If your computer system can handle more than one running program at a time, as Macs and Windows can do, you can have several Internet applications running at a time, which can be quite handy. You might be reading your electronic mail, for example, and receive a message describing a cool, new home page on the World Wide Web. You can switch immediately to your Web program (Netscape, most likely), look at the page, and then return to the mail program and pick up where you left off. The newest versions of Eudora highlight URLs (Web addresses) and enable you to go directly to your browser by clicking the URL in your e-mail.

Another advantage of PPP/SLIP access is that you're not limited to running programs your Internet provider gives you. You can download a new

Internet application from the Net and begin using it immediately — your provider is just acting as a data conduit between your computer and the rest of the Net.

The disadvantage of PPP/SLIP access is that it's somewhat more difficult to set up because you have to get an Internet access package loaded and configured on your computer. We help you get started with your PPP/SLIP account in Chapter 13.

Shell-shocked

The older type of ISP account is *shell access.* Although it's less flexible than the other kind, it's much easier to set up. For shell access, the only software you need on your computer is a terminal emulator.

With shell access, your provider's computer is considered part of the Internet, but your computer is not. When you connect to your provider, you type commands to its system, which tell it what Internet or other functions you want to perform. The program on your provider's computer that receives and acts on the commands is known as a shell (hence the name). The shell and the programs it runs for you send back to your computer some text that is displayed on your screen.

Almost without exception, shell access providers are running some version of UNIX system software, perhaps Linux, so it eventually helps to learn a little about UNIX systems. In Chapter 22, we tell you where you can find more info.

The Beauty of Bandwidth

If you're the type of person who likes to live on the edge, technologically speaking, you're the type of person who wants the fastest Internet connection available so that you can play with all the fancy graphics and download sound and video. Graphics, video, and sound are all bits of information — lots and lots of bits of information — too many for most dial-up connections to handle. High-speed connections can provide greater *bandwidth,* the amount of data transferred in a specific amount of time. The good news is that high-speed connections are becoming available and affordable by mere mortals.

Cable connections

Cable television companies have been working to provide Internet access and in some areas are successfully providing service. If cable Internet access is available in your community, it's worth checking out.

Here's how it works in the Boston area. You call the cable company. The technician comes and installs a network connection doozus (technical term), installs a standard network card in your computer, and hooks them together. Magic.

If you have cable television, the cable is split and one segment goes to your computer. If you don't have cable television, the cable company may have to install the actual cable too. When the technician goes away, however, you have a permanent high-speed connection to the Internet (as long as you pay your bills, about $50 a month). In addition to the speed and constant access at a fixed price, you aren't tying up a phone line.

ISDN, ADSL, and other four-letter words

The pair of phone wires that runs between your house and the phone company has remained unchanged in design since about 1900. Although it works just fine for voice applications, such as ordering pizza, it leaves something to be desired for transmitting Internet data. In the early 1980s, AT&T developed what was supposed to be the next generation of telephones, called ISDN, short for I Still Don't Know or Improvements Subscribers Don't Need. ISDN uses the same kind of pair of phone wires (which is important because phone companies have about 100 million of them installed) but puts boxes at each end that transmit *digital* data rather than the older *analog* data, which means that an ISDN line can transmit 128K bits per second, a considerable improvement over the 33K that a regular line permits.

Although the idea was good, phone companies, unfortunately, utterly botched the way they made ISDN available. For one thing, the way one installs ISDN is fantastically complicated, so much so that we know full-time telecom managers who have been unable to find anyone at their local phone company who knows how to install it. For another, ISDN is overpriced in most places: In New York, for example, an ISDN line costs about twice as much as a regular line, and every call you make, even local calls, costs extra. For this reason, unless you have a local Internet provider that will arrange the details of an ISDN connection for you and knows the incantations to mutter at the phone company to make the per-call charges go away (phrases such as multilocation Centrex), we don't think that it's worth the bother.

If you're a student

Most colleges and universities provide some type of Internet access for their students. Which type of access varies a great deal. In some cases, it's just a few text-only terminals in a lab somewhere on campus. Others have a complete dial-up Internet service comparable to what you would get from a commercial provider. Some universities have already taken the plunge and are wiring direct Internet access into every dorm room.

In all cases, Internet access is inexpensive or free, so if you're a student or otherwise affiliated with a college or university, check out what's available on campus before you look elsewhere. In some areas, it's cheaper to become a student than to pay for long-distance Internet access.

Some institutions even let alumni use their systems; if you live close to your alma mater, it's worth seeing whether it has some sort of alumni access.

Wait! ISDN uses 1970s computer technology, and things have moved ahead a wee bit since then. Now there's ADSL, SDSL, and HDSL (the DSL stands for Digital Subscriber Loop, and the first letter is a minor variation on the theme), which take the same pair of phone wires and run not at a piddling 128,000 bits per second but at 2, 3, and even 5 *million* bits per second using late '80s and '90s technology. ADSL was originally supposed to provide "video on demand," but it turned out that when customers demanded video, they were happy to turn on their cable TV or run down to the store and rent a movie. Now ADSL has been reborn as yet another high-speed Internet gateway.

Although phone companies are still in the early stages of advanced planning for their ADSL roll-out strategies (or in English, they don't yet have a clue how or when to offer it), they know that they have to do something pretty soon or else the cable-TV crowd will steal all their Internet customers. Stay tuned.

Picking an ISP

After you have decided that you want to go with an ISP, the next question is *which* ISP. This question is relatively complicated because you have several thousand ISPs from which to choose. Many are listed Chapter 20.

A few lines about Linux

Linux is a new, completely free, UNIX-style system that runs on PCs. Because most servers on the Net run UNIX, most server software also runs on Linux or can be easily adapted for it by someone with a little programming experience. Although it can be a pain to get Linux installed, if you find yourself wanting to put your computer on the Net many hours a day or to test out a set of interrelated Web pages you have written, Linux is the system to use. By using advanced system-software techniques known since about 1961 (but not yet fully implemented in Windows — even in Windows 95), Linux protects running programs from each other so that if one program crashes, it almost never takes the system with it. Nobody thinks it at all unusual when Linux systems run continuously for a month or more without having to be restarted.

You can download Linux from the Net if you're an extremely patient person (it takes several days). Although Linux is not as easy to set up as Windows, it's considerably cheaper and much more reliable for use as a server.

A few national ISPs are available, such as IBM Internet Connection, Netcom, Prodigy Internet, Sprint Internet Passport, and AT&T WorldNet. National ISPs have lots of dial-in numbers across the country, which can be handy if you travel much, and usually (but, sadly, not always) have an extensive support staff to help you. Their pricing varies but is usually in the $20-to-$25 per month range.

You can usually get a better deal from a regional or local ISP. They tend to compete on price more than the national ones do, and in many cases, because they stick to one geographic area, they also offer community-oriented online materials. When you're doing your comparison shopping, consider the following:

- ✔ **Price:** Obviously.
- ✔ **Support:** Call and talk to members of the support staff before you sign up. We think that good support means support 24 hours a day, not being put on hold for long periods of time, and most important, support people who don't think that your questions are stupid and can actually answer them. (You can't take this for granted.)
- ✔ **Load:** What is response time like at peak times, and do you get busy signals when you call?
- ✔ **Modem speed:** Some providers haven't upgraded their equipment in a long time. It does you no good to have a fast modem if your provider's modem speed can't match it.

ISP odds and ends

A few Internet providers don't exactly fall into any of the categories we have discussed:

> **Pipeline:** An all-in-one Internet-access package from Mindspring, a medium-size national ISP. It has been licensed by several other providers around the country. It's a decent way to get on the Net, relatively easy to set up, and relatively complete.

> **Netcruiser and NetComplete:** All-in-one package from Netcom. If you're using Netcom as your provider, give them a try and see whether you like them, because the software is free.

Back to Software

The type of access you have is intimately related to the type of software you need.

Commercial providers

Nearly all commercial providers give you program disks with software that works with their particular systems. A few of them, including CompuServe, still offer text-only access by using terminal-emulator software.

Chapter 14 describes America Online (AOL), and Chapter 15 describes CompuServe. We tell you how to use these popular commercial online services and how to get and install the software required to access them.

SLIP or PPP access

If you use an ISP with SLIP or PPP access, you need PPP/SLIP software. If your provider doesn't give you software to install, you still have lots of alternatives:

- ✔ Windows 95 has a minimal but adequate set of PPP software built right in. See Chapter 13 for advice about setting it up.

- ✔ The most popular access software for Windows is Trumpet Winsock. It's shareware, and many ISPs give their customers disks with copies of it. (Most of them, unfortunately, forget to mention that if you use the software on the disk, you owe a registration fee to the program's author in Tasmania.) It's also on the CD-ROM in the back of this book.

Winsock? Like at an airport?

No, Winsock is short for *Windows sock*ets. It's like this: Back in the dark ages of PC networking, seven years ago, several different software vendors wrote PC Internet packages. Each package provided functions so that other people could write Internet applications of their own that worked with the vendor's package.

Each vendor's functions were, unfortunately, slightly different in the details, even though functionally they all did the same things, so that applications which worked with one didn't work with another. Some vendors boasted that they had compatibility libraries for four or five other vendors so that programs which expect to use the other vendors' libraries will work. (It's similar to the situation with electrical appliances in Europe: Although all the power is the same, all the plugs are different. If you bring an English sewing machine to France, for example, you can't use it unless you can find an adapter plug.)

In 1991 all the network vendors were gearing up to produce Windows Internet packages. One day a bunch of them got together at a trade show and thrashed out a common, standard set of functions for Windows Internet applications. Every Internet software vendor, even Microsoft, quickly agreed to support this Windows Sockets standard, or Winsock. (It's called Sockets because its design is based on a well-established UNIX package by that name.)

In practice, therefore, any Windows Internet application you find that uses Winsock (whether it's commercial, shareware, or free) should work with any Windows Internet package. In the annals of software development, this degree of compatibility is virtually unprecedented, so let's hope that it's a harbinger of things to come.

- A few free access software packages are available, most notably the Chameleon Sampler. Although it's an older, buggier, and unsupported version of the commercial Chameleon software package, it works well enough for many users.

- Several commercial Windows packages are available too. Although most are pricey, two of the least expensive are the Spry, Inc., package, found in *Internet in a Box* (about $100), and Internet Chameleon, offered by some Internet providers.

- For Mac users, most of the necessary Internet software, called MacTCP, is a standard part of System 7. The missing parts are the dial-up access software and the applications, both of which are available from most ISPs and also bound in the back of this book. We tell you in Chapter 21 where to find the software you need.

- If you use Linux or a workstation running some version of UNIX, all the necessary software is part of the standard system.

Chapter 21 describes how to find software to use with your PPP/SLIP account, and the appendix describes the software on the CD-ROM in the back of this book.

Shell access

If you use an ISP and choose shell access, you use a *terminal emulator:* software that makes your computer act as though it's just a screen and keyboard hooked up to your ISP's computer. Although this process isn't something you usually have to think much about, we tell you what you need to know in Chapter 13, in the sidebar "Using a UNIX shell account."

On and off the Information Superhighway

If the computer you use is already connected to a network, you're probably familiar with such terms as user ID and login name. If you're not, keep reading.

Sixty million people are on the Internet. Only one of them is you, so it would be nice if the other 59,999,999 couldn't go snooping through your files and e-mail. No matter which type of provider you use, you have to use a security procedure to prove that you are who you say you are.

Would you sign your name in, please?

Not so different from that prehistoric TV show "What's My Line," service providers of all sorts want to know who's on the system. To track usage, users are given an account, kinda like a bank account. The account has your name and a secret password associated with it.

Your account name may also be called your user ID, or your login or logon name. Your name must be unique among all the names assigned to your provider's users.

Your password, just like those associated with bank teller machine cards, should not be a common word or something easily guessed. Stay away from names and birthdays, unless you mix them up. We have heard that the most commonly used password in the world is the name Susan. For best results, include both numbers and letters so that a bad guy using a dictionary doesn't find your password listed. You really don't want strangers using your account, and your password is your primary protection. We tend to use obscure medical terms with a few letters capitalized and a digit or two thrown into the middle.

Fire at the wall

Lots of PCs in big companies are loaded up with Internet software and have network connections with a hookup to the Internet, so if you're so blessed, you can run programs on your computer and hook right up to the Net. Right? Not quite.

If you're in a large organization that has (not altogether unreasonable) concerns about confidential company secrets leaking out by way of the Internet, a *firewall* system placed between the company network and the outside world may limit outside access to the internal network.

Because the firewall is connected to both the internal network and the Internet, any traffic between the two must go through the firewall. Special programming on the firewall limits which type of connections can be made between the inside and outside and who can make them.

In practice, you can use any Internet service that is available within the company; for outside services, however, you're limited by what can pass through the firewall system. Most standard outside services — such as logging in to remote computers, copying files from one computer to another, and sending and receiving electronic mail — should be available, although the procedures, involving something called a *proxy server,* may be somewhat more complicated than what's described in this book.

Often, you have to log in to the firewall system first and from there get to the outside. It's usually impossible for anyone outside the company to get access to systems or services on the inside network (that's what the firewall is for). Except for the most paranoid of organizations, electronic mail flows unimpeded in both directions.

Keep in mind that you probably have to get authorization to use the firewall system before you can use *any* outside service other than mail.

Please don't touch the crystal

After you begin exploring the Internet you can find yourself in many far-off, and not-so-far-off, lands on many strange computers. Those computers have information that's available to every Sally and Sam, and usually these computers are also used for lots of other things. These other things are none of your business (nor ours, for that matter.)

To protect information from the voyeurs, the ignorant, and the vile, an elaborate scheme of permissions, also known as access control, determines who can do what to what. Each data file or other resource on computers on the Net has a set of permissions that might say, for example, that anyone can look at the file but only the file's owner can change it. For more private data, it might say that no one other than the file's owner can even look at it.

When you're wandering around the Net, you may find resources whose names you can see but that you can't actually look at; it just means that the permissions don't let you look inside them. It's nothing personal.

If you have information on a networked system, you probably want to protect it in the same way. Although you can screen out ordinary users, remember that system administrators and sometimes clever intruders can override permissions. If you have something of an extremely personal nature that you feel compelled to leave on the Net, it's worth learning how to encrypt it so that no one can decode it without the encryption key you used.

To find more information about UNIX permissions, security, and encryption, see Chapter 22.

How to Get Off

After you have gotten yourself on the Internet, you're inevitably placed in the position of having to get off. There are more and less graceful ways of getting off — and, depending on how far you have gone, potentially layers of systems to exit from.

If you use a modem to dial in, you can always hang up the phone from your terminal program. A cleaner, more polite way to leave, however, means saying good-bye to everyone to whom you have said hello. The problem is that not all computers say good-bye in the same language.

Here are some commonly used exit sequences. If none of them works, try typing **help** to see whether the system has any clues for you. If you can't get help, use your terminal program to hang up the phone and don't feel guilty about it.

The most common exit sequences include:

- Type **exit**.
- Press Ctrl-D (popular on always excessively terse UNIX systems).
- Type **logout**.
- Type **bye**.

Some Other Ways to Connect to the Net

Before we leave the topic of connecting to the Net, take a last look at some other less well-known ways to hook up.

Some phone numbers

Here are the voice phone numbers for some of the national providers we have listed in this chapter. Chapter 20 has a much larger list of regional and local Internet providers.

America Online: 800-827-6364

AT&T WorldNet: 800-967-5363

CompuServe: 800-380-9535

IBM Global Network: 800-888-4103

Juno Online: 800-654-5866

MCI Mail: 800-444-6245

Microsoft Network: 800-386-5550

Netcom: 800-501-8649

Mail call

Several commercial systems are available that do just electronic mail, including AT&T Easylink Mail, SprintMail, MCI Mail, and Juno Online. A mystical connection apparently exists between long-distance telephony and e-mail. MCI started MCI Mail, and AT&T and Sprint inherited their mail systems when they bought other computer networking businesses. Although they're all low-profile, they're quite large — Easylink is reputedly bigger than America Online.

MCI Mail is unusual in that it provides 800-number access all over the United States with no hourly online charges. If you live in an area in which no other providers are a local call away or if you travel frequently, MCI Mail toll-free access makes it quite attractive. It's also unusual in that you pay only an annual fee and a per-message charge for outgoing mail. Incoming mail is free. It's just e-mail — none of the other Internet services — but it's much better than nothing. Juno Online provides a mail-only system with local and 800-number access for free, supported by advertising you watch while it's uploading and downloading your mail. At the price, it's quite nice.

Wireless

Cabling is often a problem for mobile computing. People who carry their laptops with them want to connect from wherever they are, and it's not always easy to dial in. Progress is being made toward wireless Internet connection and is already available from some providers. We have even gotten e-mail from a nerdy friend on an airplane.

Chapter 3

Intranet? Are You Sure That's Spelled Right?

In This Chapter

▶ What's an intranet?

▶ How do you use an intranet?

Sure is. Now that everyone knows about the *Internet,* the marketroids have invented intranets, which are just the same except different. The idea is simple: Take all that swell technology that has been developed for the Internet during the past 20 years and use it directly inside your company on its own network.

An *intranet* is, specifically, a bunch of services, such as Web pages, that are accessible only within an organization. The World Wide Web works over the Internet with tens of thousands of *Web servers* (computers that store Web pages) serving up Web pages to the general public. An intranet works over an organization's internal network with a few Web servers serving up Web pages to folks within the organization. An intranet is sort of a private World Wide Web — an Organization Wide Web. (Oww! — another acronym!)

What's the Big Deal?

In one sense, intranets aren't very interesting because anything you can do on an intranet, people have probably been doing on the Internet for years. Departments in your organization create Web pages that other people in the organization can see. So what?

Intranets can be a very big deal. In many (if not most) companies, a mountain of important information about the business is locked up in big old databases on big old mainframes or minicomputers. The information would be of great use to people all over the company if only they could get at it.

Another mountain of stuff is stuck in spreadsheets and word-processing files on people's computers all over the company. Intranets offer a new way to take that locked-up information and make it available to the rest of the company.

After people within a company have a basic set of Internet-style software on an intranet, particularly the Web browsers we discuss in Chapters 5 and 6, it's surprisingly easy to take that locked-up information and write software glue (often known as *middleware* — see the following sidebar) that lets people get at the formerly locked-up information. Lots of people have told us that they can make information available in weeks or months on an intranet that would have taken months or years to provide using older software tools. We have also heard of many "skunkworks" projects in which small but useful intranets were created quickly and with little or no budget using a few spare PCs.

After an organization has an intranet — its own Web server and some Web pages — anyone in the organization can see the Web pages by using a browser. Product information, human-resources information, and other stuff is suddenly easy to find, read, and print using the intranet.

Using Intranets

What your organization can do on an intranet is limited only by the imagination of the people in the organization. (We realize that this limitation is more severe in some organizations than in others, but we're optimists.) Here are some examples; (the *italicized* words are all defined in the following sidebar):

- ✔ Nearly all the paper memoranda circulated around a company can be sent more effectively as e-mail or as Web pages. This method saves paper and makes the information easier to file and find.

- ✔ Those big, dusty company manuals moldering on the shelf or perhaps holding up one corner of your desk if the floor is uneven work much better as Web pages. They're easier to search through to find the page you want. Also, the authors can update them as often as necessary, and everyone instantly has access to the most current version.

- ✔ Catalogs, parts lists, and the like are relatively easy to put on the Web by using *database publishing,* a technique which automatically creates Web pages that contain the information from the *legacy system* in which the information is actually stored.

- ✔ If you have several people working on a project, putting the project information on the Web lets each person look at and update the status of parts of the project, with everyone seeing up-to-date information. That's how the three authors and the editor of this book, who live in four different states, tracked our progress in updating the book and keeping ourselves moving in roughly the same direction, using a little Web application John whipped up in an afternoon.

✔ If your company has a flair for multimedia, now you can have animation, video, and sound right on your desktop. Slightly less dramatic but perhaps more useful are new integrated intranet products that let you put "live" links to Web pages in your e-mail. Now you can send around a memo that refers to all types of different material with a link directly to that material. Your readers have to just click the link to see the information you're referencing.

All in all, we see the technology flowing both ways. As Internet technology, particularly e-mail and Web technology, combines with traditional databases, the ways in which companies manage information are bound to change. Paper memoranda will be about as common as the IBM Selectric, and large, metal filing cabinets will fill much more slowly.

Why This Is the Last You Will Hear from Us about Internets

Because there really isn't a fundamental difference between intranets and the Internet, we're going to stop talking about them. The more you use either technology, the more you're going to expect everyone around you to get smart and get with it. Buy them a book. E-mail and Web technology are much like the telephone — much more useful when everyone has them and uses them.

You too can be an intranet consultant!

A rule of thumb in the computing industry says that a consultant is anyone more than 75 miles from home. We can't offer transportation, but here are some handy buzzwords you will want to use if you want to sound like you're an intranet expert (see whether you can use all of them in one sentence):

✔ **Client/server:** A type of computer system in which one program, the client, runs on your computer so that you can work with it directly; a separate program, the server, runs on another computer and manages all the important data; and a computer network connects the two. Although the Internet has always worked this way, it took the special insight of the large-scale business data-processing industry to realize that you could make a great deal of money in the process.

✔ **Database publishing:** The process of taking a bunch of a company's information that used to be locked away in databases where only the DP types and a few managers could see it and making it available to large numbers of people inside and even outside the company. Makes it much easier to get your job done, but makes managers nervous. ("If they know everything I know, how can I keep my job?")

✔ **Drill down:** To throw away all the confusing but important details and reduce something to one or two simple ideas a customer can understand.

✔ **Legacy:** Obsolete but still essential. "I'm looking for a pair of recapped whitewalls for my legacy vehicle here." Usually it's *legacy system,* a computer system that has been nursed along for the past 20 years and everyone who remembers how it was originally put together has retired.

✔ **Middleware:** Software that connects one piece of software to another piece of software with which nobody ever dreamed it would have to work but now it does. If you saw the movie *Apollo 13* and remember the scene in which the air scrubbers in the command module are exhausted and they have to use spares from the lunar module, only they're a completely different shape, so they concoct something from duct tape and wire and who-knows-what to make it fit, the concoction was middleware.

✔ **Platform:** The underlying computer hardware on which a system runs or sometimes the underlying software on which a system runs or both. "We're targeting a Netscape platform on a Windows 95 platform on a Pentium platform."

✔ **Solution:** A software package or a hardware and software combination that does something, preferably an expensive software package or combination.

Chapter 4
The Net, Your Kids, and You

*W*ith more than a million kids already online and an estimated 7 million online by the turn of the millennium, we think a discussion of families online critical. Obviously, if this isn't your thing, just skip it and go to the next chapter.

Stop Making Sense

We're all trying to make sense of the Internet and what it means for us and our families. Although no one has the ultimate answer, we can talk about some of the major issues being raised, the benefits we see, and potential problems. The Net has dramatic implications in the education, entertainment, and socialization of our children. The more we know and are actively involved, the better choices we can make.

What's in it for us?

We're just beginning to discover the myriad ways in which the Internet can be exciting in the context of our families' lives. Here are some of the ways in which we think that the Internet enhances our lives:

- ✔ It provides us with personal contact with new people and cultures.
- ✔ It helps us develop and improve our reading, writing, research, and language skills.
- ✔ It provides support for families with special needs.
- ✔ It is an exciting new outlet for artistic expression.

Not everything new is wonderful, and not everything wonderful is new. In talking about children, we have to make distinctions: Are these preschoolers or college kids? What makes sense for one group in this case usually doesn't map to another, so let's consider how the Internet works for different age groups.

The Internet for young children

We have to say up front that we are strong advocates of allowing children to be children, and we believe that children are better teachers than computers are. Carol doesn't even own a television set, and none of our kids watches commercial TV. Now that you know our predisposition, maybe you can guess what we're going to say next: We are not in favor of sticking a young child in front of a screen. How young is young? We feel that younger than age 7 is young. Many educators feel that unstructured computer time under age 11 is inappropriate. We recommend that children get as much human attention as possible, and we believe that computers make lousy baby-sitters. At that age, children benefit more from playing with trees, balls, clay, crayons, paint, mud, monkey bars, bicycles, and other kids.

Even if you do want to let your small kids use the Internet, frankly, there's not much out there for the prereading set anyway.

The Internet for K–12

K–12 is the label given to all the education that happens in the United States between preschool (nursery school or day care) and college. It's a broad category. We use it here because many mailing lists and newsgroups use the K–12 designation and it seems to be common ground for many people. We think that Internet access is more appropriate for somewhat older children (fourth or fifth grade and older), but your mileage may vary.

The Internet is an incredible way to expand the walls of a school. The Net can connect you to other schools and to libraries, research, museums, and other people. You can visit the Louvre and the Sistine Chapel; practice your French or Spanish or Portuguese or Russian or Japanese; and hear new music and make new friends.

School projects such as the Global Schoolhouse connect kids around the world by working collaboratively on all types of projects. The first annual global learning project drew more than 10,000 students from 360 schools in 30 different countries. The second annual project is aiming to triple participation in 1997.

You can send an e-mail message to the Global Schoolhouse at helper@gsn.org or check out its Web site at http://www.gsn.org. (We explain these funny-looking locations in Chapter 5, so you can come back here later and follow up on them.) From the Global Schoolhouse Web site, you can subscribe to lots of mailing lists. If you don't have Web access, you can subscribe to the Global Watch mailing list (Chapter 10 has all the details) by sending an e-mail message to lists@gsn.org that contains this single line in the body of the text: subscribe global-watch.

College and the Net

Although the Internet has had a home in universities for a long time, what's happening with the World Wide Web is new for everyone. Much of the inspiration and perspiration of the volunteers who are making information available to everyone is coming from universities, both students and faculty, who see the incredible potential for learning.

Many campuses provide free access to the Internet for their students and staff. Campuses that allow you to register early sometimes give you that access when you register, even months in advance. If you're going to go anyway, you can get a jump on your Internet education before you even get to campus.

Checking out colleges on the Net

Most colleges and universities have or are rapidly creating sites on the Web. Yahoo, or more correctly, Yahoo! (a Web index we tell you all about in Chapter 7) has pointers to thousands of schools. From the top level, click Education and then Universities.

After you're a little more adept at using the Net, you can research classes and professors to get a better idea of what appeals to you.

The Internet (more specifically, e-mail) is a great way for parents and college kids to stay in touch. It's much cheaper than phoning home and easier than coordinating schedules. Forwarding mail to other family members allows for broader communication. We noticed one more surprising benefit: In our experience, families tend to fight less when they're communicating by e-mail. Somehow, when folks have time to think about what they're going to say before they say it, it comes out better.

Finding a job by using the Net

Not just for students, the Net is an incredible tool for finding a job. It's especially good for students because it provides a powerful, economical way to conduct a real job search. You can publish your résumé online for prospective employers. You can check out the Monsterboard, an impressive compilation of job-related information that enables you to search by discipline (the area of study — all searches need the other kind) or geography or a host of other criteria. You can find the Monsterboard at http://www.monster.com/. You can also research companies to find ones you may want to work for.

Companies have found that posting their jobs on the Net is an effective, economical way to recruit talented people. Check out the home pages of companies that interest you, and look for their open positions. Many colleges and universities have career office home pages, many of which are grouped together for you on the Web. Ask your search engine to look for "career office home pages" to get college and university listings grouped by geography.

When the Net is college

It's no exaggeration to say that many people are learning more on the Net than they ever did in school. Although you have to consider many factors, the Net requires motivation, and motivated learning is much more fun. The Net provides equal opportunity beyond the imagination of those locked in physical settings. It is open to everyone of any color, height, belief, and description. People previously locked out of educational opportunities by physical handicap, economic need, or geography find the Net an empowering, life-altering experience.

Beyond the informal education that's already available, organizations are actively working to establish formal online colleges. Athena Virtual Online University (VOU) was founded in the spring of 1995. Although it's not yet accredited, all colleges and universities begin that way. For more information, check it out at http://www.athena.edu/.

Of Paramount Concern

High on the list of parents' concerns about the Internet is the question of children's access to inappropriate material. We have found that parents who take the time to learn about access issues understand that the threat is not so great as some would have us believe. Parents who have thought about the issues on a larger scale are very concerned that reactionary sentiment and hyperbole pose a real threat to our freedom of expression and that, ultimately, that is a much greater danger to our children. Parental involvement is essential, and we talk about family strategy a little later in this chapter. If you're interested in people thrashing out these issues, you can subscribe to the CACI (Children Accessing Controversial Information) mailing list by sending e-mail to `majordomo@cygnus.com` with the words `subscribe caci` in the body of the message. (We talk about sending e-mail in Chapter 8.)

Another problem that has surfaced which should be of concern to parents but doesn't have a strong enough titillation factor to garner a cover story in a national magazine is the targeting of children by marketing organizations. Children of middle- and upper-income families are considered the most lucrative target market, and the Net is being viewed as another way to capture this audience.

Targeting children isn't new. You're probably familiar with Joe Camel, the Camel cigarette campaign that many people claim is aimed at kids. You may know about Channel One, which brings advertising directly to the classroom. If you have ever walked into Toys 'R Us, you see the unmistakable link between television shows and toys.

You should know that astute marketing types have already designed very kid-friendly, fascinating, captivating software to help them better market to your kids. Delightful, familiar cartoon characters deftly elicit strategic marketing information directly from the keyboard in your very home. You should be aware of this situation and teach your children about what to do when someone on the Web is asking for information. You can obtain a copy of the Center for Media Education report "The Web of Deception" by sending $25 to the organization at 1511 K Street NW, Suite #518, Washington, DC 20005.

More than ever, children need to develop critical thinking skills. They have to learn how to evaluate what they read and see — most especially on the Web.

"But Time magazine said. . . ."

If you're part of mainstream America, you probably saw or heard about, in the summer of 1995, the *Time* magazine sensationalist "Cyberporn" cover story. You might not have seen its retraction in tiny print, however.

If you missed the details, here's the gist of it: A Carnegie-Mellon student-turned-entrepreneur took a look at online pornography. He wrote a lurid book about marketing pornography and sold software to dial-up computer bulletin-board systems to help them with their pornographic needs. He then "gathered data" about the widespread proliferation of pornography on these bulletin boards but for some reason made the completely insupportable leap to claim that what's available on the Internet is the same as what's on local, membership-only, pay-to-use bulletin boards.

It was as though he claimed that because glossy magazines found in certain kinds of stores are full of naughty pictures, *Reader's Digest* (which is also a magazine, after all) is full of naughty pictures. Although the student's report had not been reviewed by anyone familiar with the area of study (a standard prerequisite for all academic publications), the *Georgetown Law Review* decided to publish it, and *Time* picked it up as a "scoop."

The real problem is the gross misrepresentation of facts. With guidance, parents can go a long way toward ensuring healthy, constructive Internet experiences for their children.

Although some laws that have been proposed would outlaw "indecent" content on the Net, they miss the point (not to mention that courts have held them to be unconstitutional). The focus should be on how this manipulation of fraudulent data is being used to push for regulation and censorship of a raw communications medium. Ask yourself who stands to gain the most by controlling the content of the Internet. Ask yourself whether you believe that someone has the right to read your personal mail or listen to your personal phone calls. If you think that your privacy is something to be cherished, you will understand that the answers to protecting our children lie not in having Big Brother regulate the content of the Internet but rather in designing ways to guide our children's access and choices.

Many people are working hard to solve these problems, and most believe that we're well on our way to providing Internet access with parental guidelines. We talk about some of the forms this guidance can take and trust that you will find a solution which works for your family.

Parental Guidance Required

Parents, educators, and free-speech advocates alike agree that parental guidance has no substitute when it comes to the subject of Internet access. Just as we as parents want our children to read good books and see quality films, we also want them to find the good stuff on the Net. If you take the time to learn with your children, you have the opportunity to share the experience and to impart critical values and a sense of discrimination that your children need in all areas of their lives.

Remember that the good stuff on the Net far outweighs the bad. Today, software aids are being developed almost daily to help parents and educators tap the invaluable resources of the Net without opening Pandora's box. Remember that every child is different and that what may be appropriate for your children may not be appropriate for someone else's. You have to find what's right for you.

Establish rules for your family's use of the Net. Outline areas that are on- and off-limits, limit the time, and be explicit about the types of information kids can give out over the Net.

Setting limits

Now that America Online is charging a flat rate for service, you can't rely on economic incentive alone to curb your Internet use. If you don't let your children watch unlimited television, don't let them have unlimited computer access. Don't buy into the hype that just because it's on a computer, it's educational. We're reminded of the cartoon featuring wishful parents reading the Help Wanted section where they find that Nintendo players are making $70,000. We all know kids whose lives seem to be lost in front of a screen. Don't let it happen to your kid.

Rating the ratings

Several schemes have been proposed that involve the rating of Internet content. Who will rate the material, and whose ratings will you trust? Is the author of a Web page or other online material the right person to assign the ratings? Probably not. Internet software designers are adding provisions for third-party ratings so that you can, if you want, choose or exclude material by the ratings, although the guidelines the raters use may not be the ones you would choose.

In an attempt to address the concern of controlling access while not caving in to censorship, the World Wide Web Consortium (W3) has designed a standard for marking Web content so that third parties can rate the material. The standard is called PICS (Platform for Internet Content Selection), and you can read all about it at this Web address:

```
http://www.wellesley.edu/CS/JimMillerTalk/9601PICS/
        slide1.htm
```

Or see the W3 Web page about PICS, at `http://www.w3.org/PICS`.

Other software under development will let parents limit access by their own criteria. A parent who feels strongly about warthogs and asparagus, for example, could block all material about those subjects. More realistically, they could block heavy fictionalized violence and still permit access to medical information about sexually transmitted diseases.

Consumer's choice

Because parents are paying for online services, services that want to remain competitive are vying for parental dollars by providing features to help families control Internet access. America Online, for example, enables you to block access to chat rooms that may not be appropriate for children and to restrict access to discussion groups and newsgroups based on keywords you choose. Parental blocking is available at no extra cost.

Software sentries

More and more products are appearing on the market to help parents restrict access or monitor usage by some sort of activity report. If you choose to use one of these systems, remember that they are not a substitute for your direct involvement with your child's Internet experience; they all filter based on keywords and fixed lists of systems that are believed (by the programs' authors) to have objectionable material. None of them tells you exactly what they block, and your idea of what's appropriate and inappropriate may well not be the same as theirs. Some people claim that certain software sentries seem to have a political agenda because they block sites whose political content doesn't conform with that of the program's authors.

You can try before you buy by downloading evaluation copies of software-blocking packages. (You find out how to do that when you learn to navigate the Web in Chapters 5 and 6.) Here are a few blocking programs we're aware of:

✔ SurfWatch, from Spyglass, 175 S. San Antonio Road, Suite 102, Los Altos, CA 94022

   Phone: (888-6SPYGLASS)
   E-mail: info@surfwatch.com

   Available for both Windows and Macintosh, SurfWatch screens for newsgroups likely to contain sexually explicit material and keeps a computer from accessing specified Web, FTP, Gopher, and chat sites.

- Net Nanny, from Trove Investment Corporation

  E-mail: netnanny@netnanny.com
  URL: http://www.netnanny.com/

  This PC-based product monitors all PC activity, both online and off the Net in real-time. The parent- (or employer- or teacher-) defined dictionary enables you to determine what's not appropriate in your home. Net Nanny creates a log of children's activities.

- Cybersitter, from Solid Oak Software, Inc.

  URL: http://www.solidoak.com/cysitter.htm

  This Windows-based Internet filtering program blocks Web sites and newsgroups and filters e-mail. Cybersitter also generates a report of site visits.

Internet Resources for Kids

As you might have guessed, the Internet is replete with resources for kids — and parents, by the way. As we have learned from writing this book four times in four years, there's nothing so ephemeral as a Net address. To help keep this information as accurate as possible, we're putting our lists of resources on our Web site, both to keep them up to date and because they're too long to list here completely. From there, you can get right to the source, and we'll do our best to keep the sources current.

Visit http://net.dummies.net/kids, which puts you one mouse click away from the pages described here.

Mailing lists for parents and kids

Chapter 10 tells you how to subscribe to mailing lists. Lots of mailing lists for and about kids are listed on our Web page.

Newsgroups for parents and kids

Usenet newsgroups provide a way for Internet users around the world to hold conversations, and it's a great way for kids to converse too. Usenet also includes a number of newsgroups for parents and teachers (we describe how to read newsgroups in Chapter 11). We have on our Web site a list of newsgroups that might be of interest to you and your family.

Some Internet providers make available an entire set of K–12 groups, intended for teachers and schoolchildren in elementary and high schools. The first part of the names of these newsgroups is k12.

Web sites for kids

Okay, we admit it. Web sites can be the coolest thing since sliced bread. We have links to sites from around the world just especially for kids. To get to these sites, you have to know how to use a browser, such as Netscape, Internet Explorer, or Lynx. We tell you how in the very next chapter.

One word of warning. When we're looking for fun, we tend to think that color and graphics make all the difference. If you spend a great deal of time on the Web, you probably won't be satisfied for long with a text-only interface. To get the best from the Web, you need a color monitor and a Net connection that gives you graphics. If those aren't available to you now, by all means check stuff out anyway; just remember that you might have more fun in the text-based world of mailing lists and newsgroups, where content is more important than form.

Help for parents of kids with problems

One of the most profound and heartening human experiences available on the Net has to do with the help that total strangers freely offer one another. The incredible bonds that form from people sharing their experiences, struggles, strengths, and hopes redefine what it means to reach out and touch someone. We encourage everyone who has a concern to look for people who share that concern. Our experience of participating in mailing lists and newsgroups related to our own problems compels us to enthusiastically encourage you to check things out online. You can do so with complete anonymity. You can watch and learn for a long time, or you can jump into the fray and ask for help.

We caution you that everyone who gives advice is not a medical expert. You have to involve your own practitioners in your process. Many people have found enormous help, however, from people who have gone down similar paths before them. For many of us, it has made all the difference in the world.

We list a few of the available online mailing lists and discussion groups. There's almost certainly a mailing list or group specific to your needs regardless of whether we list it, and new groups are added every day. If you're using a commercial provider such as America Online or CompuServe, your provider has special forums that may interest you as well.

Notice that some lists are talk lists, which feature free-flow discussion; some lists have very focused discussions, and some lists are almost purely academic. It's not always obvious from the name. If it looks interesting, subscribe and see what sort of discussion is going on there. It's easy enough to unsubscribe if you don't like it.

The Internet in Schools

Schools are actively debating Internet access for their students. Teachers and parents go round and round, and ignorance seems to prevail. Find out as much as you can and get involved. The more you know, the more you can advocate for appropriate access.

A wonderful book called *The Internet For Teachers,* by David Clark (published by IDG Books Worldwide, Inc.) can help you understand all that can be gained from the Internet and can arm you with the information you need in order to face hordes of cynics, including school administrators, teachers, and other parents. The book focuses on the Net from an educator's perspective, including why it is important, how to use it, and where to find education-specific resources. Though it's aimed at teachers, it's a great find for parents.

Contractually speaking

Many kids are smart. Smart kids can find ways around rules, and smart kids can find ways around software systems designed to "protect" kids. Many institutions rely successfully on students' signed contracts that explicitly detail what is appropriate and what is inappropriate system use. Students who violate one of these contracts lose their Internet or computer privileges.

We believe that this approach is a good one. In our experience, kids are quicker and more highly motivated and have more time to spend breaking in to and out of systems than most adults we know, and this method encourages them to do something more productive than electronic lock-picking.

Industrial-strength cyberprotection

It's not just schools that are trying to restrict access to the Internet. Some corporations, fearful of their employees wasting time on personal interests, are turning to software products that limit users to what the employer deems appropriate. Although our personal experience is that the most highly creative and productive environments are the least restrictive ones, you have to verify that for yourself.

WebTrack, an institutional software product, logs Internet access and denies access to certain categories of sites. It is available from:

Webster Networks Strategies

Phone: 800-WNS-0066 or 813-261-5503
E-mail: info@webster.com
URL: http://www.webster.com/

Part II
Using Your
Internet Account

In this part . . .

We cover the basic Internet skills you need to become a full-fledged *internaut*. We tell you all about the World Wide Web and how to find things there, how to send and read e-mail, how to participate in mailing lists and newsgroups, and how to download files from the Net.

Chapter 5

The Wild, Wonderful, Wacky Web

*P*eople are talking about *the Web* today at least as much as they're talking about *the Net.* The World Wide Web and the Internet are not the same thing, but they are related. The World Wide Web (which we call the Web because we're lazy typists) lives "on top of" the Internet. The Internet's network is at the core of the Web, although the Web itself is something different.

Okay, okay, so what is it already? The Web is in some ways sort of a cross between libraries, television, computer networks, and telephones — it's all of the above and none of the above.

The Web is a bunch of "pages" of information connected to each other around the globe. Each page can be a combination of text, pictures, audio clips, video clips, animations, and other stuff. (We're vague about the other stuff because they add new types of other stuff every day.) What makes Web pages interesting is that they contain *hyperlinks,* usually called just *links* because the Net already has plenty of hype. Each link refers to another Web page, and when you click a link, your *browser* fetches the page the link connects to. (Hold your hat — we talk about browsers in a couple of pages. For now, just think of your browser as the program that talks to the Web.)

Each page your browser gets for you can have more links that take you to yet other places. Pages can be linked to other pages anywhere in the world so that after you're on the Web, you can end up looking at pages from Singapore to Calgary, from Sydney to Buenos Aires, all faster than you can say "Jack's your uncle," usually. How fast you get from one page to another depends on a number of different things we talk about later on; in theory, however, and approaching reality in many parts of the world, you're only seconds away from any site, anywhere in the world.

Where did the Web come from?

The World Wide Web was invented in 1989 at the European Particle Physics Lab in Geneva, Switzerland, an unlikely spot for a revolution in computing. The inventor was a British researcher named Tim Berners-Lee, who is now the director of the World Wide Web Consortium (W3), the organization that sets standards and loosely oversees the development of the Web. Tim is terrifically smart and hard-working and is the nicest guy you would ever want to meet. (Margy met him through Sunday school — is that wholesome or what?)

Tim invented *HTTP* (*HyperText Transport Protocol*), the way that Web browsers communicate with Web servers; *HTML* (*HyperText Markup Language*), the language in which Web pages are written; and *URLs* (*Uniform Resource Locators*), the codes used to identify Web pages and most other information on the Net. He envisioned the Web as a way for everyone to both publish and read information on the Net, and early Web browsers had editors that would let you create Web pages almost as easily as you could read them.

For more information about the development of the Web and the work of the World Wide Web Consortium, take a look at its Web site (at `http://www.w3.org`).

This system of interlinked documents is known as *hypertext*. Figure 5-1 shows a Web page: Each underlined phrase is a link to another Web page. Hypertext is the buzzword that makes the Web go. It's one of those simple ideas that turns out to have a much bigger effect than you would think.

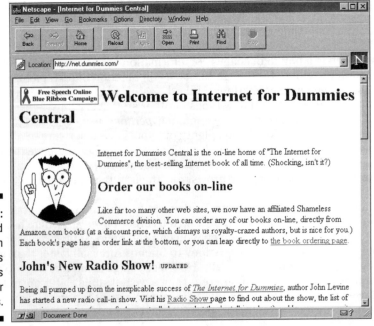

Figure 5-1: Underlined phrases on Web pages are links to other pages.

Hypertext: A reminiscence

John writes:

The term and concept of hypertext were invented around 1969 by Ted Nelson, a famous computer visionary who has been thinking about the relationship between computers and literature for at least 25 years now — starting back when most people would have considered it stupid to think that such a relationship could exist. Twenty years ago, he claimed that people would have computers in their pockets with leatherette cases and racing stripes. (I haven't seen any racing stripes yet, but otherwise he was dead on.)

Back in 1970 Ted told me that we all would have little computers with inexpensive screens on our desks with superwhizzo graphical hypertext systems. "Naah," I said. "For hypertext, you want a mainframe with gobs of memory and a high-resolution screen." We were both right, of course, because what we have on our desks in 1995 are little computers that are faster than 1970s mainframes and that have more memory and better screens.

Various hypertext projects have come and gone over the years, including one at Brown University (of which Ted was a part) and one at the Stanford Research Institute (which was arguably the most influential project in computing history because it invented screen windows and mice).

Ted's own hypertext system, Project Xanadu, has been in the works for about 15 years, under a variety of financing and management setups, with many of the same people slogging along and making it work. The project addresses many issues that other systems don't. In particular, Ted figured out how to pay authors for their work in a hypertext system, even when one document has pieces linked from others and the ensuing document consists almost entirely of a compendium of pieces of other documents. For a decade I have been hearing every year that Xanadu, and now a smaller Xanadu Light, which takes advantage of a great deal of existing software, will hit the streets the next year. This year I hope that they're right.

Margy adds:

Now that the World Wide Web has brought a limited version of hypertext to the masses, Ted is now hoping to build a Xanadu-like system on the Web. Stay tuned for developments!

Getting Hyper — the Basic Stuff

If you can get a handle on the fundamental structure of the Web, you can use it better and think about all the other ways it can be used. *Hypertext* is a way of connecting information in ways that make it easy to find — in theory. In traditional libraries (both the kinds with books and the kinds in computers), information is organized in a relatively arbitrary way, such as alphabetical order or the Dewey decimal system. These orders reflect nothing about the relationships among different pieces of information. In the world of hypertext, information is organized in relationship to other information. The relationships between different pieces of information are, in fact, often much more valuable than the pieces themselves.

Hypertext also enables the same set of information to be arranged in multiple ways at the same time. In a conventional library, a book can be on only one shelf at a time; a book about mental health, for example, is shelved under medicine or psychology, and it can't be in both places at one time. Hypertext is not so limited, and it's no problem to have links to the same document from both medical topics and psychological topics.

Suppose that you're interested in what influenced a particular historical person. You can begin by looking at the basic biographical information: where and when she was born, the names of her parents, her religion, and other basic stuff like that. Then you can expand on each fact by learning what else was happening at that time in her part of the world, what was happening in other parts of the world, and what influence her religion may have had on her. You draw a picture by pulling together all these aspects and understanding their connections — a picture that's hard to draw from just lists of names and dates.

A hypertext system creates between pieces of information the connections that enable you to find related information easily. As you draw connections between the pieces of information, you can begin to envision the Web created by the links between the pieces. What's so remarkable about the Web is that it connects pieces of information from all around the *planet,* on different machines and in different databases, all pretty much seamlessly (a feat you would be hard pressed to match with a card catalog). You might think of it as an extremely large but friendly alien centipede made of information.

The other important thing about the Web is that the information in it is searchable. For example, in about ten seconds you can get a list of all the Web pages that contain the words *domestic poultry* or your name or the name of a book you want to find out about. You can follow links to see each page on the list, to see which pages contain the information you want.

Name That Page

Hypertext is all well and good — trust us. You need to know about one more basic concept before hitting the Web. Every Web page has an address, a code by which it can be found and the name that gets attached to it so that browsers can find it. Great figures in the world of software engineering named this name *URL,* or *Uniform Resource Locator.* Every Web page has a URL. Those strings of characters that begin with `http://` or `www.` are URLs. Some people pronounce each letter ("U-R-L,"), and some think that it's a word ("URL") — it's your choice. Now you know enough to go browsing.

Duke of URL

Part of the plan of the World Wide Web is to link together all the information in the known universe, starting with all the stuff on the Internet and heading up from there. (This may be a slight exaggeration, but we don't think so.)

One of the keys to global domination is to give everything (at least everything that could be a Web resource) a name, and in particular a consistent name so that no matter what kind of thing a hypertext link refers to, a Web browser can find it and know what to do with it.

Look at this typical URL, the one for the Web page shown in Figure 5-1:

```
http://net.dummies.net/
    index.html
```

The first thing in a URL, the word before the colon, is the *scheme,* which describes the way a browser can get to the resource. Although ten schemes are defined, the most common by far is http, the *HyperText Transfer Protocol* that is the Web's native transfer technique. (Don't confuse http, which is the way pages are sent over the Net, with HTML, which is the way the pages are coded internally. We get to that in Chapter 6.)

The details of the rest of the URL depend on the scheme, but most schemes use a consistent syntax. Following the colon are two slashes (always forward slashes, never reverse slashes) and the name of the host computer on which the resource lives; in this case, net.dummies.net. Then there's another slash and a *path,* which gives the name of the resource on that host; in this case, a file named index.html.

Web URLs allow a few other optional parts. They can include a *port number,* which says, roughly speaking, which of several programs running on that host should handle the request. The port number goes after a colon after the host name, like this:

```
http://net.dummies.net:80/
    index.html
```

Because the standard http port number is 80, if that's the port you want (it usually is), you can leave it out. Finally, a Web URL can have a *search part* at the end, following a question mark, like this:

```
http://net.dummies.net:80/
    index.html?plugh
```

Although not all pages can have search parts, for those that do, it tells the host, uh, what to search for. (You rarely type a search part yourself — they're often constructed for you from fill-in fields on Web pages.)

Three other useful URL schemes are mailto, ftp, and file. A mailto URL looks like this:

```
mailto:internet4@dummies.net
```

That is, it's an e-mail address. When you choose a mailto URL in Netscape, it pops up a window in which you can enter an e-mail message to the address in the URL. In Internet Explorer, clicking a mailto URL runs the Internet Mail program, described in Chapter 8. It's most commonly used for sending comments to the owner of a page.

A URL that starts with ftp lets you download files from an FTP server on the Internet (see Chapter 12 for information about FTP servers). An ftp URL looks like this:

```
ftp://ftp.netscape5.com/
    navigator/3.0/mac/README.TXT
```

The part after the two slashes is the name of the FTP server (ftp.netscape5.com, in this case). The rest of the URL is the pathname of the file you want to download.

(continued)

(continued)

The `file` URL specifies a file on your computer. It looks like this:

`file:///C|/WWW/INDEX.HTM`

On a DOS computer, this line indicates a Web page stored in the file C:\WWW\INDEX.HTM. The colon turns into a vertical bar (because colons in URLs mean something else), and the reverse slashes turn into forward slashes. File URLs are useful mostly for looking at GIF and JPG graphics files and for looking at a Web page you just wrote and stuck in a file on your disk.

Browsing Off

Now that you know all about the Web, you undoubtedly want to check it out for yourself. To do this, you need a *browser,* the software that goes and gets Web pages and displays them on your screen. Fortunately, if you have Internet access, you probably already have one. One probably came from your Internet service provider (ISP) and you installed it when you installed the rest of your Internet software. If you don't have a browser at all or want to get a copy of Netscape Navigator or Microsoft Internet Explorer (most likely because you have one but want to try the other), see the section "Getting and Installing Netscape or Internet Explorer," later in this chapter.

Now that the Web gets more press than the rest of the Internet put together, everyone and her uncle wants to write a Web browser. We discuss three of the most popular: Netscape, the world's most popular graphical browser; Internet Explorer, the Microsoft answer to Netscape; and Lynx, the text-only browser for the UNIX shell account crowd.

If you have another window-oriented browser, such as any of the many versions of Mosaic, nearly everything we say about Netscape and Internet Explorer also applies. (It's no coincidence because Netscape was written by many of the same people who originally wrote Mosaic, and Internet Explorer is based on Mosaic too.)

If you use America Online or CompuServe, read Chapters 14 and 15 to find out how to get and install Netscape and Internet Explorer with these services. Then come back and read this chapter.

Browser Warfare

Are you sick of hearing about the war between Netscape, the "killer application" for the Internet, and Internet Explorer, the Microsoft attempt to kill off Netscape? This chapter shows you how to use both. We don't take sides here because they both work okay and they're similar enough that any reason to dislike one of them probably applies to the other.

If you already have a PPP or SLIP account or if you use an online service (such as CompuServe or America Online), you can use cool modern Web browsers, such as Netscape and Internet Explorer.

If you have a UNIX shell account, close your eyes and forget about all the pretty pictures. Many other programs, fortunately, do roughly the same thing as Netscape, including one called Lynx, which works just fine over a text-only dial-up connection. Go to the section "Life with Lynx," later in this chapter, or go get yourself a PPP or SLIP account.

Surfing with Netscape and Internet Explorer

When you start Netscape, you see a screen similar to the one that was shown in Figure 5-1. The Internet Explorer window looks like Figure 5-2. Which page your browser displays depends on how it's set up; many providers arrange to have it display their home page.

At the top of the window are a bunch of buttons and the (Netscape) Location or (Internet Explorer) Address line, which contains the *Uniform Resource Locator,* or *URL,* for the current page. (Netscape sometimes labels this box Netsite for reasons we can't fathom. Microsoft sometimes calls it a

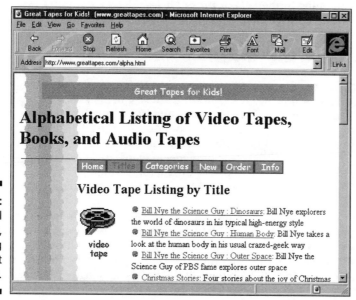

Figure 5-2:
Your typical Web page, using Internet Explorer.

Shortcut.) Remember that URLs are an important part of Web lore because they're the secret codes that name all the pages on the Web. For details, see the sidebar "Duke of URL," earlier in this chapter.

Getting around

The primary skill you need (if we can describe something as basic as a single mouse-click as a skill) is to learn how to move from page to page on the Web.

It's easy: You just click any link that looks interesting. Underlined blue text and blue-bordered pictures are links. (Links may be a color other than blue, depending on the look the Web page designer is going for, but they're always underlined unless the page is the victim of a truly awful designer.) You can tell when you're pointing to a link because the mouse pointer changes to a little hand. If you're not sure whether something is a link, click it anyway because, if it's not, it won't hurt anything. (Clicking outside a link selects the text you click, as in most other programs.)

Backward, ho!

Web browsers remember the last few pages you visited, so if you click a link and decide that you're not so crazy about the new page, you can easily go back to the preceding one. To go back, click the Back button (its icon is an arrow pointing to the left) or press Alt-←.

All over the map

Some picture links are *image maps,* such as the big picture in Figure 5-3. With a regular link, it doesn't matter where you click; in an image map, it does. The image map here is typical and has a bunch of obvious places you click for various types of information. (All the 1990 census data except private individual info is online on the Net, by the way, at http://www.census.gov.) Some image maps are actual maps — a map of the United States at the Census Bureau, for example, that shows you information about the state you click.

As you move the mouse cursor around a Web page, whenever you're pointing at a link, the place you linked to appears in small type at the bottom of the screen. Netscape shows the URL of the page, and Internet Explorer shows the name of the computer the Web page is stored on and the name of the file containing the Web page. If the link is an image map, Netscape shows

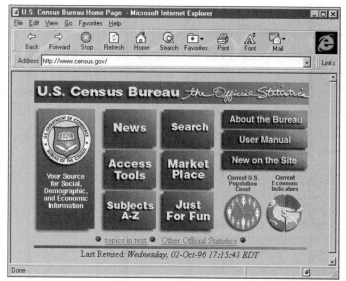

Figure 5-3:
Stand up
and be
counted at
the Census
Bureau.

the link followed by a question mark and two numbers that are the X and Y positions of where you are on the map. The numbers don't matter to you (it's up to the Web server to make sense of them); if you see a pair of numbers counting up and down when you move the mouse, however, you know that you're on an image map.

Going places

These days everyone and his dog has a home page. A *home page* is the main Web page for a person or organization. (For some samples, check out `http://users.aimnet.com/~carver/cindy.html` or you can try `http://www.rtd.com/~scs/dog/dog.html`.) Companies are advertising their home pages, and people are sending e-mail talking about cool sites. When you see a URL you want to check out, here's what you do:

1. **Click in the Location or Address box near the top of the Netscape or Internet Explorer window.**

2. **Type the URL in the box.**

   The URL is something like `http://net.dummies.net/`.

3. **Press Enter.**

If you receive URLs in electronic mail, Usenet news, or anywhere else on your Windows PC or Macintosh, you can use the standard cut-and-paste techniques and avoid retyping:

1. **Highlight the URL in whichever program is showing it.**

2. **Press Ctrl+C (⌘+C on the Mac) to copy the info to the Clipboard.**

3. **Click in the Location box in Netscape or the Address box or Internet Explorer.**

4. **Press Ctrl+V (⌘+V on the Mac) to paste the URL, and then press Enter.**

Newer versions of Eudora highlight any URLs in e-mail messages. All you have to do is click the highlighted link to open the Web page.

You can leave the `http://` off the front of URLs when you type them in the Location or Address box. If you use Netscape, you can leave the `www` off the front and the `com` off the back — that is, rather than type `http://www.idgbooks.com`, you can just type `idgbooks`.

Where to start?

You learn more about how to find things on the Web in Chapter 7; for now, here's a good way to get started: Go to the Yahoo! page. (Yes, the name of the Web page includes an exclamation point — they're very excitable.) That is, type this URL in the Location or Address box and then press Enter:

```
http://www.yahoo.com
```

You go to the Yahoo! page (there it is again), a directory of millions of Web pages by topic. Just nose around, and you will find something interesting.

For updates to the very book you are holding, go to this URL:

```
http://net.dummies.net/update
```

Follow the links to the page about our books, and then select the pages for readers of *The Internet For Dummies*, 4th Edition. If we have any late-breaking news about the Internet or updates and corrections to this book, you can find them there. If you find mistakes in this book, by the way, please send e-mail to us at `internet4@dummies.net`.

This page looks funny

Sometimes a Web page gets garbled on the way in or you interrupt it (by clicking the Stop button on the toolbar). You can tell your browser to get the information on the page again: In Netscape, click the Reload button or press Ctrl+R; in Internet Explorer, click the Refresh button or press F5.

Netscape and Internet Explorer are not in a hurry

When Netscape announced Version 3.0, it publicized tests which showed that it was 200 percent faster than its rival program, Internet Explorer. Microsoft retaliated with studies and statistics of its own. This is not unlike a battle to claim the title of the world's slimmest hippopotamus — they're both big and slow.

The programs have two separate slowness problems. One is that fancy multimedia screens require a great deal of data, which means that they take a long time to transfer over any except the fastest networks. The other is that both programs are, to use a technical computer term, pigs. (They're not as piggish as some other Net browsers, though.) The standard rule of thumb says that you need a 486/33MHz computer with 8 megabytes of RAM to get reasonable performance, and we can report from experience that if you run either program on a computer of that size, they still spend an awful lot of time swapping pieces of program back and forth from the disk. If you have a Pentium and 32 megabytes of RAM, they're reasonably but not breathtakingly fast.

You can do a few things to speed up Netscape and Internet Explorer, which we address in Chapter 6. (This is a ploy to keep you reading.)

Get me outta here

Sooner or later even the most dedicated Web surfer has to stop to eat or attend to other bodily needs. You leave Netscape or Internet Explorer in the same way as you leave any other Mac or Windows program: by choosing File⇨Exit (File⇨Close for Windows Internet Explorer, we were surprised to notice) or pressing Alt+F4.

Getting and Installing Netscape or Internet Explorer

With luck, Netscape or Internet Explorer is already installed on your computer. The two programs are so similar that if you have one of them, we suggest that you stick with it (for now, anyway). Without luck, you don't have either program, but they are, fortunately, not difficult to get and install.

Netscape Navigator (the real name of the program everyone calls Netscape) comes in several varieties: Windows 3.1 (the 16-bit version), Windows 95 (the 32-bit version), Mac, and versions for a bunch of UNIX workstations. Netscape also comes as part of a suite of programs called Netscape

Communicator (we talk about the other programs in Chapters 8 and 11). Netscape 4.0 includes a Web page editor too, in case you want to create your own Web pages. (See Chapter 22 to find information about creating Web pages.)

Although Internet Explorer was originally available for only Windows 95, Microsoft now has versions for Windows 3.1 and the Mac.

Even if you already have a copy of Netscape or Internet Explorer, new versions come out every 20 minutes or so, and it's worth knowing how to upgrade because occasionally the new versions fix some bugs so that they're better than the old ones. The steps are relatively simple:

1. **Get a copy of the Netscape or Internet Explorer installation package on your computer.**

2. **Unpack the installation package.**

3. **Install the software.**

Because computers are involved, each of these steps is, naturally, a little more difficult than necessary.

Getting the package

Your Internet provider may have given you a copy of Netscape or Internet Explorer on a disk. The AT&T WorldNet Service software, for example, includes a licensed version of Netscape or Internet Explorer, as do the sign-up packages for IBM Advantis, EarthLink, and many other Internet providers.

Because Internet Explorer comes as part of Windows 95, Windows 95 users already have it, but it may be an elderly version. Microsoft gives away Internet Explorer. (One can complain about many aspects of Explorer, but not the price.)

You can also download both Netscape and Internet Explorer from the Net. If you have access to any Web browser, try one of these Web sites:

- ✔ **TUCOWS (The Ultimate Collection of Internet Software):**
  http://www.tucows.com

- ✔ **The Consummate WinSock Applications page:**
  http://www.cwsapps.com

- ✔ **Netscape home page (for Netscape only):**
  http://home.netscape.com

- ✔ **Microsoft home page (for Internet Explorer only):**
  http://www.microsoft.com

Use your Web browser to go to the page, and then follow the instructions for finding and downloading the program. You may also want to consult Chapter 12 for more information about downloading files from the Internet.

If you don't have Web access yet but you do have access to an FTP program (described in Chapter 12), you can use it to download the Netscape or Internet Explorer program:

✔ Netscape can be downloaded from ftp.netscape.com (if it's busy, try ftp1.netscape.com, ftp2.netscape.com, up to about ftp15.) Move to the navigator directory and then to the directory for the version you want (which is 3.01 as we write this book but is probably at least 4.0 by the time you read it). Then choose the directory for the type of computer you have (mac, unix, or windows). Finally, choose the file to download. Currently, the filenames are n16e301.exe for Windows 3.1 and n32e301.exe for Windows 95 — the 301 in the filename will change for future versions. If you want the version with extra features, or *plug-ins,* choose n16e301p.exe or n32e301p.exe.

✔ Internet Explorer is available from ftp.microsoft.com. Move to the msdownload directory. Then choose ie2 for Version 2.0 for Windows, ie3 for Version 3.0 for Windows, or iemac for the Mac version — these directory names may change as Microsoft releases new versions. Finally, choose the filename to download. The filenames are currently ntie30.exe for Version 3.0 for Windows, IE21_68K.exe for Version 2.1 for 68K Macs, and IE21_PPC.exe for Version 2.1 for PowerPC Macs.

Another option is to stroll into a software store and buy Netscape — you get a license, a manual, and the phone number for tech support, which you don't get when you download Netscape or buy the CD-ROM version of this book.

We're home — let's unpack and install

After you have the program, you have to unpack it and install it. If you get Netscape or Internet Explorer on floppy disks or CD-ROM, follow the instructions that come with it. If you have the Netscape or Internet Explorer distribution file or your hard disk, follow these instructions (assuming that you use Windows 3.1 or Windows 95). Macintosh users, check the tips at the end of this section — installing on the Mac is even simpler.

To avoid excess user comprehension, the thing that Microsoft called a directory in MS-DOS and Windows 3.1 is now called a folder in Windows 95. We use the official newspeak term; if you're a Win 3.1 user, however, pretend that we said "directory" wherever you read "folder."

1. **Create a folder called something like \Inst.**

   This folder is just for installing the program — it's not where Netscape or Internet Explorer will live permanently. From the Windows 3.1 File Manager, choose File➪Create Directory. From Windows 95 My Computer or Explorer, choose File➪New➪Folder.

2. **Put the Netscape or Internet Explorer distribution file in that folder.**

   The Netscape filename probably begins with N16 or N32. The Internet Explorer filename usually begins with MSIE, although we just downloaded one named DLMIN30.exe, so you never can tell. Just drag the distribution file to your new folder in File Manager, My Computer, or Windows Explorer.

3. **The distribution file contains a program — run it.**

   A bunch of files will burst forth from the distribution file, reminiscent of the movie *Alien*. (It's called, in the lingo, a *self-extracting archive*.) Although you can run the program in a couple of ways, the simplest is just to double-click the filename in File Manager, My Computer, or Windows Explorer.

   Some versions of the Internet Explorer go right ahead and begin installing the program — if you see a window with instructions about how to install Internet Explorer, skip to Step 5.

   Otherwise, you now have several dozen files in your \Inst folder, including a file called Setup.exe.

4. **Run the setup program (Setup.exe) to install the program.**

   The program begins installing Netscape or Internet Explorer.

5. **Follow the instructions on-screen.**

   Although the installation program asks a bunch of questions, the default answers for all of them are usually okay. If the Internet Explorer installation program asks whether you want to select optional components, choose Yes, and select the additional programs you want to install. (They may include Internet Mail and Internet News, the Microsoft e-mail and Usenet newsgroup programs, respectively; see Chapters 8 and 11 to find out how to use them.)

   When the Internet Explorer installation is done, you may have to restart your computer; if so, you see a message offering to restart it now. Click Yes unless you're in the middle of other work — then finish your work and restart your computer.

6. **Connect to your Internet provider or online service.**

   The first thing your new browser will want to do is display a Web page, so you had better be connected to the Internet.

7. **Try out Netscape or Internet Explorer.**

   Click the attractive new icon — the Netscape icon is labeled Netscape Navigator, which is the real name of the program, and the Internet Explorer icon goes by the intriguingly vague name The Internet.

   The first time you run Netscape, you see a bunch of legal boilerplate stuff describing the license conditions for the program. If you can stand the conditions (many people can), click to indicate your acceptance. The program then starts up. It may want to connect to the Netscape Web page so that you can register your copy of Netscape — follow its instructions.

   The first time you run Internet Explorer, it may run the Internet Connection Wizard, which offers to help you get connected to the Internet. If so, follow the instructions on-screen. If you already have an Internet connection that works, you have a chance to tell it so.

8. **When you're happy with the program, delete the \Inst folder.**

   You don't need the installation files anymore, and they take up a great deal of disk space.

Attention Mac users: The installation tips for a Mac are almost exactly the same. If you download your browser from the Net and you're lucky, it should arrive as an executable program in your download folder. Click it and follow its directions in order to install it. It may arrive as a StuffIt file that self-extracts if you have StuffIt installed.

If you're upgrading from an older version of Netscape to a newer one, you can install the new version to replace the old one. When the installation program asks whether to replace Netscape.ini, choose No to keep your existing Netscape settings.

If you have installed the excellent shareware WinZip program, you can use it to automate the entire Netscape or Internet Explorer installation process. As soon as you have downloaded the distribution file, open it in WinZip. (Even though it ends with EXE, it's really a ZIP file.) Then click Install. WinZip creates a temporary folder, extracts the files, and runs Setup. Later, when you return to WinZip, it gets rid of the junk. (See Chapter 12 for more information about WinZip.)

Life with Lynx

Netscape and Internet Explorer require PPP or SLIP connections. What if you're stuck with a UNIX shell account? Those of you living a mouse-free existence can still do some serious Web surfing using Lynx.

Because Lynx is a text-only browser, it can't do some things, such as show pictures, play audio and video clips, or display news-ticker-style moving messages at the bottom of your screen (a real advantage, in this last case). Within those limitations, though, it's a good program.

Because Lynx *is* text-only, in fact, it's much faster than the graphics-based browsers, which leaves you at least one thing to feel good about.

All UNIX shell providers should have Lynx available because it's free. To start it, you type **lynx** at the UNIX shell prompt. It starts up and displays a home page on the screen, as shown in Figure 5-4, which shows the same Web page as in Figure 5-1.

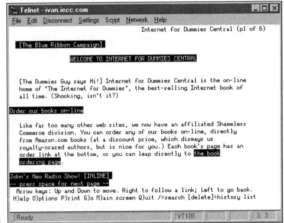

Figure 5-4:
Look, Ma,
no pictures!

Because most text screens can't do underlining, the links are shown in reverse video. Bracketed text or the word [IMAGE] appears where a picture would be displayed. One link on the screen is *current* and is highlighted in a different color. (On our screen, it's yellow rather than white text, which doesn't show up on a black-and-white page. Use your imagination, or go get a yellow highlighting pen.) Lynx thoughtfully puts some help information on the bottom two lines, which makes it much easier to use.

Wandering around

Nearly all Lynx commands are single keystrokes. Pressing the ↑ and ↓ keys moves you from link to link on the current page. If the page is more than one screenful, the page scrolls as necessary. To move to the next screen of the current page, press the spacebar or press + and – to move forward and backward a screen at a time.

You press ↑ and ↓ to move from link to link, even when the links are next to each other on a line. For example, you might have a few lines on the screen like this:

```
Famous philosophers:

[Moe] [Larry] [Curly] [Socrates]
```

If the highlight is on Larry, you press the ↑ key to go to Moe and press the ↓ key to go to Curly. The ← and → keys mean something else, as you will see in a second.

After you have highlighted a link you like, press the → key or Enter to follow that link (Pressing→ is the Lynx equivalent of clicking a link.) After Lynx fetches the new page, you can press the arrow keys to move around the new page. Pressing ← takes you back to the preceding page. You can press the ← key several times to go back several pages.

Lynx just can't do some things, most notably image maps. Although it tells you that there's an image, because you can't see the image and you can't use a mouse, there's no way to click it. Fortunately, any sensible Web page that has an image map offers some other way to get to the places the image map would otherwise take you. The page has either a set of text links under the image or, in some cases, a link that says something like "Click here for a text-only version of this page." Lynx gives you a nice, clean, image-free page from which to work.

To go to a specific URL, press **g** for *go-to* and then type the URL on the line that Lynx provides, followed by pressing Enter.

Leaving Lynx

When you're finished with Lynx, press **q** to exit. Lynx asks whether you're sure that you want to quit; press **y**.

Is that all there is?

Of course not. Lynx is bristling with features, just like any other modern computer program. Just about every possible keystroke means something to Lynx (we discuss some of them in Chapter 6). The arrow keys and g and q are all you really need to get going.

If all else fails. . . .

If you don't even have access to Lynx on your system, a few systems offer public access to it. If you have access to Telnet (Chapter 22 gives you information about Telnet and other UNIX commands), these systems let you Lynx around:

- ✔ `lynx.cc.ukans.edu` (Kansas, log in as *lynx*)
- ✔ `sailor.lib.md.us` (Maryland, log in as *guest*)

Although they're not as good as running Lynx on your own provider's system (they're slower, and some options don't work), they're better than nothing.

Chapter 6

Wrangling with the Web

. . . .

. . . .

*N*ow that you have begun to find your way around the Web, we introduce you to some comparatively advanced features so that you can start to feel like a Web pro in no time. Remember that Netscape Navigator (commonly called just Netscape), Internet Explorer, and Lynx aren't the only browsers. If you're using something else, most of the features we cover here are probably also available to you. Try poking around. The best way to learn what you can do is by trying everything. If you have a manual or online Help, of course, you might resort to reading them, but, hey, why spoil all the fun?

My Favorite Things

The Web really does have cool places to visit. Some you will want to visit over and over again. All the makers of fine browsers have, fortunately, provided a handy way for you to remember those spots and not have to write down those nasty URLs just to have to type them in again later.

The name varies, but the idea is simple. Your browser lets you mark a spot and then adds the URL to a list. Later, when you want to go back, you just go to your list and pick it out. Netscape calls these hot spots Bookmarks; Internet Explorer calls them Favorites.

Bookmarks can be handled in two general ways. One is to think of them as a menu so that you can choose individual bookmarks from the menu bar of your browser. The other is to think of them as a custom-built page of links so that you go to that page and then choose the link you want. Lynx takes the latter, custom Web page approach. Netscape, a prime example of the Great Expanding Blob approach to software design, does both. Internet Explorer takes yet another tack: It adds your Web pages to a folder of favorite places you might want to come back to.

Marking Netscape

Netscape bookmarks lurk under the Bookmarks menu. To add a bookmark for the currently displayed Web page in Netscape 3.0, choose Bookmarks⇨ Add Bookmark or press Ctrl+D. In Netscape 4.0, choose Window⇨ Bookmarks⇨Add Bookmark, or press Ctrl+D. The bookmarks appear as entries on the Bookmarks menu (in Netscape 3.0) or on the menu that appears when you click the Bookmarks Quick File button, to the left of the Location box (in Netscape 4.0). To go to one of the pages on your bookmark list, just choose its entry from this menu.

If you're like most users, your bookmark menu will get bigger and bigger and crawl down your screen and eventually end up flopping down on the floor, which is both unattractive and unsanitary. Fortunately, you can smoosh (technical term) your menu into a more tractable form. Choose Bookmarks⇨Go to Bookmarks (in Netscape 3.0) or Window⇨Bookmarks⇨ Edit Bookmarks (in Netscape 4.0), or press Ctrl+B (in either version) to display your Bookmarks window, as shown in Figure 6-1.

Figure 6-1:
The
Netscape
Bookmarks
window
shows the
list of Web
pages you
want to
come
back to.

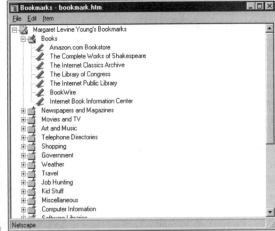

Because all these bookmarks are "live," you can go to any of them by clicking them. (You can leave this window open while you move around the Web in your main browser window.) You can also add separator lines and submenus to organize your bookmarks and make the individual menus less unwieldy. Submenus look like folders in the Bookmarks window.

In the Bookmarks window, choose Item⇨Insert Separator to add a separator line and Item⇨Insert Folder to add a new submenu. (Netscape asks you to type the name of the submenu before it creates the folder.) You can then drag the bookmarks, separators, and folders up and down to where you want them in the Bookmarks window. Drag an item to a folder to put it in that folder's submenu, and double-click a folder to display or hide that submenu. Because any changes you make in the Bookmarks window are immediately reflected on the Bookmarks menu, it's easy to fiddle with the bookmarks until you get something you like.

When you're done fooling with your bookmarks, choose File⇨Close or press Ctrl+W to close the Bookmarks window.

Netscape also has a cool feature that enables you to see which of the items in your bookmark list have been updated since you last looked at them. Open the Bookmarks window by choosing Bookmarks⇨Go to Bookmarks from the menu and then choosing File⇨What's New from the menu in the Bookmarks window. You see a little box asking which bookmarks you want to check. Click the Start Checking button. When Netscape is done checking the Web pages on your bookmarks list, it displays a message telling you how many have changed. The icons in the Bookmarks window reveal which pages have changed: The ones with little sparkles have new material, the ones with question marks Netscape isn't sure about, and the ones that look normal haven't changed.

Marking Internet Explorer

Internet Explorer uses a system similar to the one Netscape uses: You can add the current page to your Favorites folder and then look at and organize your Favorites folder. If you use Windows 95, however, this Favorites folder is shared with other programs on your computer. Other programs also can add things to your Favorites folder, so it's a jumble (in our opinion) of Web pages, files, and other things.

To add the current page to your Favorites folder, choose Favorites⇨Add to Favorites from the menu. To see your Favorites folder, choose Favorites⇨ Organize Favorites or Open Favorites from the menu.

Exactly how the Favorites folder works depends on which version of Internet Explorer you are running. The Windows 95 version is shown in Figure 6-2. This version of the Favorites folder lets you create subfolders in the Favorites folder so that you can store different types of files in different folders (the Windows 3.1 version just lets you look at the Favorites list, but you can't reorganize it). To create a folder, click the Create New Folder button (the button with the yellow folder with a little sparkle, near the upper right corner of the window). To move an item in the Favorites window into a folder, click it, click the Mo<u>v</u>e button, and select the folder to move it to. You can see the contents of a folder by double-clicking it. When you are done organizing your favorite items, click the <u>C</u>lose button.

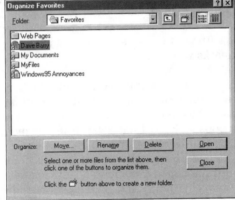

Figure 6-2:
Your
favorite
Web pages,
word-
processing
files, and
other items
all appear
in this
window.

The folders you create in the Organize Favorites window appear on your F<u>a</u>vorites menu, and the items you put in the folders appear on submenus. To return to a Web page you added to your Favorites folder, just choose it from the F<u>a</u>vorites menu.

In Windows 95, the Favorites folder usually appears on your desktop. You can double-click the folder to open it and double-click an item to return to that item. If the item is a Web page, your browser fires up and (if you're connected to the Internet) displays the Web page.

Marking Lynx

The Lynx bookmark scheme is a complete anticlimax compared to Netscape and Internet Explorer. It's controlled by two (count 'em — two) letters.

To add the current page to your bookmark list, press **a**. Lynx gives you the choice of adding a link to the page on the screen (**d** for document) or copying the highlighted link (**c** for current).

To look at (view) your current bookmark list, press **v**. When you're looking at your bookmark list, you move through it and choose links in the same way as you do on any other Web page. You can remove links from the bookmark page by pressing **r**.

 If you're using Lynx on your own UNIX account, your bookmarks are saved in a file between Lynx sessions. On the other hand, if you're using Telnet to connect to a Lynx system somewhere else, the bookmarks exist only through a single Lynx session, and they're discarded when you quit.

Speeding Things Up

Unless you have a high-speed dedicated connection rather than a normal dial-up account, you probably spend a great deal of time wishing that getting to stuff on the Web was much faster. (John has a high-speed dedicated connection, and he spends a certain amount of time waiting for the Web anyway.) Here are a handful of tricks you can use to try to speed things up.

Where do we start?

In Netscape Navigator: When Netscape starts up, by default it loads the large and attractive Netscape home page. After one or two times, beautiful though the home page is, you will probably find that you can do without it. You can tell Netscape not to load any Web page when you start the program:

1. **Choose Options⇨General Preferences (in Netscape 3.0) or Edit⇨Preferences⇨General Preferences (in Netscape 4.0).**

   You see the Preferences dialog box.

2. **Click the Appearance tab.**

   Under Startup, you see a setting called Browser Starts With.

3. **If you want to start with no Web page, click Blank Page. If you want to start with a page you specify, click Home Page Location, click in the box below it, and type the name of a page you would rather see (your provider's home page, for example).**

4. **Click OK.**

In Internet Explorer: Internet Explorer starts by displaying the Microsoft home page or a Web page stored on your own hard disk, depending on which version of Internet Explorer you have. You can change that start page, but you can't tell Internet Explorer not to load any page at all. (Loading a home page from your disk is, fortunately, pretty fast.) Follow these steps to change your start page:

1. **Display the Web page you want to use as your start page.**

   For example, you might want to start at the Yahoo! page, which we describe in Chapter 7, or Internet For Dummies Central, at `http://net.dummies.net`.

2. **Choose View⇨Options from the menu.**

   You see the Options dialog box.

3. **If you see a Navigation tab along the top of the dialog box, click it. Otherwise, skip to Step 7.**

   You can set the addresses of several Web pages.

4. **Make sure that the Page box is set to Start Page (if it's not, click it and choose Start Page from the list that appears.)**

   You are telling Internet Explorer to display the address of the start page in the Address box.

5. **Click the Use Current button.**

   The URL of the current page appears in the Address box.

6. **Click OK. You're done — skip the rest of these steps.**

7. **Click the Start and Search Pages tab along the top of the Options dialog box.**

   The dialog box says, "Your Start Page is currently:" followed by the URL of the page on which you start. If you don't see "Start Page" in the box, click in the box and choose Start Page from the list that appears.

8. **To change the start page to the page Internet Explorer is currently displaying, click the Use Current button. To change the start page to the Microsoft home page, click the Use Default button.**

   The URL changes.

9. **Click OK.**

Choose a start page that doesn't have many pictures: By starting with a Web page that loads faster or with no start page at all, you don't have to wait so long to start browsing.

Switching to ugly mode

You can save a great deal of time when you're browsing the Web by skipping the pictures. True, the pages don't look as snazzy, but they load like the wind. If you decide that you want to see the missing pictures after all, you can still do so.

In Netscape Navigator: On the Netscape Options menu (in Netscape 3.0) or the Edit⇨ Preferences menu (in Netscape 4.0), uncheck Auto Load Images. (That is, choose Options or Edit⇨Preferences from the menu and look to see whether a check mark appears to the left of the Auto Load Images command. If it does, choose the command — this action removes the check mark. If there is no check mark, *don't* choose the command — press Esc instead.) Turning Auto Load Images off tells Netscape to load the text part of Web pages, which is small, and to hold off on the larger images. It displays a box with three colored shapes where the images go. To see a particular image, click the three-shape box with the *right* mouse button and choose Load Image from the menu that appears. You can turn image-loading back on by choosing the Options⇨Auto Load Images or Edit⇨Preferences⇨Auto Load Images command again.

In Internet Explorer: You can tell Internet Explorer not to bother loading images by choosing View⇨Options from the menu and clicking the General or Appearance tab. If a check mark or X appears in the Show pictures box, click in the box to remove the check mark or X. Then click OK. Where pictures usually appear, you see a little box with three shapes in it. If you want to see a particular picture, right-click the little box and choose Show Picture from the menu that appears. You can turn image-loading back on by choosing View⇨Options again, clicking Show pictures, and clicking OK.

Cold, hard cache

When Netscape Navigator or Internet Explorer retrieves a page you have asked to see, it stores the page on your disk. If you ask for the same page again five minutes later, the program doesn't have to retrieve the page again — it can reuse the copy it already has. If you tell the program not to load images, for example, you get a fair number of them anyway because they were already downloaded.

The space your browser uses to store pages is called its *cache* (pronounced "cash" because it's French and gives your *cache* more *cachet*). The more space you tell your browser to use for its cache, the faster pages appear the second time you look at them.

In Netscape Navigator: To set the size of the Netscape cache, follow these steps:

1. **Choose Options⇨Network Preferences (in Netscape 3.0) or Edit⇨Preferences⇨Network Preferences from the menu.**

   You see the Preferences dialog box.

2. **Click the Cache tab along the top of the dialog box.**

   The Disk Cache box shows the maximum size of the cache in kilobytes (K): We like to set Disk Cache to at least 1024 K (that is, 1 MB). Set it to a higher number if you have a large hard disk with loads of free space — the more space your cache can occupy, the more often you can load a Web page quickly from the cache rather than slowly from the Net.

3. **Click OK.**

In Internet Explorer: To set the size of the Internet Explorer cache, follow these steps:

1. **Choose View⇨Options from the menu.**

   You see the Options dialog box.

2. **Click the Advanced tab.**

3. **Click the Settings button in the Temporary Internet files box.**

   You see the Settings dialog box, with information about the cache. (Many versions of Internet Explorer never call it a cache — guess they don't speak French.)

4. **Click the slider on the Amount of disk space to use or Maximum size line and move it to about 10 percent.**

   If you have tons of empty disk space, you could slide it rightward to 20 percent. If you're short on space, move it leftward to 1 or 2 percent.

5. **Click OK twice.**

Some of us hardly ever exit out of our browsers, which is probably not a good idea for our long-term mental stability. If you are one of us, however, remember that the pages your browser has cached aren't reloaded from the Web (they're taken from your disk) until you reload them. If you want to make sure that you're getting fresh pages, reload pages that you think might have changed since you last visited. Your browser is supposed to check whether a saved page has changed, but because the check sometimes doesn't work perfectly, an occasional Reload command for pages that change frequently, such as stock prices or the weather report, is advisable.

Getting the Big Picture

Netscape and Internet Explorer have so many buttons, icons, and boxes near the top of the window that not much space is left to display the Web page.

In Netscape Navigator: You can clear off a little more space in the Netscape window by using commands on the Options or View⇨Toolbars menu:

✔ To eliminate directory buttons (the bottommost row of buttons, just above the Web page area, that say "What's New?" and "What's Cool?"), choose Options⇨Show Directory Buttons. Netscape 4.0 eliminates these buttons permanently (a good move, in our opinion).

✔ To clear off the Location box, choose Options⇨Show Location (in Netscape 3.0) or View⇨Toolbars⇨Hide Location Toolbar (in Netscape 4.0). This isn't such a good idea most of the time because the Location box shows you the URL of the page you're looking at and lets you type a new URL to go to.

✔ To say sayonara to the toolbar (the row of buttons just below the menu), choose Options⇨Show Toolbar (in Netscape 3.0) or View⇨ Toolbars⇨Hide Command Toolbar (in Netscape 4.0). Most people use the Back button all the time, but you won't miss it if you remember that pressing Alt+← does the same thing.

To restore any of the things you just blew away, give the same command again. We find that we never use the directory buttons and that we would rather keep the toolbar and Location box.

In Internet Explorer: You can reclaim screen real estate by giving these commands:

✔ To get rid of the toolbar (the row of buttons just below the menu), choose View⇨Toolbar. Most buttons on the toolbar have keyboard equivalents, some of which we describe in this chapter.

✔ To get rid of the status bar (the gray bar at the bottom of the Internet Explorer window), choose View⇨Status Bar.

Give the same command again to restore the item you got rid of. We prefer to keep these items on-screen most of the time, but your tastes may differ, and we have pretty big screens.

Filling In the Forms

Back in the Dark Ages of the Web (that is, in 1993), Web pages were just pages to look at. Because that wasn't anywhere near enough fun nor compli-cated enough, Web forms were invented. A *form* is sort of like a paper form, with fields you can fill out and then send in. Figure 6-3 shows a typical form.

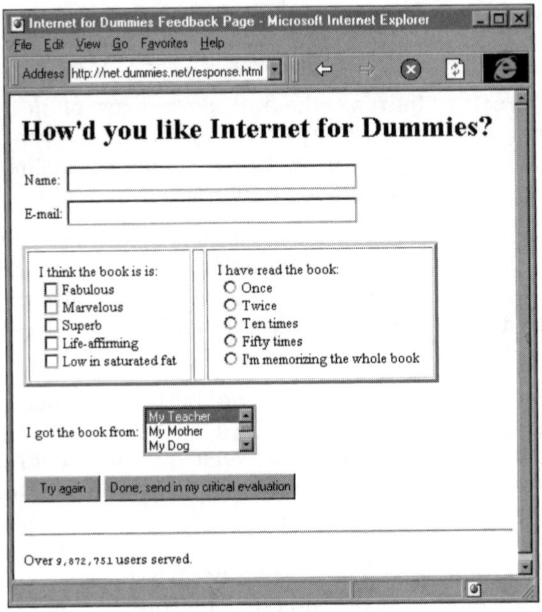

Figure 6-3:
Form-ally
speaking.

The top two lines in the form are fill-in text boxes in which you type, in this case, your name and e-mail address. Under that is a set of *check boxes,* in which you check whichever ones apply (all of them, we hope), and a set of *radio buttons,* which are similar to check boxes except that you can choose only one of them. Under that is a *list box,* in which you can choose one of the possibilities in the box. In most cases there are more entries than can fit in the box, so you scroll them up and down. You can usually choose only one entry, but some list boxes let you choose more.

At the bottom of the form are two buttons. The one on the left clears the form fields to their initial state and sends nothing; the one on the right, known as the *Submit* button, sends the filled-out form back to the Web server for processing.

After the data is sent from the form back to the Web server, it's entirely up to the server how to interpret it.

Lynx handles forms just like Netscape and Internet Explorer do (one of the best Lynx features), as shown in Figure 6-4. You move from field to field on a Lynx form by pressing the ↑ and ↓ keys, the same as always. To submit a form, move to the Submit button and press Enter.

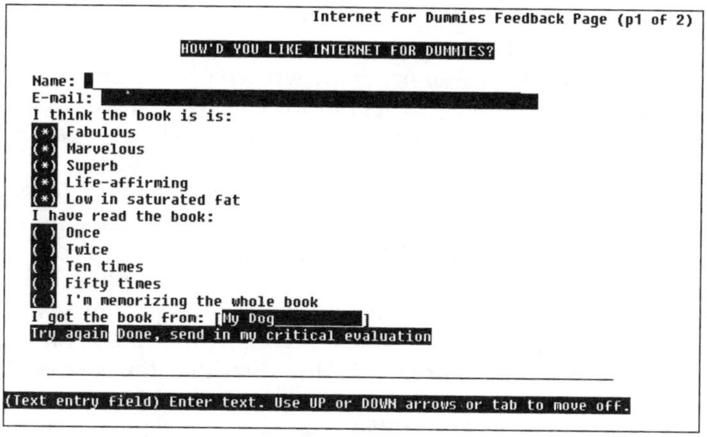

```
                                    Internet for Dummies Feedback Page (p1 of 2)
                              HOW'D YOU LIKE INTERNET FOR DUMMIES?
          Name: █
          E-mail: ███████████████████████████████
          I think the book is is:
          (*) Fabulous
          (*) Marvelous
          (*) Superb
          (*) Life-affirming
          (*) Low in saturated fat
          I have read the book:
          ( ) Once
          ( ) Twice
          ( ) Ten times
          ( ) Fifty times
          ( ) I'm memorizing the whole book
          I got the book from: [My Dog_____]
          Try again Done, send in my critical evaluation

          (Text entry field) Enter text. Use UP or DOWN arrows or tab to move off.
```

Figure 6-4:
Form-ally
speaking in
Lynx.

Some Web pages have *search items*, which are simplified one-line forms that let you type some text, usually interpreted as keywords to search for. Depending on the browser, a Submit button may be displayed to the right of the text area, or you may just press Enter to send the search words to the server.

Save Me!

Frequently you see something on a Web page that's worth saving for later. Sometimes it's a Web page full of interesting information or a picture or some other type of file. Fortunately, saving stuff is easy.

May we have your credit card number, please?

More and more things are being sold over the Web, and the most common way to pay for them is by credit card. Web forms often include a space for you to fill in your credit card number. Some sites offer secure servers — your credit card number is coded in such a way that it can't be seen as it zips its way across the wire. Some sites offer the option of placing your order and calling your credit card in over the phone. Many sites verify your transaction and get the credit approval while you're still at their site. We tend to think that these are pretty safe practices. We buy lots of stuff over the Web and feel no less comfortable about sending our credit card number over the wire than speaking it over the telephone or using it in a restaurant. (Who knows what the server does with your credit card between the time he takes it and the time he brings it back with the slip.) If you're somewhat paranoid, limit your transactions to secure servers; keep in mind, however, that in the United States, by law the most you can lose from credit card fraud is $50.

When you save a Web page, you have to decide whether to save only the text that appears or the entire contents of the page in HTML, the programming language in which Web pages are written (for a glimpse of HTML, see the sidebar "Skimpy little instructions for making your own Web page," later in this chapter). You can also save the pictures that appear on Web pages.

In either Netscape Navigator or Internet Explorer, choose File⇨Save As to save the current Web page in a file. (Actually, Internet Explorer calls this command File⇨Save As File.) You see the standard Save As dialog box, in which you specify the name to save the incoming file. Click in the Save as type box to determine how to save the page: Choose Plain Text to save only the text of the page, with little notes where pictures occur. Choose HTML or HMTL Files to save the entire HTML file. Then click the Save or OK button.

To save an image you see on a Web page, right-click the image (click the image with your right mouse button). Choose Save Image As or Save Picture As from the menu that appears. When you see the Save As dialog box, move to the folder or directory in which you want to save the graphics file, type a filename in the File name box, and click the Save or OK button.

A note about copyright: Contrary to popular belief, almost all Web pages, along with almost everything else on the Internet, are copyrighted by their authors. If you save a Web page or a picture from a Web page, you don't necessarily have permission to use it any way you want. Before you reuse the text or pictures in any way, send an e-mail message to the owner of the site. If an address doesn't appear on the page, you have to write to `webmaster@domain.com`, replacing `domain.com` with the domain name part of the URL of the Web page. For permission to use information on the `http://net.dummies.net/books.html` page, for example, write to `webmaster@dummies.net`.

Saving Lynx pages

Saving files in Lynx is a little more complicated but still not too difficult. How you do it depends on whether you want to save a page that Lynx knows how to display or to do something else.

Whenever Lynx saves something to disk, it saves it to your *provider's* disk. If you want it on your own PC, you have to download it yourself.

To save a page that Lynx can display, first move to the page so that it's displayed on your screen. Then press **d** for download. Lynx prompts you with the various ways it knows to save the page; usually the only option is to save to disk, which lets you specify on your provider's system a filename in which to save it. Alternatively, you can press **p** for print, which gives you three options:

> ✔ Save to disk, just like **d**.
>
> ✔ Mail to yourself, frequently the most convenient option.
>
> ✔ Print to screen. Turn on "screen capture" in the terminal program in your PC, which saves the contents of the page as it goes by on the screen.

Saving anything else in Lynx

Saving is the easiest part. If you choose a link that goes to an image, program, or other sort of document that Lynx can't handle, it stops and tells you that it can't display this link. You press **d** to download it to a local file, for which you specify the name, or **c** to cancel and forget that link.

Doing Doing Two Two Things Things at at Once Once

Netscape and Internet Explorer are what are known in the trade as *multi-threaded* programs. What this means in practice is that the program can do several things at a time.

If you ask Netscape or Internet Explorer to begin downloading a big file, it displays, most usefully, a small window in the corner of your screen. The Netscape version of this window displays a "thermometer" showing the download progress; Internet Explorer shows tiny pages flying from one folder to another. Some people consider watching the thermometer grow or the pages fly enough entertainment (we do when we're tired enough), but you can click back to the main Netscape or Internet Explorer window and continue surfing. You can also have several Web browser windows open at a time. Press Ctrl+N or choose File➪New Web Browser (in Netscape 3.0) or File➪New➪Browser Window (in Netscape 4.0) or File➪New Window (in Internet Explorer) to create a new window. We find this the most useful way to look at two related pages side by side (or overlapping) on-screen.

Doing two or three things at a time in your browser when you have a dial-up Net connection is not unlike squeezing blood from a turnip — only so much blood can be squeezed. In this case, the blood is the amount of data it can pump through your modem. A single download task can keep your modem close to 100 percent busy, and anything else you do shares the modem with the download. When you do two things at a time, therefore, each one happens more slowly than it would by itself.

If one task is a big download and the other is perusing Web pages, it usually works okay because you spend a fair amount of time looking at what the Web browser is displaying; the download can then run while you think. On the other hand, although Netscape and Internet Explorer let you start two download tasks at a time (or a dozen if you're so inclined), there's no point in doing more than one at a time because it's no faster to do them in parallel than one after another, and it can get confusing.

Lynx users are in a somewhat different situation because Lynx displays only one window at a time. In theory you can run two copies of Lynx and switch back and forth, but in practice it's not worth the trouble. Because Lynx is running on your provider's system, it can take advantage of your provider's high-speed Net connection, and even large files load pretty quickly.

The Dead-Tree Thing (Printing)

For about the first year that there were Web browsers, they all had print commands that didn't work. People finally figured out how to print Web pages, and now they all can do it.

To print a page from Netscape or Internet Explorer, just click the Print button, press Ctrl+P, or choose File⇨Print (or File⇨Print page in Netscape 4.0). Reformatting the page to print it can take a while, so patience is a virtue. Fortunately, Netscape and Internet Explorer each display a progress window to keep you apprised of how it's doing.

Printing in Lynx is easy in principle: You press **p**. If you're dialed in to your provider, however, printing on your provider's computer doesn't do you much good, so Lynx gives you some options, the most useful of which are save to disk (so that you can download it and print it locally) or e-mail it to yourself (so that you can download it and print it locally). Are you detecting a pattern here?

Getting Plugged In: Singing, Dancing, and Chatting with Your Browser

As Netscape Navigator has evolved from an unknown newcomer in the Web biz to the big gorilla on the block, it has gained a few new features. Lots and lots of features. Lots and lots and lots of features. Netscape already had about as many features as any single human could comprehend, but just in case someone somewhere understood the whole thing, you can now extend Netscape capabilities with *plug-ins*, or add-on programs that glue themselves to Netscape and add yet more features.

Not to be outdone, each version of Internet Explorer tries to match the Netscape features. In addition to using plug-ins, you can also extend the already massive Internet Explorer capabilities using things called *ActiveX* controls (formerly called OCX controls, but they changed the name when people started to figure out what they are), which are another type of add-on program.

Web pages with pictures are old hat. Now Web pages have to have pictures that sing and dance or ticker-style messages that move across the page or video clips. Every month, new types of information appear on the Web.

What's a Web browser to do with all these new kinds of information? Get the plug-in program which handles that kind of information and glue it to Netscape or Internet Explorer. You "Star Trek" fans can think of plug-ins as parasitic life forms that attach themselves to your browser and enhance its intelligence.

Cool plug-ins

Here are some useful plug-ins:

- **RealAudio:** Plays sound files as you download them (other programs have to wait until the entire file has downloaded before beginning to play)
- **QuickTime:** Plays video files and VDOLive, which plays video files as you download them
- **Shockwave:** Plays both audio and video files as well as other types of animation
- **CyberSpell:** Adds a spelling checker to Netscape
- **ichat:** Lets you use your Web browser to participate in online chats
- **Netscape Live3D, WIRL, Liquid Reality, and other "VR" plug-ins:** Let you move around inside 3-D "virtual reality" worlds on Web pages

What's inside a Web page?

Web pages are stored as text files containing a mixture of text and HTML commands. Here's a sample from Margy's home page, at http://www.gurus.com/margy:

```
<HTML>
<HEAD>
<TITLE>Margy Levine Young's Home
  Page</TITLE>
</HEAD>
<BODY>
<H1>Who Cares Who Margy Levine
  Young Is?</H1>
```

Why do you care who I am? Because I've co-written a bunch of the "...For Dummies" <A HREF="books.htm">books</A> for IDG Books Worldwide, that's why. One of my co-authors is none other than the internationally famous John Levine (alias my brother), and another is the multi-talented Carol Baroudi (a.k.a. Josh's mom)!

```
<P>
```

How to use plug-ins with your browser

You can find Netscape plug-ins and Internet Explorer ActiveX controls at TUCOWS (http://www.tucows.com), Stroud's Consummate Winsock Applications page (http://www.stroud.com), or other sources of software on the Web (see Chapter 21).

After you have downloaded a plug-in from the Net, run it (that is, double-click its filename in My Computer, Windows Explorer, or File Manager) to install it. Depending on what the plug-in does, you follow different steps to try it out. Here are some examples:

- **RealAudio:** Go to the http://www.realaudio.com Web page for a list of sites that include RealAudio sound files. Our favorite site is the National Public Radio Web site (http://www.npr.org), where you can hear recent NPR radio stories, and John's site at http://iecc.com, where you can listen to his radio show.

- **CyberSpell:** See Chapter 8 to find out how to compose an e-mail message using Netscape. With CyberSpell installed, the menu includes a comment to check your spelling.

- **ichat:** Go to the ichat Web site, at http://www.ichat.com, to join chats with other ichat users or to participate in Internet Relay Chat (IRC) conversations. (Chapter 22 tells you where to get more information about IRC.)

Skimpy little instructions for making your own Web page

After a while, every Web user thinks about putting up her own personal Web page. Although creating a Web page is not inordinately difficult, we think that it's pretty complicated for a new computer user. If you have a background in computers and have done some programming, the following few paragraphs may be all you need to get yourself started. If you're new to all this stuff, go ahead and read through this section. When you're ready to take on creating a home page, go get more in-depth instructions. We give you the blow-by-blow at `http://net.dummies.net/webpage`, this book's Website. If you prefer your instructions offline, check Chapter 22 to read about entire books on the subject .

Store your Web pages directly on your own hard disk while you're getting them set up. Create each page as a separate file on your disk by using a text editor (if you're hard-core) or a specialized HTML editor (if you're more normal). Netscape Navigator Gold 3.0 and Netscape Navigator 4.0 have a built-in Web page editor that works nicely. Some word-processing programs can create Web pages too, including WordPerfect 7 for Windows and Microsoft Word (using Microsoft Internet Assistant, which you can download from the Microsoft Web site). These pages consist of the text for the page interspersed with HTML codes that tell the Web browser how to format the page, which text is a heading, which text is a link, and the Web page the link links to.

For pictures, you can download pictures from the Web (but remember — you need the owner's permission to use them on your own Web pages), scan in pictures you have taken or drawn, or create pictures using a graphics editor (such as Paint Shop Pro, a popular program you can download from the Net). Each picture on the Web page is stored in a separate file, usually in GIF or JPG format (two standard graphics formats). You add an HTML code to the Web page on which the picture should appear.

Then test your pages with Netscape, Internet Explorer, and other browsers to make sure that they work the way you want them to. Just because a page looks terrific with Netscape doesn't mean that it might not look like it was run over by a truck when it's displayed in a different browser. Make sure that the links work.

Most Internet providers and online services have some arrangement to let you install your pages on their Web server so that your Web pages can be seen by the general Web-surfing public. Sometimes this is part of the basic package, and sometimes it costs extra. If your pages become wildly popular, the provider invariably will charge extra for the extra load it causes on the system.

Upload your Web pages to your Internet provider's or online service's computer and put them in the appropriate place (wherever the provider says). Then take a look at them again with a few different browsers.

Update the pages often enough to keep them interesting. If you create some pages and never change them, no one will come back for a second look.

Chapter 7

Needles and Haystacks: Finding Stuff on the Net

"*O*kay, all this great stuff is out there on the Net. How do I find it?" That's an excellent question. Thanks for asking that question. Questions like that are what makes this country strong and vibrant. We salute you and say, "Keep asking questions!" Next question, please.

Oh, you want an *answer* to your question. Fortunately, quite a bit of (technical term follows) stuff-finding stuff is on the Net. More particularly, indexes and directories of much of the interesting material are available on the Net.

The Net has different types of indexes and directories for different types of material. Because the indexes tend to be organized, unfortunately, by the type of Internet service they provide rather than by the nature of the material, you find Web resources in one place, e-mail resources in another place, and so on. You can search in dozens of hundreds of different ways, depending on what you're looking for and how you prefer to search. (John has remarked that his ideal restaurant has only one item on the menu, but it's just what he wanted. The Internet is about as far from that ideal as you can possibly imagine.)

To provide a smidgen of structure to this discussion, we look at several different sorts of searches:

✔ **Topics:** Places, things, ideas — anything you want to find out more about

✔ **Companies:** Organizations that you think have a Web site or other Net presence

✔ **People:** Actual human beings whom you want to contact or spy on

Index, directory — what's the difference?

When we talk about a *directory,* we mean a listing that's divided up into named categories and the entries assigned to categories partly or entirely by humans. You look things up by finding a category you want and seeing what it contains. In this book, we would think of the table of contents as a directory.

An *index,* on the other hand, simply collects all the items, extracts keywords from them (often by taking all the words except for *the, and,* and the like), and makes a big list. You search it by giving some words that seem likely, and it finds all the entries that contain that word. The index in the back of this book is more like an index.

Each has its advantages and disadvantages. Directories are organized so that when you find a category of interest, all the items in that category are likely to be related to what you want. Because indexes, on the other hand, don't know what the words mean, if you look for `program`, it finds computer programs, educational programs, theater programs, and anything else that contains the word. Because indexes can be created largely or completely automatically, however, indexes on the Net tend to contain many more entries and to be updated more often than directories, which need human catalogers.

Some overlap exists between indexes and directories — Yahoo!, the best known Web page directory, lets you search by keyword, and many of the indexes divide their entries into general categories that let you limit the search.

To find topics, we use the various online indexes and directories, such as Yahoo! and AltaVista. To find companies, we also use *whois,* the main directory of Internet domains. To find people, however, we use directories of people, which are (fortunately) different from directories of Web pages.

Your Basic Search Strategy

When we're looking for topics on the Net, we always begin with one of the Web guides (indexes and directories) discussed in this section.

You use them all in more or less the same way:

1. **Start your Web browser, such as Netscape Navigator.**

2. **Pick a directory or index you like, and tell your browser to go to the index or directory's home page.**

   We list the URLs (page names) of the home pages later in this section.

   After you get there, you can choose between two approaches.

3a. If a Search box is available, type some keywords in the box and click Search.

This is the "index" approach, to look for topic areas that match your keywords.

After a perhaps long delay (the Web is pretty big), an index page is returned with links to pages that match your keywords.

or

3b. If you see a list of links to topic areas, click a topic area of interest.

The "directory" approach is to begin at a general topic and get more and more specific. Each page has links to subpages, which get more and more specific until they link to actual pages likely to be of interest.

After some clicking around to get the hang of it, you find all sorts of good stuff.

You hear a great deal of talk around the Web about search engines. *Search engines* is a fancy way to say stuff-finding stuff. All the directories and indexes we're about to describe are in the broad category called search engines. So don't get upset by some high falutin'-sounding terms.

Search-a-Roo

So much for the theory of searching for stuff on the Net. Now for some practice. (Theory and practice are much further apart in practice than they are in theory.) We use our two favorite search systems for examples: Yahoo!, which is a directory, and AltaVista, which is an index.

The lazy searcher's search page

You may feel a wee bit overwhelmed with all the search directories and indexes we discuss in this chapter. If it makes you feel any better, so do we.

To make a little sense of all this, we made ourselves a search page that connects to all the directories and indexes we use so that we get one-stop searching. You can use it too. Give it a try, at http://net.dummies.net/search/.

In the not unlikely event that new search systems are created or some of the existing ones have moved or died, the page gives you our latest greatest list.

Yahoo!-a-roo

There are two ways to find stuff in Yahoo!. (Yes, it's spelled with an exclamation point. Last year's fad was funny CapITallzaTion; this year's seems to be !funny? &punc@@tuation!) The easier way is just to click from category to category until you find something you like.

We start our Yahoo! visit at its home page, at `http://www.Yahoo.com` (at least the page name doesn't use an exclamation point), which looks like Figure 7-1. A whole bunch of categories and subcategories are listed. You can click any of them to see another page that has yet more subcategories and links to actual Web pages. You can click a link to a page if you see one you like or on a sub-subcategory, and so on.

At the top of each Yahoo! page is the list of categories, subcategories, and so on, separated by colons, that lead to that page. If you want to back up a few levels and look at different subcategories, just click the place on that list to which you want to back up. After a little clicking up and down, it's second nature. Many pages appear in more than one place in the directory because they fall into more than one category. An advantage of a Web page directory over a card catalog in a library is that a book can be in only one place on the shelf in the library, and Web pages can have as many links referring to them as they want.

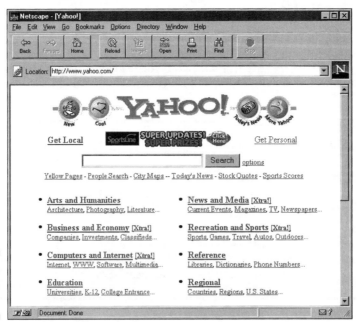

Figure 7-1:
Ready to
Yahoo!

(Text and artwork copyright 1996 by YAHOO!, INC. All rights reserved. YAHOO! and the YAHOO! logo are trademarks of YAHOO!, INC.)

Although all the categories in the Yahoo! list have plenty of subcategories under them, some have much more than others. If you're looking for a business-related page, it helps to know that Yahoo! sticks just about everything commercial under the category Business and Economy, as shown in Figure 7-2. If we were looking for Internet for Dummies Central, for example (which we think people should look for several times a day, at least), we could click our way to it from the Yahoo! home page by clicking Business and Economy, then on that page click Companies, then Books, then Titles, and then Internet; on that page, you would find links to pages with lots of Internet books, including ours.

If you know in general but not in detail what you're looking for, clicking up and down through the Yahoo! directory pages is a good way to narrow your search and find pages of interest.

Yahoo!-a-roo, Part II

"Click on Business and Economy, then on that page click Companies, then Books, then Titles, and then Internet? How the heck did they know which categories to click?" you're doubtless asking. We admit it: We cheated.

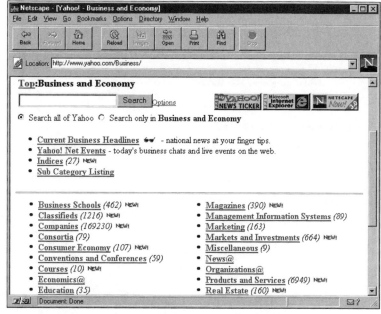

Figure 7-2:
A store-
house of
commercial
information
at Yahoo!

Yahoo! also lets you search its index by keyword, which is the best way to use it if you have some idea of the title of the page you're looking for. Every Yahoo! screen has near the top a search box in which you can type words you want to find in the Yahoo! entry for pages of interest. For example, we typed `internet dummies books`, clicked the Search button next to the type-in box, and got the answer shown in Figure 7-3, with two entries for our Web site (it appears in two different places in the Yahoo! index) and one book by Dan Gookin, who has written the occasional *...For Dummies* book as well.

Above each entry it finds, Yahoo! reports the category in which it found the entry. Even if the entry isn't quite right, if you click on the category, you find other related titles and some of them may well do the trick.

If Yahoo! finds hundreds of pages or categories, you should refine your search. One way to do that is to add extra words to make more specific what you're looking for. If you were looking for a key lime pie recipe (John sent out a good one on the Net about ten years ago) and you search for `baking`, you get 71 fairly random pages; if you search for `key lime pie`, however, you get three pages, one of which is on the Entertainment:Food and Eating: Recipes:Pie page, which has links to lots of tasty pie recipes.

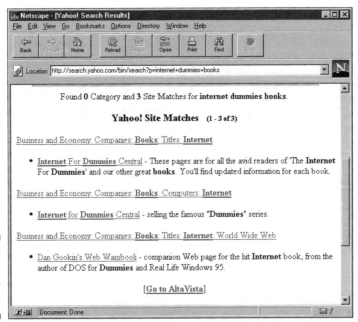

Figure 7-3:
Zeroing in
on quality
literature.

You can click Options, next to the Search button, to get to the slightly more advanced Yahoo! search page. It lets you limit how far back you want to see pages (three years is the default), and you can tell it to look for either all the words or any of the words you typed.

Yahoo-a-roo, toodle-oo

Although Yahoo! is primarily a directory of resources available on the Web, it has other databases available, each with a link you can click just under the box in which you would enter search terms:

- ✓ **Yellow Pages:** A business directory (but not our favorite — see the section "Finding Companies," later in this chapter)
- ✓ **People Search:** Finds addresses and phone numbers, like a white pages directory (see the "Finding People" section, later in this chapter)
- ✓ **City Maps:** Lets you type a street address to get a more or less accurate map
- ✓ **Today's News, Stock Quotes, and Sports Scores:** News from Reuters

AltaVista-a-rista

If you examine Figure 7-3 carefully, you notice a link to AltaVista at the bottom. Yahoo! and we agree that AltaVista is the best index on the Net.

AltaVista has a little robot named Scooter that spends its time merrily visiting Web pages all over the Net and reporting back what it saw. AltaVista makes a humongous index of which words occurred in which pages; when you search AltaVista, it picks pages from that index which contain the words you asked for.

AltaVista is an index, not a directory. The good news is that it has about ten times as many pages as Yahoo!; the bad news is that finding the one you want can be difficult. Regardless of what you ask for, you probably will get 15,000 pages on your first try. After you refine your request a little, however, you can usually get the number of pages down to a somewhat more manageable number.

Using AltaVista, or any index, effectively is an exercise in remote-control mind reading because you have to guess words that will appear on the pages you're looking for. Sometimes that's easy — if you're looking for recipes for key lime pie, `key lime pie` is a good set of search words because you know the name of what you're looking for. On the other hand, if you have forgotten that the capital of Germany is Bonn, it's hard to tease a useful page out of AltaVista because you don't know what words to look for. (If you try `Germany capital`, you find stuff about investment banking.)

Now that we have you all discouraged, let's try some AltaVista searches. Direct your browser to `http://altavista.digital.com` (notice the `digital` in there because it's brought to us by Digital Equipment, the large computer maker). You see a screen like the one shown in Figure 7-4.

Type some search terms, and AltaVista finds the pages that best match your terms. That's "best match," not "match" — if it can't match all the terms, it finds pages that match as well as possible. AltaVista ignores words that occur too often to be usable as index terms, both the obvious ones, such as *and, the,* and *of,* but also terms such as *internet* and *mail.* This sounds somewhat discouraging, but in fact it's still not hard to tease useful results out of AltaVista. You just have to think up good search terms. Try that key lime pie example, by typing **key lime pie** and pressing the Search button. You get the response shown in Figure 7-5.

It might not look exactly like Figure 7-5 because we told it to display the results in compact form rather than standard form (see the box just above and to the right of the keyword box) so that the example would fit on this page. All the pages it found do, in fact, have something to do with key lime pie, and the first page on that list has a pretty good recipe. Notice that it found about 60,000 matches. That's probably more than you wanted to look at, but you should at least look at the next couple of screens of matches if the first screen doesn't have what you want. At the bottom of the AltaVista screen are page numbers; click Next to go to the next page.

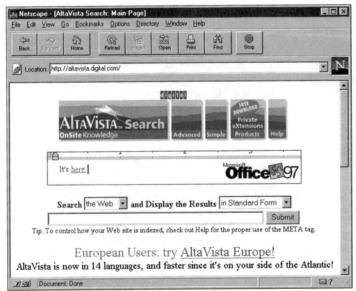

Figure 7-4:
AltaVista,
ready to
roll.

(Reproduced with the permission of Digital Equipment Corporation. AltaVista, the AltaVista logo, and the Digital logo are trademarks of Digital Equipment Corporation.)

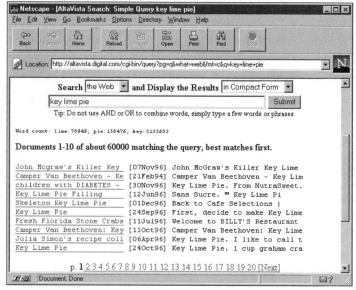

Figure 7-5:
A plethora
of pages
of pie.

(Reproduced with the permission of Digital Equipment Corporation. AltaVista, the AltaVista
logo, and the Digital logo are trademarks of Digital Equipment Corporation.)

Handy AltaVista tips

AltaVista, unlike Yahoo!, makes it easy to refine your search to target the
pages you want to find more exactly. After each search, your search terms
appear in a box at the top of the page so that you can change them and try
again. Here are some tips on how you might want to change your terms:

✔ Type most search words in lowercase. Type proper names with a single
capital letter, such as `Elvis`. Don't type any words in all capital letters.

✔ If two or more words should appear together, put quotes around them,
as in `"Elvis Presley"`.

✔ Use + and – to indicate words that must appear or must not appear,
such as `+Elvis +Costello -Presley` if you're looking for the modern
Elvis, not the classic one.

The number-one reason your searches don't find anything

Well, maybe not *your* number-one reason, but *our* number-one reason: We spelled one of the search words wrong. Check carefully. John notes that his fingers insist on typing "Interent," which doesn't find much other than Web pages from other people who can't spell. (Thanks to our friend Jean Armour Polly, for reminding us about this.)

TIP

The 404 blues

More often than we want to admit, when you click a link that Yahoo! or one of its competitors found, instead of getting the promised page, you get a message such as 404 Not Found. What did you do wrong? Nothing. Web pages come and go and move around with great velocity, and the various search systems do a lousy job, frankly, of cleaning out links to old, dead pages that have gone away.

The automated indexes, such as AltaVista and Lycos, are better in this regard than the manual directories, such as Yahoo!. The automated ones have software robots that revisit all the indexed pages every once in a while and note whether they no longer exist; even so, many lonely months can pass between robot visits, and a great deal can happen to a page in the meantime.

It's just part of life on the online frontier — the high-tech equivalent of riding your horse along the trail in the Old West and noticing that there sure are a lot of bleached white cattle skulls lying around.

Yahoo! and AltaVista, together at last

It occurred to us that a rather effective way to search the Web is to look in the Yahoo! directory and then, if you don't find what you want, try AltaVista. Because great minds (or maybe tiny minds) think alike, the Yahoo! and AltaVista people got together to make it easy to do just that.

If you go back and rescrutinize Figure 7-3, which shows the result of a Yahoo! search, notice the AltaVista links we mentioned earlier, at both the top and bottom of the page. (These Yahoo! people aren't subtle, but considering what they call themselves, are you surprised?) Click either of those links, and you're flipped into an AltaVista-in-Yahoo! page that shows the results of an AltaVista search using the same terms you just used for a Yahoo! search. The pages of links look a little different from the "native" AltaVista pages because they're aesthetically designed to match the Yahoo! pages, but the search finds the same pages either way.

AltaVista away

AltaVista has a few other options that can be handy.

Rather than search Web pages, you can search Usenet, the giant collection of Internet newsgroups we discuss in Chapter 11. Simply click the box that says Search the Web and flip to Search Usenet. If a topic has been discussed recently on Usenet, this is the best way to find the messages about that topic.

WHOOSH

Who pays for all this stuff?

You may be wondering who pays for all these wonderful search systems. All except one of them are supported by advertising. On every page of Yahoo!, Lycos, and most other search systems, you see lots and lots of ads. In theory, the advertising pays the costs. In reality, the independent advertising-supported search systems Excite, Infoseek, Lycos, and Yahoo!, have all lost pots of money. (In this case, a pot is sized in millions of bucks.) Fortunately for all of them, because they issued stock to the public at the height of the 1996 Internet investment craze, each has plenty of cash to burn up while they try to find out how to turn a profit. WebCrawler belongs to AOL, which lost 500 pots in 1996, though it's hard to tell how much of that was the fault of WebCrawler.

The exception is AltaVista, originally a research project to measure just how fast the new Alpha line of workstations at Digital Equipment was. The new line turned out to be extremely fast, blowing the socks off most of the competition. Because DEC knew a good thing when it saw it, it turned AltaVista into a product line that it licenses to other search systems (such as Yahoo! and CNET, Inc.) and that companies can use to create their own internal indexes. Some folks thought that DEC might issue stock in its AltaVista Internet Software division as well (if the Excite, Infoseek, Lycos, and Yahoo! guys can raise all that money, you might as well get in on the party); as of early 1997, it hasn't done so yet, but it has cashed in on its popularity by accepting a few ads.

Some think that there's a big "bubble" in the search biz and that we can expect some of these search systems to run out of money and shut down or merge with others. Visit http://net.dummies.net/search/ for the latest up- or down-dates.

You can choose how detailed a report you want to get, in compact or detailed form. The Compact option gives you a single line per item found; Detailed, about three lines per item. AltaVista normally uses Standard form, which tells AltaVista to use Compact if you're doing a Usenet search or Detailed if you're doing a Web search.

Because the Compact report is much smaller, it loads faster. If you have a slow dial-up Net connection, Compact form makes searching much snappier, at the cost of not being able to tell quite so easily what's in each item found. If you're searching for a particular page or Usenet item that you will recognize when you see it, compact form is definitely quicker.

The Usual Suspects

After you have surfed around Yahoo! and AltaVista for a while, you might want to check out the competition as well.

WebCrawler

http://www.webcrawler.com

WebCrawler is an automated indexer that crawls around the Web cataloging and indexing every page it comes across — again, sort of like AltaVista. Although America Online (AOL) owns WebCrawler, anyone can use it. It's a reasonable alternative to AltaVista.

Infoseek

http://www.infoseek.com

Infoseek is an index similar to AltaVista rather than a directory: You give it some keywords to look for, and it finds the pages that match the best. It also has a directory of useful Web pages. It can search the Web, Usenet, Reuters news, and a few other odds and ends.

Excite

http://www.excite.com

Excite is primarily an index, like AltaVista, with a "concept search," which is supposed to find relevant pages even if you don't type exactly the same words the pages themselves use. We don't find that its concept search helps much, but perhaps we were too wordy to start with. Excite also has sections with reviews of Web pages, city directories, white pages, and more.

HotBot

http://www.hotbot.com

HotBot is yet another index, like AltaVista. It's affiliated with *Wired* magazine and in the classic *Wired* style uses bright clashing colors that make your head hurt. If you can deal with that (try sunglasses), it's not a bad index.

Lycos

http://www.lycos.com

Lycos is a largely automated index, sort of like AltaVista. It began as a project at Carnegie-Mellon University and has also gone commercial. It also has a directory called Top 5% of Web Sites. Lycos was one of the earliest Web search systems, but, honestly, at this point AltaVista has a better index and Yahoo! has a better directory. Lycos also has headline news and local pages for some cities around the United States.

Other Web guides

Lots of other Web guides are available, including many specialized guides put together for particular interests (there's Femina, for example, a feminist guide, at http://www.femina.com).

Yahoo! has a directory of other guides: Start at the Yahoo! page (http://www.Yahoo!.com), choose WWW (which appears under Computers), and then Searching the Web.

Finding Companies

The first way to search for companies is to search for the company name as a topic. That is, if you're looking for the Egg Farm Dairy, search for Egg Farm Dairy in Yahoo!, AltaVista, or any of the other search systems. (You'll find it, too. We like the Muscoot.)

After you have done that, a few other places are worth checking for business-related info.

Whois that?

http://www.internic.net/wp/whois.html

Every registered Internet domain has a listed owner and contacts. The whois facility lets you look up domains and contacts. Although some separate whois programs exist, for most purposes, you can do just as well by visiting the InterNIC whois Web page.

On that page, you get to choose which whois server to use and what to search for. It has two servers, one for U.S. military addresses and one for everyone else. By default, it uses both, which is usually okay.

In the Search strings box, enter the name of the company or contact person or network you're interested in and click Search. With luck, you get back one entry that matches. More likely, you get back a list of all the matches. When we searched for IBM.COM, here's part of what we got:

```
International Business Machines (IBM-DOM)  IBM.COM
International Business Machines (IBM4-HST) IBM.COM
129.34.139.30
To single out one record, look it up with "!xxx", where xxx
        is the handle, shown in parenthesis following
        the name, which comes first.
```

Two possible matches are listed: the IBM.COM domain and the single computer that happens to be called IBM.COM. To tell it which one we want (the domain, this time), we take the hint it gives and search for !IBM-DOM with an exclamation point in front. Because a new search box is at the bottom of the whois page, we can enter our new search string (using cut and paste because we're lazy typists), and we get a more concrete answer with the full name of the company and the e-mail address of the person responsible for the domain.

In a company as large as IBM, the domain contact is doubtless a technical network specialist; in small companies, however, it's usually someone who can answer short, polite questions, such as "What's the e-mail address of your sales department?" or "Does Jim Smith still work there?"

Hoovering in

```
http://www.hoovers.com
```

Although whois tells you about a company's connection to the Internet, it doesn't tell you much about the company itself. Hoover's is a business information company that has been publishing paper business directories for quite a while. Now it's on the Net as well. Its Web site offers free company capsules, stock prices, and other company info. If you sign up for its paid service, it offers considerably more. Even the free stuff is quite useful.

Ask EDGAR

```
http://edgar.sec.gov (government)
http://www.edgar-online.com (private)
```

The U.S. Securities and Exchange Commission (SEC), the people who regulate stock and bond markets, has a system called EDGAR that collects all the financial material that publicly traded companies have to file with the government. Although most of this stuff is dry and financial, if you can read financial statements, you can find all sorts of interesting information, such as Bill Gates' salary.

The government EDGAR site is run directly by the SEC, and the private site, EDGAR ONLINE, is run by an independent company, Cybernet Data Systems, Inc. Although they have pretty much the same information, the private site offers free limited access and charges a modest price (about $5 per month) for more complete access and automatic e-mail updates when a company you're interested in files EDGAR documents. Because EDGAR ONLINE has partner arrangements with several other companies, including Hoover's, if you check on a company in Hoover's and then click the EDGAR link to get to EDGAR ONLINE, you can often get documents not directly available from the EDGAR ONLINE home page. If you use EDGAR ONLINE often, however, pay the five bucks.

Lots of other business directories

Tons of business information is available on the Net. Here are a few places to begin:

Companies Online

```
http://www.CompaniesOnline.com
```

Companies Online is a joint project between Dun & Bradstreet and Lycos. You enter the name of a company you're interested in, and they tell you about it.

Inc. magazine

```
http://www.inc.com
http://www.inc.com/500
```

Inc. magazine concentrates on small, fast-growing companies. Each year its Inc. 500 features the 500 companies it likes the best. Many hot little companies are listed here, with contact information.

Yellow Pages

```
http://www.bigyellow.com
http://yp.gte.net
http://www.yellow.com
http://www.switchboard.com
http://www.abii.com    (click on American Yellow Pages)
```

Quite a few yellow pages business directories are on the Net, both national and local. The ones in this list are some of the national ones. We like Big Yellow the best (even though it's run by NYNEX, which is otherwise not our favorite telephone company), but they're all worth a look. The American Yellow Pages even offers credit reports, though we can't vouch for its reliability.

Finding People

Finding people on the Net is surprisingly easy. It's so easy that, indeed, sometimes it's creepy. Two overlapping categories of people finders are available: those that look for people on the Net with e-mail and Web addresses and those that look for people in real life with phone numbers and street addresses.

In real life

The real-life directories are compiled mostly from telephone directories. If you haven't had a listed phone number in the past few years, you probably aren't in any of these directories.

On the Net

Finding e-mail and Web addresses is somewhat hit-and-miss. Because there has never been any online equivalent to the official phone book the telephone company produces, directories of e-mail addresses are collected from addresses used in Usenet messages, mailing lists, and other more or less public places on the Net. Because the different directories use different sources, if you don't find someone in one directory, you can try another. Remember that because the e-mail directories are incomplete, there's no substitute for calling someone up and asking, "What's your e-mail address?"

If you're wondering whether someone has a Web page, use AltaVista to search for his or her name. If you're wondering whether you're famous, use AltaVista to search for your own name and see how many people have linked to you.

Yahoo! People Search

```
http://www.Yahoo.com/search/people
```

Yahoo! has a nice directory that looks people up by name and optionally the address, and gives you the full address and phone number. This is the same system as Four-11 (below), but with Yahoo!-ish screens.

Four11 (Four-eleven)

```
http://www.four11.com
```

You can search for addresses and phone numbers (same as with the Yahoo! people search) and e-mail addresses. If you don't like your own listing, you can add, update, or delete it.

American Directory Assistance

```
http://www.abii.com
```

(Click on American Directory Assistance.)

This is another white pages directory. After you have found the entry you want, you can ask for a graphical street map of the address.

WhoWhere

```
http://www.whowhere.com
```

WhoWhere is another e-mail address directory. Although we find that Four11 usually gives better results, some people are listed in WhoWhere who aren't listed in other places.

Canada 411

http://www.canada411.com

Canada 411 is a complete Canadian telephone book, sponsored by the major Canadian telephone companies. Aussi disponible en français, eh?

Bigfoot

http://www.bigfoot.com

Bigfoot provides a way to search for people and also provides permanent, free e-mail addresses for life (it promises to forward mail from your Bigfoot address to your Internet account forever, for free).

While You're Looking

Although you may think from the hype that all of human knowledge is found on the Web, it's not true. Sometimes it works better to ask human beings who use e-mail and Usenet messages.

What's in the news?

Among the mountains of dross in Usenet news, described in Chapter 11, is some good stuff. This section lists some tips for finding what you want:

✔ Most newsgroups have FAQ (frequently asked questions) messages posted regularly to the group. These FAQs are a treasure trove of useful and interesting information. You can find all the FAQs in the newsgroup news.answers. The comp.answers newsgroup also has FAQs for the comp newsgroups; misc.answers has FAQs for misc groups; FAQs for alt groups are in alt.answers; rec.answers has FAQs for rec groups; and soc.answers has FAQs for soc groups. There's also an FTP archive of the FAQs at rtfm.mit.edu.

✔ Some newsgroups are archived and have keyword indexes to search them. This is a good way to look for articles about particular topics. You generally have to look at the FAQ in a particular group to see whether it has an index.

✔ A couple of online search systems let you search through news postings. Look at http://www.dejanews.com for a public news-search system. AltaVista and Infoseek, described earlier in this chapter, both let you search Usenet articles from the past few months.

The ten-minute challenge

Our friend Doug Hacker claims to be able to find the answer to any factual query on the Net in less than ten minutes. Carol challenged him to find a quote she vaguely knew from the liner notes of a Duke Ellington album, whose title she couldn't remember. He had the complete quote in about hour but spent less than five minutes himself. How? He found a mailing list about Duke Ellington, subscribed, and asked the question. Several members replied in short order. The more time you spend learning your way around the Net, the more you know where to go for the information you need.

Mail, one more time

Mailing lists are another important resource. Most lists (but not all — check before you ask) welcome concrete, politely phrased questions related to the list's topic. See Chapter 10 for more information about mailing lists, including how to look for lists of particular topics of interest to you.

Chapter 8

Mailing Hither, Mailing Thither

*E*lectronic mail is without a doubt the most popular Internet service. Although it doesn't get as much press as the World Wide Web, more people use it. Every system on the Net supports some sort of mail service, which means that, no matter what kind of computer you're using, if it's on the Internet, you can send and receive mail.

Because mail, much more than any other Internet service, is connected to many non-Internet systems, you can exchange mail with lots of people who are not on the Internet in addition to all the people who *are* on it (see Chapter 17 for details).

What's My Address?

Everyone with e-mail access to the Net has an *e-mail address,* which is the cyberspace equivalent of a postal address or a phone number. When you send an e-mail message, you enter the address or addresses of the recipients so that the computer knows who to send it to.

Before you do much mailing, you have to figure out your electronic-mail address so that you can give it to people who want to get in touch with you. And you have to figure out some of their addresses so that you can write to them. (If you have no friends or plan to send only anonymous hate mail, you can skip this section.)

Internet mail addresses have two parts, separated by an @ (the *at* sign). The part before the @ is the *mailbox,* which is (roughly speaking) your personal name, and the part after that is the *domain,* usually the name of your Internet provider, such as `aol.com` or `tiac.net`.

The username part

The mailbox is usually your *username,* the name your provider assigns to your account. If you're lucky, you get to choose it; in other cases, providers have standardized the naming conventions and you get what you get. Some usernames include first names, last names, initials, first name and last initial, first initial and last name, or anything else, including completely *made-up* names. Over the years, for example, John has had usernames such as `john`, `john1`, `jrl`, `jlevine`, `jlevine3` (must have been at least three `jlevine`s there), and even `q0246`; Carol has been `carol`, `carolb`, `cbaroudi`, and `carol377` (the provider threw in a random number); and Margy tries to stick with `margy` but has ended up with `margy1` or `73727,2305` on occasion. A few systems assign names such as `usd31516`. Ugh.

For example, you can write to the President of the United States at `president@whitehouse.gov`. The President's mailbox is `president`, and the domain that stores that mailbox is `whitehouse.gov` — reasonable enough.

Back when many fewer e-mail users were around and most users of any particular system knew each other directly, it wasn't all that difficult to figure out who had what username. These days, because it's becoming much more of a problem, many organizations are creating consistent mailbox names for all users, most often by using the user's first and last names with a dot between them. In this type of scheme, your mailbox name may be something like `elvis.presley@bluesuede.org`, even though your username is something else. (If your name isn't Elvis Presley, adjust this example suitably. On the other hand, if your name *is* Elvis Presley, please contact us immediately. We know some people who are looking for you.)

Having several names for the same mailbox is no problem, so the new, longer, consistent usernames are invariably created in addition to — rather than instead of — the traditional short nicknames.

The domain name part

The domain name for Internet providers in the United States usually ends with three letters (called the *zone*) that give you a clue to what kind of place it is. *Commercial* organizations end with .com, which includes both providers such as America Online (AOL) and CompuServe and many companies that aren't public providers but that are commercial entities, such as `amrcorp.com` (AMR Corporation, better known as American Airlines), `creamery.com` (Egg Farm Dairy in New York state, which makes really good French-style soft cheeses), and `iecc.com` (the Invincible Electronic Calculator Company). Educational institutions end with `.edu` (like `yale.edu`), networking organizations end with `.net`, U.S. government sites end with `.gov`, military sites end with `.mil`, and organizations that don't fall into any of those categories end with `.org`. Outside the United States, domains usually end with a country code, such as `fr` for France or `zm` for Zambia. See our Web site (at `http://net.dummies.net/countries`) for a listing of country codes. New domains are being registered at a ferocious rate, many thousands per month, particularly in the extremely trendy `.com` zone, and the near future holds some possibility for new zones named `.biz` or `.www`.

Putting it all together

Capitalization never matters in domains and rarely matters in mailbox names. To make it easy on your eyes, therefore, most of the domain and mailbox names in this book are shown in lowercase.

If you're sending a message to another user in your domain (same machine or group of machines), you can leave out the domain part altogether when you type the address. If you and a friend both use AOL, for example, you can leave out the `@aol.com` part of the address when you're writing to each other.

If you don't know what your e-mail address is, a good approach is to send yourself a message and use your login name as the mailbox name. Then examine the return address on the message. Or you can send a message to Internet For Dummies Mail Central at `internet4@dummies.net`, and a friendly robot will send back a message with your address. (While you're at it, tell us whether you like this book because we authors see that mail too.) Chapter 17 has more suggestions for finding e-mail addresses.

My Mail Is Where?

You have an e-mail address. Cool. Next we tell you how to send and receive mail — and what you can do with it. First, there's the tiny detail of where your mail is stored. When your mail arrives, unless you're one of the lucky (or rich) few whose computers have a permanent Internet connection, the mail doesn't get delivered to your computer automatically. Mail gets delivered instead to a *mail server,* which is sort of like your local post office. To get your mail, you have to go and get it. Actually, your *mail* program has to go and get it. For you to be able to send mail, your *mail* program has to take it to the post office. It's sort of like having a post office box rather than home delivery — you have to pick it up at the post office and also deliver your outgoing mail there. (Strange but true: Margy and Carol, being normal, get their e-mail via a mail server and have their "snail" mail delivered to their homes; John, who's abnormal, has his e-mail delivered directly to his home computer but walks to the post office every day, often in the freezing drizzle, to get his regular mail.)

If you're using a PPP/SLIP account, you have to tell your e-mail program the name of your mail server. When your mail program picks up the mail, it sucks your mail from your provider's mail server to your PC or Mac at top speed. After you have downloaded your mail to your own computer, you can disconnect, which is a good idea if your provider charges by the hour. Then you can read and respond to your mail while the meter isn't running — while you're *off-line.* After you're ready to send your responses or new messages, you can reconnect and transmit your outgoing mail, again at top network speed. (If you don't know what to type here, ask your provider.)

If you use a commercial online service or UNIX shell account, the mail server is the same computer you connect to when you dial in (this explanation is an oversimplification, but it's close enough) so that when you run your provider's e-mail program, your mail is right there for you to read, and your provider can drop outgoing messages directly in the virtual mail chute.

Too Many E-Mail Programs

It's time for some hand-to-hand combat with your e-mail system. The bad news is that countless e-mail programs exist — programs that read and write electronic-mail messages. (At least there are so many that none of us felt up to the task of counting them.) You've got your freeware, you've got your shareware and your commercial stuff, and stuff probably came with your computer. They all do more or less the same thing because they're all mail programs, after all.

Here's a quick rundown of e-mail programs:

   ✔ **Windows PC or Mac with a PPP/SLIP Internet account:** The most widely used e-mail programs for this type of account are Eudora (which is on the CD-ROM in the back of this book), described later in this chapter, and Netscape Navigator, usually called just Netscape. (Versions 2.0 and later include a mail program.) Eudora works pretty well, and one version (Eudora Light) is free. Microsoft offers Internet Mail, another free mail program that you might have received along with Microsoft Internet Explorer. Pegasus is another excellent e-mail program for this type of Internet account, and it's available for free from the Net. See Chapter 21 to get hold of Eudora, Pegasus, Netscape, and Internet Mail.

✔ **UNIX shell accounts:** You almost certainly can use Pine (also described later in this chapter). If your Internet provider doesn't have it, demand it.

✔ **America Online (AOL), CompuServe, or NetCom:** The access software you use to connect to your account includes an e-mail program. After you read this chapter, AOL users can turn to Chapter 14 and CompuServe users to Chapter 15 for detailed instructions.

✔ **Microsoft Network (MSN):** You use Microsoft Exchange, which comes with Windows 95, or Microsoft Outlook, which comes with Microsoft Office 97.

✔ **Free e-mail accounts:** At least one service is available that gives you free dial-up accounts for e-mail only. The price you pay is having advertisements appear on-screen as you read your messages. Juno Online is this type of service (call 800-654-JUNO to ask for a software disk). If you use a service like this one, you have to use its e-mail software (otherwise, their advertisements won't appear).

If you're connected in some other way, you probably have a different mail program. For example, you may be using a PC in your company's local-area network that runs cc:Mail, Lotus Notes, or Microsoft Mail and has a mail-only link to the outside world. We don't describe local-area network mail programs here (Chapter 22 tells you where to find out more about them).

Regardless of which type of mail you're using, the basics of reading, sending, addressing, and filing mail work in pretty much the same way, so it's worth looking through this chapter even if you're not using any of the mail programs we describe here.

Four Popular E-Mail Programs

After you understand what an e-mail program is supposed to do, it's much easier to figure out how to make a specific e-mail program do what you want it to, so we picked the four most popular e-mail programs to show you the ropes. For the PPP and SLIP users, we picked Eudora, Netscape, and Microsoft Internet Mail. AOL and CompuServe users should take a look in Chapters 14 and 15, respectively. For UNIX account users, we picked Pine.

✔ **Eudora:** This popular e-mail program runs under Microsoft Windows (3.1 and 95) and on Macintoshes. Eudora up- and downloads mail to your mail server too and is popular for two reasons: It's easy to use, and it's cheap. You can get a freeware version (Eudora Light, which is on the CD-ROM in the back of this book) for free, and an enhanced commercial version (Eudora Pro) costs only about $65. The examples here are made by using Eudora Light, and the professional version looks even better. See Chapter 21 to find out how to get either version.

✔ **Netscape:** Yes, it's the same Netscape you met in Chapter 5 while surfing the World Wide Web. All except the oldest versions (from 2.0 on up) of Netscape make it an adequate if not superb mail program as well as a Web browser. It runs on your own computer and up- and down-loads mail to your mail server. We strongly prefer Eudora, but because some people are stuck with Netscape, we mention it here.

✔ **Internet Mail:** When Netscape began including an e-mail program with its browser, Microsoft felt compelled to follow suit. When you get a copy of the Microsoft Web browser, Internet Explorer, you may get Internet Mail too. If not, you can download it from the Net (see Chapter 21).

✔ **Pine:** This rather nice mail program comes with a full-screen terminal interface. It's generally available from most UNIX shell providers because it's (no! wait! you guessed!) free. If you're using a UNIX shell system, Pine runs on your provider's computer, and you type commands at it using a terminal program on your computer.

Sending Mail Is Easy

Sending mail is easy enough that we show you a few examples rather than waste time explaining the theory.

Sending mail with Eudora

Here's how to run Eudora and send some mail:

1. **From your PC or Mac, start Eudora.**

   From Windows 3.1, start Eudora by clicking her Program Manager icon, which looks like an envelope. In Windows 95, her icon is on the desktop or in a folder. Mac users click the Eudora icon. You should see an introductory "splash" window that goes away after a few seconds and then a window like the one shown in Figure 8-1. Exactly what's in the window varies depending on what you were looking at the last time you ran Eudora.

2. **To send a message, click the New message button on the toolbar (the button with the paper and pencil). Or choose Message⇨New message from the menu. (If you can remember shortcut keys, you can also press Ctrl+N.)**

   Eudora pops up a new message window, with spaces to type the address, subject, and text of a message.

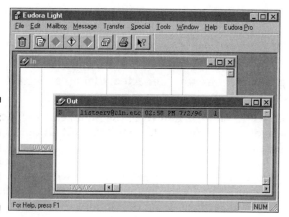

Figure 8-1:
Eudora
(Eudora
Light, in this
case) says
hello.

3. **On the To line, type the recipient's address**
   (`internet4@dummies.net`, **for example**).

   For your first e-mail message, you might want to write to us (because we will send you back a message confirming what your e-mail address is) or to yourself.

4. **Press Tab to skip to the Subject line (because Eudora already knows who you are, you skip the From line), and type a subject.**

   Make the subject line short and specific.

5. **Press Tab a few more times to skip the Cc: and Bcc: fields (or type the addresses of people who should get carbon copies and blind carbon copies of the message).**

   The term "carbon copy" should be familiar to those of you who were born before 1960 and remember the ancient practice of putting sheets of carbon-coated paper between sheets of regular paper to make extra copies when using a typewriter. (Please don't ask us what a typewriter is.) In e-mail, a carbon copy is simply a copy of the message you send. All recipients, on both the To: and Cc: lines, see who's getting this message. *Blind carbon copies* are copies sent to people without their names on the message. *You* can figure out why you might send a copy to someone but not want everyone to know you sent it.

6. **Press Tab to move to the large area, and then type your message.**

7. **To send the message, click the Send or Queue button in the upper right corner of the message window (what the button says depends on how Eudora is set up).**

   If the button is marked Send, as soon as you click it, Eudora tries to send the message and puts up a little status window that contains incomprehensible status messages. If, on the other hand, it's marked Queue, your message is stashed in your outbox to be sent later.

The usual reason to have a Queue button is that you have a dial-up PPP or SLIP connection so that your computer isn't connected to the Net all the time. After you have queued a few messages, you can send them all at one time.

8. **If your computer isn't already connected, dial up and get it connected to your provider.**

9. **Then switch back to Eudora, and from the menu choose File⇨Send Queued Messages (Ctrl+T for the lazy) to transmit all the messages you have queued up.**

Even if you leave your computer connected while you write your mail, it's not a bad idea to set Eudora to queue the mail and not send it until you tell it to. (Choose Special⇨Settings or Tools⇨Options from the Eudora menu, go to the Sending Mail category, and be sure that Immediate Send isn't checked.) That way, you get a few minutes after you write each message to ponder whether you really want to send it. Even though we have been using e-mail for almost 20 years, we still throw away many of the messages we have written before we send them.

After you have sent a piece of e-mail, there's no way to cancel it!

The same idea, using Netscape

The steps for sending mail from Netscape are almost identical to those for sending mail from Eudora (you're doing the same thing, after all):

1. **Start Netscape.**

   The instructions from here on depend on whether you're using Netscape Version 3.0 or 4.0.

2. **Choose Window⇨Netscape Mail (in Netscape 3.0) or Window⇨Inbox (in Netscape 4.0).**

   This step opens the Netscape Mail or Inbox window. The first time you give the command, Netscape asks you for the password for your mailbox, which is usually the same as the password for your Internet account.

   If you see an error message about a POP3 mailbox, Netscape is complaining that it doesn't know the name of the computer on which your mail is stored. Click OK to make the error message go away. When you see the Netscape Mail or Inbox window, choose Options⇨Mail and News Preferences (in Netscape 3.0) or Edit⇨Mail and News Preferences (in Netscape 4.0) from the menu, click the Servers or Mail Server tab along the top of the Preferences window that appears, and fill in the first three boxes you see. Type the name of your Internet provider's mail server in the first two boxes (all providers we know of use the same server for incoming and outgoing mail — if you don't know what to type, call and ask your provider) and your username in the third box. Click OK.

Netscape may try to retrieve any waiting mail; click Cancel or the red stop sign if you don't want it to bother. You see the Netscape Mail window, shown in Figure 8-2, if you use Netscape 3.0; Netscape 4.0 users see the Inbox window, which looks similar.

3. **Click the To:Mail (in Netscape 3.0) or Compose (in Netscape 4.0) button on the icon bar.**

Yet another window opens, the Message Composition window, with a blank message template.

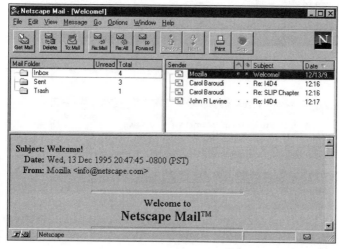

Figure 8-2:
Netscape
shows you
your e-mail.

If Netscape complains that it doesn't know your e-mail address, click OK, choose Options⇨Mail and News Preferences (in Netscape 3.0) or Edit⇨Mail and News Preferences (in Netscape 4.0), click the Identity tab, fill in the first three blanks, and click OK. Then click the To:Mail or Compose button again.

4. **Fill in the recipient's address (or addresses) in the Mail To box, type the subject, and type the message.**

5. **Click Send to send the message.**

The message wings its way to your Internet provider and on to the addressee.

Sending mail with Internet Mail

If you have Microsoft Internet Mail, here's how to send mail:

1. **Start Internet Mail. You don't have to connect to your Internet provider (yet).**

   Click the Internet Mail icon, or (in Windows 95) choose it from the Start⇨Programs menu. The Internet Mail window (shown in Figure 8-3) features a nice, shiny New Message icon for composing a message.

Figure 8-3: Internet Mail shows a list of messages in the current folder and the text of the selected message.

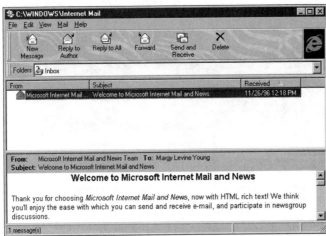

2. **Click the New Message button (the leftmost button on the toolbar), press Ctrl+N, or choose Mail⇨New Message from the menu bar.**

   You see a New Message window, with boxes to fill in to address the message.

3. **In the To box, type the address to send the message to, and then press Tab.**

   Don't press Enter unless you want to add another line to the To box so that you can type an additional address to send the message to.

4. **If you want to send a copy of the message to anyone, type the address in the Cc box. Then press Tab. In the Subject box, type a succinct summary of the message. Then press Tab.**

   Your cursor should be blinking in the message area, the large empty box where the actual message goes.

5. **In the large empty box, type the text of the message.**

   When you have typed your message, you can press F7 to check its spelling.

6. **To send the message, click the Send button on the toolbar (the leftmost button), press Alt+S (not Ctrl+S, for some strange reason), or choose File⇨Send Message from the menu.**

   Internet Mail sticks the message in your Outbox folder, waiting to be sent.

7. **Connect to your Internet provider.**

   To send the message, you have to climb on the Net.

8. **Click the Send and Receive button on the toolbar, press Ctrl+M, or choose Mail⇨Send and Receive from the menu.**

   Your message is on its way.

Sending mail with Pine

We presume that your UNIX shell provider has Pine all installed and ready to go (if not, call up and complain; there's no excuse not to have it available). Here's how to send a message:

If you have been using a PC with Windows or a Macintosh and have never experienced the utter thrill of computing without being able to point and click, you might — right this minute — be on the brink of a profound moment that will make you thank the stars for all you have now and have taken for granted. Hide your mouse. It's of no use to you now. It will only frustrate you even more if you try to use it. All the navigation you will do requires you to use letters or arrow keys.

1. **Run Pine by typing** pine **and pressing Enter (or Return — same thing)**.

   You see the Pine main menu, a list of commands that includes Compose Message.

2. **Press** c **to compose a new message.**

   Pine displays a nice, blank message, all ready for you to fill in.

3. **On the To line, type the address you want to send mail to and press Enter.**

   At the bottom of the screen, you now see a bunch of options preceded by a funny-looking caret sign and a letter. The caret sign indicates the Ctrl key on your keyboard. To choose an option, press the Ctrl key and the letter of the option that interests you (such as Ctrl-G for ^G to get help).

4. **On the Cc: line, you can enter addresses of other people to whom you want to send a copy of this message.**

5. **Press Enter to get to the line labeled** Attchmnt:

Whether the programmers can't spell or the lazy typists have struck or they abbreviate things so that people won't know that they can't spell, no one really knows. This line is for *attachments* — files you want to send along with your message. You can enter the name of a file, even a file that contains stuff that isn't text, and Pine sends it along with your message.

6. **Press Enter to get to the subject of your message, and then enter something descriptive about the content of your message.**

   Subject lines that say something like "A message from Fred" are somewhat less useful than something specific, such as "Re: Pizza dinner tomorrow at eight."

7. **Press Enter to get to the part we have all been waiting for and enter your message.**

   It can say anything you want, and it can be as long as you want. To enter the message text, Pine automatically runs the simple text editor Pico, which, with any luck, you already know how to use. If you don't know how to run Pico but you know how to run another UNIX editor, ask your Internet service provider to help you set up Pine to use the editor you do know how to run. (Some providers ask you when they configure your account.) You have to be able to stumble through some type of editor, so if you don't know any, starting with Pico is as good a place as any.

   Type the message. If you don't know how to use any editor features, just type your message. Press the arrow keys on the keyboard to move around if you need to make changes.

8. **When you're finished, press Ctrl+X to save the message and return to Pine.**

   Pine asks whether you really want to send the message.

9. **Press y or Enter to send your message.**

   The Pine program responds with a cheery [Sending mail.....] message, and you're all set.

Pine lets you do all sorts of other nifty things; to see where to find more info, see Chapter 22.

Mail Coming Your Way

If you begin sending e-mail (and in most cases even if you don't), you begin receiving it. The arrival of e-mail is always exciting, even when you get 200 messages a day.

Getting ANSI

If, when you're trying to run Pine on your UNIX shell account, you get a strange message that looks something like this:

```
Your terminal, of type "ansi,"
is lacking functions needed to
run pine.
```

you have to utter a magic spell before continuing. Type this line:

```
setenv TERM vt100
```

or if your provider's system doesn't grok that:

```
TERM=vt100 ; export TERM
```

Be sure to capitalize the commands exactly as you see here. Then try again. (You're giving it some hints about which kind of terminal your computer is pretending to be. Trust us — the details aren't worth knowing.)

Reading mail with Eudora

One seriously cool feature of Eudora is that you can do much of what you do with mail while you're not connected to your account and paying by the minute. On the other hand, when you really do want to check your mail, you have to be connected. Eudora allegedly can figure out that you're not connected and dial in for you; in our experience, however, this "feature" doesn't always work.

If you don't have a full-time Net connection, follow these steps to get your mail:

1. **Make your Net connection, if you're not already connected.**

2. **Start up Eudora, if she's not already running.**

3. **If Eudora doesn't retrieve mail automatically, choose File⇨Check Mail (or press Ctrl+M) to retrieve your mail.**

   If you have a full-time Net connection, Eudora probably is set up to retrieve your mail automatically, in which case you only have to start Eudora and she gets your mail. (In addition, if you leave Eudora running, even hidden at the bottom of your screen as an icon, she automatically checks for new mail every once in a while.)

   If you have mail on the Mac, Eudora blows a horn and shows you a cute picture of a mailman delivering a letter. If you don't have any mail, you don't get any sound effects, but you do get a nice picture of a letter with a big red X through it. Windows users who have a sound card hear a little song that announces new mail.

   The mail appears in your inbox, a window that Eudora labels In, one line per message.

4. **To see a message, double-click the line or click the line and press Enter.**

   To stop looking at a message, double-click the box in the upper left corner of the message window (the standard way to get rid of a window) or press Ctrl+W or Ctrl+F4.

Buttons at the top of the In window or at the top of your screen (depending on your version of Eudora) let you dispose of your mail. First click (once) the message you want, to highlight it. Windows users can click the trashcan button to discard the message or the printer icon to print it. Macintosh users can press Delete to delete it or choose File⇨Print to print it.

There's much more you can do to messages, which we discuss in Chapter 9, but that's enough for now.

Reading mail with Netscape

Reading mail with Netscape is similar to reading it with Eudora:

1. **Start Netscape and connect to your Internet provider.**

   The rest of these steps depend somewhat on whether you're running Netscape Version 3.0 or 4.0.

2. **In Netscape 3.0, choose Window⇨Netscape Mail or click the little envelope in the lower right corner of the Netscape window. In Netscape 4.0, choose Window⇨Inbox from the menu or click the Inbox icon in the lower right corner of the Netscape window, the second of the four icons.**

   This step opens the Netscape Mail or Inbox window. Netscape may try to retrieve any waiting mail immediately; if it doesn't, click the Get Mail button. Incoming mail is filed in your Inbox folder.

   Netscape 3.0: The upper left part of the Netscape Mail window lists your mail folders (including Inbox and Sent — more folders appear later). The upper right part lists the messages in the selected folder. The bottom part of the window displays the selected message.

   Netscape 4.0: The box just under the toolbar shows the current folder, and the rest of the window lists the messages in that folder. The current folder is usually Inbox, your incoming mail.

3. **In Netscape 3.0, click the Inbox icon in the list of folders. In Netscape 4.0, if the box just under the toolbar doesn't say Inbox, click in the box and choose Inbox from the list that appears.**

   You see the subject lines for incoming mail. (In Netscape 3.0, the list appears in the upper right part of the window.)

4. Click each message to read it (double-click it in Netscape 4.0), or click Next or Previous to read messages in order.

In Netscape 3.0, the text of the message appears in the bottom part of the Netscape window. In Netscape 4.0, the message appears in a new window.

When you see the text of a message, you can click the Print, Delete, and other buttons to dispose of it. We discuss the other buttons in Chapter 9.

Reading mail with Internet Mail

If you have Microsoft Internet Mail, here's how to get your mail:

1. Run Internet Mail and connect to your Internet provider.

2. Click the Send and Receive button on the toolbar, press Ctrl+M, or choose Mail⇨Send and Receive from the menu bar.

Internet Mail downloads your incoming mail on your computer and stashes the message in your Inbox folder. See the Folders box right below the toolbar? You can choose which folder full of mail to look at. Right now, you should be looking at your Inbox.

The box in the middle of the Internet Mail window lists the senders and subjects of messages in the Inbox. The box at the bottom of the window shows the text of the message you select.

3. Click a message header on the list of messages to see the text of the message at the bottom of the Internet Mail window. Or double-click the message header to see the message in a new, big window.

If you see a message in its own window, click the Close button (in Windows 95), choose File⇨Close from the menu, or press Alt+F4 to get rid of the window.

You can delete, reply to, forward, or print a message after you have seen it (Chapter 9 tells you how).

Reading mail with Pine

When you log in to your shell account, you usually get a little message that says "You have new mail" if you do or "You have mail" if stuff you have already seen is hanging around. Depending on some obscure parameter, your mail gets checked periodically, and when you have new mail you get the "You have new mail" message again.

Here are the steps to follow:

1. **Type the** pine **command.**

   The Pine main menu lets you choose from a variety of activities; if you have mail, the choice L (Folder List) is highlighted.

2. **Press Enter to see the list of folders you can choose from.**

   When you're just starting out, you don't have much to choose from, but that can change. Right now you're interested in the one labeled INBOX. INBOX should be highlighted. Press Enter to see your mail. Pine displays a list of messages.

3. **The message that is highlighted is the current message. To choose a different one, press the arrow keys or press** P **for the preceding message or** N **for the next message.**

   When you have chosen the message you want to read, press Enter. Pine displays your message.

   After you have read a message, you have several choices about what to do with it. We talk about the details of deleting, forwarding, and filing messages in Chapter 9.

4. **To read your next message, press** N; **to read the preceding message, press** P; **to return to the index of messages in the folder you're reading (in this case, INBOX), press** I.

5. **When you're finished reading mail, press** Q **to quit.**

   Pine asks you whether you really want to do that. (What — leave this fabulous program? It's so wonderful!) Reassure it by pressing **Y**.

A Few Words from the Etiquette Ladies

Sadly, the Great Ladies of Etiquette, such as Emily Post and Amy Vanderbilt, died before the invention of e-mail. Here's what they might have suggested about what to say and, more important, what *not* to say in electronic mail.

E-mail is a funny hybrid, something between a phone call (or voice mail) and a letter. On one hand, it's quick and usually informal; on the other hand, because it's written rather than spoken, you don't see a person's facial expressions or hear her tone of voice.

A few words of advice:

✔ When you send a message, watch your tone of voice.

✔ Don't use all capital letters — it looks like you're SHOUTING.

✔ If someone sends you an incredibly obnoxious and offensive message, as likely as not it's a mistake or a joke gone awry. In particular, be on the lookout for failed sarcasm.

Flame off!

Pointless and excessive outrage in electronic mail is so common that it has a name of its own: *flaming*. Don't flame. It makes you look like a jerk.

When you get a message so offensive that you just *have* to reply, stick it back in your electronic inbox for a while and wait until after lunch. Then, don't flame back. The sender probably didn't realize how the message would look. In about 20 years of using electronic mail, we can testify that we have never, never, regretted *not* sending an angry message (although we *have* regretted sending a few — ouch).

When you're sending mail, keep in mind that someone reading it will have no idea of what you *intended* to say — just what you *did* say. Subtle sarcasm and irony are almost impossible to use in e-mail and usually come across as annoying or dumb instead. (If you're an extremely superb writer, you can disregard this advice — just don't say that we didn't warn you.)

Another possibility to keep in the back of your mind is that it is technically not difficult to forge e-mail return addresses. If you get a totally off-the-wall message from someone that seems out of character for that person, some-body else may have forged it as a prank. (No, we won't tell you how to forge e-mail. How dumb do you think we are?)

Smile!

Sometimes it helps to put in a : -) (called a *smiley*), which means "this is a joke." (Try leaning way over to the left if you don't see why it's a smile.) In some communities, notably CompuServe, <g> or <grin> serves the same purpose. Here's a typical example:

```
People who don't believe that we are all part of a warm,
caring community who love and support each other are no
better than rabid dogs and should be hunted down and shot.
:-)
```

Although smileys sometimes help, if a joke needs a smiley, maybe it wasn't worth making. It may sound as though all your e-mail is supposed to be humorless. It's not that bad; until you have the hang of it, though, limit the humor. You'll be glad you did.

How Private Is E-Mail?

Relatively, but not totally. Any recipient of your mail might forward it to other people. Some mail addresses are really mailing lists that redistribute messages to many other people. In one famous case, a mistaken mail address sent a message to tens of thousands of readers. It began, "Darling, at last we have a way to send messages that is completely private."

If you send mail from work or to someone at work, your mail is not private. You and your friend may work for companies of the highest integrity whose employees would never dream of reading private e-mail. When push comes to shove, however, and someone accuses your company of leaking confidential information and its corporate lawyer says, "Examine the e-mail," someone reads all the e-mail. (This actually happened to a friend of ours, who was none too pleased to find that all his intimate correspondence with his fiancee had been read.) E-mail you send and receive is stored on your disk, and most companies back up their disks regularly. Reading your e-mail is very easy for someone who really wants to, unless you encrypt it.

The usual rule of thumb is not to send anything you wouldn't want to see posted next to the water cooler or perhaps scribbled next to a pay phone. The latest e-mail systems are beginning to include encryption features that make the privacy situation somewhat better so that anyone who doesn't know the keyword used to scramble a message can't decode it.

The most common tools for encrypted mail are known as *PEM* (privacy-enhanced mail) and *PGP* (pretty good privacy). PGP is one of the most widely used encryption programs, both in the United States and abroad. Many experts think that it is so strong that even the National Security Agency can't crack it. We don't know, but if the NSA wants to read your mail, you have more complicated problems than we can help you solve.

BTW, what does IMHO mean? RTFM!

E-mail users are often lazy typists, and many abbreviations are common. Here are some of the most widely used:

Abbreviation	What It Means	Abbreviation	What It Means
BTW	By the way	RTFM	Read the, er, fine manual — you could have and should have looked it up yourself
IMHO	In my humble opinion		
ROFL	Rolling on floor laughing	TIA	Thanks in advance
RSN	Real soon now (vaporware)	TLA	Three-letter acronym

Hey, Mr. Postmaster

Every Internet host that can send or receive mail has a special mail address called `postmaster` that is guaranteed to get a message to the person responsible for that host. If you send mail to someone and get back strange failure messages, you might try sending a message to the postmaster. For example, if `king@bluesuede.org` returns an error from `bluesuede.org`, you might try a polite question to `postmaster@bluesuede.org`. Because the postmaster is usually an over-worked volunteer system administrator, it is considered poor form to ask a postmaster for favors much greater than "Does so-and-so have a mailbox on this system?"

PGP is available for free on the Net. To find more information about privacy and security issues, including how to get started with PGP, see Chapter 22.

To Whom Do I Write?

Now that you know how to use e-mail, you will want to send some messages. See Chapter 17 to find out how to find the e-mail address of someone you know. Chapter 10 tells you how to find other people to write to and how to get interesting information by e-mail.

Mail Prowess

Learning the basics of electronic mail is simple for many people. If you find it difficult or if you want to become a power e-mail user, we tell you where to get more information in Chapter 22.

Chapter 9

Putting Your Mail in Its Place

· ·

In This Chapter

▶ Deleting mail

▶ Responding to mail

▶ Forwarding and filing mail

▶ Spotting and avoiding chain letters

▶ Sending and receiving exotic mail and mail attachments

▶ Exchanging mail with robots and fax machines

· ·

*O*kay, now you know how to send and receive mail. It's time for some tips and tricks to make you into a real mail aficionado. We describe Eudora, Netscape Navigator (Versions 3.0 and 4.0), Microsoft Internet Mail, and Pine (see Chapter 8 for descriptions of these programs).

After you have seen a message, you can do a bunch of different things with it (much the same as with paper mail). Here are your usual choices:

✔ Throw it away

✔ Reply to it

✔ Forward it to other people

✔ File it

Unlike with paper mail, you can do any or all of these things to each message. If you don't tell your mail program what to do to a message, the message either stays in your mailbox for later perusal or sometimes, when you're using Pine, for example, the message gets saved to a `read-messages` folder.

If your mail program automatically saves messages in a `read-messages`, Sent, or Outbox folder, be sure to go through the folder every week or so or else it will become enormous and unmanageable.

Deleting Mail

When you first begin to get e-mail, it's so exciting that it's difficult to imagine just throwing it away. Eventually, however, you *have* to learn how to do this or else you will run out of room. Start early. Delete often.

The physical act of throwing away mail is easy enough that you probably have figured out how to do it already. Using the Windows version of Eudora, you click a message and then click the trashcan or press Ctrl+D. In the Macintosh version of Eudora, you can click the message and press Delete. If the message is open, press ⌘+D or choose Delete from the Message menu. In Netscape (either the Netscape Navigator 3.0 Mail window or the Netscape 4.0 Messenger program), click the message and then the Delete button on the toolbar or press the Del key. In Internet Mail, click the message and then the Delete button on the toolbar, press Ctrl+D, or choose File⇨Delete. From Pine, press **D** for Delete.

You can often delete mail without even reading it. If you subscribe to mailing lists, certain topics might not interest you. After you see the subject line, you might want to delete it without reading it. If you're the type of person who reads everything Ed McMahon sends to you, you may have problems with junk e-mail too. Consider getting professional help.

Back to You, Sam: Replying to Mail

You should know a couple of things about replying to mail. It's easy enough to do: In Eudora, choose Message⇨Reply or click the icon that looks like a U-turn sign; in Netscape, click the Re:Mail icon on the toolbar or choose Message⇨Reply from the menu or press Ctrl+R; in Internet Mail, click the Reply to Author button on the toolbar or press Ctrl+R or choose Mail⇨Reply to Author; in Pine, press **R**.

Pay attention to two things in particular:

  ✔ To whom does the reply go? Look carefully at the To: line your mail program has filled out for you. Is that who you thought you were addressing? If the reply is to a mailing list, did you really intend to post to that list, or is your message of a more personal nature and might be better addressed to the individual who sent the message? Did you mean to reply to a group? Are all the addresses you think you're replying to included in the To: list? If the To: list isn't right, you can move the cursor to it and edit it as necessary.

✔ Do you want to include the content of the message you're replying to? Most e-mail programs begin your reply message with the content of the message you're replying to. Netscape has a Quote button on the toolbar that sticks the quoted text of the original message into your reply. We suggest that you begin by including it and then edit the text to just the relevant material. If you don't give some context to people who get a great deal of e-mail, your reply will make no sense. If you're answering a question, include the question in the response. You don't have to include the entire text, but give your reader a break. She may have read 50 messages since she sent you mail and may not have a clue what you're talking about unless you remind her.

When you reply to a message, most mail programs fill in the Subject field with the letters *Re:* (short for *re*garding) and the Subject field of the message you're replying to.

Hot Potatoes: Forwarding Mail

You can forward e-mail along to someone else. It's easy. It's cheap. Forwarding is one of the nicest things about electronic mail and at the same time one of the worst. It's good because you can easily pass along messages to people who need to know about them. It's bad because you (not you personally, but, um, people around you — that's it) can just as easily send out floods of messages to recipients who would just as soon not hear yet another press release from the local Ministry of Truth. You have to think a little about whether you will enhance someone's quality of life by forwarding a message to him. (If you don't care about quality of life, pick some other criterion.)

What's usually called *forwarding* a message involves wrapping the message in a new message of your own, sort of like sticking Post-It notes all over a copy of it and mailing the copy and Post-Its to someone else.

Forwarding mail is almost as easy as replying to it. In Eudora, choose Message⇨Forward or click the icon of a road sign with an arrow pointing up; in Netscape, click the Forward icon on the toolbar or choose Message⇨Forward from the menu or press Ctrl+L; in Internet Mail, click the Forward button on the toolbar or press Ctrl+F or choose Mail⇨Forward; in Pine, press **F**. The mail program composes a message containing the text of the message you want to forward; all you have to do is address it, add a few snappy comments, and send it.

Keeping track of your friends

After you begin using e-mail, you quickly find that you have enough regular correspondents that it's a pain to keep track of their e-mail addresses. Fortunately, every popular e-mail program provides an *address book* in which you can save your friends' addresses so that you can send mail to Mom, for example, and have it automatically addressed to chairman@exec.hq.giant-corp.com. You can also create address lists so that you can send mail to family, for example, and it goes to Mom, Dad, your brother, both sisters, and your dog, all of whom have e-mail addresses.

All address books let you do the same things: save in your address book the address from a message you have just read, use addresses you have saved, and edit your address book.

Netscape: Netscape has an adequate if uninspired address book. When you're reading a message, you can add the sender's address to your address book by choosing Message➪ Add to Address Book. It pops up a window in which you can enter the nickname to use and then click OK to add it to the address book. To use the address book when you're creating a message, click the Mail To: or Cc: buttons (in Netscape 3.0) or the To button (in Netscape 4.0) in the message-creation window. This action pops up a window that lists the contents of your address book. Double-click the address or addresses you want, and then click OK to continue composing your message. To edit your address book, choose Window➪Address Book. You can create a mailing list by choosing Item➪Add List, which creates an empty list, and then dragging existing addresses from the address book into the list. (Yes, this means that first you have to put all the people for the list into the address book separately and then drag them into the list. We

said that it was uninspired.) The address book window is deliberately similar to the Netscape bookmark window, so if you remember how to edit bookmarks, you edit the address book in the same way.

Eudora: Eudora has a very nice address book. If you're reading a message, choose Special➪Make Address Book Entry (or press Ctrl+K). It suggests using the person's real name as the nickname, which is usually fine. Then click OK. To use the address book while you're composing a message, you can open the address book with Tools➪Address Book (Ctrl+L), click the nickname to use, and then click the To:, Cc:, or Bcc: button in the address book window to add the selected address to the message. Or use this shortcut: Type the first few letters of the nickname on the To: or Cc: line, enough to distinguish the nickname you want from other nicknames, and press Ctrl+,. Eudora finishes the nickname for you. To make a mailing list, open the address book by choosing Tools➪Address Book (Ctrl+L), click New to create a new nickname, and then click in the Address(es) subwindow in the address book and type the addresses you want, one to a line. Alternatively, if you have received mail in your inbox from all the people you want to put on your list, you can highlight all those messages in the inbox list, using Ctrl+click, and then press Ctrl+K to make a new address book entry, which is a list of all the authors of the selected messages.

Internet Mail: The Windows 95 version of Internet Mail has a barely adequate address book. (The Windows 3.1 version of Internet Mail doesn't.) There is, as far as we can tell, no direct way to copy a correspondent's address into the address book; the best you can do is to click Reply to Author, highlight the person's name on the To: line, and press Ctrl+C to copy the address to the Clipboard. Then close the message you just started (unless you want to write to him right now), choose File⇨Address Book to open the address book, click New Contact to create a new address book entry, type the person's real name, click in the address book area for e-mail addresses, press Ctrl+V to paste in the address you just copied, press Enter, and then click OK. If this procedure sounds like more trouble than it's worth, we agree. (Perhaps this would be a good time to download Eudora Light.) If you have managed to get some entries into your address book, you use them while creating a new message by clicking the little icon on the To: or Cc: line that looks like a Rolodex card. This step opens the address book. Double-click the address book entry or entries you want to use, and then click OK to make the address book go away.

✔ Eudora and Internet Mail provide the forwarded text in the message part of the window. In Eudora, each line is preceded by the greater-than sign (>); in Internet Mail, the forwarded message is at the bottom of the outgoing message. You then get to edit the message and add your own comments. See the nearby "Fast forward" sidebar for tips about pruning forwarded mail.

✔ Netscape doesn't show you the text of the original message — you just have to trust it to send the text along. (Netscape treats the message as an *attached file,* which you learn about later in this chapter.) The comments you type in the message box appear along with the text of the original message.

If you want Netscape to include the text of the original message in the usual way (with each line preceded by a >), choose the Message⇨ Forward Quoted command instead.

Sometimes the mail you get might really have been intended for someone else. You probably will want to pass it along as is, without sticking the greater-than character at the beginning of every line, and you should leave the sender and reply-to information intact so that if the new recipient of the mail wants to respond, the response goes to the originator of the mail, not to you just because you passed it on. Some mail programs call this feature *remailing* or *bouncing,* and it's the electronic version of scribbling another address on the outside of an envelope and dropping it back in the mailbox.

Eudora calls this process *redirecting;* you can redirect mail by choosing Message⇨Redirect from the menu or clicking the right-turn arrow icon. Eudora sticks in a polite by-way-of notice to let the new reader know how the message found her. Pine uses B for Bounce; Netscape has no redirection, so you have to forward messages instead.

TIP

Fast forward

When you're forwarding mail, it's generally a good idea to get rid of uninteresting parts. All the glop in the message header is frequently included automatically in the forwarded message, and almost none of it is comprehensible, much less interesting, so get rid of it.

The tricky part is editing down the text. If the message is short, a screenful or so, you probably should leave it alone:

```
>Is there a lot of demand for
 >fruit pizza?
```

In answer to your question, I checked with our research department and found that the favorite pizza toppings in the 18-34 age group are pepperoni, sausage,ham, pineapple, olives, peppers, mushrooms, hamburger,and broccoli. I specifically asked about prunes andthey said that there was no statistically significant response about them.

If the text is really long and only part of it is relevant, you should, as a courtesy to the reader, cut it down to the interesting part. We can tell you from experience that people pay much more attention to a concise, one-line e-mail message than they do to 12 pages of quoted stuff followed by a two-line question.

Sometimes it makes sense to edit material even more, particularly to emphasize one specific part. When you do so, of course, be sure not to edit to the point where you put words in the original author's mouth or garble the sense of the message, as in the following reply:

```
>In answer to your question, I
 checked with our research
 department and found that the
 favorite pizza toppings ...
 and they said that there was
 no statistically significant
 response about them.
```

That's an excellent way to make new enemies. Sometimes it makes sense to paraphrase a little — in that case, put the paraphrased part in square brackets, like this:

```
>[When asked about prunes on
 pizza, research] said that
 there was no statistically
 significant response about
 them.
```

People disagree about whether paraphrasing to shorten quotes is a good idea. On one hand, if you do it well, it saves everyone time. On the other hand, if you do it badly and someone takes offense, you're in for a week of accusations and apologies that will wipe out whatever time you may have saved. The decision is up to you.

Cold Potatoes: Saving Mail

Saving e-mail for later reference is similar to putting potatoes in the fridge for later (don't knock it if you haven't tried it — day-old boiled potatoes are yummy with enough butter or sour cream). Lots of your e-mail is worth saving, just like lots of your paper mail is worth saving. (Lots of it *isn't*, of course, but we already covered that subject.)

You can save e-mail in a few different ways:

- ✔ Save it in a folder full of messages.
- ✔ Save it in a regular file.
- ✔ Print it and put it in a file cabinet with paper mail.

The easiest method usually is to stick messages in a folder (a folder is usually no more than a file full of messages with some sort of separator between each message).

Two general approaches are used in filing mail: by sender and by topic. Whether you use one or the other or both is mostly a matter of taste. Some mail programs (such as Pine) help you file stuff by the sender's name. If your friend Fred has the username fred@something.or.other, when you press S to save a message from him, Pine asks whether you want to put it in a folder called fred. Of course, if some crazed system administrator has given him the username z921h8t@something.or.other, the automatic naming can leave something to be desired, so make up names of your own.

For filing by topic, it's entirely up to you to come up with the folder names. The most difficult part is coming up with memorable names. If you're not careful, you end up with four folders with slightly different names, each with a quarter of the messages about a particular topic. Try to come up with names that are obvious, and don't abbreviate. If the topic is accounting, call the folder accounting because if you abbreviate you will never remember whether it's called acctng, acct, or acntng.

If you use Windows or a Mac, you can save all or part of a message by copying it into a text file or word-processing document. Select the text of the message using your mouse. In Windows, press Ctrl+C (⌘+C on a Mac) or choose Edit⇨Copy to copy the text to the Clipboard. Switch to your word processor (or whatever program you want to copy the text into) and press Ctrl+V (⌘+V on the Mac) or choose Edit⇨Paste to make the message appear where your cursor is.

Filing with Eudora

To file a message in Eudora, click the message and choose Transfer from the menu. The Transfer menu that appears lists all your mailboxes — all the choices you have for where to file your message. Highlight the mailbox in which you want to stick your message. Poof — it's there.

The first time you try to file something, you will notice that you don't have anywhere to file it. Create a new mailbox to stick the message in by choosing New from the Transfer menu. Every time you want to create a new file, use the New selection. Although you will eventually have enough mailboxes to handle most of your mail, for a while it may seem as though you're choosing New all the time.

You can see all the messages in a folder by choosing Mailbox from the menu — a window appears listing all the messages in the folder.

If you want to save the message in a text file, click the message, choose File⇨Save As from the menu, move to the folder in which you want to save the message, type a filename, and click OK.

The commercial Eudora Pro and the new 3.0 version of Eudora Light can file messages for you automatically: You can create *filters* that tell Eudora, for example, "Any message that comes from the POULTRY-L mailing list should be automatically filed in the Chickens folder." (The freeware version of Eudora has a less flexible version of this feature — they had to give you *some* reason to buy Eudora Pro.)

Filing with Netscape Navigator

In the Netscape 3.0 Mail window, you can save a message by clicking the message and choosing Message⇨Move from the menu. Then select the folder name from the list that appears. An easier way to move a message is to drag it from the list of messages to another folder on the list of folders. To make a new folder, choose File⇨New Folder from the menu.

Netscape 4.0 has a new window, the Netscape Message Center, in which you can fool around with folders, so its filing commands work a little differently. In the Netscape 4.0 Inbox window, you can save a message by clicking the message, choosing Message⇨File message from the menu, and choosing the folder from the list that appears. To make a new folder, choose Window⇨ Folders from the menu to display the Netscape Message Center window, and then choose File⇨New Folder. This window lists your mail folders and the Usenet newsgroups to which you subscribe. (Chapter 11 tells you what a newsgroup is and how to subscribe to one.) To move a message to folder, you can click it in your Inbox window and drag it to the folder in your Message Center window.

To save a message or several messages in a text file (in either version of Netscape), select the message or messages and choose File⇨Save As from the menu. Click in the Save as type box and choose Plain Text (*.txt) from the list that appears. Type a filename and click the Save button.

Filing with Internet Mail

To save a message in Internet Mail, you stick it in a folder. You start out with folders named Inbox, Deleted Items, Outbox, and Sent Items. To make a new folder, choose File⇨Folder⇨Create from the menu and give the folder a name. (Make one called Personal just to give it a try.) Then move messages into it by clicking a message header in your Inbox and choosing Mail⇨Move to from the menu. You can see the list of message headers for any folder by clicking in the Folders box just below the toolbar and choosing a folder name.

You can save the text of a message in a text file by clicking the message and choosing File⇨Save As from the menu, clicking in the Save as type box and choosing Text (*.txt), typing a filename, and clicking the Save button.

Filing with Pine

To save a message in a folder, press **s** when you're looking at the message or when it is highlighted on your list of messages. To create a new folder, tell Pine to save a message to a folder that doesn't exist (yet). Pine asks whether you want to create it — press **y** to do so.

Exotic Mail and Mail Attachments

Sooner or later, just plain, old, everyday e-mail isn't good enough for you. Someone's gonna send you a picture you just have to see or you're gonna want to send something cool to your new best friend in Paris. When we talk about sending stuff other than text through the mail, we're talking about using special file formats and systems that can read them. Sometimes the entire message is in a special format (such as MIME, which we talk about in a minute), and sometimes people *attach* things to their mail. Attachments come in three flavors:

- ✔ **MIME:** Stands for *m*ultipurpose *I*nternet *m*ail *e*xtensions
- ✔ **Uuencoding:** A method of including information in e-mail; invented back in the days of UNIX-to-UNIX e-mail (hence the *uu* in the name)
- ✔ **BinHex:** Stands for *bin*ary-to-*hex*adecimal, as far as we can tell

Chain letters: Arrrrrggghhh!

One of the most obnoxious things you can do with e-mail is to pass around chain letters. Because all mail programs have forwarding commands, with only a few keystrokes you can send a chain letter along to hundreds of other people. Don't do it. Chain letters are cute for about two seconds, and then they're just annoying. After 15 years of using e-mail, we have *never* received a chain letter worth passing along.

A few chain letters just keep coming around and around, despite our best efforts to stamp them out. Learn to recognize them now and avoid embarrassment later.

The Good Times virus hoax: In late 1994 a chain letter appeared on America Online disguised as a warning that a horrible computer virus capable of erasing your hard disk was being spread by e-mail. The virus allegedly arrived in e-mail bearing the words *Good Times*. Well-intentioned individuals quickly sent it to everyone they knew. The chain letter, not the non-existent virus, spread rapidly throughout the Internet. Computer viruses are spread though infected programs that, after they are run, can have malicious effects. E-mail is stored as text — not as a program — that cannot cause damage to your disk unless you give specific commands to run a program.

Dying boy wants greeting (or business) cards: Not anymore, he doesn't. A decade ago an English boy named Craig Shergold was hospitalized with a serious brain tumor. Craig wanted to set the world record for most greeting cards. Word got out, and Craig received millions of cards and eventually got into the *Guinness Book of World Records.* Then U.S. TV billionaire John Kluge paid for Craig to fly to the United States for a successful operation. Craig is okay now and doesn't want any

more cards. (You can read all about this story on page 24 of the July 29, 1990, edition of the *New York Times.*) Guinness is so sick of the whole business that it closed the category — no more records for the most cards are accepted. To help dying children, give the two dollars that a card and stamp would have cost to a children's welfare organization, such as UNICEF.

The modem-tax rumor: In 1987 the U.S. Federal Communications Commission (FCC) proposed changing the rules governing the way online services are billed for their phone connections. The proposal would have had the effect of raising the prices these services charge. Online service customers made their opposition clear immediately and loudly, members of Congress made concerned inquiries, and the proposal was *dropped.* Undated notices about the proposal unfortunately have circulated ever since. If you see yet another modem-tax scare, demand the current FCC docket number because the FCC — as a government bureaucracy — can't blow its nose without making announcements, accepting comments, and so on. No docket means no action, which means that it's the same old rumor.

Make big bucks with a chain letter: These types of letters usually have the subject MAKE.MONEY.FAST, are signed by "Dave Rhodes," contain lots of testimonials from people who are now rolling in dough, and tell you to send $5 to the name at the top of the list, put your name at the bottom, and send the message to a zillion other suckers. Some even say "This isn't a chain letter" (you're supposedly helping to compile a mailing list or something — your 100 percent guaranteed tip-off that it's a chain letter). Don't even think about it. These chain letters are extremely illegal even when they say they aren't, and, besides, they don't even work. (Why send any money? Why not just add your name and send it on?) Think of them as gullibility viruses. Send a polite note to the sender's postmaster to encourage her to tell users not to send any more chain letters. If you don't believe that they're illegal, see the Postal Service Web site, at `http://www.usps.gov/websites/depart/inspect/chainlet.htm`.

The "two-fifty" cookie recipe: According to this one, someone was eating chocolate-chip cookies somewhere (Mrs. Fields and Neiman-Marcus are frequently cited) and asked for the recipe. "Sure," came the answer, "that'll be two-fifty, charged to your credit card." When the credit card statement came, it turned out to be 250 *dollars,* not two dollars and fifty cents. In retribution, the message concludes with the recipe, sent to you for free. The story is pure hooey: Mrs. Fields' recipes are in her cookbook; and Neiman's doesn't give theirs out. The recipe makes perfectly okay cookies, but no better than the one on the back of the bag of chips. This same story, by the way, circulated hand-to-hand in the 1940s and 1950s, except that the recipe was for a red-velvet cake served at a New York hotel.

Send e-mail to a publisher so that they give books to children's hospitals: This brief, ill-considered marketing gimmick lasted for a few days in late 1996. Needless to say, they got all the mail they wanted in a few hours after word got around and now don't want any more.

The technical details of these three methods are totally uninteresting and irrelevant: What matters to you is that your e-mail program must be capable of attaching files by using at least one of these methods and that it be capable of detaching incoming files that other people send you, preferably using any of the three methods.

You can generally send a file as an e-mail attachment by using your regular mail program to compose a regular message and then give a command to attach a file to the message. You send the message using the program's usual commands.

When you receive a file that is attached to an e-mail message, your mail program is responsible for noticing the attached file and doing something intelligent with it. Most of the time, your mail program saves the attached file as a separate file in the folder or directory you specify. After the file has been saved, you can use it just like any other file.

For example, you can send these types of files as attachments:

- ✔ Pictures, in image files
- ✔ Word-processing documents
- ✔ Sounds, in audio files

> ✔ Movies, in video files
> ✔ Programs, in executable files
> ✔ Compressed files, such as ZIP files

See Chapter 18 for a description of the types of files you may encounter as attachments. On the other hand, if you successfully receive a program as an attachment, don't run it unless you know the person who sent it —the program could have a virus.

If you receive a message with an attachment that uses a method (MIME, uuencoding, or BinHex) that your mail program doesn't know, the attached file shows up as a large message in your mailbox. If the attached file contains text, about half the kinds of tarted-up text are readable as is, give or take some ugly punctuation. If the attached file contains sound or pictures, on the other hand, the message is totally hopeless because the message just contains binary digitized versions of the images and not any sort of text approximation.

If you get a picture or sound MIME message and your mail program doesn't automatically handle it, clunky but usable methods may exist for saving the message to a file and extracting the contents with separate programs. Consult your Internet service provider's help desk.

Eudora attachments

To attach a file to a message with Eudora, compose a message as usual. Then choose Message⇨Attach File from the menu or click the Attach icon (a disk in front of a folder) or press Ctrl+H. Eudora helps you choose the document you want to attach. Eudora Light (the freeware version of Eudora) always sends files as MIME attachments and can handle incoming files by using any of the three attachment methods.

If you drag a file from Windows Explorer, My Computer, or File Manager to Eudora, she attaches it to the message you're writing. If you're not writing a message, she starts one for you.

When Eudora receives mail with attachments, she automatically saves them to your disk and tells you where they are and what they're called.

Netscape attachments

In Netscape, you click the Attach button to attach a file to the message you're composing. Unlike most other mail programs, Netscape lets you attach any file or document you can describe with a *Uniform Resource Locator,* or *URL* (the naming scheme used on the Web, as explained in

Chapter 5). It gives you your choice of attaching a document, by default the last message or page you were looking at, or attaching a file — click Document or File (Netscape 4.0 gives you even more choices). If you attach a file, you can click the Browse button to choose the file to attach. When you have decided what to attach, click OK to attach the file to the outgoing message. Netscape attaches files by using MIME.

For incoming mail, Netscape displays any attachments that it knows how to display itself (Web pages and GIF and JPEG image files). For other types of attachments, it displays a little description of the file, which you can click on, at which point Netscape runs an appropriate display program, if it knows of one, or asks you whether to save the attachment to a file or to configure a display program, which it then runs in order to display it. Netscape can handle all three attachment methods.

Internet Mail attachments

In Internet Mail, you attach a file to a message by choosing Insert⇨File Attachments from the menu while you're composing a message. Then select the file to attach. Send the message as usual.

When an incoming message contains an attachment, a paper clip appears by the message on your list of incoming messages and in the upper right corner of the message when you view it. Click the paper clip to see the filename — double-click to see the attachment itself.

Hey, Mr. Robot

Not every mail address has an actual person behind it. Some are mailing lists (which we talk about in Chapter 10), and some are *robots,* programs that automatically reply to messages. Mail robots have become popular as a way to query databases and retrieve files because it's much easier to set up a connection for electronic mail than it is to set up one that handles the more standard file transfer. You send a message to the robot (usually referred to as a *mailbot* or *mail server*), it takes some action based on the contents of your message, and it sends back a response. If you send a message to internet4@dummies.net, for example, you get a response telling you your e-mail address.

The most common use for mail servers is to get on and off *mailing lists,* which we explore in gruesome detail in Chapter 10. Companies also often use the lists to send back canned responses to requests for information sent to info@whatever.com.

Your Own, Personal Mail Manager

After you begin sending e-mail, you probably will find that you are receiving quite a bit of it, particularly if you put yourself on some mailing lists (see Chapter 10). Your incoming mail soon becomes a trickle, and then a stream, and then a torrent, and pretty soon you can't walk past your keyboard without getting soaking wet, metaphorically speaking.

Fortunately, most mail systems provide ways for you to manage the flow and avoid ruining your clothes (enough of this metaphor already). If most of your messages come from mailing lists, you should check to see whether the lists are available instead as *Usenet* newsgroups (see Chapter 11). Usenet newsreading programs generally enable you to look through the messages and find the interesting ones more quickly than your mail program does and to automatically sort the messages so that you can quickly read or ignore an entire *thread* (conversation) of messages about a particular topic. Your system manager can usually arrange to make particularly chatty mailing lists look like Usenet newsgroups. At our site, we handle about 40 mailing lists that way.

Eudora Pro users and, as of Version 3.0, Eudora Light users can create *filters* that can automatically check incoming messages against a list of senders and subjects and file them in appropriate folders. Internet Mail has the Inbox Assistant, which can sort your mail automatically. Some other mail programs have similar filtering features.

All this automatic-sorting nonsense may seem like overkill, and if you get only five or ten messages a day, it is. After the mail really gets flowing, however, dealing with your mail takes much more of your time than it used to. Keep those automated tools in mind — if not for now, for later.

One More Reason We Like Eudora Best

Beginning with Version 3.0, Eudora turns all URLs (Web site addresses) that she finds in an e-mail message into links to the Web site. You no longer have to type these addresses in your browser. All you have to do is double-click the highlighted link in the e-mail message and poof! — you're at the Web site.

Chapter 10

Mail, Mail, the Gang's All Here

• •

In This Chapter

▶ Mailing lists

▶ Getting more or less junk mail

▶ A few interesting mailing lists

▶ Mail servers

• •

Are You Sure That This Isn't Junk Mail?

Now that you know all about how to send and receive mail, only one thing stands between you and a rich, fulfilling, mail-blessed life: You don't know many people with whom you can exchange mail. Fortunately, you can get yourself on lots of mailing lists, which ensures that you arrive every morning to a mailbox with 400 new messages. (Maybe you should start out with one or two lists.)

The point of a mailing list is simple. The list has its own special e-mail address, and anything that someone sends to that address is sent to all the people on the list. Because they in turn often respond to the messages, the result is a running conversation.

Different lists have different styles. Some are relatively formal, hewing closely to the official topic of the list. Others tend to go flying off into outer space, topicwise. You have to read them for a while to be able to tell which list works which way.

Usenet newsgroups are another way to have running e-mail-like conversations, and the distinction between the two is blurry. (Because some topics are available both as mailing lists and on Usenet, people with and without access to news can participate.) Chapter 11 discusses Usenet.

Getting On and Off Mailing Lists

The way you get on or off a mailing list is simple: You send a mail message. Two general schools of mailing-list management exist: the *manual* and the *automatic.* Manual management is the more traditional way: Your message is read by a human being who updates the files to put people on or take them off the list. The advantage of manual management is that you get personal service; the disadvantage is that the list maintainer may not get around to servicing you for quite a while if more pressing business (such as her real job) intervenes.

These days it's more common to have lists maintained automatically, which saves human attention for times when things are fouled up. The most widely used automatic mailing managers are families of programs known as LISTSERV, Majordomo, and Listproc, which get their own sections later in this chapter.

Manual lists have a widely observed convention regarding list and maintainer addresses. Suppose that you want to join a list for fans of James Buchanan (the 15th President of the United States and the only one who never married, in case you slept through that part of history class), and the list's name is `buchanan-lovers@dummies.net`. The manager's address is almost certainly `buchanan-lovers-request@dummies.net`. In other words, just add `-request` to the list's address to get the manager's address. Because the list is maintained by hand, your request to be added or dropped doesn't have to take any particular form, as long as it's polite. `Please add me to the buchanan-lovers list` does quite well. When you decide that you have had all the Buchanan you can stand, another message saying `Please remove me from the buchanan-lovers list` does equally well.

Messages to `-request` addresses are read and handled by human beings who sometimes eat, sleep, and work regular jobs as well as maintain mailing lists. Therefore, they don't necessarily read your request the moment it arrives. It can take a day or so to be added to or removed from a list, and after you ask to be removed you usually get a few more messages before they remove you. If it takes longer than you want, be patient. *Don't* send cranky follow-ups — they just cheese off the list maintainer.

LISTSERV, the studly computer's mail manager

The BITNET network (a network of large computers, now mostly merged into the Internet) was set up so that the only thing it could do was ship files and messages from one system to another. As a result, BITNET users quickly developed lots and lots of mailing lists because no other convenient way — such as Usenet news — was available to stay in touch.

How to avoid looking like an idiot

Here's a handy tip: After you subscribe to a list, don't send anything to it until you have been reading it for a week. Trust us — it has been getting along without your insights since it began, and it can get along without them for one more week.

This method gives you a chance to learn the sorts of topics that people really discuss, the tone of the list, and so on. It also gives you a fair idea about which topics people are tired of. The classic newcomer gaffe is to subscribe to a list and immediately send a message asking a dumb question that isn't really germane to the topic and that was beaten to death three days earlier. Bide your time, and don't let this happen to you.

The number-two newcomer gaffe is to send a message directly to the list asking to subscribe or unsubscribe. This type of message should go to a request or LISTSERV, Majordomo, or Listproc address, where the list maintainer (human or robotic) can handle it, *not* to the list itself, where all the other subscribers can see that you screwed up.

To summarize: The first message you send, to join a list, should go to a `something-request` or `LISTSERV` or `majordomo` or `listproc` address, *not* to the list itself. After you have joined the list and read it for a while, *then* you can send messages to the list.

Because maintaining all those mailing lists was (and still is) a great deal of work, in order to manage the mailing lists the BITNET crowd came up with a program called *LISTSERV,* which originally ran on great big IBM mainframe computers. (The IBM mainframe types have an inordinate fondness for eight-letter uppercase names EVEN THOUGH TO MOST OF US IT SEEMS LIKE SHOUTING.) Although only users on machines directly connected to BITNET could originally use LISTSERV, current versions have been improved so that anyone with an Internet address can use them. Indeed, LISTSERV has grown to the point that it is an all-singing, all-dancing mailing-list program with about 15 zillion features and options, almost none of which you care about.

Although LISTSERV is a little clunky to use, it has the great advantage of being able to easily handle enormous mailing lists that contain thousands of members, something that makes the regular Internet mail programs choke. (LISTSERV can send mail to 1,000 addresses in about five minutes, for example, whereas that would take the regular Internet `sendmail` program more than an hour.)

You put yourself on and off a LISTSERV mailing list by sending mail to `LISTSERV@some.machine.or.other`, where `some.machine.or.other` is the name of the particular machine on which the mailing list lives. Because they're computer programs, LISTSERV list managers are pretty simple-minded, so you have to speak to them clearly and distinctly.

Urrp! Computers digest messages!

Some mailing lists are *digested*. No, they're not dripping with digital gastric juices — they're digested more in the sense of *Reader's Digest*. All the messages over a particular period (usually a day or two) are gathered into one big message with a table of contents added at the front. Many people find this method more convenient than getting messages separately because you can easily look at all the messages on the topic at one time.

Some mail and newsreading programs give you the option of dividing digests back into the individual messages so that you can see them one at a time yet still grouped together. This option is sometimes known as *undigestifying*, or *exploding*, a digest. (First it's digested, and then it explodes, sort of like a burrito.) Check the specifics of your particular mail program to see whether it has an option for digest-exploding.

Suppose that you want to join a list called SNUFLE-L (LISTSERV mailing lists usually end with -L), which lives at bluesuede.org. To join, send to LISTSERV@bluesuede.org a message that contains this line:

```
SUB SNUFLE-L Roger Sherman
```

You don't have to add a subject line or anything else to this message. SUB is short for subscribe, SNUFLE-L is the name of the list, and anything after that is supposed to be your real name. (You can put whatever you want there, but keep in mind that it will show up in the return address of anything you send to the list.) Shortly afterward, you should get two messages back:

✔ A chatty, machine-generated welcoming message telling you that you have joined the list, along with a description of some commands you can use to fiddle with your mailing-list membership. Sometimes this message includes a request to confirm that you got this message. Follow the instructions by replying to this message with the single word *OK* in the body of the message. This helps lists ensure that they aren't mailing into the void and that it was indeed you who asked to put your name on that list. If you don't provide this confirmation, you don't get on the list.

✔ An incredibly boring message telling you that the IBM mainframe ran a program to handle your request and reporting the exact number of milliseconds of computer time and number of disk operations the request took. Whoopee. (It's sobering to think that somewhere there are people who find these messages interesting.)

Keep the chatty, informative message that tells you about all the commands you can use when you're dealing with the list. For one thing, it tells you how to get *off* the mailing list if it's not to your liking. We have in our mail program a folder called Mailing Lists in which we store the welcome messages from all the mailing lists we join.

After you're subscribed, to send a message to this list, mail to the list name at the same machine — in this case, SNUFLE-L@bluesuede.org. Be sure to provide a descriptive Subject: for the multitudes who will benefit from your pearls of wisdom. Within a matter of minutes, people from all over the world will read your message.

To get off a list, you again write to LISTSERV@some.machine.or.other, this time sending

```
SIGNOFF SNUFLE-L
```

or whatever the list's name is. You don't have to give your name again because after you're off the list, LISTSERV has no more interest in you and forgets that you ever existed.

Some lists are more difficult to get on and off than others are. Usually you ask to get on a list, and you're on the list. In some cases, however, the list isn't open to all comers, and the human list owner screens requests to join the list, in which case you may get some messages from the list owner to discuss your request to join.

To contact the actual human being who runs a particular list, the mail address is OWNER- followed by the list name (OWNER-SNUFLE-L, for example). The owner can do all sorts of things to lists that mere mortals can't do. In particular, the owner can fix screwed-up names on the list or add a name that for some reason the automatic method doesn't handle. You have to appeal for manual intervention if your mail system doesn't put your correct network mail address on the From: line of your messages, as sometimes happens when your local mail system isn't set up quite right.

Stupid LISTSERV tricks

The people who maintain the LISTSERV program have added so many bells and whistles to it that it would take an entire book to describe them all, and, frankly, they're not that interesting. This section describes a few stupid LISTSERV tricks you can try out. For each of them, you send a message to LISTSERV@some.machine.or.other to talk to the LISTSERV program. You can send several commands in the same message if you want to do two or three tricks at one time:

✔ **Temporarily stop mail:** Sometimes you're going to be away for a week or two, and you don't want to get a bunch of mailing-list mail in the meantime. Because you're planning to come back, though, you don't want to take yourself off all the lists either. To stop mail temporarily from the SNUFLE-L mailing list, send

```
SET SNUFLE-L NOMAIL
```

and it will stop sending you messages. To turn the mail back on, send this message:

```
SET SNUFLE-L MAIL
```

✔ **Get messages as a digest:** If you're getting a large number of messages from a list and would rather get them all at one time as a daily digest, send this message:

```
SET SNUFLE-L DIGEST
```

Although not all lists can be digested (again, think of burritos), the indigestible ones let you know and don't take offense.

✔ **Find out who's on a list:** To find out who subscribes to a list, send this message:

```
REVIEW SNUFLE-L
```

Some lists can be reviewed only by people on the list, and others not at all. Because some lists are enormous, be prepared to get back an enormous message listing thousands of subscribers.

✔ **Get or not get your own mail:** When you send mail to a LISTSERV list of which you're a member, it usually sends you a copy of your own message to confirm that it got there okay. Some people find this process needlessly redundant. ("Your message has been sent. You will be receiving it shortly." Huh?) To avoid getting copies of your own messages, send this message:

```
SET SNUFLE-L NOACK
```

To resume getting copies of your own messages, send this one:

```
SET SNUFLE-L ACK
```

✔ **Get files:** Most LISTSERV servers have a library of files available, usually documents contributed by the mailing-list members. To find out which files are available, send

```
INDEX
```

To have LISTSERV send you a particular file by e-mail, send this message:

```
GET listname filename
```

where *listname* is the name of the list and *filename* is the name of a file from the INDEX command. For example, to get the article on Social Security number security from the LISTSERV that hosts the privacy forum, send the message `GET privacy prc.ssn-10` to `LISTSERV@vortex.com`.

✔ **Find out which lists are available:** To find out which LISTSERV mailing lists are available on a particular host, send this message:

```
LIST
```

Note: Keep in mind that just because a list exists doesn't necessarily mean that you can subscribe to it. It never hurts to try.

✔ **Get LISTSERV to do other things:** Lots of other commands lurk in LISTSERV, most of which apply only to people on IBM mainframes. If you're one of these people or if you're just nosy, send a message containing this line:

```
HELP
```

You receive a helpful response that lists other commands.

An excellent choice, Sir

The other widely used mailing-list manager is Brent Chapman's *Majordomo*. It started out as a LISTSERV wannabe for workstations but has evolved into a system that works quite well. Because of its wannabe origins, Majordomo commands are almost but (pretend to be surprised now) not quite the same as their LISTSERV equivalents.

The mailing address for Majordomo commands, as you might expect, is `majordomo@some.machine.or.other`. Majordomo lists tend to have long and expressive names. One of our favorites is called `explosive-cargo`, a funny weekly column written by a guy in Boston who in real life is a computer technical writer. To subscribe, because the list is maintained on host `world.std.com`, send this message to `Majordomo@world.std.com`:

```
subscribe explosive-cargo
```

Note: Unlike with LISTSERV, you *don't* put your real name in the subscribe command. Like LISTSERV, Majordomo may send back a confirmation question to make sure that it was you who wanted to subscribe.

To unsubscribe:

```
unsubscribe explosive-cargo
```

After you have subscribed, you can send a message to everyone on the mailing list by addressing it to `listname@some.machine.or.other`. (You can't post messages to `explosive-cargo` because it's an announcements-only list: Only the guy in Boston who runs it is allowed to post messages.)

Stupid Majordomo tricks

Not to be outdone by LISTSERV, Majordomo has its own set of not particularly useful commands (as with LISTSERV, you can send in a single message as many of these as you want):

✔ To find out which lists at a Majordomo system you're subscribed to:

```
which
```

✔ To find all the lists managed by a Majordomo system:

```
lists
```

✔ Majordomo also can keep files related to its lists. To find the names of the files for a particular list:

```
index name-of-list
```

✔ To tell Majordomo to send you one of the files by e-mail:

```
get name-of-list name-of-file
```

✔ To find out the rest of the goofy things Majordomo can do:

```
help
```

✔ If you want to contact the human manager of a Majordomo system because you can't get off a list or otherwise have an insoluble problem, send a polite message to `owner-majordomo@hostname`. Remember that because humans eat, sleep, and have real jobs, it may take a day or two to get an answer.

Listproc — third-place list manager

Although Listproc is not as widely used as LISTSERV and Majordomo, it is increasing in popularity because it is easier to install than LISTSERV, cheaper, and almost as powerful.

To subscribe to a Listproc mailing list, you send the message

```
subscribe listname yourname
```

to `listproc@some-computer`. To subscribe to the (hypothetical) `chickens` mailing list on `dummies.net`, for example, you send the message

```
subscribe chickens George Washington
```

to `listproc@dummies.net` (assuming that you were named after the same person that the first President of the United States was).

To get off the mailing list, send this message to the same address:

```
signoff listname
```

You don't have to provide your name — the Listproc program should already know it.

After you have subscribed to the list, you can send messages to every one on the list by addressing e-mail to `listname@some-computer` — `chickens@dummies.net`, for example (don't try it — there's no such mailing list!).

To find out other things that Listproc can do, send the message `help` to `listproc@whatever`, where *whatever* is the name of the computer on which the Listproc mailing list lives.

LISTSERV, Listproc, and Majordomo: They could have made them the same, but n-o-o-o-o

Because LISTSERV, Listproc, and Majordomo work in sort of in the same way, even experienced mailing-list mavens get their commands confused. Here are the important differences:

✔ The address for LISTSERV is `LISTSERV@hostname`, the address for Majordomo is `majordomo@hostname`, and the address for Listproc is `listproc@hostname`.

✔ To subscribe to a LISTSERV list, send `SUB` followed by the list name followed by your real name. To subscribe to a Majordomo list, just send `subscribe` and the list name. To subscribe to a Listproc list, send `subscribe` followed by your real name.

Sending messages to mailing lists

Okay, you're signed up on a mailing list. Now what? First, as we said a few pages back, wait a week or so to see what sort of messages arrive from the list — that way, you can get an idea of what you should or should not send to it. When you think that you have seen enough to avoid embarrassing yourself, try sending something in. That's easy: You mail a message to the mailing list. The list's address is the same as the name of the list — buchanan-lovers@dummies.net or snufle-1@bluesuede.org or whatever. Keep in mind that because hundreds or thousands of people will be reading your pearls of wisdom, you should at least try to spell things correctly. (You may have thought that this advice is obvious, but you would be sadly mistaken.) On popular lists, you may begin to get back responses within a few minutes of sending a message.

Some lists encourage new subscribers to send in a message introducing themselves and saying briefly what their interests are. Others don't. Don't send anything until you have something to say.

After you watch the flow of messages on a list for a while, all this stuff becomes obvious.

Some mailing lists have rules about who is allowed to send messages, meaning that just because you're on the list doesn't automatically mean that any messages you send appear on the list. Some lists are *moderated:* Any message you send in gets sent to a human *moderator,* who decides what goes to the list and what doesn't. Although this may sound sort of fascist, in practice the arrangement makes a list about 50 times more interesting than it would be otherwise because a good moderator can filter out the boring and irrelevant messages and keep the list on track. Indeed, the people who complain the loudest about moderator censorship are usually the ones whose messages most deserve to be filtered out.

Another rule that sometimes causes trouble is that many lists allow messages to be sent only from people whose addresses appear on the list. This rule becomes a pain if your mailing address changes. Suppose that you get a well-organized new mail administrator and that your official e-mail address changes from jj@shamu.pol.bluesuede.org to John.Jay@bluesuede.org, although your old address still works. You may find that some lists begin *bouncing* your messages (sending them back to you rather than to the list) because they don't understand that John.Jay@bluesuede.org, the name under which you now send messages, is the same as jj@shamu.pol. bluesuede.org, the name under which you originally subscribed to the list. Worse, LISTSERV doesn't let you take yourself off the list, for the same reason. To resolve this mess, you have to write to the human list owners of any lists in which this problem arises and ask them to fix the problem by hand.

Boing!

Computer accounts are created and deleted often enough and mail addresses change often enough that a large list always contains, at any given moment, some addresses that are no longer valid. If you send a message to the list, your message is forwarded to these invalid addresses, and a return message reporting the bad addresses is generated for each of them. Mailing-list managers (both human and computer) normally try to deflect the error messages so that they go to the list owner, who can do something about them, rather than go to you. As often as not, however, a persistently dumb mail system sends one of these failure messages directly to you. Just ignore it because there isn't anything you can do about it.

The Fine Points of Replying to Mailing-List Messages

Often you receive an interesting message from a list and want to respond to it. When you send your answer, does it go *just* to the person who sent the original message, or does it go to the *entire list?* It depends, mostly on how the list owner set up the software that handles the list. About half the list owners set it up so that replies automatically go just to the person who sent the original message, on the theory that your response is likely to be of interest only to the original author. The other half set it up so that replies go to the entire list, on the theory that the list is a running public discussion. In messages coming from the list, the mailing-list software automatically sets the Reply-To: header line to the address where replies should be sent.

Fortunately, you're in charge. When you start to create a reply, your mail program should show you the address it's replying to. If you don't like the address it's using, change it. Check the To: and Cc: fields to make sure that you're sending your message where you want.

While you're fixing the recipient's address, you may also want to fix the Subject: line. After a few rounds of replies to replies to replies, the topic of discussion often wanders away from the original topic, and it's nice to change the subject to better describe what is really under discussion.

Mailing lists versus Usenet news

Many mailing lists are "gatewayed" to Usenet newsgroups (see Chapter 11), which means that all the messages you would receive if you subscribed to the mailing list appear as items in the newsgroup and vice versa. Most gateways are two-way: Anything you mail to the list shows up also in the newsgroup, and anything you post as a news item also goes to the list. A few are one-way, usually because of sloppy gateway management, and many of them are moderated, which means that you have to mail any items to the human moderator, who filters out inappropriate messages.

Whether you get a particular list as mail or news is largely a matter of personal taste. The advantages of receiving lists as mail are that mail items tend to arrive faster than news items do (usually by only a few hours); mail

items stick around until you explicitly delete them, whereas news is deleted automatically after a few days; and some mail programs are more flexible than the newsreading programs. The advantages of news are that items are collected in a newsgroup rather than mixed in with your mail; items are automatically deleted unless you save them, avoiding mailbox bloat if you don't read and clean up your mail every day; and news programs usually do a better job than mail programs of collecting threads of related messages so that you can read them in order.

If you don't care which way you get your stuff, get it as news because the load on both your local computer and the network in general is considerably lower that way.

Some Interesting Lists

Thousands of lists reside on the Internet — so many, in fact, that entire *books* have been written that just enumerate all the *lists*. To get you started, here are some lists we find interesting in addition to short descriptions of what they are. These addresses change relatively frequently, and we keep finding new and interesting lists. For our latest list of lists, check out our Web update at `http://net.dummies.net/lists`. For a complete list of lists — thousands exist — check out one of the mailing list directory sites, such as `http://www.liszt.com`.

If you don't have access to the Web, send e-mail to `lists@dummies.net` and we'll send you back our current list. If you have a favorite list you want to share, send us mail at `list-suggestions@dummies.net`.

Each list in our list of lists is accompanied by at least one of the following codes, describing what kind of list it is:

- **Manual:** Manually maintained list. To get on or off or to contact the human who maintains the list, write to `whatever-request@sitename`. In the text of your e-mail, state what you want. A human being handles these requests.

✔ **LISTSERV:** LISTSERV-type list. To get on or off, send e-mail to `listserv@sitename`. In the body of the e-mail, use the LISTSERV commands detailed earlier in this chapter. For example:

```
sub LISTNAME Your Name
signoff LISTNAME
```

To contact the relevant human, send mail to this address:

```
owner-whatever@sitename
```

✔ **Majordomo:** A Majordomo list. To get on or off, send a "subscribe" or "unsubscribe" message to `Majordomo@sitename` asking to subscribe to the list name we give. For example:

```
subscribe listname
unsubscribe listname
```

✔ **Listproc:** A Listproc list. To get on or off, send a "subscribe" or "signoff" message to `listproc@sitename` asking to subscribe to the list name we give. Put your name after the list name. For example:

```
subscribe listname yourname
unsubscribe listname
```

✔ **Moderated:** Moderated list. Messages are filtered by the human list owner (moderator).

✔ **News:** The list is also available as Usenet news, which is usually the better way to receive it (see the preceding sidebar, "Mailing lists versus Usenet news"). Although nearly all BITNET lists are also available as a special type of newsgroup, this list marks only lists available as regular news.

✔ **Digest:** Messages normally arrive as a digest rather than one at a time.

Subscribing to BITNET lists

Several lists have old-fashioned BITNET addresses, such as `LISTSERV@gwuvm.bitnet`. It turns out that these aren't valid Internet addresses, although most Internet systems know how to send mail to them anyway.

If your system doesn't grok BITNET addresses, fool it this way:

`LISTSERV%gwuvm.bitnet@cunyvm.cuny.edu`

Change the original at-sign (@) to a percent sign (%) and add `@cunyvm.cuny.edu` at the end. This line tells your system to forward your message to a system (CUNYVM at the City University of New York) that is well-connected to BITNET and sends it on for you.

Risks Digest
Majordomo@csl.sri.com
Majordomo (list name risks) Moderated, News, Digest

This forum discusses risks to the public in computers and related systems. It covers the risks of modern technology, particularly of computer technology (lots of great war stories).

Privacy Forum Digest
LISTSERV@vortex.com
LISTSERV (list name PRIVACY) Moderated

This running discussion of privacy in the computer age has lots of creepy reports about people and organizations you would never expect were snooping on you (ambulance drivers, for example).

Tourism Discussions
LISTSERV@trearn.bitnet
LISTSERV (list name TRAVEL-L)

The TRAVEL-L list covers travel and tourism, airlines, guidebooks, places to stay — you name it. Because participants come from all over the world (the system host is in France), you get lots of tips you would never get locally.

The Jazz Lover's List
LISTSERV@brownvm.brown.edu
LISTSERV (list name JAZZ-L)

This friendly, laid-back, ongoing discussion makes no claim to staying on-topic but rather to creating a salon-type atmosphere in which "like-minded intelligent people from diverse backgrounds" can make real connections.

Tall Ships
LISTSERV@vccscent.bitnet
LISTSERV (list name TALLSHIP)

The discussion in this list is all about sailing and operating traditional sailing vessels.

Liberal Judaism
Listproc@shamash.org
Listproc (list name MLJ) Moderated, Digest

Nonjudgmental discussions of liberal Judaism (Reform, Reconstructionist, conservative, secular humanist, and so on), issues, practices, opinions, and beliefs take place here. Include your real first and last name in your request — `subscribe MLJ yourfirstname yourlastname`.

Chapter 11

All the News That Fits and Considerably More

Whose News Do You Use?

There's news, and then there's *Usenet news.* For more than 15 years, a gigantic, ever-growing, all-encompassing news system has been insinuating itself into computers and wrapping itself around the globe. *Usenet* (also referred to as *Net news,* the name of the system that manages and transports its messages) consists of *articles* created by and posted by ordinary people, or *users.* Articles bear a striking similarity to e-mail messages, and programs that read news often read e-mail too. *Newsgroups,* the name given to the interest groups that comprise Usenet, are not all that different from mailing lists except that the articles aren't distributed to people who have signed up for them. Instead, they're posted where those who are interested can read them. It's like the world's largest bulletin board.

You will find news you won't find on TV, on the radio, or in a newspaper or magazine. And Usenet news isn't limited to what commercial sponsors know will sell.

Big bags o' news

Although mailing lists are an okay way to send messages to a small number of people, they're a lousy way to send messages to a large number of people. For one thing, just maintaining a big list with thousands of people is a great deal of work for a list manager, even if you automate most of it with something like LISTSERV, which we discuss in Chapter 10. (On a large list, a few of the addresses go bad every day as people move around and system managers reconfigure addresses.) For another thing, just shipping the contents of messages to thousands and thousands of addresses puts a huge load on the system that sends them out.

Usenet solves that problem while creating a host of others. The principle is simple: Every Usenet site ships a copy of all articles it has received to all its neighbors several times a day. (To avoid wasted effort, each article contains a list of sites it has already been sent to.) It's sort of a global game of Whisper Down the Lane, although computers don't scramble the messages at each stage the way people do. Although different connections run at different speeds, for the most part news articles slosh around to all except the most remote parts of Usenet within a day or two. If your host is directly on the Internet rather than connected over the phone, most news arrives within a few hours.

Depending on your Internet provider or commercial online account (you were waiting for us to say that, weren't you?), the way you access Usenet newsgroups, and to some extent what news is available to you, varies. For the details of how to read news if you use AOL or CompuServe, check the chapter for your provider in Part III.

Being a newsgroupie

Every day more than 100,000 articles containing a gigabyte of text appear at a typical, well-connected news machine. To make it possible to sort through this mass of stuff, all items are assigned to *newsgroups,* which are topic headings. More than 20,000 newsgroups exist, ranging from the staid and technical (computer data communications, for example) to the totally goofy (urban legends, such as the one about the poodle in the microwave). You have to choose a small number of groups to read and ignore the rest because more news arrives every day than even the late Evelyn Wood could read.

You can easily *subscribe* and *unsubscribe* to any group received by your machine. Although the details vary depending on your newsreader, it's much easier than subscribing and unsubscribing from mailing lists. Many people begin reading a group by looking at a few articles and then stop reading it if it looks boring. Depending on how much time you plan to spend reading news, you may add several groups when you're less busy and then drop all except the ones directly related to work when the crunch hits. We suppose that you could theoretically stop reading news altogether, just as you could stop drinking coffee altogether — way too painful to contemplate.

Where did Usenet come from?

North Carolina, originally. In 1980 two students came up with the first version to run on a couple of UNIX machines. Their original version, now known as *A news,* seemed pretty cool because it could transfer as many as a dozen articles a day from one machine to another by using a networking scheme called *UUCP* (*UNIX-to-UNIX copy*), which is a clunky but reliable dial-up communications program that comes with all UNIX systems. Within a few years Usenet had spread to several other universities and several software companies in a completely rewritten version called *B news,* then transferring as many as a thousand messages a day. Usenet was established enough to be featured in an article in the October 1983 issue of *Byte* magazine, which boasted that more than 500 news sites were in existence. (John can't resist pointing out that his site was called `ima` — you can find it near the upper right corner of the network map on page 224 of the issue.)

Throughout the ensuing decade, Usenet has spread like a disease. Now more than 50,000 sites send out news, and probably at least that many more sites just read it. Most of the original dial-up links have been replaced by permanently connected Internet network links using a communications scheme called *NNTP,* for *network news transfer protocol.* (And you thought that all acronyms were obscure.) Although some news is still sent over the telephone by way of UUCP, an increasing amount of it is sent by way of exotic means, including satellite (using a spare channel that belongs to a national beeper company), CD-ROM, and even magnetic tapes (the tapes are sent to such countries as Malaysia, where long modem phone calls are impractical, and also to such places as the FBI, where internal computer users are prohibited from connecting to outside networks).

The volume of news has increased from a few hundred articles per day in 1983 to upward of 100,000 articles (more than a gigabyte of text) per day now. And Usenet is still growing.

Some sites still use B news, even though its own authors officially pronounced it dead more than five years ago. Current news systems include *C news,* which is a faster, more maintainable, complete rewrite of B news, and INN, a new version designed to work well in Internet networked environments. Fortunately, because they all function in pretty much the same way, you don't have to worry about which version you're using.

The newsgroup thicket

Newsgroups have multipart names separated by dots, as in `comp.dcom.fax` (a group devoted to fax machines and fax modems). Some providers hide the real names from you in an attempt to be user-friendly. Although sometimes they also hide certain groups from you too (usually those of a prurient nature), if you know the name of the group you're looking for, you usually can get to it.

The plan is that newsgroups are arranged in *hierarchies*. The first part of the name describes the general type of newsgroup. When a bunch of newsgroups are related, their names are related too. For example, all the newsgroups having to do with data communications are filed as `comp.dcom.something`. Here are the top-level names of the seven *official* Usenet hierarchies distributed to nearly every news site:

- ✔ **comp:** Topics having something to do with computers (lots of fairly meaty discussions)

- ✔ **sci:** Topics having something to do with one of the sciences (also fairly meaty)

- ✔ **rec:** Recreational newsgroups (sports, hobbies, the arts, and other fun endeavors)

- ✔ **soc:** Social newsgroups (both social interests and plain socializing)

- ✔ **news:** Topics having to do with Net news itself (a few groups with introductory material and the occasional important announcement should be read by everyone — otherwise, not very interesting unless you're a news *weenie*)

- ✔ **misc:** Miscellaneous topics that don't fit anywhere else (the ultimate miscellaneous newsgroup is called `misc.misc`)

- ✔ **talk:** Long arguments, frequently political (widely considered to be totally uninteresting except to the participants)

Note: Lots of less widely distributed, or less widely sanctioned, sets of newsgroups are mentioned later in this chapter, particularly the highly popular yet completely unofficial `alt` hierarchy.

Regional groups

All the mainstream groups are, in theory at least, of interest to people regardless of where they live. Many topics, however, are specific to a particular place. Suppose that you live near Boston and you want recommendations for restaurants where you can take small children and not be snarled at. (This topic really came up.) Although some newsgroups in the `rec` hierarchy discuss food, because most readers are likely to be nowhere near Boston, you're more likely to get snappy comments than useful restaurant tips (someone in Texas, for example, may note that if you don't mind driving to Dallas for dinner, you can find one there).

Fortunately, local and regional groups exist for local and regional discussions. An `ne` hierarchy for topics of interest to New England includes such groups as `ne.food`, which is just the place to ask about kiddie restaurants. (The answers, by the way, turned out to be practically any ethnic restaurant and one yuppie place in the suburbs that makes a big deal about having an annex featuring hot dogs and baby-sitters so that Mom and Dad can eat their fancy meal in elegant silence.) State and regional hierarchies exist for most places that have enough Usenet sites to make it worthwhile: ny for New York, vt for Vermont, ba for the San Francisco Bay Area, and so on.

Spam wars

One of the worst innovations in recent Usenet history is *spamming,* or sending thousands of copies of a message, invariably advertising something you don't want to buy, to thousands of newsgroups. It's a guaranteed way to let millions of people know that you're a jerk. One fellow in New Mexico has even styled himself the Spam King and used to spam for you for a fee of several hundred dollars. (You provide the Internet account and take the flak when your provider finds out what you have done. He's no fool. Although he claims that he has stopped, we have seen conflicting reports.) A great deal of spam also comes from commercial providers, such as AOL, despite the providers' efforts to prevent it. Every day AOL sends out a list of accounts it has canceled for Net abuse.

Usenet has always had a way to cancel articles, for the benefit of people who have second thoughts about something they have posted and for places that send out updated news articles to replace older ones. Some concerned users (or Net vigilantes, depending on your point of view) wrote *cancelbots,* which automatically send out cancellations for all the messages in a spam. The best known cancelbot is the CancelMoose, run by an anonymous user who seems to be in Norway, and others are located all over the world. You can read all about who's canceling which spams in these newsgroups:

news.admin.net-abuse.announce
news.admin.net-abuse.misc

One more cancel war involves the *cancelpoodle,* another anonymous user who cancels postings to the extremely contentious group alt.religion.scientology, a group that has sparked some real-world legal battles because the church claims that some of the messages, posted by a former church member, contain copyrighted and trade secret church material. The poodle invariably cancels postings critical of the church, and again, nobody knows who's really behind it.

Some e-mail spams also occur. They used to be less frequent because they're more work (why send e-mail to individuals when you can send news that will be seen by millions?); since mid-1996, however, far too many entrepreneur wannabes and political kooks have decided that this is the ideal way to advertise.

One of the most peculiar e-mail spams was the Crusader spam in mid-1995, which was a virulently racist neo-Nazi diatribe, mailed by an anonymous person who had broken into and taken over some workstations in France, Germany, and Italy. Although the message was real to the extent that it was an actual piece written by a group in West Virginia, it fairly quickly became apparent that the person sending it out wasn't a member of the group. Was he trying to discredit them (as though they needed much discrediting)? Trying to distract attention from someone else? Nobody seems to know. Unfortunately, e-mail spam has become an increasing problem, with no end in sight for now.

Universities and other organizations large enough to have a large number of Net news users often have hierarchies of their own, such as `mit` for MIT. Many companies have their own local sets of newsgroups for announcements and discussions about company matters. At a software company where one of us used to work, for example, every time someone logged in a change to one of our programs, the description of the change was sent out as a local news item so that everyone else could keep up with what was changing. Local company groups are sent around, naturally, only within the company. Ask around to find out which organization or regional newsgroups your system gets, because it's basically up to your Internet provider to decide what to get.

Enough Already — Let's Read Some News

Lots and lots of news programs are available, for every type of computer that's attached to the Net. In our examples, we use Free Agent, a widely used Windows news reader because

- ✔ It's easy to install.
- ✔ It works well.
- ✔ It's free.

Free Agent is the junior version of an inexpensive commercial program called Agent, which does all the same things as Free Agent and more (such as reading e-mail).

Netscape Navigator (Versions 3.0 and 4.0) and Microsoft Internet Explorer (Version 3.0), the famous Web browsers we discuss in Chapters 5 and 6, also can be used as newsreaders. They aren't as good as Free Agent, but if you already have one of these programs installed, go ahead and start out by using it.

- ✔ **Netscape Navigator 3.0:** The Netscape newsreader looks a great deal like Free Agent (probably not a coincidence because Free Agent is so good). In Version 3.0, choose Window➪Netscape News to open a News window.

  Netscape Navigator may complain that your news system isn't set up. Fortunately, it needs only one item to get going — the name of your Internet provider's news server. Choose Options➪Mail and News Preferences and click the Servers tab. The bottom half of that window has a line for News (NNTP) Server, where you type the name of your provider's news server, which you should have received in your sign-up package. (If not, call and ask. If no one can answer that question in less than two minutes, consider getting another provider.) Then click OK, and your news should be ready to go.

✔ **Netscape Navigator 4.0:** In Version 4, mail and news have been separated out into a new program called Messenger, but Netscape has tried to combine mail and news in a consistent way. Choose <u>W</u>indow⇨<u>D</u>iscussions, or bypass the Netscape program altogether and just run Netscape Collabra, to open the Message Center, which combines e-mail and newsgroups. If the progam can't connect to your news server, choose <u>E</u>dit⇨Mail Pre<u>f</u>erences from the menu, click the News Server tab, and fill in the name of your Internet provider's news (NNTP) server.

✔ **Internet Explorer or Internet News**: In Internet Explorer (the Microsoft Web browser), click the Mail and News icon, if one appears, and then click Read News in the window that pops up. Or choose <u>G</u>o⇨Read <u>N</u>ews from the menu. Or skip Internet Explorer altogether and just run the Internet News program, which comes with Internet Explorer.

If you haven't told it about your news server yet, Internet Mail complains and lets you do so.

Getting Free Agent Installed

Back to Free Agent, our favorite Windows newsreader. Free Agent is a blessedly simple program to install. You retrieve it, unpack the files, and run it. (If you have decided to use Netscape or Internet News to read newsgroups, just skip this section.)

1. **See the appendix, which explains how to get Free Agent from the CD-ROM in the back of theis book, or use your Web browser to visit** `http://www.forteinc.com/agent/freagent.htm` **and click the Get Free Agent icon to get to the download page.**

   Download the current 32-bit version for Windows 95 or the 16-bit version for Windows 3.1. (The latest version of the program files is `fa32-11.exe` for 32-bit and `fa16-11.exe` for 16-bit.)

   See Chapter 12 for more details about downloading.

"Hey — not everyone uses Windows"

Oh, right. Mac users also have a variety of newsreaders, including the new InterNews, Nuntius, NewsWatcher (on the CD-ROM), and, of course, Netscape Navigator.

No matter which newsreader you use, you follow the same basic steps (it's all the same news, after all), so the examples here still point the way.

2. **Run the downloaded file to install Free Agent.**

It creates a directory (C:\Agent unless you say otherwise), installs Free Agent into it, and adds icons to your Program Manager or Start menu.

3. **Run Free Agent to complete the setup process.**

First, Free Agent displays a terms-and-conditions window. Assuming that you accept the terms, click OK.

4. **Enter the info that Free Agent needs to start reading news.**

Free Agent asks for the name of your NNTP server (the computer at your provider where the news is stored) and the SMTP server (the computer that handles outgoing mail). These names usually are the same; your Internet provider should have given the name (or names) to you. If not, ask.

Free Agent also wants your e-mail address and full name so that it can put them in the headers of mail you send while reading news (responses to articles, mostly). Finally, you can set the time zone your computer is in. Then click OK.

If you already have another news program installed, click the bar Use Information from Another Program so that Free Agent can copy the configuration you already have. It even picks up the names of newsgroups to which you have subscribed and which articles you have already seen.

5. **Free Agent suggests going online and getting the available newsgroups.**

Do so. Although it takes awhile because most providers carry more than 10,000 groups, you have to do it only once. (It skips this step if it copied subscription info from another program.)

Finally, Some Newsreading

After you have done all the setting up, reading news is relatively easy. Here's what Free Agent, Netscape, and Internet News show you:

✔ **Free Agent:** The basic Free Agent screen, shown in Figure 11-1, has three windows. In the upper left corner is a list of newsgroups. In the upper right corner is a list of available articles in a newsgroup; at the bottom is an article in that group.

Although Free Agent has a wonderful little row of icons on its toolbar, it's not easy to guess what they might do. Luckily, you don't have to guess. Position the mouse pointer over an icon for a few seconds *without clicking,* and the name of the icon appears. The leftmost icon, the lightning bolt, for example, turns out to be called Get New Headers in Subscribed Groups. (In this case, a picture is worth six words.)

Figure 11-1:
The Free
Agent
window
shows the
list of
newsgroups,
the list of
articles
in the
selected
newsgroups,
and the text
of the
selected
article —
whew!

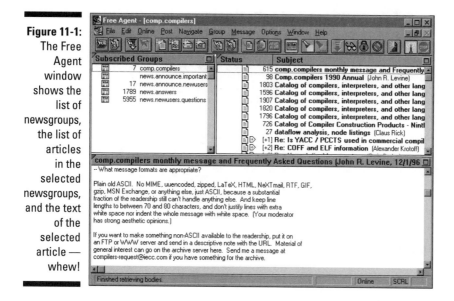

▶ **Netscape:** Figure 11-2 shows the Netscape 3.0 News window when it's
ready to show you some news. Version 4.0 uses the Message Center
window, which lists your e-mail folders along with your newsgroups.

Figure 11-2:
Netscape
News, such
as it is.

▶ **Internet News:** The Internet News window shows the current newsgroup
in the Newsgroups box, right below the toolbar, as shown in Figure 11-3.
The top half of the window lists the articles in the current newsgroup,
and the bottom half displays the current article in that newsgroup.

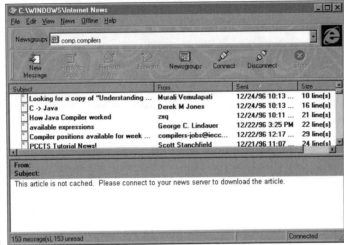

Figure 11-3:
Internet
Explorer
shows you
the news in
the Internet
News
window.

First, subscribe

You begin by subscribing to some likely groups, by scrolling through the list of groups:

- **Free Agent:** You can zoom the list of newsgroups to full screen by clicking in the group list and then pressing **Z**. (Press **Z** again to unzoom.) To subscribe to a group, click that group and then choose Group⇨Subscribe or press Ctrl+S. If you're not sure what to subscribe to, start with news.announce.newusers.

  Even though the list is in alphabetical order, finding group names can be difficult. You can use the usual Windows text search (choose Edit⇨Find, press Ctrl+F, or click the flashlight icon) to search for group names.

- **Netscape 3.0:** The upper left quarter of your news window lists the newsgroups to which you are subscribed. If you want to change that list, choose Options⇨Show All Newsgroups. After a considerable delay (there are many groups, and the program isn't particularly fast), it shows you all the newsgroups, arranged in a folderlike way, with all the groups that start with comp in a folder named comp. You can open and close the folders by double-clicking the folder's icon. After you have opened a folder and discovered a newsgroup that looks interesting, click the little box to the right of the group's name, and a check mark appears in the box, indicating that you have subscribed to the group. (Click again to unsubscribe.)

After you have picked a few groups — and we stress a few, not many — choose Options⇨Show Subscribed Newsgroups to make all except the ones you have chosen disappear.

Netscape 4.0: Double-click the Messenger folder for your news server to see the newsgroups to which you're subscribed. To browse through a list of the newsgroups available, choose File⇨Choose Newsgroup from the menu, double-click a hierarchy that looks interesting, click a newsgroup you want to read, and click the Subscribe button.

If you want to add a newsgroup and you know its exact name, click the Add button at the top of the screen and type the name of the group.

✔ **Internet News:** Internet Explorer shows you the first newsgroup to which you have subscribed. To change your subscriptions, click the Newsgroups icon, which gives you a long list of newsgroups you can double-click to subscribe or unsubscribe. Tabs at the bottom of the newsgroups window let you look at your subscribed groups, all groups, or new groups since the last time you checked. After you're happy with your subscriptions, click OK to return to reading news.

The current newsgroup is displayed in a line at the top of the news window. Click the arrow to the right of that line to pull down a list of subscribed newsgroups, and pick the one you want to read.

Second, get the headers

After you have subscribed to a group or two, you can retrieve some article headers.

✔ **Free Agent:** Click the Get New Headers in Subscribed Groups icon (the leftmost icon on the toolbar, the lightning bolt over three little folders) to retrieve the headers (titles and authors) of articles in the groups in which you're interested.

✔ **Netscape Navigator:** Click the name of a newsgroup (double-click in Version 4.0) to see the articles in the group, which appear in the upper right quarter of the window after a delay to download all the article topic lines.

✔ **Internet News:** When you choose the newsgroup you want to read, Internet News fetches the list of articles in that group.

Third, get the articles

After you have seen the headers for a newsgroups, you can read the articles with a few clicks of the mouse. Articles are grouped into *threads,* or related articles on (theoretically) the same topic so that you can follow the thread of the topic, as it were.

✔ **Free Agent:** After you have retrieved the headers, whenever you click a newsgroup name the available articles in that group are displayed in the right window. Double-click an article, and it fetches the contents and you can read it. (Wow! At last!)

When you're looking at an article in a thread, press **N** to highlight the header for the next article in the thread, or the next thread if that's the last article in this thread, or Ctrl+N to go to the next article in the thread and retrieve it automatically.

✔ **Netscape Navigator:** Double-click an article that looks interesting. In Version 3.0, it appears in the bottom half of the window; Version 4.0 displays articles in their own windows.

Click the Next and Previous buttons to go from one hitherto unread message to another. If you find a topic boring, click the Thread button to go to the next thread (messages on a different topic.) Click another group name to switch groups.

If a topic is getting boring, you can choose Go⇨Next Unread to go to a different topic. To switch newsgroups, close the article and message list windows and click a different newsgroup in the message center. (Or, in the message list window, click the arrow to the right of the news-group name to pop down a menu of mail folders and newsgroups, and click one of them.)

✔ **Internet News:** A list of articles in the current newsgroup appears in the upper part of the Internet News window. If you read news online, click the Connect button to tell it to go online. Internet Explorer fetches and displays each article as you click its title. You can also press Ctrl+> and Ctrl+< to move to the next and previous unread article in the current group.

To read news offline, see the sidebar "Saving phone time with Internet News," later in this chapter.

Now you can click groups and articles to find and read the articles in which you're interested.

Offline reading

Free Agent is set up so that you can read articles offline (for reasons why you would want to do that, see the nearby sidebar "Saving dough: Reading news offline with Free Agent"). Internet News does offline reading too (see the sidebar "Saving phone time with Internet News," later in this chapter).

In Free Agent, the second icon from the right on the toolbar, the one that looks like a radio antenna, is the Go Online/Offline button; it shows whether Free Agent is online (connected to the news server) or offline.

Saving dough: Reading news offline with Free Agent

If you discover that you're a news junkie (or maybe you already knew it) *and* you're paying an arm and a leg for Net access, you're a good candidate for an offline newsreader such as Free Agent. The idea is that you tell Free Agent to suck down news from your provider at top speed and then hang up and read at your leisure without the meter running.

When you first fire up Free Agent, you can tell it to download a list of the titles of all the new articles in the groups to which you subscribe.

Then you can disconnect. Now you can, without hurry or worry, look at the titles and choose the articles that look interesting. You reconnect, download the contents of those articles, and hang up again. Now you can read the articles at your convenience.

Although this process sounds like a pain in the neck, a good news program can make it easy.

Commercial providers vary in whether they support offline reading. Check your provider's chapter in Part III for the best strategy for you.

To avoid having to connect and disconnect to your provider manually, set your Internet software to "dial on demand" (so that it connects to your provider when Free Agent goes online), and set the disconnect time-out to one minute (so that it disconnects a minute after Free Agent goes offline).

To get the new available articles, connect to your provider, start Free Agent, and click the Get New Headers in Subscribed Groups icon (the leftmost icon on the toolbar). Free Agent retrieves all the headers at top speed. Now click the Go Online/Offline icon (the antenna) to tell Free Agent to go offline. Your Internet software should hang up soon after.

Next look at the headers as just discussed; rather than double-click the interesting articles, however, press **M** to mark them for later retrieval. It marks them with a little downward-pointing arrow, to say that they will be downloaded.

When you have marked all the articles you want, click the Get Marked Article Bodies icon, the third icon from the left — it's a download arrow with a lightning bolt. Free Agent connects to your provider and downloads only the articles you asked for. As each article is loaded, its download arrow changes to a little sheet of paper to show that the article is present. Click the Go Online/Offline icon to go offline again, and you can go back and read the articles you downloaded. Press Ctrl+B to move automatically from one downloaded article to the next.

Saving phone time with Internet News

The Internet Explorer newsreader makes it reasonably possible to read your news offline, while your computer isn't connected to your Internet provider. The offline features are all hiding on the Offline menu in the news window.

When you start up news for the day, choose Offline⇨Mark Newsgroups, which lets you download the headers (authors and titles) or entire articles for new news. You can either tell it to download all the groups to which you're subscribed or just select particular groups.

After you have downloaded message headers, you can look through the groups and pick articles or threads that look interesting. To mark an article or thread for download, click the article's title and then choose Offline⇨Mark Message for Download, Offline⇨Mark Thread for Download, or, if it's a particularly interesting group, Offline⇨Mark All for Download to select all the messages in the group.

After you have marked interesting-looking stuff, choose Offline⇨Post and Download, which uploads any new articles you have written and then downloads the stuff you have selected. After you have downloaded the articles, you can read them by clicking them.

Honest, It's a Work of Art

Usenet allows exactly one type of message: plain old text. (A few versions of news handle MIME messages, which were mentioned in Chapter 9, and versions exist for Japanese and Russian characters, but this chapter is confusing enough without worrying about them.) A few widely used conventions exist, though, for sneaking through other types of files.

Binary files

Some newsgroups consist partly or entirely of encoded binary files, most often executable programs for IBM PCs, Macs, or other personal computers, or GIF or JPEG bitmap files (see Chapter 18 for details about file formats) of, um, artistic images. (If you absolutely must know, the newsgroup with the largest amount of traffic, measured in megabytes per day, is called `alt.binaries.pictures.erotica`, and it contains exactly what it sounds like. It's an equal-opportunity group — it has about the same number of pictures of unclad men as of unclad women. Not that we know from personal experience, of course!) The usual way to pass around binary files of whatever type is called `uuencode`. You can recognize uuencoded messages because they start with a `begin` line followed by lines of what looks like garbage, as in this example:

```
begin elvis.gif 644
M390GNM4L-REP3PT45G00I-05[I5-6
M3OME,MRMK760PI5LPTMETLMKPY
MEOT39I4905B05YOPV30IXKRTL5KWL
MJROJTOU,6P5;3;MRUO5OI4J5OI4
```

Extracting binary files

Here's how to look at a binary file using Free Agent, Netscape Navigator, and Internet News:

- **Free Agent:** Handles uuencoded files with a single click. Click the Launch Binary Applications icon (the third one from the right, the one that looks like a lighthouse) to extract the encoded file and automatically run an appropriate program to view it. The appropriate programs are the same ones File Manager or My Computer uses. Some binary files are sent in several messages — highlight all the messages and click the lighthouse to glue the pieces back together. For example, if you read the alt.binaries.pictures.fractals newsgroup and you see a set of messages with names like "CUTE.GIF: Cute Fractal, Part 1 of 7," highlight the whole set of headers and click the lighthouse icon. Free Agent downloads the messages, uudecodes them to turn them into the original GIF (graphics) file, and runs whatever program you have on your computer that can display a GIF graphics file.

- **Netscape Navigator and Internet News:** Handle uuencoded files nicely too — just double-click an article that contains a GIF file. Netscape displays the picture right in a window, and Internet News pops up an icon you can double-click to display the picture in an Internet Explorer window.

For commercial providers, such as AOL and CompuServe, check your provider's chapter in Part III to learn the best way to unscramble uuencoded messages on your service.

What's in a Number?

Every Usenet message has a *message ID,* which is supposed to be different from the message ID of any other message ever, from the beginning to the end of time. (These people thought big.) A typical message ID looks like this:

```
<1997Mar18.055259.15278@chico.iecc.com>
```

The part after the @ is the name of the site where the article originated; the part before the @ is some garbage made up to be unique and usually includes the date, time, and phase of the moon.

Messages also have numbers, which are assigned in order at each newsgroup as articles arrive: The first message in `rec.fooble` is number 1, the second is number 2, and so on.

An important difference distinguishes the IDs and the numbers: Although the IDs are the same everywhere, the numbers apply to only *your local system*. Don't refer to articles' message numbers when you write a response, because people at other sites can't tell which articles you mean.

So You Want to Be Famous?

Sooner or later, unless you're an extraordinarily reticent person, you will want to send out some messages of your own so that people all over the world can at last find out just how clever you are. (This urge can be a mixed blessing, of course.) In this section, we look at general guidelines for responding to an article and give instructions for Free Agent, Netscape, and Internet News. For the details of how to do this stuff from AOL or CompuServe, look in your provider's chapter in Part III.

Before posting a follow-up article, consider replying by e-mail to the article's author. For example, a response such as "Good point!" or "Nice article!" is of interest only to the author. Post a follow-up only if you're adding significant new information to the discussion.

That's a roger, Roger

The easiest and usually most appropriate way to respond to an article is to send e-mail to its author in case you want to ask a question or offer a comment.

- ✔ **Free Agent:** Write a mailed response to an article by pressing **R** or clicking the Post Reply Via Email icon, the little envelope icon that says `Re:`. Free Agent opens a new window in which you can edit the message and, if necessary, the headers. Then click Send Now to connect to your provider and send it immediately or, if you're offline, Send Later to stash the message for later. To send all your stashed messages after you're online, choose Online⇨Post Articles and Emails.

- ✔ **Netscape Navigator:** Click the Re:Mail button in Version 3.0 to reply via e-mail. In Version 4.0, click the Re:News button, and then choose Reply to Sender from the menu that appears. Either way, you then compose your reply and click the Send button.

- ✔ **Internet News:** Respond to an article via e-mail by clicking the Reply to Author button on the toolbar or choosing News⇨Reply to Author from the menu or pressing Ctrl+R. If you see a confusing window asking what profile you want to use, just click OK; Internet News may insist on using Microsoft Exchange to compose your e-mail. Type the text of your message and click the send button (the flying yellow envelope).

I'll follow you anywhere

If you have a comment about an article that is of general interest, you can post it as a Usenet article. Here's how:

- ✔ **Free Agent**: Press **F** for Followup or click the Post Followup Article icon, the tiny picture of a page of paper with Re: over it. Again, when you're finished, you can send it now or stash it for later if you're offline.

- ✔ **Netscape Navigator:** In Version 3.0, click the Re:News button on the toolbar or choose Message⇨Post Reply from the menu. In Version 4.0, click Re:News, and then choose Post and Mail Reply from the menu that appears. Delete all except the relevant parts of the original article, which appears quoted in your response, and add your article at the top. Click the Send button to distribute your message to tens of thousands of potential Usenet readers.

- ✔ **Internet News:** Click the Reply to Group button on the toolbar or choose News⇨Reply to Newsgroup from the menu. Delete all except the interesting part of the original message and add your reply. Then click the Post Message button on the toolbar (the one with the pushpin) to send the article out over Usenet.

  To post a response with a courtesy copy to the author, choose News⇨Reply to Newsgroup and Author (no button equivalent.)

  Internet Explorer and Netscape 4.0 offer you the option of putting Weblike HTML codes in your news messages so that you can add extra formatting. *Don't do it!* Because the vast majority of news users don't use news programs that handle HTML, they see illegible coding glop instead.

When you send your follow-up, the article is in most cases posted either immediately or in a few minutes (the next time a background posting program runs). Some groups are moderated, which means that you can't post to them directly. In moderated groups, your message is mailed to the group's moderator, who posts it if it meets the group's guidelines. Because moderators are all volunteers and have work to do other than run their moderated groups, it may take a while for your message to appear. Although most moderators handle messages every day or two, the slowest ones can take as long as two weeks. Remember: Patience is a virtue. As a newsgroup moderator (John runs one called `comp.compilers`, a technoid group that discusses techniques of translating one computer language to another), one of the authors of this book can assure you that writing cranky letters to a moderator — in which you complain that it's taking too long to process your pearls of wisdom — is utterly counterproductive.

Many news systems reject messages that contain more quoted text than new material to discourage lazy typists who quote an entire 100-line message and add a 2-line comment. Some people are under the peculiar impression that if an article is rejected with too much quoted text, they should add garbage lines at the end to pad out the unquoted part. *Don't ever do that.* It instantly marks you as a pompous ass. Edit the text — your readers will thank you.

I have something new to say

Here's what to to if you want to start a new topic rather than comment on a thread that's already in progress:

- ✔ **Free Agent:** Click the Post New Usenet Message button, which looks like a sheet of paper with a twinkle, or press P. Posting a new message is similar to posting a response except that you have to type a subject line. (Free Agent is a fine program, but it's not clairvoyant.)

- ✔ **Netscape Navigator:** To create a new news article about a new topic, click the To:News button on the toolbar, fill out the headings, write your article, and send it off.

- ✔ **Internet News:** To compose a new article, click the new message button on the toolbar or choose News⇨New Message to Newsgroup from the menu or press Ctrl+N. Internet News assumes that you want to post the article to the current newsgroup.

Distributions Are Your Friends

Even though Usenet is a worldwide network, many times you're posting an article that doesn't really need to go to the whole world. If you're posting something to `misc.forsale.computers`, for example, to advertise an old disk drive you want to sell and you're in the United States, there's no point in sending the article outside the country because it wouldn't be worth the shipping and customs hassles to sell it overseas. Usenet distributions enable you to limit where an article is sent. A line such as the following in your article header limits its distribution to the United States:

```
Distribution: usa
```

Here's how to add a distribution line to your article:

- ✔ **Free Agent:** Click the <u>A</u>ll Fields button to open a subwindow in which one line says `Distribution`. Click that line to open a Distribution window in which you can type the distribution you want.

- ✔ **Netscape Navigator:** Netscape doesn't let you set distributions. Consider switching to Free Agent.

- ✔ **Internet News:** Choose <u>V</u>iew⇨Full Headers while composing your article. A bunch of headers you can use, including the Distribution header, appear at the top of your message.

A long list of possible distributions exists. Some commonly used distributions are shown in this list:

- ✔ **world:** Everywhere (default)
- ✔ **na:** North America
- ✔ **usa:** United States
- ✔ **can:** Canada
- ✔ **uk:** United Kingdom
- ✔ **ne:** New England
- ✔ **ba:** Bay Area (California)

TIP

Dying boy makes mailing list about modem tax

Back in Chapter 9, a sidebar lists well-known topics about which you should never, *never,* write to any mailing list. The same warning applies to Usenet news. For review, the top four topics *not* to write about are listed here.

Chapter 9 gives you the details about why nobody wants to hear about any of these things — ever.

- ✔ Dying boy wants cards to set Guinness world record
- ✔ FCC will pass modem tax and impoverish us all
- ✔ Good Times virus erases hard disk
- ✔ Make money fast with a chain letter

Unless you're sure that people on the other side of the world will be as fascinated by what you say as people next door, you should use the smallest appropriate distribution for any articles you post, both originals and follow-ups.

In practice, distributions are leaky; because of peculiarities in the way news is passed from one system to the next, articles often get sent to places the distribution says that they shouldn't go. It's a courtesy to faraway readers to at least *try* to avoid sending articles to places where the articles are not interesting. Keep in mind that because international phone links are expensive, if you avoid sending an article to countries in which people aren't interested, you can save people some money.

All the News that Fits

Eventually you have your fill of news. Exit Free Agent, Netscape Navigator, or Internet News in the usual Windows way, by choosing File⇨Exit or pressing Alt+F4. On the way out, Free Agent may ask whether it should compact its databases, a complicated way of asking whether it should free up space from old articles it deleted. (They go away after a week or so unless you specifically save them.) Unless you're in a big hurry, let it do so.

So What Is There to Read Already?

New newsgroups appear every day, old groups occasionally go away, and system managers can reject any groups they want to for lack of interest or other reasons. Because this book is getting fat and it's easy to get a current and complete list from your newsreader, we spend just a little space to give you a taste of what's out there. Trust us. If you can imagine a topic of interest to more than one person, there's probably a newsgroup about it already. Some newsgroups may not even meet that criterion, in fact. We first present some popular groups to get you acquainted with the mainstream hierarchies, and then we tell you about hierarchies that are a tad more obscure.

To see the latest list of newsgroups, subscribe to news.announce.newgroups and look for articles entitled List of Active Newsgroups Part I and List of Active Newsgroups Part II. For lists of the alt groups, look for articles with titles such as Alternative Newsgroup Hierarchies Part I.

Or, to save some time, visit our Usenet newsgroups update page at `http://net.dummies.net/usenet` to see searchable lists of groups and other Usenet info.

Here are a few groups you should start with:

news.announce.newusers

Every new user should at least skim this group, which contains introductory material for new news users. One of the messages is pretty funny, but you have to read them to find out which one.

news.newusers.questions

This is the one newsgroup in which it's appropriate to ask and answer neophyte-type questions. Although it has a great deal of noise, it's worth looking through to see whether someone else has already asked the same question you were about to ask.

news.answers

This group contains all the periodic (mostly weekly and monthly) postings to all the groups on the Net. Many postings have evolved into pithy and well-written introductions to their subjects. When you want to learn something fast about something that might have been discussed on the Net, start here.

rec.humor.funny

This highly competitive, moderated group contains jokes, most of which are funny. Compare it to `rec.humor`, which contains articles that the authors think are funny but that usually aren't.

comp.risks

The *Risks Digest* has lots of swell war stories about computer screw-ups.

comp.compilers

John thinks that it's interesting, but then he's the moderator.

xx.general

Replace *xx* with the two-letter abbreviation of your state or (for non-U.S. folks) your country code. These newsgroups usually have news and views about your state or country.

alt.sex

Although everybody reads it, nobody admits to doing so. We certainly don't.

Listen to the ClariNet

It had to happen someday — Usenet meets real life. A guy named Brad (the same guy who created `rec.humor.funny`, the most widely read Usenet group) had a simple goal for his computer: He wanted to get his weekly Dave Barry column in his electronic mail. How hard could that be, considering that newspaper features are all distributed by satellite, anyway? Pretty hard, it turned out, mostly because of the legal issues of who owns what on the satellite.

Brad kept at it, though, and ended up with the right to distribute by network not just Dave Barry but also the entire UPI newswire and many other features. Because that was *much* too much data to send out as e-mail, Brad did the obvious thing and decided to use Usenet software instead. The result is a group of about 250 newsgroups known as ClariNet. Each group contains a particular category of news (actual newspaper-type news, not just Net news), such as `clari.news.economy` for stories about the economy.

If your system has a direct (not just dial-up) Internet connection, you can get ClariNet news about as fast as the news comes off the ticker. Although it costs money, of course, for a site with dozens or hundreds of users, the price per user is low — on the order of a few dollars per user per month. For information, send e-mail to `info@clarinet.com`.

Brad also did get his e-mail Dave Barry, for about two years until the syndicate that distributed him decided that there was more copyright piracy of Dave's articles than they cared for. You can still get other syndicated columns, including Mike Royko, Miss Manners, and Joe Bob Briggs, for less than $10 per year (less than the cost of a Sunday paper every week). If your system gets ClariNet news, it may already be filed under `clari.feature.*`. If not, send e-mail to `info@clarinet.com` to get subscription details.

Netscape bookmarks and newsgroups

Although Netscape Navigator can use a bookmark that refers to a newsgroup, it doesn't have any easy way to create one. Here's how *you* do it: Choose Window➪Bookmarks to open the Bookmarks window. In that window, choose Item➪Insert Bookmark to create a new bookmark. A little window pops up in which you can set the name of the bookmark, the line that appears on the Bookmarks menu, and the URL for the bookmark. The URL for any newsgroup is `news:` followed by the name of the group (`news:rec.humor.funny`, for example). Then click OK to create the bookmark and close the bookmark window.

Now, whenever you click that bookmark, the program opens the News or Message Center window and selects that newsgroup. Pretty handy if it's a newsgroup you visit often.

Although it's also possible to create a bookmark for an individual news message, that's not very useful because the bookmark works only as long as that message is available on your news server, usually only a few days. If a message is particularly interesting, save it to a file, print it, or click the Forward button and e-mail a copy to yourself.

More Hierarchies

Along with the standard hierarchies we discussed at the beginning of this chapter are a bunch of less widely distributed ones. For example, Table 11-1 shows a bunch of *regional hierarchies* that discuss topics of interest to people in various parts of the world.

Table 11-1	Regional Hierarchies
Hierarchy	**Description**
aus.*	Australia
ba.*	San Francisco Bay area
ca.*	Canada
fr.*	France
de.*	Germany
ne.*	New England
ny.*	New York
nz.*	New Zealand
uk.*	United Kingdom

alt

This name designates so-called *alternative* groups. Setting up a group in a regular hierarchy is relatively difficult because it requires a formal charter and an online vote by its prospective readers and nonreaders. On the other hand, any fool can (and often does) set up an alt group. After an alt has been around awhile, its proponents often go through the procedure to create a corresponding mainstream group, and the alt group goes away. The quintessential stupid alt group is called alt.barney.die.die.die.

aol

This one (accessible only from America Online) is for groups for and about AOL users.

bionet

This bunch of groups is of interest to *biologists,* with the latest news about fruit flies and the like. If you're not a biologist, don't bother.

bit

These groups are mailing lists (see Chapter 10) made available on some systems as Usenet news.

biz

Designates *business* groups that are more commercial than the generally noncommercial traffic in the mainstream groups.

clari

This one refers to ClariNet (see the sidebar "Listen to the ClariNet," earlier in this chapter).

compuserve

Groups for and about CompuServe users (accessible only from CompuServe).

gnu

The *GNU project* develops freely available software, including, eventually, a complete reimplementation of the UNIX system. (GNU, by the way, stands for *GNU's not UNIX*.)

ieee

This one is IEEE, the professional organization for electrical and electronics engineers.

k12

The K-12 Net is for elementary and high school students and teachers. Although students and teachers are welcome on all the other groups, of course, these groups contain topics of particular interest.

relcom

These Russian-language groups are unintelligible unless you have a newsreading program that handles Cyrillic characters. You have to be able to read Russian too.

vmsnet

These groups discuss the VMS system that runs on some DEC (Digital Electronic Corporation) computers. They are primarily for VMS fans.

Of all these hierarchies, only `alt` has many groups that are of general interest. The character of `alt` groups varies wildly. Some, such as `alt.dcom.telecom`, are just as staid as any `comp` group. Others, such as `alt.buddha.short.fat.guy`, verge on the indescribable.

Chapter 12

Swiping Files from the Net

· ·

· ·

*F*irst, the fancy terminology: *File transfer* means to copy files from one system to another. You can copy files from other systems to your system and from your system to others. On the Internet, everyone uses either the *FTP* (*file-transfer protocol*) system or the Web HTTP system for transferring files.

Why copy a file from one system to another? Because lots of cool stuff out there on the Internet is available for free. You can download programs, pictures, and text to your computer by using FTP or the Web — it's relatively quick, and the price is right. Much of the Internet software we use with PPP and SLIP accounts, for example, comes via FTP, and you can get nice clip art, recipes — you name it!

Getting Files over the Web

Getting files over the Web is simplicity itself. You probably have been doing it for ages and didn't even know. Every Web page, every icon or image on a Web page, every ornate Web background is a file. Every time you click a link or type a URL to go to a Web page, you're getting at least one file. (If it's a page with a great deal of graphics, you're getting a great deal of files.)

Getting a program file is not much different from getting any other type of file — you just type the file's URL or click a link to it. Your Web browser will probably stop and ask you what to do with the file. If it's a program (a Windows EXE or the like) or a ZIP file, the most reasonable thing for your browser to do is to save it to disk so that you can run it or unzip it later. If

it's a ZIP file and you have WinZip (mentioned later in this chapter) installed, you can also tell the browser to run WinZip directly, by making
WinZip the handler program for ZIP files; we find that method less handy
than you might think.

To make absolutely sure that your browser simply downloads to the disk a
file for which you have a Web link, rather than try to run it, display it, or
otherwise get clever, hold down the Shift key while you click the link.

How FTP Works

Transferring a file via FTP requires two participants: an *FTP client program*
and an *FTP server program.* The FTP client is the program that we, the Joe
Six-Pack Users of the world, run on our computers. The FTP server is the
program that runs on the huge mainframe somewhere (or these days, likely
as not, a PC under someone's desk) and stores tens of thousands of files.
The FTP server is similar to an online library of files. The FTP client can
upload (send) files to the FTP server or, more commonly, *download* (receive)
files from the FTP server.

Thousands of publicly accessible FTP servers exist, and they store hundreds
of thousands of files. Many of the files are freeware or shareware programs.
Some FTP servers are so popular that they can't handle the number of file
requests they receive. When FTP servers are inundated, other FTP servers,
called *mirrors,* with copies of the same files, are set up to handle the over-
flow traffic.

Hello, this is anonymous

To use an FTP server, you have to log in. What happens if you don't have an
account on the FTP server machine? No problem, if it's a publicly accessible
FTP server. You log in as anonymous and type your e-mail address as your
password. Voilà! You have access to lots of files! This method of using public
FTP servers is called *anonymous FTP.*

When is a file not a file?

When it's a text file. The FTP definition specifies six different types of files,
of which only two types are useful: ASCII and binary. An ASCII file is a text
file. A binary file is anything else. FTP has two modes: *ASCII* and *binary* (also
called *image* mode), to transfer the two types of files. When you transfer an
ASCII file between different types of computers that store files differently,
ASCII mode automatically adjusts the file during the transfer so that the file
is a valid text file when it's stored on the receiving end. A binary file is left
alone and transferred verbatim.

A few anonymous FTP tips

Some FTP servers limit the number of anonymous users or the times of day that anonymous FTP is allowed. Please respect these limits because no law says that the owner of the system can't turn off anonymous access.

Don't store files on the FTP server unless the owner invites you to do so. A directory called INCOMING or something similar is usually available where you can put stuff.

Some FTP servers allow anonymous FTP only from host computers that have names. That is, if you try to FTP anonymously from a host that has a number but no name, these hosts don't let you in. This problem occurs most often with PPP accounts, which, because they generally offer no services that are useful to other people, don't always have names assigned.

Getting your FTP client

If you want to get files by FTP, you need an FTP client program. Luckily, you have several excellent ways to do so:

- ✔ Use your Web browser. Most Web browsers can handle anonymous FTP for downloading files (no anonymous uploading — you probably didn't want to do that anyway).

- ✔ If you have a SLIP or PPP account, you also use a Winsock or MacTCP FTP program. The most popular freeware FTP program that's Winsock-compatible is WS_FTP, and you find out how to use it in this chapter. If you have a Mac, you can use a shareware program called Fetch. These programs can handle both uploading and downloading files by using both anonymous FTP or private accounts on an FTP server.

- ✔ If you use America Online (AOL) or CompuServe, it's easy to get files via anonymous FTP. On both services, use the keyword `ftp`. If you use AOL, see the section in Chapter 14 about grabbing files from FTP servers. If you use CompuServe, see the section about getting files via FTP in Chapter 15.

Get with the program

Getting a file over the Web is easy: You click a link if one is handy or you type its URL (Web address) to your browser. We discuss this procedure in more detail later in this chapter.

The basic steps you follow to FTP, no matter which program you use, are somewhat more complicated:

- ✔ If you use a UNIX shell provider and you want to upload files to an FTP server, first upload them from your own computer to the provider's computer.
- ✔ Log in to the FTP server.
- ✔ Move to the directory on the server that contains the files you want to download, or move to the directory to which you want to upload files.
- ✔ Tell the program which type of files (ASCII or binary) you will be moving.
- ✔ Download or upload the files.
- ✔ Log off the FTP server.

The rest of this chapter describes how to use a Web browser and the WS_FTP program.

FTP-ing on the Web

Most Web browsers can do much more than just browse the Web — among other things, they can act as FTP client programs. They all handle downloading via anonymous FTP.

Interestingly, Web browsers are smart enough to tell which files are ASCII and which are binary. You don't have to worry about it!

The URL of FTP

To tell your Web browser to log in to an FTP server, you tell it to load the URL of the FTP server. An FTP server's URL looks like this:

```
ftp://servername/directoryname/filename
```

You can leave out the directory name and filename, if you like, and you get the top-level directory of that FTP server. For example, the URL of the Microsoft FTP server (at `ftp.microsoft.com`) is

```
ftp://ftp.microsoft.com/
```

This URL has no filename part: If you omit the filename, the server displays the top-level directory to which you have access.

Some Web browsers can handle only anonymous FTP. If you have an account on a server at your provider's system, however (many do, so you can upload your own Web pages), you can include your account name, like this:

```
ftp://elvis@ftp.dummies.net
```

When it logs in to the server, your browser asks you to type the password, which on your provider's system is probably the same password it uses when you first connect.

The big file-grabbing picture

No matter which Web browser you use, you follow the same general steps to retrieve files via FTP:

1. **Run your Web browser as usual.**

2. **To tell your browser to load the URL of the FTP server, type the URL in the Address, URL, or Netsite box just below the toolbar, and press Enter.**

   If you use a browser in which you can't type a URL in a box below the toolbar, you must give a command to tell it which URL to go to. In older versions of Mosaic, for example, you choose File⇨Open (or press Ctrl+O) and then type the URL in the dialog box that's displayed.

   The browser logs in to the FTP server and displays its home directory, as shown in Figure 12-1. Each file and directory in the current directory appears as a link. Depending on the Web browser you use, the format may differ from the one shown in the figure.

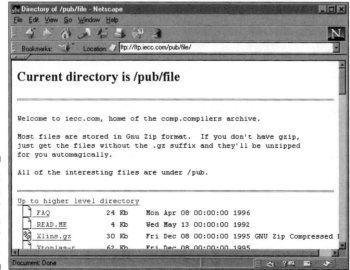

Figure 12-1:
Netscape
Navigator
can act as
your FTP
program.

3. **Move to the directory that contains the file you want, by clicking the directory name.**

   When you click a directory name, you move to that directory and your browser displays its contents.

At this point, what you do depends on which browser you use.

If you use Netscape Navigator

When you have found the file you want to download (as described in the section "Getting Files over the Web," earlier in this chapter), follow these steps:

1. **Download the file you want by clicking its filename.**

   If you download a text file or another file your browser knows how to display, the browser displays it after it downloads. If you click the filename readme.txt, for example, the browser displays the text file. If you want to save it after you look at it, choose File⇨Save As from the menu and tell Navigator the filename to use.

   If you download a file your browser doesn't know how to display, such as a program, it asks what to do (see Figure 12-2).

2. **If the program asks what to do with the file, click Save File and then choose the directory and filename in which to save it.**

   Navigator downloads the file.

Figure 12-2:
Navigator
asks what
to do with
the file.

If you use Internet Explorer

Internet Explorer works almost identically to Netscape Navigator, FTP-wise. You enter the URL in the Address box and it visits that FTP site. Click the desired file to download it. Unless it's a type of file that Explorer already knows how to run, it asks whether to open the file or save it to disk. Tell it to save the file to disk.

If you use another Web browser

Check your Web browser's documentation to find out how to save files that are downloaded. Or just try it — click the filename of a file that looks interesting and see what happens. If you don't like what happens, try holding down the Shift key and clicking again.

Using WS_FTP: FTP-ing Using a SLIP or PPP Account

If you use a SLIP or PPP account, you can also use a Winsock (for Windows users) or MacTCP (for Mac users) FTP client program. Many good freeware and shareware FTP programs are available right off the Internet. Our favorites are WS_FTP for Windows and Fetch for the Mac. This section describes how to use WS_FTP.

Cool features of WS_FTP include

✔ Scrollable and selectable windows for the names of local and remote files and directories

✔ Clickable buttons for such common operations as connect and set binary mode

✔ Connection profiles, which save the host name, login name and password, and remote host directory of your favorite FTP sites; comes with a bunch of useful profiles already set

WS_FTP is good enough that even when we're using commercial Winsock packages that come with their own FTP programs, we still use WS_FTP because we like it better.

You can also use your Web browser, of course, to download files via anonymous FTP, as described earlier in this chapter.

Getting WS_FTP

Our favorite Winsock FTP program is called WS_FTP. It's available for free by FTP from a variety of places, including its "home," the United States Military Academy. (And you thought that they only learned how to fight wars!) Because we get a little better service from a mirror site, that's what we encourage you to use:

1. **In Windows File Manager (or My Computer or Windows Explorer in Windows 95), make a directory in which to put WS_FTP.**

2. **See the appendix to find out how to get WS_FTP from the CD-ROM in the back of this book or, following the instructions earlier in this chapter, use your Web browser to FTP to**

   `ftp://papa.indstate.edu/winsock-1/ftp/ws_ftp.zip`

   (That is, FTP to `papa.indstate.edu`, go to the `/winsock-1/ftp` directory, and download the file `ws_ftp.zip`.) If you can't find it on that particular FTP server, go to the TUCOWS Web page at `http://www.tucows.com` to find other locations that store the file.

3. **Unzip the `WS_FTP.ZIP` file.**

   You end up with a bunch of files, including the install program, which is named INST.EXE (Windows 3.1) or INST32.EXE (Windows 95 or NT).

4. **Run the installation program.**

   It asks a bunch of questions, such as whether you agree to the terms for noncommercial use (if you're a home user, you probably do), which directories to use, and which version of the program to use. In each case, the suggested answer is fine.

You're ready to FTP by using WS_FTP!

Dialing for files

Here's how to use the WS_FTP program to swipe files from or put files on an FTP server:

1. **Run the WS_FTP program by double-clicking its icon.**

   You see the FTP Client Connect To dialog box, shown in Figure 12-3. This dialog box lets you enter information about the FTP server you want to connect to. After you have entered this information, WS_FTP saves it so that you can easily connect to the saved FTP server again.

2. **In the Config name box, enter the name you want to use for this FTP server.**

   If you want to FTP to `rtfm.mit.edu`, for example, which contains FAQs for all the Usenet newsgroups, you might enter **Usenet FAQ Central**.

3. **In the Host name box, enter the name of the FTP server.**

   This name can be a regular Internet name (such as `oak.oakland.edu`, another useful FTP server) or a numeric address.

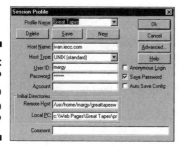

Figure 12-3:
Which FTP
server do
you want to
talk to?

4. **Leave the Host Type box set to auto-detect.**

   This step tells WS_FTP to guess which operating system the FTP server is using.

5. **If you really have a username on the FTP server, enter your username and password in the User ID and Password boxes.**

   Otherwise, click the Anonymous FTP box. WS_FTP asks for your e-mail address, which it uses as your password (this is the usual thing to do when you FTP anonymously).

6. **Enter your address and click OK.**

   WS_FTP fills in the User ID and Password boxes for you.

   If you want WS_FTP to store the password in the Password box rather than ask you for it every time you connect to the FTP server, click the Save Password box so that it contains an X.

   Leave the account box blank, unless you have your own username on the FTP server and you know which account to enter.

7. **In the Remote Dir box, enter the directory in which you want to look on the FTP server.**

   Alternatively, you can leave this box blank and look around yourself.

8. **In the Local Dir box, enter on your own PC the directory in which you want to store downloaded files.**

9. **Click the Save Config button to save this information.**

10. **Click OK.**

   WS_FTP tries to connect to the FTP server.

"It won't speak to me!"

If you have a problem connecting to the FTP server, messages appear in the two-line box at the bottom of the WS_FTP window. You can scroll this little window up and down to see what happened. For example, `rtfm.mit.edu` is frequently overloaded and doesn't let you log on. When this happens, it displays some helpful messages about other FTP sites that might have the information you want. You can see these messages in this box.

If you really want to see the messages the FTP server sent, double-click them. WS_FTP opens a big window so that you can see them better. To close it, click the Close button.

Do you copy?

After you're connected to the FTP server, you see the WS_FTP window, shown in Figure 12-4. WS_FTP displays information about the files on your own computer on the left side of the window (labeled Local PC) and the directories and files on the FTP server on the right side (labeled Remote Host). On each side are buttons that enable you to change directories (ChgDir), make directories (MkDir), delete directories (RmDir), view files, and so on. Naturally, you don't have permission to delete or change anything on most FTP servers, so don't even try.

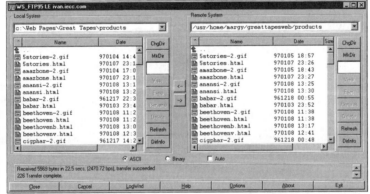

Figure 12-4:
Prepare to
receive
some files!

To move from directory to directory on the FTP server, choose directory names from the list box. Or you can click the ChDir button and enter the full pathname of the directory to go to.

Here's how to copy a file:

1. **Choose ASCII or Binary by clicking the buttons at the bottom of the window.**

   For files that consist entirely of text, choose ASCII. For anything else, choose Binary.

2. **Choose the file you want on the FTP server.**

3. **Choose the directory to put it in on your own computer.**

4. **Click the left-pointing arrow button in the middle of the window.**

WS_FTP downloads the file. For large files, this step can take some time; WS_FTP displays your progress as a percentage completed.

Hang up!

To disconnect from the FTP server after you're finished, click the Close button at the bottom of the WS_FTP window.

Connecting again

To call someone else, click the Connect button. You see the FTP Client Connect To window again. Fill in different information and click OK to make the connection.

To call an FTP server you have called before, click Connect. In the FTP Client Connect To window, click the arrow button to the right of the Config name box. You see a list of the configurations you entered before — choose one and then click OK.

For Mac users

It's not that we want you to feel slighted by the in-depth coverage of WS_FTP. Things on the Mac are just always much simpler, and because we have a tight page budget, we try not to spend a bunch of words on things that work the way they should.

When it comes to FTP, we like the excellent shareware program Fetch, by Jim Mathews. There's a copy on the CD-ROM in the back of this book; see the appendix for installation instructions.

Fetch gives you a choice between downloading files as raw data and MacBinary. The

MacBinary format combines the parts (*forks*) of Macintosh files into one file so that they can travel together when they're being FTP'd. Use MacBinary for Mac-specific stuff that only other Macs can understand, such as Macintosh software. When you download Mac software from a Mac software archive, for example, use MacBinary. Don't use MacBinary for text files, graphics files, and other non-Mac-specific stuff. MacBinary formatted files usually have the filename extension .bin.

How to foul up your files in FTP

The most common error inexperienced Internet users make (and some *experienced* users, for that matter) is transferring a file in the wrong mode. If you transfer a text file in binary mode from a UNIX system to an MS-DOS or Macintosh system, the file looks something like this (on a DOS machine):

```
This file
        should have been
                        copied in
                                ASCII mode.
```

On a Mac, the entire file looks like it's on one line. When you look at the file with a text editor on a UNIX system, you see strange ^M symbols at the end of every line. You don't necessarily have to retransfer the file. Many networking packages come with programs that do ex-post facto conversion from one format to the other.

If, on the other hand, you copy something in ASCII mode that isn't a text file, it gets scrambled. Compressed files don't decompress; executable files don't execute (or they crash or hang the machine); images look unimaginably bad. When a file is corrupted, the first thing you should suspect is the wrong mode in FTP.

If you're FTP-ing (Is that a verb? It is now!) files between two computers of the same type, such as from one Windows system to another, you can and should do all your transfers in binary mode. Whether you're transferring a text file or a nontext file, it doesn't require any conversion, so binary mode does the right thing.

About face!

Okay, now you know how to retrieve files from other computers. How about copying the other way? If you write your own Web pages and want to upload them to your Internet provider's computer, this is how you do it: FTP them to the provider's Web server.

In Navigator, you have to log in to the Web server as yourself by using a URL like this:

```
ftp://yourid@www.yourprovider.com/
```

Why is it called FTP?

We could say that FTP is short for *file-transfer program* and you probably would believe us, but that would be wrong. It really stands for *file-transfer protocol.* Way back in 1971, the Internet Powers That Be decided on a *protocol,* a set of conventions for copying files from one place to another on the Net. Then many people wrote programs that implemented the protocol and called them all FTP. Is this clear? Never mind.

Use your login ID rather than *yourid* and the name of your provider's Web server, which most likely is www followed by the provider's name but might also be something like ftp.www.fargle.net. (Ask your provider if this info isn't in the sign-up packet it gave you.) Navigator asks for your password; use the same one you use when you dial in. If this password works, you see your home Web directory listed on-screen. If you want to upload files to a different directory, click that directory's name so that you see that directory.

After you have the directory you want on-screen, just drag the file to upload from any other program (such as File Manager or Windows Explorer) into the Navigator window. Way cool. You can also choose File⇨Upload File from the menu if you find dragging to be a drag.

Microsoft Internet Explorer doesn't handle uploading. You have to install WS_FTP or (gasp!) Netscape Navigator if you want to use FTP to upload files to your server.

In WS_FTP, log in as we just described, using your login ID and password. After you have the desired local and remote directories in their respective windows in WS_FTP, just click the local file you want to upload and then click the arrow button pointing to the remote window.

If you're uploading a Web page to a Web server, be sure to upload the page itself (in ASCII mode because the HTML file that contains the Web page is a text file) along with any graphics files that contain pictures that appear on the page (in binary mode).

Patience is a virtue

The Internet is pretty fast, but not infinitely so. When you're copying stuff between two computers on the same local network, information can move at about 200,000 characters per second. When the two machines are separated by a great deal of intervening Internet, the speed drops — often to 1,000 characters per second or fewer. If you're copying a file that's 500,000 characters long (the size of your typical inspirational GIF image), it takes only a few seconds over a local network, but it can take several minutes over a long-haul connection.

It's often comforting to look at the directory listing before retrieving a file so that you know how big the file is and can have an idea of how long the copy will take. Because programs get inexorably larger, even with faster modems, patience remains as the key to successful downloading.

Other FTP shenanigans

A bunch of other file-manipulation commands are sometimes useful. In particular, you can delete and rename files on both your computer and (if permissions allow) the remote computer you're connected to.

In WS_FTP, click a file of interest, and then click the Delete or Rename buttons to delete and rename it. WS_FTP asks for confirmation for deleting and asks you to type the new name if you're renaming. If the remote system doesn't let you delete or rename stuff, you don't find out until after you try to do so.

If you plan to do much file deleting, directory creating, and the like, it's usually much quicker to log in to the other system by using the Telnet remote terminal program to do your work by using the usual local commands. For information about where to find out more about Telnet and other UNIX commands, turn to Chapter 22.

"Waahhh! I Can't FTP!"

Oh, no! You have only an e-mail connection to the Internet, so you can't FTP any of this swell stuff! Life isn't worth living!

Wait. There's hope. Several kind-hearted Internet hosts provide FTP-by-mail service. You e-mail a request to them, and a helpful robot retrieves the file and mails it to you. Although it's not as nice as direct FTP, it's better than nothing. Only a few FTP-by-mail servers exist, so treat them as a precious resource. In particular, observe the following guidelines:

✔ Be moderate in what you request. When one of these servers mails you a nontext file (remember that compressed or archived files are nontext for FTP purposes, even if what they contain is text), it has to use a textlike encoding that makes the mailed messages 35 percent larger than the file itself. If you retrieve a 100KB file, for example, you get 135KB of mail, which is a great deal of mail. If you use a system in which you pay for incoming mail, you probably will find FTP by mail to be prohibitively expensive. (In that case, try a service such as AT&T Mail or MCI Mail that doesn't charge for incoming mail or a public Internet provider that provides direct FTP access.)

✔ Be patient. Nearly all FTP-by-mail systems ration their service. If many people are using the service (which is always true), you may have to wait several days until they can get to your request. If you send in a request and don't hear back right away, *don't send it again.*

✔ Before you use a general-purpose FTP-by-mail server, check to see whether the system from which you want to retrieve stuff has a server of its own that can send you files from just that system. If it does, use it because that's much quicker than one of the general servers.

The most widely available FTP-by-mail server is known as *BITFTP.* It was originally intended for users of *BITNET,* an older, mostly IBM network that has great mail facilities but no FTP. In the United States, a BITFTP server is at Princeton University, at `bitftp@pucc.princeton.edu`. European users should try `bitftp@vm.gmd.de` in Germany.

Table 12-1 lists some other FTP-by-mail servers. To minimize expensive international network traffic, please use one in your own country.

Table 12-1	FTP-by-Mail Servers
E-Mail Address	*Location*
`ftpmail@ftp.ramona.vix.com`	California, USA
`ftpmail@ieunet.ie`	Ireland
`bitftp@plearn.edu.pl`	Poland
`ftpmail@doc.ic.ac.uk`	Britain

Before you send any requests to an FTP-by-mail server, send a one-line message containing the word *help.* You should do this for two reasons: to see whether the help message contains anything interesting and to verify that you and the server can send messages to each other. Don't try to retrieve any files until you get the help message.

The message you send to a BITFTP server is more or less the sequence of commands you would issue in an interactive command-line FTP session. For example, to retrieve a text file with the index of FYI notes from InterNIC (Internet Network Information Center), send this message to BITFTP:

```
FTP ftp.internic.net
USER anonymous
cd fyi
get fyi-index.txt
quit
```

The cd changes to the fyi directory, and get retrieves the file. Although you can enter multiple cd and get commands if necessary, keep in mind that you don't want to overwhelm your mailbox with huge numbers of incoming messages full of files.

"How am I supposed to know which files to ask for?"

An excellent question. We're glad you asked. When you use FTP by mail, you can't see which files the FTP server has. If you're lucky, someone has sent you a note that tells you what to look for. Failing that, you can get a directory listing and then ask for a file in a later request, like this:

```
FTP ftp.internic.net
USER anonymous
cd fyi
dir
quit
```

Many systems have a complete directory listing available as a file in the top-level directory. The file is usually called something like ls-1R or ls-1R.Z. (The odd name comes from the name of the UNIX command used to create it.) If such a file exists, try getting it instead of doing a zillion dir commands. If no ls-1R is available but the file README is, get that one because it often tells you where the directory listing is hidden.

If u cn rd ths u mst b a cmptr

So far we have considered retrieving text files by mail. What about the 95 percent of available files, however, that aren't text? For those files, you can use a subterfuge called *uuencode.* (This is the same way binary files are sent as Usenet news.) The uuencode program disguises binary files as text, something like this:

```
begin plugh.exe 644
M390GNM4L-REP3PT45G0OI-05[I5-6M3OME,MRMK76OPI5LPTMETLMKPY
ME0T39I4905B05YOPV3OIXKRTL5KWLJROJTOU,6P5;3;MRUO5OI4J5OI4
. . .

end
```

Because Eudora and Agent (the payware version of Free Agent, which handles mail in addition to news) automatically decode uuencoded messages, most users can unscramble uuencoded messages easily enough.

Otherwise, you have to feed the message through the program *uudecode* (or, for Windows users, WinCode) to get back the original file. If a file is really big, its uuencoded version is sent as multiple mail messages, in which case you have to save to a file all the messages in the correct order and then uudecode that file. (Agent handles multiple parts, but Eudora doesn't.)

To retrieve a binary file by mail, you give a uuencode *keyword* on the FTP line to tell it to uuencode what it retrieves and, as always, a binary command to tell it to FTP the file in binary mode. For example, to retrieve the compressed directory listing from /INFO on wuarchive.wustl.edu, send this message to BITFTP:

```
FTP wuarchhive.wustl.edu uuencode
USER anonymous
binary
cd info
get ls-lR.Z
quit
```

After you have uudecoded this file, you uncompress it (just like a file you FTP-ed directly) to get the file listing.

It's Not Just a File — It's Software

Using FTP, you can download freeware and shareware programs and install them and use them. You need a few well-chosen software tools, including a program to uncompress compressed files. (Useful little programs like this are usually called *utilities* in the jargon.)

Installing FTP'd software usually requires three steps:

1. Using FTP, download the file that contains the software.

2. **If the software isn't in a self-installing file, it's usually in a compressed format, so uncompress it.**

3. **Run the installation program that comes with it, or at least create an icon for the program.**

The first part of this chapter described how to do Step 1, the FTP part. The rest of this chapter describes Steps 2 and 3: uncompressing and installing. Here goes!

Decompressing and unzipping

A large amount of software is stored on FTP servers in a compressed format, to save both storage space on the server and transmission time when you download the file. An increasing amount of software is self-installing — the file is a program that does the necessary uncompressing and installing. Self-installing Windows files end with EXE, and non-self-installing compressed files end with ZIP.

If a file is compressed, you need a program to deal with compressed files, specifically those with the file extension .zip (these files are called, amazingly, *ZIP files*). Programs with names such as PKZIP, PKUNZIP, and UNZIP have been around for years for DOS users. Although UNZIP and its brethren work fine, they are DOS programs and not really convenient to use from Windows. It's annoying to use the MS-DOS icon every time you want to run one. Luckily, someone (a guy named Nico Mak) wrote a nice little Windows program called WinZip that can both unzip and zip things for you, directly from Windows. Mac users can get a program named unzip.

You can install WinZip from the CD-ROM in the back of this book—the appendix tells you how. If you have and love PKZIP and PKUNZIP or UNZIP and don't mind running them from DOS, you can use them. You can get a Windows version of PKUNZIP, which isn't as nice as WinZip, but some people like it. It works fine.

To get WinZip on the Web, go to http://www.winzip.com/, a page full of pictures of outer-space-type blobs. Click the blob marked Download Evaluation to get to the download page. On that page, download either the Windows 3.1 or Windows 95 version, as appropriate.

To install WinZip:

1. **Run WINZIP31.EXE or WINZIP95.EXE.**

   That's the program you just downloaded.

2. **Follow the installation instructions WinZip gives you.**

   Although you have a bunch of options, you can accept the suggested defaults for all of them.

Mac users say StuffIt

Mac users can download an unzip program from `ftp.uu.net` in the /pub/ archiving/zip/MAC directory or from `ftp.doc.ic.ac.uk` in the /packages/ zip/MAC directory or from `quest.jpl.nasa.gov` in the /pub/MAC directory. The file that contains the unzip program is called something like `unz512x.hqx`.

More popular than zip and unzip for the Mac crowd is a shareware program, by Raymond Lau, known as StuffIt. StuffIt comes in many flavors, including a commercially available version called StuffIt Deluxe. StuffIt files of all varieties generally end with the extension .SIT.

For decompression, you can use the freeware programs UnStuffIt, StuffIt Expander (which is on the CD-ROM in the back of this book), or Extractor.

Running WinZip

Give it a try! Double-click that icon! WinZip looks like Figure 12-5.

Figure 12-5:
WinZip is
ready to
deal with
your ZIP
files.

To open a ZIP file (which the WinZip folks call an *archive*), click the Open button and choose the directory and filename for the ZIP file. Poof! WinZip displays a list of the files in the archive, with their dates and sizes.

Unzip it!

Sounds suggestive, we know, but it's not as much fun as it sounds. If you want to use a file from a ZIP file, after you have opened the ZIP file, you *extract* it — that is, you ask WinZip to uncompress it and store it in a new file.

To extract a file:

1. **Choose it from the list of files.**

   You can choose a group of files that are listed together by clicking the first one and then Shift+clicking the last one. To select an additional file, Ctrl+click it.

2. **Click the Extract button.**

   A dialog box asks which directory you want to put the file in and whether you want to extract all the files in the archive or just the one you selected.

3. **Select the directory in which to store the unzipped files.**

4. **Click OK.**

   WinZip unzips the file. The ZIP file is unchanged, but now you have the uncompressed file (or files) also.

Zipped out?

When you're all finished zipping and unzipping, quit WinZip by choosing File⇨Exit.

Although WinZip can do a bunch of other things too, such as add files to a ZIP file and create your own ZIP file, you don't need to know how to perform these tasks in order to swipe software from the Net, so we skip them. (We bet that you can figure them out, just by looking at the buttons on the WinZip toolbar.)

Now that you know how to unzip software you get from the Internet, you're ready for the next topic: safe software.

Scanning for viruses

We all know that you practice safe software: You check every new program you get to make sure that it doesn't contain any hidden software viruses that might display obnoxious messages or trash your hard disk. If this is true of you, you can skip this section.

For the rest of you, it would be a good idea to run a virus-scanning program. You never know what naughty piece of code you might otherwise unwittingly FTP to your defenseless computer!

If you use Windows 3.1 with DOS 6.2, you have a virus checker built right into File Manager. Here's how to run the virus checker:

1. **Run File Manager.**

2. **Choose Tools⇨Antivirus from the menu.**

   You see the Microsoft Anti-Virus window, shown in Figure 12-6.

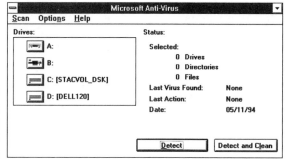

Figure 12-6:
Evict those
viruses!

3. **Choose a disk drive, by clicking it in the Drives box.**

4. **Click the Detect and Clean button.**

   If you're scanning a large hard disk for viruses, this step can take
   several minutes.

 It's a good idea to run Anti-Virus after you have obtained and run any new
piece of software. Although the FTP servers on the Internet make every
effort to keep their software archives virusfree, nobody is perfect. Don't get
caught by some prankster's idea of a joke!

 Although Windows 95 doesn't come with a virus checker, several commercial ones are available, including the McAfee VirusScan program, which you
can download from its Web page, at `http://www.mcafee.com`.

Installing the program

Now you have downloaded the software, unzipped it (if it's a ZIP file), and
the program is ready to run, but there's no icon for it. Here's how to make
one in Windows 3.1:

1. **Open both Program Manager and File Manager and arrange the
   screen so that you can see the program group in which you want to
   put the icon (in Program Manager) and the program name (in File
   Manager).**

   2. **Drag the program name from File Manager into Program Manager, and place it in the program group where you want it.**

      You see a new icon in the program group.

To run your new program, you can just double-click the icon. Cool!

In Windows 95, follow these steps:

   1. **Run either My Computer or Explorer, and select the program file (the file with the extension EXE, or occasionally COM).**

   2. **Use your right mouse button to drag the filename out on the desktop or into an open folder on the desktop.**

      An icon for the program appears.

Configuring the program

Now you can run the program by double-clicking its icon. Hooray!

You may have to tell the program, however, about your Internet address or your computer or who knows what before it can do its job. Refer to the text files, if any, that came with the program or choose Help from the program's menu bar to get more information about how to configure and run your new program.

Where Is It?

"The world of FTP sounds fine and dandy," you may say, "but what's out there, and where can I find it?" We have collected our favorite lists of resources into one handy place, Chapter 22.

Also look at Chapter 7, which tells you how to look for stuff on the Net, and visit our online favorite software page, with our current updated list of greatest hits:

    http://net.dummies.net/software

Part III
Getting an Internet Account: Some Popular Entrance Ramps

In this part . . .

Millions of Internet users use a commercial provider as their entrance ramp to the information superhighway (known in some circles as the information supercollider or the information supersoaker). We look in detail at the most popular ones: Internet service providers that provide PPP and SLIP accounts, and America Online and CompuServe.

Chapter 13

Using the Internet via an Internet Service Provider

· ·

· ·

*T*o connect to the Internet, you have two major choices — or three, if you're lucky:

✔ **Choice 1: Sign up with an online service, such as America Online or CompuServe.** Online services tend to be easier to use, and they provide information in a more organized way. They usually don't give you the full range of Internet services, however. Unless services have a flat rate for unlimited use, they can be expensive if you use them for more than a few hours a month. Because the demand is growing faster than some providers are able to support, access is sometimes slow.

✔ **Choice 2: Sign up with an Internet provider for an Internet account.** These days, most providers provide you with a PPP or SLIP account (we promise that we will explain them again in a few paragraphs). Most still also provide UNIX shell accounts or both shell and PPP accounts. You need PPP or SLIP to use all the cool, new programs, such as Netscape Navigator, Microsoft Internet Explorer, and Eudora.

✔ **Choice 3 (if you're lucky): Sign up for cable access.** We say "if you're lucky" because cable access is not widely available yet. If it is, however, all you have to do is call your cable company and arrange for them to come and install a network card in your computer and some cable to your home (if you don't already have cable TV). If you choose this option, you can skip the rest of this chapter and the next two chapters and just gloat. You don't need a phone, you don't need a modem, and you don't need a TV.

If you're interested in using America Online to access the Internet, skip ahead to Chapter 14; for a description of CompuServe Internet services, see Chapter 15. This chapter describes The Real Thing: an honest-to-goodness Internet account. And not just any account — a PPP or SLIP account, the kind that lets you use cool programs, such as Netscape and Internet Explorer and their multimedia add-ons. We give you a few hints about how to use a UNIX shell account and tell you where to go if you're serious about it.

What Are PPP and SLIP Again?

We had better explain what PPP and SLIP are. Here are the three incomprehensible acronyms you need to know:

  ✔ **PPP (Point-to-Point Protocol):** Enables your PC to connect to the Internet not as a terminal but as a full-fledged member of the Net, at least while your computer is on the phone to its Internet provider

  ✔ **SLIP (Serial Line Internet Protocol):** An older version of the same thing

  ✔ **CSLIP (Compressed SLIP):** A faster version of SLIP

Because these three protocols are identical for our purposes, we refer to them all as PPP. (If you care about the differences, turn to Chapter 22 — we tell you where to find out about them.) All three are versions of IP (Internet Protocol), the underlying part of TCP/IP (Transmission Control Protocol/ Internet Protocol), which is the way that all computers on the Internet communicate with each other. All three are cool because many network operations are much simpler when your own computer is on the Net instead of acting as a terminal to someone else's big computer — programs running on your own computer can do much nicer sound, graphics, and animation than a terminal can.

You provide the programs

To use a PPP account, you need two types of programs:

  ✔ **A program to get you connected to the account:** The technical term for this type of program is a *TCP/IP stack,* although normal mortal human beings usually call it something like an Internet dialer program. Windows 95 comes with one, called Dial-Up Networking. Windows 3.1 users need to get their own Internet dialer; we tell you how, in the section "Connecting, for Windows 3.1 Users," later in this chapter. If you use Windows, your Internet dialer program comes with a file called WINSOCK.DLL. Macintoshes have the basic TCP/IP stuff, called MacTCP, built in as of System 7. You also need MacPPP, MacSLIP, or InterSLIP to handle the telephone-dialing stuff. (New Macintoshes come with it already installed.)

✓ **Programs to use various Internet services:** These programs give you access to e-mail, the Web, and information over the Internet. They're known as *client programs* because they're part of a two-part strategy — part of the programs run on your computer; the other part, the *server programs,* run on your provider's computer.

You want an e-mail program to read and send e-mail, a Web browser to surf the Web, and a newsreader program to read Usenet newsgroups. Or you can get a program that does all three, such as Netscape. If you use Windows, you can use any *Winsock-compatible* program (any program that works with the WINSOCK.DLL file that's part of your Internet dialer program). If you use a Mac, you can use any MacTCP-compatible program.

Cool programs you can use

All the cool Internet programs you have heard about are either WinSock- or MacTCP-compatible, and many work on both Windows and Macs. Here are some famous programs available for Windows 95, Windows 3.1, and the Mac:

✓ **Netscape and Internet Explorer:** The former is the world's most popular Web browser; the latter, the Microsoft answer to Netscape (Chapters 5 and 6 tell you how to use them).

✓ **RealAudio and Shockwave:** You have to be running Netscape or Internet Explorer to use these and lots of other cool plug-in programs for Netscape and Internet Explorer, as described in Chapters 5 and 6.

✓ **Eudora:** This one is our favorite e-mail program. Pegasus and Microsoft Internet Mail are other e-mail programs that share the advantage of being totally free. (Chapter 9 describes how to use them.)

✓ **Free Agent (for Windows) and Newswatcher (for the Mac):** These are great programs for reading Usenet newsgroups (see Chapter 11 for an introduction to newsgroups).

✓ **mIRC (for Windows) and Ircle (for the Mac):** These programs let you participate in Internet Relay Chat (IRC). We don't have space in this book to describe IRC, but you can find an introduction on our Web site:

```
http://net.dummies.net/irc
```

Chapter 21 lists places you can get these programs. Eudora, Free Agent, Newswatcher, mIRC, and Ircle are all on the CD-ROM in the back of this book.

PPP connections are easy enough to use, but they can be tricky to set up. In fact, connecting can be the hardest part of your Internet experience. Installing and setting up TCP/IP software requires entering lots of scary-looking numeric Internet addresses, host names, communications ports — you name it. Make sure that your provider is helpful and available, or choose another provider. If you have a friend or relative whom you can bribe or coerce into helping you, do so. (Hint: Look for someone roughly between the ages of 12 and 16 — we find them very knowledgeable and very patient.)

Because each provider is just a tad different from the next, we can't go into exact step-by-step directions for everyone. We give the usual steps, help you understand the terms, and coax you through. If you find this process totally impossible and have no one you can press into service or just don't like the thought of doing this, don't despair. If you're a Windows 95 user, turn to Chapter 22, in which we tell you where you can find detailed, step-by-step instructions. If you're not, consider using America Online or CompuServe to get started.

Getting Connected

Okay, you're raring to go. What are the steps you have to follow? What hardware and software will you need? This section tells all.

Do you have what it takes?

Hardware-wise, here's what you need to cruise the Net:

- ✔ **A modem that connects your computer to a phone line:** The faster the modem, the better. Try to get a modem that talks at 14.4 Kbps (bits per second), 28.8 Kbps, or even 33 Kbps. Otherwise, things will be sluggish.

- ✔ **A phone line (you probably guessed that):** Make sure that your phone line doesn't have call waiting. If it does, you have to type ***70** or **1170** at the beginning of your provider's phone number to tell your phone company to turn off call waiting for this phone call.

- ✔ **A computer capable of running Winsock- or MacTCP-compatible programs:** Any computer that can run Windows 3.1 or Windows 95 or any Macintosh will do fine. Note, however, that the World Wide Web is full of pictures that take up a large amount of hard disk space. To get the full effect, you probably want more than the minimal amount of memory that came with older machines, and you may need more disk space. Before you upgrade an older machine, look at the brand-spanking new ones — they have changed a great deal in the past couple of years, and now may be the time to trade yours in.

The big picture, PPP-wise

To get your Windows PC set up for PPP, follow these steps:

1. **Arrange for a PPP account from a local provider.**

   In the following section, we give you ideas about how to choose one.

2. **Get the basic TCP/IP software loaded into your computer somehow, either from a disk or over the phone.**

   Use the software your PPP provider gives you, if any, or get a friend to download it from the Internet for you and give it to you on a floppy disk. Some providers mail you a disk. Others start you off with a UNIX shell account that they tell you over the phone how to set up and then provide a program to download the rest of the software you need.

   Later in this chapter are sections about TCP/IP and dialer software for Windows 95, Windows 3.1, and Macs.

3. **Type about a thousand setup parameters, if you're not lucky.**

   Your Internet provider (if it provided the software) or the software vendor should have given you instructions for when to type what. If you're lucky, your software has an automatic configuration program to set most or all of the setup parameters. In the section "Many mysterious numbers," later in this chapter, we tell you as much as we know about the parameters you might encounter.

4. **Crank up your TCP/IP program, and fiddle with it until it works.**

   Hey, sometimes it works the first time. If it doesn't, call and ask your provider to help you. You may find it difficult and frustrating if you have only one phone line, and you have to hang up to call your provider. We can only sympathize and tell you that, yes, it's a real pain, it shouldn't be this difficult, and one day it won't be. For now, it is.

   After you have done it, you can go on to load the swell applications described in Part II.

Who Will Provide?

Dozens of national Internet providers have phone numbers all over the United States, and hundreds (probably thousands, by now) of regional and local providers have phone numbers in limited areas. Be sure to find a provider that

- Offers PPP accounts
- Has a phone number that is an untimed local call for you so that you don't have to pay per-minute phone charges

✔ Has reasonable phone support (a good clue is how they treat you when you call to ask about an account—if they put you on hold for ten minutes, look for another provider)

✔ You can afford (otherwise, you never use it!)

Where to look for a provider

To find an Internet provider:

✔ Look in your local newspaper, especially in the business pages.

✔ Ask friends which providers they use.

✔ Ask a reference librarian at your local public library.

✔ Find someone who has an online account, and go to the following World Wide Web site, which contains a huge listing of Internet providers by area code:

```
http://thelist.com/
```

✔ See Chapter 20 for more ways to find an Internet provider.

When you open your account, ask your Internet provider to provide you with connection software. Most providers give you a disk containing a nice set of freeware and shareware software for connecting to the Net, along with instructions.

Using Microsoft Network

When Microsoft introduced Windows 95, it also introduced Microsoft Network (MSN), the new online service that was going to eat America Online's and CompuServe's lunch. A year or two later, MSN is still undergoing growing pains, has given up its original proprietary design, and is moving to become an Internet provider with special Web pages that you can see only if you're an MSN subscriber.

Signing up with MSN is easy if you use Windows 95, because an MSN icon sits right on your desktop. MSN is not available if you use any other operating system — Windows 3.1 and Mac users are out of luck (or in luck, depending on your point of view). For more information, take a look at its Web page, at `http://www.msn.com`.

Many mysterious numbers

Your TCP/IP program uses a bunch of scary-looking technical information to connect to your PPP account. Although in theory you should never need any of this information after your account is first set up, we find that it's useful to have on hand, particularly if you have to call your provider for help. Feel free to write it down in Table 13-1.

Table 13-1	Information about Your PPP Connection	
Information	*Description*	*Example*
Your domain name	The name of your Internet provider's domain. It looks like the last part of an Internet address and usually ends with .net or .com (in the United States, anyway).	dummies.net
Your communications port	The communications port on your own PC to which your modem is attached, usually COM1 or COM2. (Mac owners don't worry about this stuff.) Even if your modem lives inside your computer and doesn't look as though it's connected to a port, it is.	COM1
Your modem speed	The fastest speed that both your modem and your Internet provider's modem can go. If your modem can go at 14.4 Kbps or 28.8 Kbps, for example, but your Internet provider can handle only 14.4 Kbps, choose 14.4 Kbps. Conversely, if your modem can do only 9600 bps (which seems really slow when you get connected), choose 9600 bps.	28.8K

(continued)

Table 13-1 (continued)

Information	Description	Example
Your modem	The type of modem you have. Most dialer packages are only dimly aware of the details of different types of modems. A regular PC-type modem is probably similar enough to a Hayes model to fool the programs you use.	Hayes
Phone number	The number you call to connect to your Internet provider, exactly as you would dial it by hand. If it's a long-distance call, include the 1 and the area code at the beginning. If you have to dial 9 and pause a few seconds to get an outside line, include 9,, at the beginning (each comma tells your modem to pause for about a second, so stick in extra commas as necessary to get the timing right). Many modems have speakers, so you can hear them dialing. The noise is useful when you're trying to figure out whether you have succeeded in getting an outside line when you dial out.)	1-617-555-1234
Username	The name on your account with your Internet provider, also called a *login name*.	myoung
User password	The password for your account.	3friedRice
Start-up command	The command your Internet provider should run when you call in. Your Internet provider can tell you this command. If the provider starts PPP or SLIP right away when you log in, you may not need a start-up command, so you may be able to leave this entry blank when the time comes to type it.	PPP

Information	Description	Example
Domain name server (DNS) address _____	The numeric Internet address of the computer that can translate between regular Internet addresses and their numeric equivalents (between `net.dummies.net` and `205.238.207.74`, for example). Your Internet provider should give you this address.	123.45.67.99
Interface type _____	The exact type of interface the provider uses. The three choices are PPP, CSLIP, and SLIP. Some TCP/IP packages can't handle them all. If your software and provider handle it, use PPP; the next-best choice is CSLIP; the worst (but still okay) choice is SLIP.	PPP
MTU _____	Some providers limit the size of individual packets of data sent over the SLIP link, or the *maximum transfer unit (MTU).* If your provider has an MTU, it lets you know.	
Your own numeric Internet address _____	Your PC's own numeric Internet address. Although it's for your computer, you get this number from your Internet provider. Some providers issue you a number every time you call, in which case it doesn't give you a permanent number.	123.45.67.89
Your own host name _____	The name of your computer. Although most Internet providers don't give each user's computer a name, if yours does, make it short and spellable and perhaps cute.	meg

Where Does All This Software Come From?

You can find a TCP/IP program that connects your computer to the Internet using a PPP account in several places:

- ✔ **Your Internet provider may offer the program on a disk.** That's certainly the easiest way to get it. If your Internet provider gives you software, use it. That way, when you call for help, your provider knows what to do (one hopes!). Note that the software your provider gives you is probably shareware — which means that, if you use it, you're honor-bound to send a donation to the author, who is probably on the other side of the world in Tasmania (yes, really).

- ✔ **You can buy it.** If you buy Netscape Navigator in a box from a store, for example, the program (a Web browser) comes with a TCP/IP program and dialer program.

- ✔ **You can get someone to download it from the Internet for you.** If you have a friend with an Internet account, induce him or her to download the programs you need, copy them on one or more floppy disks, and give them to you. Then buy your friend lunch.

Read the rest of this chapter to find out exactly which programs you might need, depending on which type of computer system you use (Windows 95, Windows 3.1, or the Mac).

A Home for Your Programs

Before you begin filling your computer's disk with network software, make a folder in which to put these new programs. (Windows 3.1 users, make a directory.) You can use this folder for the programs you download in this chapter in addition to useful little programs you find on the Net.

In Windows 95, run My Computer or Windows Explorer, move to the Program Files folder, and choose File⇨New⇨Folder from the menu.

In Windows 3.1 File Manager, move to the directory in which you want to create the new directory (probably the root, a.k.a. C:\), and choose File⇨Create Directory.

On a Macintosh, choose New Folder from the File menu.

If you don't already have one, you should also make a folder or directory for storing things temporarily. You need it when you install the software you download from the Internet. On a PC, we recommend calling the directory C:\temp.

Connecting, for Windows 95 Users

Windows 95 comes with all the software you need to connect to a PPP account, using Dial-Up Networking. Except for the first versions of Windows 95 that shipped, Windows 95 also comes with the Internet Setup Wizard. Run the wizard by clicking the Start button and choosing Programs⇨Accessories⇨Internet Tools⇨Internet Setup Wizard. You need the information you wrote down in Table 13-1 as you follow the wizard's instructions.

When you're done, you have a Dial-Up Networking icon (and choice on the Programs menu) for your Internet provider. To call your account, run the Dial-Up Networking program and click the Connect button.

Connecting, for Windows 3.1 Users

Windows 3.1 doesn't come with the software you need to connect to a PPP account. Most Internet providers give you a copy of the Trumpet Winsock shareware TCP/IP package or else the Shiva TCP/IP package that comes with Netscape. They chose Trumpet Winsock because it's freely available shareware (we thought that you would like that). They may also give you a copy of Eudora Light, the freeware version of the popular Eudora e-mail program, and possibly Netscape Navigator. Trumpet Winsock and Eudora Light are on the CD-ROM in the back of this book.

Some Internet providers give you an automated sign-up program; AT&T WorldNet, Concentric, and other nationwide providers do, which makes setting up your account easy. Otherwise, your Internet provider should give you detailed installation and configuration instructions. If they do the latter, plan to spend some time on the phone getting your software set up correctly.

After you're done setting up Trumpet Winsock, you have a Trumpet icon in one or your Windows program groups. Double-click the Trumpet icon and follow the instructions your Internet provider gave you to get connected.

Your provider should also have given you, at the very least, an e-mail program and Web browser. If your provider gave you Netscape 2.0 or 3.0, you have an excellent Web browser and an acceptable e-mail and news-reader program. Because Microsoft Internet Explorer also runs on Windows 3.1 and is free, your provider might give it to you along with Internet Mail and Internet News. Part II tells you how to use these programs.

Using a UNIX shell account

In the early days of the Internet, before Netscape, before America Online, before the World Wide Web itself (can you remember back that far? — we're talking about 1989), intrepid Internet explorers dealt with the Internet using UNIX accounts. UNIX is an operating system that, in its purest form, requires you to type short, cryptic, and totally unmemorable commands to get anything done. UNIX is a very powerful system and programmers love it, but most mere mortals find it a pain in the neck to use. Because most of the computers on the Internet run UNIX, however, early Internet users didn't have any choice. UNIX accounts are also called *shell accounts,* for the name of the part of UNIX that listens to the commands you type.

UNIX accounts used to be widely available, before PPP and SLIP accounts took the world by storm. Most Internet providers can still give you one, if you ask specifically. Some providers give you one for free when you sign up for a PPP or SLIP account.

One big advantage of UNIX accounts is that you don't need any fancy programs on your computer to get connected. All you need is a *terminal emulator* program, one that dials the phone and pretends to be a terminal attached to the UNIX computer at the other end of the phone line. Almost every computer comes with a terminal emulator program; Windows 3.1 comes with Windows Terminal, Windows 95 comes with HyperTerminal, and Macs come with MacTerminal.

When you use a UNIX account, all the programs you run (except the terminal emulator) run on the Internet provider's computer, not on your computer. To read your e-mail, you run a UNIX e-mail program on your Internet provider's computer; the most popular UNIX e-mail program is called Pine — we describe Pine in Chapter 9. To browse the Web, you run a UNIX browser, usually one called Lynx, which we describe in Chapter 5. To read Usenet newsgroups, you run a UNIX newsreader program, such as trn or tin (see Chapter 11). Because these programs don't do graphics and you don't use your mouse, you end up learning lots of one-letter commands.

If you use a UNIX account because you never liked using your mouse in the first place or because you get a UNIX account for free from your school, see Chapter 22 to find out how to use it.

Connecting, for Mac Users

Mac users, stop right here. You already have most of the software you need to connect to the Internet because System 7.5 comes with MacTCP. Upgrade to System 7.5 to get it. You also need a Mac TCP/IP modem program, such as MacSLIP, MacPPP, or InterSlip, which your Internet provider should be able to give you. (If not, consider finding a provider who has more clues about Macs or else you will always be on your own when you have problems.) Most newer Macs come with modem software installed. The excellent modem program FreePPP is on the CD-ROM in the back of this book.

Chapter 14

Using the Internet via America Online

*A*merica Online (AOL, to its friends), the world's largest online service, provides access to both the Internet and its own proprietary services. AOL has more than six million subscribers and is still growing. To use AOL, you use software it provides. (Windows, Mac, and even DOS versions are available.) You can also use other software with your AOL account, such as Netscape Navigator and Microsoft Internet Explorer. This chapter describes the AOL Internet-related capabilities, including e-mail and the World Wide Web.

This chapter describes AOL software Version 3.0. Because AOL updates its software and the graphics that appear in its dialog boxes all the time, your screen may not match exactly the figures in this chapter.

The pros and cons of AOL

AOL is easier to use than most commercial online services and Internet accounts because one big AOL access program does it all for you. AOL also does a nice job of providing users with online software updates — it can update your AOL access software for you right over the phone, and connect-time is usually free when it does so.

Signing up for an AOL account is easy too — many magazines come with free AOL sign-up disks. It also has lots of discussion groups and information available only to AOL subscribers.

With the new AOL flat rate of $19.95 a month (as of the beginning of 1997), it's competitive with regular Internet PPP and SLIP accounts and provides both AOL-specific content and adequate Internet access.

On the other hand, getting tech support can be a trick — you can wait a long time for phone support, and getting help from the online tech-support chat rooms can be painfully slow and not always informative.

Signing Up for America Online

Ready to sign up? No problem! In the unlikely event that you don't already have a stack of AOL disks or CD-ROMs lying around, call 1-800-827-6364 and ask for a trial membership. Specify whether you want the CD-ROM or a floppy disk with the Windows version (works with Windows 3.1 and Windows 95), the Mac version, or the DOS version. The introductory package has instructions and a disk containing the AOL access program. After you have the introductory package, follow the instructions on its cover to install the program and sign up for an account. You need a credit card to sign up.

Note: America Online, despite its name, is available outside America. AOL has access numbers in all major Canadian cities, at no extra charge. Although you can also use AOL from other parts of Canada or from other countries, you pay a steep surcharge.

The installation program creates a cute triangular icon named America Online. If you have trouble installing the AOL software, call AOL at 1-800-827-3338.

Running AOL from Windows and the Mac are similar processes. Although we took pictures of the Windows version, we don't think that it matters much. You can tell that you're on the right Mac screen.

Setting Up Your AOL Account

After you have installed the AOL software, you can use it to sign up for an account. When you sign up, you have to tell it which *screen name* (account name) you want to use and how you want AOL to bill you after you have used up your free hours.

Follow these steps to set up your account:

1. **Double-click the America Online icon.**

2. **Follow the instructions on-screen.**

   First, AOL calls up an 800 number to find out the local-access number closest to you. Then it asks for your *registration certificate,* which comes with AOL disks and CD-ROMs — it's a long number with a couple of dashes. (We love it — ours was *SPECS-RICHES,* and our editor's was *ANGER-PASTRY.* Who or what thinks these things up?)

3. **Choose an account name (which AOL calls a *screen name* — sounds glamorous) for yourself, along with a password.**

   Your screen name can be as long as ten characters and can contain spaces. You can use a combination of capital and small letters, as in MargyL or LoveAOL. When AOL asks you to enter the screen name, it checks its list of existing names. If someone is already using that name (John Smith, for example), you have to invent another one. By now, most of the obvious names have been taken, so get creative. If the screen name you want is already taken, try adding a number to the end to make it unique. For example, if NetHead is taken (and we're sure that it is), you can be NetHead326.

4. **Enter a credit card number and expiration date.**

   When you finish, you see the Welcome window in the America Online window, as shown in Figure 14-1. You're ready to boogie!

The America Online window always displays the menu bar and, underneath it, the *Flashbar* (a row of cute little icons).

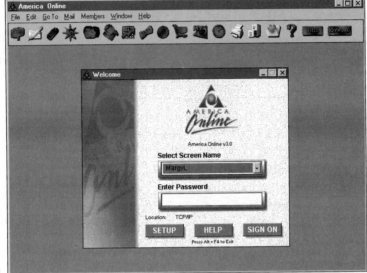

Figure 14-1:
The
America
Online
Welcome
window
suggests
that you log
right in!

Calling America!

To connect your computer to AOL:

1. Type your password in the Enter Password box.

2. Click the Sign On button.

A window appears, showing the progress of the connection. The graphic changes as the AOL program dials the phone, establishes a connection with the big AOL computer in the sky, and logs you in.

You see the online Welcome window. Behind the Welcome window is the Main Menu window. (Its edges peek out from behind the Welcome window.)

Now you're connected to AOL. You can click the buttons to read the day's news stories. If e-mail is waiting for you, you can click the You Have Mail button.

3. Minimize the Welcome window by clicking its Minimize button (in the upper right corner of the window).

You see the Channels window, with buttons for the AOL main subject areas.

If your PC has a sound board or you're using a Mac, don't be surprised if your computer suddenly says "Welcome!" when you log on to AOL. If you have e-mail, it says "You have mail!" Try not to jump right out of your chair when this happens.

I'm Outta Here!

With all the friendly little pictures on the screen, you would think that one of them would show a door or an EXIT sign or something. But no. To get out of AOL, choose File⇨Exit from the menu or press Alt+F4. AOL asks whether you really, truly want to leave. Choose Yes to sign off from AOL but remain in the America Online for Windows program (unlikely) or choose Exit Application to end everything.

The next time you want to use AOL, double-click the AOL icon, fill in your screen name and password, and click the Sign On button or just press Enter. You're ready to surf the Net when you see the online Welcome window.

Internet, Ho!

AOL has organized its Internet services in one dialog box so that they're easy to find. To get at the AOL Internet services, click the Internet Connection button on the Channels window. Alternatively, you can choose Go To⇨ Keyword from the menu (or press Ctrl+K) and enter the keyword INTERNET. You see the Internet Center window, as shown in Figure 14-2.

Figure 14-2: The Internet Connection window, with buttons for the World Wide Web, Usenet newsgroups, and more.

The Internet Connection window has the following icons you can use:

- ✔ **World Wide Web:** Lets you browse the Web

- ✔ **Gopher and WAIS Databases:** Enables you to search the Internet for the information you want. These services have largely been replaced by the World Wide Web.

- **FAQ:** Frequently asked questions (and their answers) about the Internet Connection; this free area contains lots of useful information about how to use Internet services from your AOL account — highly recommended!

- **FTP:** Lets you download (copy) files from archives (FTP servers) to your own computer

- **News Groups:** Enables you to read Usenet newsgroups

In addition, the right side of the Internet Connection window lists other Internet-related "channels," including information about how to join Internet mailing lists and download Internet-related programs.

When you finish using the Internet Connection, double-click the little box in the upper left corner of its window to close the window.

AOL has a number of other keywords you can go to for Internet information, including

- **Net Highlights:** Similar to the Internet Connection, with buttons for Internet services

- **Internet Newsstand:** Interesting sites on the Net

- **Netguide:** Information for Net beginners

To find other Internet information on AOL, press Ctrl+K (or choose <u>G</u>o To⇨ Keyword from the menu), type **internet** and click Search.

E-Mailing from AOL

You can send messages to other AOL members and to folks on the Internet.

Your Internet address is your screen name (omitting any spaces) plus @aol.com. If your screen name is John Smith, for example, your Internet address is JohnSmith@aol.com.

"Do I have mail?"

When you sign on to AOL, it tells you whether you have any mail. On the left side of the Welcome! window you see a button saying either Mail Center or You Have Mail. Another way to tell whether mail is waiting for you is to look at the Read New Mail icon on the Flashbar — it's the first one, a picture of a little mailbox. If the little red flag is *up,* you have mail.

Reading your mail

You probably *do* have mail, in fact, because every new member gets a nice note from the president of AOL and because AOL members tend to get mountains of junk mail, far more than people with other types of accounts. To read your unread mail, follow these steps:

1. **Click the leftmost icon on the Flashbar.**

   It's the Read New Mail icon. Alternatively, you can click the You Have Mail button in the Welcome window, choose Mail⇨Read New Mail from the menu, or press Ctrl+R.

   In the New Mail window, each line on the list describes one incoming mail message with the date it was sent, the sender's e-mail address, and the subject.

2. **To read a message, highlight it on the list and click Read or press Enter.**

   You see the text of your message in another cute little window.

3. **To reply to the message, click the Reply button. Type the text of your message in the box in the lower part of the window that appears. Then click the Send button.**

4. **To forward the message to someone else, click the Forward button. Fill in the e-mail address to which you want to forward the message. You can add a message to go along with the original message, too, by typing it in the large message area box. Then click Send Now (if you're online) or Send Later (if not).**

5. **To see the next message, click the Next button.**

6. **When you finish, double-click the little box in the upper left corner of each window you're finished with.**

It's not always a good idea to respond to messages right away. You may have to get some information or cool off after reading the brainless message some jerk sent you.

Composing a new message

You don't have to reply to other messages — you can begin an exchange of messages, assuming that you know the e-mail address of the person you want to write to:

1. **Click the second icon from the left on the Flashbar, the picture of a pencil and paper.**

   Alternatively, you can choose Mail⇨Compose Mail from the menu or press Ctrl+M. You see the Compose Mail dialog box, which looks just like the one shown in Figure 14-3.

Figure 14-3:
Send a
message to
anyone with
an AOL,
CompuServe,
Prodigy, or
Internet
account.

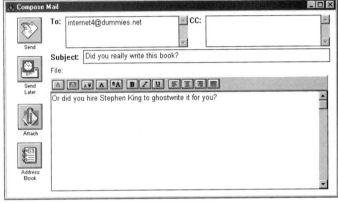

2. **Enter the recipient's address in the To box.**

   For AOL members, just enter the username. For others on the Net, type the entire Internet address.

3. **In the CC box, enter the addresses of anyone to whom you want to send a copy.**

   You don't have to send a copy to yourself — AOL keeps copies of mail you have sent.

4. **Enter a brief subject line in the Subject box.**

5. **In the box with no name, type the text of your message.**

   Don't press the Tab key because it moves your cursor from one box to the next in the dialog box. You can press Enter, though, to begin a new paragraph.

6. **When you like what you see, click the Send button.**

   AOL confirms that the mail is winging on its way.

7. **Click OK to make the message go away.**

Attaching a file to your message

If you want to send a file from your computer to someone as an e-mail message, AOL makes this process easy. When you're writing the message, click the Attach button. The Attach File dialog box is displayed, which lets you choose any file from your PC. Select a file and click OK.

AOL attaches the file using MIME, a method that most other e-mail programs can deal with.

Saving a message on your PC

If you get a message on AOL that you want to download to your computer, display it on-screen as described in the section "Reading your mail," earlier in this chapter. Then choose File⇨Save from the menu bar or press Ctrl+S. AOL lets you choose the directory and filename in which to save the file on your computer. When you click OK, it saves the e-mail message as a text file. Nice and easy!

Stop the junk mail!

America Online users get more junk e-mail messages than users of any other online system. Most of the messages are for fraudulent (in our opinion) get-rich-quick schemes and offers to advertise *your* product by e-mail to millions of people who are just as unenthusiastic about getting those types of messages as you are.

As you can imagine, AOL has gotten many complaints about the level of junk mail, especially from users who have to pay by the hour to read it. (Even with the new flat rates, some people still pay by the minute for phone calls.) The folks at AOL have been fighting the junk e-mailers for some time, including trying to block their messages, and have fought several court battles with the online spammers. Because many junk e-mail messages have forged return addresses, however, it isn't always easy to trace or block them. What's an e-mail reader to do?

Go to the keyword MAIL CONTROLS, that's what. (That is, press Ctrl+K or choose Go To⇨ Keyword from the menu. Then type **mail controls** and click Go.) For each screen name on your account, you can turn off receiving all e-mail, e-mail from sites that you select, or e-mail attachments only. AOL automatically blocks e-mail from sites they have identified as spammers; click the Preferred Mail link in the Welcome to Mail Controls window to turn off this blocking (but you would be crazy to do so!).

If kids use your AOL account, you can create a separate screen name for each kid and control what each kid can do on AOL; go to the keyword PARENTAL CONTROLS.

Web Browsing from AOL

The AOL software includes a built-in Web browser, so it's easy to learn how to use it. You can add Web pages to your Favorite Places list. You can have a Web browser window open at the same time that other AOL windows are open.

The Web browser requires that you use AOL software Version 2.5 or higher. If you don't yet have AOL Version 3.0, you should download it — the built-in Web browser is much better than earlier versions. Go to the keyword UPGRADE and follow the directions on-screen. The good news is that it's easy and that AOL doesn't charge you for the connect-time while you're downloading the Web browser program. The bad news is that it takes a while (several minutes to half an hour, depending on your modem speed) to download the program.

Starting the Web browser

Here are three ways to start the AOL Web browser:

- ✔ Choose Internet Connection from the Main Menu, and then click the World Wide Web button.
- ✔ Press Ctrl+K (or choose Go To⇨Keyword from the menu), type **internet**, and click Go.
- ✔ Press Ctrl+K (or choose Go To⇨Keyword from the menu), type the URL of the Web page you want to see, and click Go.

Whichever method you use, AOL runs its Web browser. Unless you configured it otherwise, it displays the AOL home page on the Web.

To use the browser, click any picture that has a blue border or any button or any text that appears underlined. (Chapter 5 tells you how to find information on the World Wide Web.)

Creating your own Web page

Although it's fun to look at Web pages that other people have created, what about making your own? AOL lets you create your own *home page* (a page about you).

Press Ctrl+K (or choose Go To⇨Keyword from the menu), type **my page**, and click OK to go to the Build Your Own Web Site window. Follow the instructions to create your own home page on the Web.

Reading Newsgroups

Although AOL has some interesting channels, in our minds Usenet newsgroups are where the action is. (We're probably just old-fashioned.) Chapter 11 describes how newsgroups work — in a nutshell, they're a large collection of discussion groups, each about a particular topic. Topics range from recipe swaps (rec.food.cooking) to arguments about abortion issues (talk.abortion) to technical discussions of multimedia computing (comp.multimedia).

To use newsgroups from AOL, click the News Groups button in the Internet Center window. Or press Ctrl+K (or choose Go To⇨Keyword from the menu), type **newsgroups**, and click OK. You see the Newsgroups window, with information and buttons for reading newsgroups.

Thousands of newsgroups exist, so you aren't going to read all of them. The idea is to find the ones which discuss subjects that interest you. After you have chosen one or more newsgroups, you still have to sift through the messages (also known as *postings*) to find the ones you want to read — some newsgroups get hundreds of postings a day.

Reading newsgroup messages

AOL remembers which newsgroups you're interested in. To get you started, those nice AOL folks even suggest a few. When you click the Read My Newsgroups icon in the Newsgroups window, you see the list of "your" newsgroups (see Figure 14-4).

If you aren't interested in the newsgroups AOL has suggested, don't worry. You can delete them from your list of newsgroups.

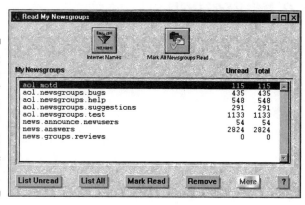

Figure 14-4:
You can add or delete groups from your own, personal list of newsgroups.

For each newsgroup on your list, you can see the total number of messages in addition to the number you haven't read yet. Yikes!

To read the messages in a newsgroup, follow these steps:

1. **Choose the newsgroup from the list in the Read My Newsgroups window.**

   If the newsgroup isn't on that list, see the section "Finding a newsgroup," later in this chapter.

2. **Click the List Unread button to see a list of the subjects of all the messages in that newsgroup you haven't read yet.**

   There may be several messages about the same topic (an exchange of messages on the same topic is called a *thread*), and the number of messages is shown for each subject.

3. **Choose a subject that looks interesting.**

4. **Click the Read button.**

   The message appears in its own window.

5. **Click the Next and Previous buttons to read the other messages for this subject, if there are any.**

6. **When you have read the messages, double-click in the upper left corner of the window to make it go away.**

In the window that lists the subjects of the messages in the newsgroup, after you have read the messages that interest you, you can "dismiss" the rest of them. Click the Mark Read button to mark all the messages in this newsgroup as having been read by you. The next time you read this newsgroup, those moldy old messages don't appear.

Finding a newsgroup

Although the kind AOL suggestions about newsgroups may be helpful, you will want to choose your own. After all, what's the point of Internet access if you can't read the newsgroup devoted to your favorite musical group, television show, or sports team?

TIP

What's all that garbage in this article?

Some newsgroups' articles contain *uuencoded information,* which is nontext information that has been encoded as text. (See Chapter 11 for a more in-depth explanation of uuencoding.) For example, the group `alt.binaries.pictures.fractals` contains lots of beautiful GIF (graphics) files that have been uuencoded. Because these files are usually too big to fit in one newsgroup posting, most appear as a series of articles with names such as `fish.gif (1/3)`, indicating that it's file number 1 of three files. File 0 in each series usually contains a description of the picture.

AOL has a feature it calls FileGrabber that helps you download these files (even large files that have been split up into several messages) and uudecode them to re-create the original file. To see a uuencoded file, double-click file 1 of the series. When you read a post that contains uuencoded information, AOL notices and displays a message from FileGrabber. If you click the Download File button, AOL asks where you want to store the file on your computer. Then it downloads and displays the file. If the file uses a graphics format

AOL can't handle, it only downloads the file. (For you graphics aficionados, AOL can handle GIF, JPEG, and PCX files on Windows systems and GIF, JPEG, and PICT files on Macs.)

You may see a message telling you that your parental controls don't allow you to download pictures. To prevent unwanted indecent material from making its way into your home or office, AOL prevents you from decoding uuencoded files unless you expressly turn this feature on. Press Ctrl+K (or choose Go To↪ Keyword), type **parental controls**, and press Enter. Click the Custom Controls button, click the Newsgroups button, click the Newsgroup Controls button, choose the screen name for which you want to allow downloading uuencoded stuff, and click Edit to see the Blocking Criteria dialog box. Click the Block binary downloads box to remove the check mark, click OK, and close the Custom Controls window.

If you have kids, you might want to read the information in the Custom Controls window and create for your kids special screen names that have these controls turned on.

To find a newsgroup and add it to the list of newsgroups you read, follow these steps:

1. **In the Newsgroups window, click the Add Newsgroups button.**

   You see the Add Newsgroups — Categories window.

2. **Browse down through the list and look for the type of newsgroup you want.**

   The list is so long that AOL sends it to you a section at a time. When you get to the end of the list, click the More button for the next section. You have really seen all of them when the More button is gray.

   For suggestions about which categories to try, see Chapter 11.

3. **Double-click a likely-looking category.**

AOL displays — no, you're not finished yet! — the list of *topics* within that category. To the right of each topic is the number of newsgroups about that topic.

4. **Double-click a topic that interests you.**

You see a list of the newsgroups about that topic, with the number of articles in the newsgroup.

5. **Double-click a newsgroup to look at the subjects of the messages in it and read the messages, just as we described in the section "Reading newsgroup messages," earlier in this chapter.**

Before subscribing to the newsgroup, you might as well take a look at its articles to see whether they're what you're looking for. When you finish, close the windows that display the individual messages and the list of articles in the newsgroup.

6. **If you plan to read the newsgroup regularly, click the Add button to add it to your list of newsgroups.**

The newsgroup now appears on the list of newsgroups you get when you click the Read My Newsgroups button in the Newsgroups window.

7. **When you finish, double-click the little box in the upper left corner of each window you're finished with.**

Finding a newsgroup if you know its name

Finding a newsgroup by using the procedure described in the preceding section can take all day, although it's nice to be able to browse around and see what's there.

If you already know the name of the newsgroup you want to read, there's a faster way:

1. **Click the Expert Add button in the Newsgroups window.**

AOL asks you for the Internet name of the newsgroup (that's the newsgroup name with dots between the words, usually all in small letters).

2. **Enter the newsgroup name and click the Add button.**

AOL confirms the addition of the newsgroup.

3. **Click OK.**

4. **When you finish, double-click the little box in the upper left corner of the window.**

AOL offers every newsgroup in the known universe — even the notably uncensored ones. If you know the name of the group you want, you can add it to your list, even if it's not in the list that AOL displays. Complete lists of newsgroups are posted in the group `news.lists` on the first day of each month under the titles List of Active Newsgroups and Alternative Newsgroup Hierarchies. Some of them can get raunchy, so if you or your family members who use AOL are young, impressionable, or easily offended, don't say that we didn't warn you. If you stick to the groups in the AOL lists, the worst thing you will find, other than some incredibly bad spelling, is an occasional rude word uttered (typed, actually) in frustration.

Searching for a newsgroup

If you don't know the name of the newsgroup you want to read, another way to find it is to click the Search All Newsgroups button in the Newsgroups window. You can then enter a word in the Search Newsgroups dialog box that is displayed, and AOL shows you the newsgroup names which contain that word.

Removing boring newsgroups

Although you cannot get rid of a newsgroup (what would all those people who *like* it do?), you can delete it from your own list of newsgroups. Out of sight, out of mind.

To delete a newsgroup from your list, choose it from the list in the Read My Newsgroups dialog box and click the Remove button. Although the newsgroups don't disappear from the list immediately (who knows why not?), the next time you choose the Read My Newsgroups button from the Newsgroups window, they don't appear.

Mouthing off

Always read a newsgroup for at least a week before you send anything to it. AOL users have a reputation (well-earned, unfortunately) of barging into newsgroups and having no idea of what the group is about or what people on it are discussing. *Please* restrain your creative impulses for a few days before contributing to a group. The rest of Usenet will thank you.

After you have read a message, you can send a response. Make sure, however, that you read all the existing responses first! Someone may already have made the excellent point you want to make.

Instead of replying to the newsgroup, consider sending e-mail to the person who posted the original message. If the information in your response will be of interest mainly to the original poster, send e-mail. If you're sure that it will interest lots of people in the newsgroup, post it.

To reply by e-mail to the person who posted the original article, click the Email to Author button. To post a response to the newsgroup, click Reply to Group. Either way, you see a Reply dialog box, which lets you enter the text of your message. If you're changing the subject, be sure to change the Subject of the posting also. When you have written your message, click the Send button.

In addition to making sure that you're not repeating what someone may have already said, be sure to write clearly, proofread your message, stay calm rather than get emotional (emotional responses don't work well in newsgroups), be polite (Net surfers are people too), and keep it brief. After all, tens of thousands of people are likely to read your posting, so don't waste their time!

If you begin to compose a reply and then think better of it, you can cancel sending the reply. Double-click the button in the upper left corner of the Reply dialog box rather than click the Send button.

Grabbing Files from FTP Servers

AOL lets you download files from FTP servers on the Internet. AOL can do anonymous FTP (in which you connect to an FTP server you don't have an account on) or FTP-ing in which you do have an account. To use the AOL FTP service, you have to know which file you want to download, which FTP server has it, and which directory the file is in. For information about FTP, see Chapter 12.

Most people now download software via the Web. Links on Web pages may be FTP links — that is, clicking the link starts downloading a file.

If you need to use FTP directly, here's how to download a file:

1. **Press Ctrl+K (or choose Go To⇨Keyword from the menu), type** ftp, **and click Go.**

   You see the FTP – File Transfer Protocol window.

2. **Click the Go To FTP button.**

   The Anonymous FTP dialog box appears.

3. **If the FTP server that has the file you want is listed, select it and click Connect. If not, click Other Site, type the Internet name of the FTP server, and click Connect.**

   When you have connected to the FTP server of your choice, AOL may display an informational message about it — click OK when you have read it. Then you see a list of the contents of the current directory on the FTP server.

4. **To move to the directory that contains the file you want, double-click the directory names.**

   AOL shows little file-folder icons by directory names and little sheet-of-paper icons by filenames. For files, look at the size of each file (in bytes, or characters) — the larger the file, the longer it takes to download.

5. **To download a file to your computer, choose the file and click Download Now.**

   The Download Manager dialog box appears, asking where to put the file on your computer.

6. **Choose the directory in which you want to put the file on your own computer, and edit the filename. Then click OK.**

   AOL downloads the file to your computer's disk. Depending on the size of the file and the speed of your modem, this step can take seconds, minutes, or hours.

7. **Close dialog boxes in AOL when you're finished.**

   You can even close dialog boxes while AOL is transferring the file.

If you have an account on the FTP server (and therefore have access to files not available to the public), use the Other Site button and click the button named Ask for login name and password.

Some FTP servers are extremely busy, and you may not be able to connect. Try again during off-hours, or try another server. AOL keeps copies of most or all of the files on some of the busiest servers, to alleviate the traffic jams online.

Using AOL As a SLIP Account

It's a tough decision, choosing between a commercial online service such as America Online and an Internet account. Although America Online has lots of AOL-only information, an Internet SLIP account lets you use all that snazzy, new Winsock software, such as Netscape Navigator. What's a cybernaut to do?

Connecting to AOL via your Internet account

If you have an existing flat-rate Internet account, you can use AOL and your Winsock software at the same time without installing any new software. You do that by making AOL itself run over the Internet. Rather than use your AOL account as a SLIP account, you can use your AOL software as Winsock software.

Start up the AOL software, but *don't* connect yet. Then go to the Modem menu and choose a "Winsock" modem. Connect to your Internet provider in the usual way, and, after that connection is made, connect to AOL. AOL connects via your Internet provider as just another Winsock program, and you can start any other Internet programs you want and click back and forth between AOL and the other programs. When you're finished with

AOL, disconnect from AOL and then disconnect from your AOL provider. One caveat: Your AOL password goes out over the Net unsecured, so some highly motivated person might be able, in theory, to find it and read it.

If you have an Internet provider that charges by the hour, you probably don't want to connect this way because you pay its hourly charges. If your provider has a flat rate or nearly so (a large number of free hours are included each month), however, it can be the best way to go because your provider may have faster modems than your local AOL dial-in; rural customers may not even have a local AOL dial-in. AOL has a special price of $9.95 per month price if you always connect via your Internet account.

Now you don't have to choose — you can have it all. AOL has created a special version of the WINSOCK.DLL program that all Winsock programs use to talk to PPP and SLIP accounts. (See Chapter 13 for an explanation of Winsock and SLIP accounts.) Using the AOL WINSOCK.DLL program, your Winsock programs talk to your AOL account.

Confused? So were we. Here's how it works: When you run the AOL program, it checks to see whether a WINSOCK.DLL is loaded in your computer's memory. If it isn't, AOL loads its own WINSOCK.DLL. Either way, you're now ready to run Winsock software. (Older versions of AOL software require you to download and install the WINSOCK.DLL program yourself.)

Getting Winsock-compatible programs

Lots of freeware and shareware Winsock software is available from AOL and from the World Wide Web! Here are places to look for Winsock programs:

✔ Go to Winsock Central in AOL (keyword WINSOCK) and click the Software Library button. You see a list of Winsock programs that AOL promises will work with its Winsock software.

✔ Look at the TUCOWS (The Ultimate Collection Of Windows Software) Web site or Forrest Stroud's Consummate Winsock Apps List. Press Ctrl+K (or choose Go To⇨Keyword from the menu) and type the URL (address) of the Web page:

```
http://www.cwsapps.com
```

or

```
http://www.tucows.com
```

When you click Go, the AOL Web browser is displayed (see the "Web Browsing with AOL" section, earlier in this chapter) and displays an extensive list of Winsock programs. Click the type of program you want (Web browsers or newsreaders, for example) and you see names, descriptions, and even reviews of the programs. Click the Location section of the program description to download the program.

Using a Winsock program

Suppose that you want to use Navigator rather than the AOL Web browser. Assuming that you're running a new version of the AOL software that includes a WINSOCK.DLL and you have downloaded the Navigator program (or bought a commercial version), here's all you have to do to use Navigator:

1. Run it.

That's it. That's all you do. To be specific, run AOL and log in to your account. Then run Navigator (or any other Winsock-compatible program). It works, using your AOL account as its connection to the Internet.

When you finish, exit from the Winsock program. Then log off from AOL.

For more information about where to get nifty Winsock programs you might want to use, see Chapter 21.

Doing Other Things

Because America Online offers tons of information that has nothing to do with the Internet, after you sign up, you might as well check it out. The Computing and Software channel (department) lets you exchange messages with others about the software you use or download shareware. The Reference channel offers all kinds of online reference materials, including the Library of Congress database of books, *Compton's Encyclopedia,* and *Webster's Dictionary of Computer Terms.* The Kids Only channel has fun and educational stuff for kids, including games, homework help, and AOL-supervised chat rooms. The Travel channel lets you make and check your own airline reservations.

Overall, AOL has one of the nicest *front ends* (as we say in the software biz — it means the way a human being actually uses the system) of any of the Internet shell providers. For all except the most seasoned hackers, all these nice icons and menus make the system easy to use. Although AOL can be slow at times, especially evenings and weekends, it keeps promising to speed things up soon. The trial membership is free — try it out!

We have heard lots of complaints about how hard it is to *cancel* an AOL account if you decide that you don't want it. You may have to make several phone calls and let your credit card company know that you refuse any additional charges from AOL.)

If you want to read other books about America Online, see Chapter 22.

Whatever happened to Prodigy?

Although Prodigy was one of the first consumer-oriented online services, it has been losing members for several years. Prodigy wasn't as quick as AOL to add the Internet, especially the World Wide Web, to its offerings. It's still out there, with more than one million members, though. In an effort to regain lost ground, Prodigy has started a new service called Prodigy Internet, which gives you a PPP Internet account (see Chapter 13 to find out how these work) and a copy of Netscape Navigator. For information about Prodigy, call 800-PRODIGY.

Chapter 15

Using the Internet via CompuServe

· ·

In This Chapter

▶ Signing up for a CompuServe account

▶ Climbing online

▶ Telling CompuServe where to go

▶ Sending e-mail

▶ Browsing the Web

▶ Reading newsgroups

▶ Getting files by using FTP

▶ Using other programs with CompuServe

· ·

C ompuServe is a very successful online service that caters to business and professional users. It has lots of information about computer hardware and software, including support forums for hundreds of software and hardware vendors. CompuServe is the oldest of the major online services; with its easy-to-use access programs — WinCIM, MacCIM, and the new CompuServe 3.0 for Windows — a CompuServe account is as user-friendly as newer online services, such as America Online.

This chapter describes the CompuServe Internet-related capabilities, including e-mail and the World Wide Web, using CompuServe 3.0 for Windows.

This chapter describes how to use the CompuServe 3.0 for Windows program; CompuServe 3.0 for Macintosh should look very similar. If you're using its older Windows or Macintosh software, WinCIM or MacCIM, your screens will look different from the ones shown in this chapter. See the nearby sidebar "The Windows 3.1 way of using CompuServe" if you use the Windows 3.1 operating system and the WinCIM 2.5 program.

TIP

The pros and cons of CompuServe

CompuServe has been around for a while and has lots of fascinating forums available only to CompuServe subscribers. If you're a serious PC user, you will love the many technical-support forums provided by hundreds of hardware and software vendors. We find that shareware programs and bug fixes are easier to find on CompuServe than on the Internet because CompuServe is better organized (almost anything is better organized than the Internet!). Downloads usually go faster too. Its new software makes it as easy to use as America Online.

Another big plus about CompuServe is that its phone network extends around the world. If you travel frequently, especially overseas, this feature is invaluable.

On the other hand, as of January 1997, CompuServe costs more than most other types of accounts, with no flat rate for unlimited hours.

Signing Up for CompuServe

To sign up for a CompuServe account, get hold of one of its disk packages. (Call 1-800-848-8199 to get yours.) It contains a disk and instructions for installing it. Make sure that you have the right disk for your computer (Windows or Mac). Both disk and CD-ROM versions are available. While you're on the phone, ask for the current pricing plan because pricing changes often in the online world.

The disk contains both the CompuServe software, which lets you connect to and use CompuServe, and an automated sign-up program that lets you sign up for a new CompuServe account over the phone. You need a credit card to make this process work. You get some free hours when you sign up for a new account, so you can figure out whether CompuServe is for you before spending too much dough.

To install the CompuServe software, follow the instructions on the package. Install the software, call CompuServe to find out the closest access phone number, and then call CompuServe using that phone number. When you're done, you have a CompuServe account and software configured to connect to it.

After you have signed up for your CompuServe account, you're ready to roll! Remove the CompuServe disk from the drive and stash it somewhere, in case you ever have to install it again. If you have trouble, call CompuServe at 1-800-487-0453 for billing questions or 1-800-944-9871 for technical support.

The Windows 3.1 way of using CompuServe

The CompuServe program for Windows 3.1 users is called CompuServe Information Manager 2.5, or WinCIM 2.5, for short. This program works a little differently from the CompuServe 3.0 program described in this chapter. Although the information you get from CompuServe is exactly the same, its on-screen presentation and the menu choices and toolbar buttons you use are different. Here's how to use WinCIM in a nutshell:

 ✔ To start the WinCIM program, double-click its icon in Windows Program Manager. To connect to your CompuServe account, click an icon to tell WinCIM what information you want.

 ✔ To get your mail, click the Get New Mail button on the toolbar, the one with an addressed envelope.

 ✔ To go to a CompuServe service if you know the exact name of the service, click the Go button on the toolbar, the button with the green traffic light, and then type the name of the service.

 ✔ To find the CompuServe service about a topic, click the Find button on the toolbar, the one with a magnifying glass.

 ✔ To see information about using the Internet, click the Explore button on the toolbar (the indescribable button to the left of the Go button). When you see the Explore Services window, click the Internet button. You see the Internet window. Bingo!

 ✔ To browse the Web, click the Go button on the toolbar, type the URL of the Web page you want to see, and press Enter. Or click the Explore button on the WinCIM 2.5 toolbar, click the Internet button, and click the Enter the Internet button. WinCIM 2.5 comes with a Web browser, Internet Explorer. To go to a particular Web page, type its URL in the Address box after you see the Internet Explorer window.

 ✔ The process of reading Usenet newsgroups and downloading files via FTP works the same in WinCIM 2.5 as it does in CompuServe 3.0, so follow the instructions in the sections "Go, Newsgroups!" and "Getting Files via FTP," later in this chapter.

 ✔ To hang up, click the Exit button, the rightmost button on the toolbar.

WinCIM 2.5 lets you use other Winsock programs too; see the section "Using Other Programs with Your CompuServe Account," near the end of this chapter.

My user ID is what?!

Unlike most other online services and Internet providers, CompuServe assigns you a number that looks like this:

77777,7777

Although the exact number of digits varies, your user ID is always a number with a bunch of digits and a comma somewhere in the middle. Users in the United States and Canada usually have numbers that begin with a 7, and overseas users usually have numbers that begin with 1. (This numbering scheme dates back to the stone age of computing, in the late 1960s. The numbers are base 8, by the way.)

Your Internet e-mail address is not the same as your CompuServe ID — you have to modify it to include the information that it's a CompuServe account number. To figure out your e-mail address, change the comma in your user ID to a period and add @compuserve.com to the end. If your CompuServe ID is 77777,7777, for example, your Internet e-mail address is

77777.7777@compuserve.com

CompuServe has just begun allowing members to register for names too, for use in sending and receiving e-mail. To register for a name, click Go and type register. After you have signed up for a name, you can use the name followed by @compuserve.com as your e-mail address rather than the long strings of digits.

Revving Up CompuServe

Now you're ready to use your CompuServe account. Here's how to use the CompuServe 3.0 for Windows software running under Windows 95 (CompuServe 3.0 for Macintosh works similarly):

1. **Click the Start button and then choose <u>P</u>rograms⇨CompuServe⇨ CompuServe from the menu. Or click the CompuServe icon on the your desktop.**

   You see the Home Desktop window, with buttons down the side and folder tabs across the top (see Figure 15-1).

2. **To call up CompuServe and do something, click the button for what you want to do.**

   The rest of this chapter contains ideas for things you might want to do, primarily Internet-related things. As soon as you click a button that tells your CompuServe program what you want to do, it calls up CompuServe on the phone, logs you in, and displays the information you want.

Desktop buttons   Toolbar   Folder tabs

Figure 15-1:
The
CompuServe
window
looks like
this when
you start
the
program.

3. **When you're done using CompuServe, click the Disconnect button on the toolbar, the rightmost button, with two hands gripping each other. Or choose Access⇨Disconnect from the menu or press Ctrl+D.**

   Because you pay for the time you're connected to CompuServe, be sure to disconnect before wandering off for a bite to eat. (CompuServe thoughtfully displays the amount of time you have been online on the toolbar, just to the right of the big yellow question-mark icon.)

4. **To leave the CompuServe program, choose File⇨Exit from the menu or click the window's Close button.**

Click the Main Menu button to return to the menu you saw when you started the program.

Go, CompuServe!

CompuServe has hundreds of *services,* or material on a particular topic. Some services contain ongoing discussions (called *forums*), some have libraries of files you might find useful, and some let you ask questions of technical experts.

Go where?

Each CompuServe service has an official name. To go to the service, you click the Go button on the toolbar, type the service name, and click OK. If you're not already connected to CompuServe, your program dials up, connects, and goes where you asked. Even easier, if the Page box appears in the upper left corner of your CompuServe window (right under the left end of the menu bar), click the Page box, type the service name, and press Enter.

In addition to CompuServe services, CompuServe has zillions of Web pages. Sometimes when you ask to go somewhere, you see a CompuServe service page, and at other times you see a Web page. You don't need to care which is which — the good news is that CompuServe shows you the information you want, whichever format it's in.

Finding where to go

How do you find the service you want? Click the Search button on the toolbar — it's the one with the flashlight. If you see a Find button, you can click that too. Type a topic, such as cats or investing or eggplants, in the box. When you click the Search button, CompuServe searches its own services for the topic.

You see a list of CompuServe services that contain the word you searched for, with descriptions and service names (the name to type to go there). If one of the services on the left list looks interesting, you can go to it by double-clicking it.

Some services ask you to join before using them. They tend to be services with *forums,* or ongoing discussion groups. Go ahead — fill in the information the forum asks for and click the Join button. You can always quit later. If CompuServe changes extra for the forum, you see a message telling you so.

Go, Internet!

CompuServe has a Browse the Internet button right on the toolbar — it's the globe. When you click it, CompuServe (after dialing up and logging in, if necessary) displays its Welcome to the Internet window, which lists all the CompuServe Internet-related services in one handy spot.

In the next few sections of this chapter, you find out how to use the Internet via CompuServe.

Go, E-Mail!

CompuServe has a mail service for sending messages to and from other CompuServe users. The same mail service works for sending and receiving e-mail to Internet addresses. To deal with your mail, click the Main Menu button and then the Mail Center button. You see tabs across the top of your CompuServe window to read messages, create messages, use your Address Book to store addresses, or search the messages you have saved.

If you have messages waiting to be read, CompuServe startles you with a cheery "You have mail!" when you connect (at least, it does if your computer has a speaker). Also, the bottom line of the CompuServe window, to the right of the envelope button, tells you how many messages are waiting.

Reading your mail the cheap and easy way

The most efficient way to read your mail is to read it *offline* — while you're not connected to CompuServe — so that you can do your reading and writing without the CompuServe meter running. Here's how it works:

- ✔ You tell CompuServe to grab all your mail and download it (copy it) from CompuServe into your Filing Cabinet, a storage area on your hard disk.

- ✔ You disconnect from CompuServe.

- ✔ While you're disconnected (and therefore not paying connect-time charges), you read your e-mail at a leisurely pace. You can even write replies or compose messages to other people. Messages you write are stored in your Out Basket, which is also on your hard disk.

- ✔ When you finish reading your mail, you tell CompuServe to send the messages in your Out Basket and pick up any additional messages in your In Basket.

The result is that you're online only long enough to download your incoming mail and upload your outgoing mail.

Ready to try it? Follow these steps:

1. **In the CompuServe program, click the Mail Center button (if you don't see it, click the Main menu button first) and then click the Get Mail button. Or choose Mail⇨Get New Mail from the menu.**

If you're not already connected to CompuServe, your program dials it up and downloads your list of messages to your computer. If you composed any messages since you last connected to CompuServe, your program sends them.

2. **When CompuServe is done, click the Disconnect button on the toolbar, the rightmost button, with two hands gripping each other. Or choose <u>A</u>ccess⇨<u>D</u>isconnect from the menu or press Ctrl+D.**

CompuServe hangs up. There! You stop paying connect charges. Your messages are listed in the CompuServe window.

3. **To read a message, double-click it (or select it and click <u>O</u>pen).**

You see the Read Mail window with a message (Figure 15-2).

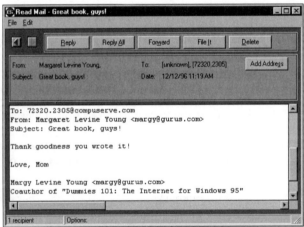

Figure 15-2: After you read a message, you can reply to it, forward it, or file it (in the circular file, if you want).

4. **To reply to a message, click the <u>R</u>eply button, compose a response, and click <u>S</u>end (if you want to connect to CompuServe and send it right now) or Send <u>L</u>ater (to put the message in your Out Basket, to be sent the next time you connect to CompuServe).**

When you reply to a message, CompuServe addresses the message for you. All you have to do is type your response.

5. **To forward a message to someone else, click For<u>w</u>ard, address the message, and click <u>S</u>end or Send <u>L</u>ater.**

See the following section to learn how to use the address book to address a message.

6. **To see the next message in your In Basket, click the right-pointing triangle button near the upper left corner of the Read Mail window.**

7. **When you're done reading your messages, close the Read Mail window by clicking its Close button or double-clicking the button in its upper left corner.**

   You see the list of incoming messages again.

8. **Compose new messages by clicking the Create button along the top of the CompuServe window, below the toolbar, and then clicking the New button. Or choose Mail⇨Create New Mail from the menu.**

9. **When you see the Create Mail window, fill in the Name (real name), Address (e-mail address), and Subject boxes.**

   See the following section later to learn how to use the address book to address a message.

10. **Type the text of the message in the large, white box and then click Send or Send Later.**

11. **When you finish reading and composing mail, choose Mail⇨Send/ Retrieve All Mail from the menu. Or click the Create button and then the Send All button if you don't care about retrieving any new messages.**

    Your program calls CompuServe again, sends all the mail you composed, and checks for any mail that has arrived since you last checked it.

You can see the messages you have sent, or that are waiting to be sent, by clicking the Create button along the top of the CompuServe window, below the toolbar.

Using your little black book

When you send mail to another CompuServe user, address a message to that person's CompuServe ID (the one that looks like *77777,7777*) or the person's personal CompuServe name, if any. When you send mail to someone on the Internet, address the message to

```
INTERNET:username@host
```

For example, you can send a test message to us authors here at Internet For Dummies Central by addressing it to

```
INTERNET:internet4@dummies.net
```

When you compose a message or forward an existing message, you have to address it. Here's how:

1. **In the Name box, type the person's real name.**

2. **In the Address box, type the person's CompuServe ID number, CompuServe personal name, or e-mail address. To send e-mail to someone not on CompuServe, add** INTERNET: **to the beginning of the address, to tell CompuServe how to send this message.**

3. **Click the Recipients button to tell CompuServe to take a look at the address you have entered.**

   If the name doesn't appear in your address book, you see the Define Address Book Entry window, as shown in Figure 15-3. The name you type appears in the Name box. The Address type box shows whether this is an Internet address, a CompuServe address, or an address on one of a number of other e-mail systems. The e-mail address itself appears in the Address box.

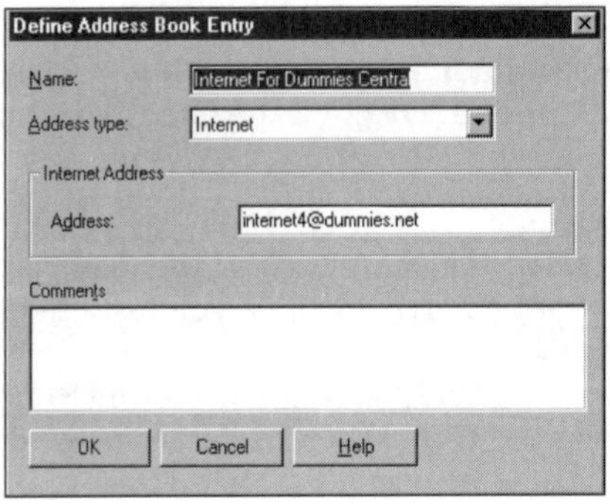

Figure 15-3:
CompuServe
maintains
an address
book of
your
favorite
addresses.

4. **To add this address to your address book, click OK.**

   Next you see the Message Recipients window, listing the people your message is addressed to. Click OK. You see the Message Recipients window, as shown in Figure 15-4. You can add addresses if you want to send the message to more than one person. You can also "cc" people (send them a copy for their information).

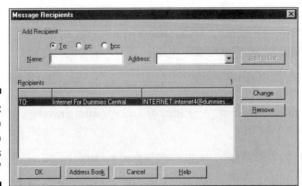

Figure 15-4:
To whom do
you want to
address this
message?

5. **To address the message to another person too, type the name and address in the first two boxes in the window. (For a cc recipient, click the cc button.) Then click the Add to List button.**

6. **To remove an addressee, select the name from the list and click the Remove button.**

7. **When you're done adding addresses, click OK.**

   You return to the window in which you were creating your mail message, and you're ready to continue composing.

Another way to address messages is by choosing addresses from your address book. To do so, click the Recipients button in the Create Mail window. Then click the Address Book button in the Message Recipients window. You see the Select Recipients window, listing everyone in your address book. To address the message to someone on the list, click the person and then click OK.

To look at your address book at any time, click the Mail Center button in the CompuServe window, and then click the Address Book tab along the top of the window, below the toolbar. You can edit or delete people on your list (well, you can edit or delete the *people,* but you can work on the entries in your address book).

Sending along a file too

You can use the Windows or Macintosh Clipboard to copy text from another Windows program into your mail messages. To include text from a word-processing document, for example, select the text in your word processor, copy it to the Clipboard (in most programs, you choose the Edit⇨Copy command or press Ctrl+C — ⌘+C on the Mac), place your cursor where you want the text to appear in your message, and choose Edit⇨Paste from the menu or press Ctrl+V (⌘+V on the Mac).

Another way of sending information along with an e-mail message is to *attach* the file to the message. If it's a text file, you can send it to anyone. In the old days (1996), if a file were not text, you could send it only to other CompuServe users. Luckily, CompuServe is adding a *MIME gateway* (sounds like something that clowns would walk through very quietly), which enables you to send any type of file to the Internet. The file is attached to the message by using MIME encoding (see Chapter 9), which most e-mail programs can handle. Try it — CompuServe probably has it working by now.

To attach a file to a message:

1. **Begin composing the message as usual.**

2. In the Create Mail window, click the Attach File button.

You see the Open dialog box.

3. If you're sending a file that contains something other than text, click the Files of type box and choose the type of file to display.

4. Move to the folder that contains the file and select the file.

5. Click the Open button.

You see the Attach Files window, listing the filename you just selected.

6. Click OK.

The Attach File button now has a little 1 on it, showing that one file is attached.

7. Finish composing the message and send it as usual.

When you receive a file attached to an e-mail message, the message arrives in several parts. The first part is the text of the message, and the second part is the attached file. If more than one file is attached, it may have more parts. Just below the subject line of the messages, you see left- and right-pointing triangle buttons and a line that looks like Part 1 of 2. To see the attached file, click the right-pointing triangle button. If the attached file is a picture that CompuServe knows how to display, the picture appears directly in the message section of the Read Mail window! CompuServe saves the file in the Download folder in your CompuServe program folder (usually something like C:\Program Files\CompuServe\Download) — the bottom line of the Read Mail window tells you the exact path and filename of the attached file.

Go, World Wide Web!

CompuServe used to get lots of grief for making the Web less accessible than its main competitor, AOL. Now that the new CompuServe software has the Microsoft Internet Explorer browser built right in, browsing the Web is as easy as using the rest of the CompuServe services.

To go directly to a Web page if you know its URL (Web address), click the Go button, type the URL, and click OK. To see the Internet For Dummies Central Web page, for example, click Go, type **http://net.dummies.net**, and then click OK. Even easier, you can click the Page box in the upper left corner of the CompuServe window, type the URL, and press Enter.

When you're typing a URL in the Page box, you can usually leave off the http:// at the beginning. CompuServe adds it for you.

To search the Web, click the Search button on the toolbar, the one with the flashlight. Then click the Start Internet Search button. You see the Csi Find page (a special version of the popular Lycos page), which lets you type a word or phrase and click Find It. Or type the address of a Web search page in the Page box.

Here are some Web search pages that work well:

```
www.yahoo.com
altavista.digital.com
www.excite.com
www.infoseek.com
```

For more information about searching the Web, see Chapter 7.

Go, Newsgroups!

The CompuServe services include hundreds (thousands?) of *forums,* online discussion groups about specific topics. CompuServe forums are restricted to CompuServe members, however. If you want to converse with people on other online services and people with Internet accounts, try joining Usenet newsgroups. Chapter 11 has general information about Usenet, like what the heck it is.

To read Usenet newsgroups, click the Internet button on the toolbar to display the Welcome to the Internet window, and then click the Newsgroups button. Or click the Go icon, type **usenet**, and click Go. Or just click the Page box in the upper left corner of the CompuServe window, type **usenet**, and press Enter. You see the Usenet newsgroups, with a list of topics about reading newsgroups.

If you're new to Usenet newsgroups, try choosing the introductory topics on this list. When you're ready to read some newsgroups, double-click Usenet Newsreader (CIM). You see another Usenet Newsgroups dialog box, as shown in Figure 15-5.

This window is mission control for reading and posting newsgroup articles. It's not really part of the CompuServe for Windows program — it's a separate program, called the CIM Usenet newsreader. All the other windows you have open within CompuServe are minimized (they shrink to little boxes in the CompuServe window) while you're running the CIM Usenet newsreader.

When you finish reading newsgroups, exit from the newsreader program by clicking the Cancel button.

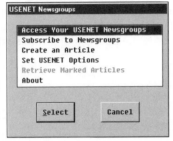

Figure 15-5:
Use the
CIM Usenet
newsreader
to read
and post
articles to
Usenet
newsgroups.

Finding a newsgroup

The first step to reading newsgroups is to subscribe to newsgroups that in-terest you. Double-click Subscribe to Newsgroups option in the Usenet Newsgroups window (the one that was shown in Figure 15-5). You see the Subscribe to Newsgroups window, with a listing of the major newsgroup hierarchies (the first part of the newsgroup name, such as comp or rec).

Here are ways to find the newsgroups you want:

✔ The dialog box lists newsgroups by hierarchy. To see the newsgroups in a hierarchy, double-click it. To see recreational newsgroups (those with names beginning with rec), for example, double-click Recreational (rec.*) on the list. You see a list of the newsgroups of that type, as shown in Figure 15-6. To subscribe to one, select it, and an X appears in the little box to the left of the newsgroup name. When you have chosen the newsgroups you want, click Subscribe. (To take a peek at the newsgroup without subscribing, click Preview.) Then click Cancel to close the window listing the newsgroups.

```
Recreational (rec.*): Found 558 Newsgroups
┌────────────────────────────────────────────────────────────┐
│ ☐ rec.animals.wildlife                                    ▲ │
│     Wildlife related discussions/information.               │
│ ☐ rec.answers                                               │
│     Repository for periodic USENET articles. (Moderated)    │
│ ☐ rec.antiques                                              │
│     Discussing antiques and vintage items.                  │
│ ☐ rec.antiques.marketplace                                  │
│     Buying/selling/trading antiques.                        │
│ ☐ rec.antiques.radio+phono                                  │
│     Audio devices and materials of yesteryear.           ▼ │
└────────────────────────────────────────────────────────────┘
      [ Subscribe ]      [ Preview ]      [ Cancel ]
```

Figure 15-6:
Here are
some
recreational
news-
groups —
pick one!

✔ To search for a newsgroup about a particular topic that interests you, type a word or phrase in the <u>K</u>eyword box in the Subscribe to Newsgroups window, and then click S<u>e</u>arch. CompuServe searches for newsgroups that contain the word or phrase in the newsgroup name or description. On the list that results, you can choose the groups to which you want to subscribe.

✔ If you know the exact name of the newsgroup you want, click Subscribe by <u>N</u>ame, type the name of the newsgroup in the box, and click OK.

When you finish, click Close to return to the Usenet Newsgroups window.

Reading newsgroup messages

To see the newsgroups you're subscribed to — whether you want to read an article or post your own — double-click Access Your Usenet Newsgroups in the Usenet Newsgroups window. You see a list of the groups you're sub-scribed to. For each newsgroup, you see the number of articles you haven't yet read (a daunting number, in most cases).

To read the articles in a newsgroup, double-click the newsgroup name. You see a list of the threads (articles grouped by topic) in the newsgroup, as shown in Figure 15-7.

Figure 15-7:
Each thread listed is a group of articles, starting with a post and including all the responses to that post.

✔ To read articles on the spot, while you're connected to CompuServe, choose the threads that look interesting and click <u>G</u>et.

✔ To save money and download the threads to your hard disk so that you can read them after disconnecting from CompuServe, choose the threads you want and click <u>R</u>etrieve. CompuServe asks where to save the articles on your hard disk.

✔ When you're looking at an article, you can respond to it, either by e-mail or by posting an article, by clicking Reply. (See the section "Mouthing off," later in this chapter.)

✔ To write a new article for this newsgroup, click Create. (Again, see the section "Mouthing off.")

When you finish reading the articles in the newsgroup, click Cancel.

Telling the CIM newsreader who you are

Before you can post articles to Usenet newsgroups by using the CIM Usenet Newsreader, you have to tell it who you are. It's just one of those rules — the program balks otherwise. To make it feel better, double-click Set Usenet Options in the Usenet Newsgroups window. You see the Options dialog box.

Fill in the blanks. For the signature, type as many as three lines of text to be added to the end of every article you post to Usenet. Be sure to include your name and e-mail address. (Remember that your e-mail address is your CompuServe ID, with the comma changed to a period, followed by @compuserve.com.) Click OK when you're done.

TIP

Tell that jerk to shut up!

Jerks lurk in almost every newsgroup, and telling them to shut up doesn't help at all. They just send *more* messages, in fact, pointing out to you why they are right and you are wrong. The intelligent tack is to *ignore* them. CompuServe makes this technique easy — it ignores people for you!

Here's how it's done:

1. Double-click Set Usenet Options in the Usenet Newsgroups window.

2. Click the Set Ignore Options button.

3. You see a list of the newsgroups to which you're subscribed. Double-click the one that contains the jerk in question.

4. You see the Ignore Criteria dialog box. Click Author for the Ignore By setting (to ignore articles based on their author), and then click OK.

5. Click Insert to enter the name of the jerk whose articles you want to ignore.

6. Type the Internet address of the jerk and the number of days you want to ignore his articles, or click Non-Expiring to ignore all additional articles from this person. Then click OK.

7. The information about whom you're ignoring, and for how long, is displayed in the dialog box.

8. Click Close, Cancel, and then OK to back out of the dialog boxes you have open.

You can use the same system for ignoring all articles about a particular topic. If the folks in a newsgroup are talking endlessly about a pointless, boring subject, you can ignore all the articles about that subject. Click Subject and then OK in the Ignore Criteria dialog box, and enter the subject you want to ignore.

Mouthing off

The best way to respond to a newsgroup article is by sending e-mail to the person who wrote the article. After all, not everyone who reads the newsgroup may be interested in your response. Sometimes you just can't restrain yourself from posting an article, however, even though you take the chance of making a fool of yourself in front of tens of thousands of people around the world.

When you read an article that demands a response, whether you're determined to post an article or have wisely decided to respond by e-mail, you can use the same button: Click Reply. If you decide to post an article about a new subject, not in response to another article, double-click Create an Article from the Usenet Newsgroups window or display the list of threads in the newsgroup and click Create.

You see the Reply to Usenet Message or Create Usenet Message window. You can use this window for posting articles to newsgroups or for sending e-mail.

Here's how to proceed:

1. **Type the subject of the e-mail or article in the Subject box.**

2. **If you want to post an article to a newsgroup, click the Post to Newsgroup(s) option and choose the newsgroup (or newsgroups) from the Newsgroups list. If you want to send an e-mail message, click Send via E-mail.**

   The Newsgroups list contains the list of newsgroups to which you subscribe. (It's rude to post articles to newsgroups you don't subscribe to — how do you know what they're talking about?)

3. **Type the article or message in the Message Contents box (the big one).**

   If you want to include text you have stored on your hard disk, you can upload it (copy the text from a file on your hard disk into the Message Contents box). Just click Upload and click the File button to choose the text file you want to include in the message. You can upload only text files — other types of files don't work.

4. **Click Send.**

   When you click Send, if you're sending the message via e-mail, the program prompts you for the e-mail address to which to send the message. Type it and click OK. You *don't* have to type *INTERNET:* before Internet addresses. Because Usenet is part of the Internet, all addresses are Internet addresses. To send a message to a CompuServe user, use her Internet address (change the comma in her user ID to a period and add @compuserve.com to the end).

If you're posting a newsgroup article, the program confirms that the article was posted.

Remember never to post in anger! Take a walk instead! If you have to write an outraged message, mail it to yourself and then consider the following day whether you still really want to send it to a newsgroup.

Dealing with boring newsgroups

If you *don't* want to continue subscribing to a newsgroup, you can unsubscribe from it. (Yes, *unsubscribe* is now a word.) In the Usenet Newsgroups window (the one that was shown in Figure 15-5), double-click Access Your Usenet Newsgroups. Choose the newsgroup you're sick of and click Remove. The program asks whether you're absolutely, positively sure that you want to unsubscribe. Click Yes to go for it. Poof! The newsgroup disappears from your list of newsgroups, never to return (unless you resubscribe).

Leaving the Usenet newsreader

When you're done reading newsgroups, click Cancel in the Usenet Newsgroups window. After a minute, you return to the first Usenet Newsgroups window you saw. Now you can use the Page box or the Go button to use another service.

Getting Files via FTP

CompuServe has oodles of files you can download. So does the Internet. FTP (File Transfer Protocol) is the Internet service that enables you to transfer files from one computer to another, usually from large public file archives to your own PC. See Chapter 12 for more information about FTP, including which types of files you're likely to find and likely places to look for them.

Why use FTP if you can get the file from CompuServe?

CompuServe has libraries with tens of thousands — perhaps hundreds of thousands — of files. You might want to check whether the file you want is available from CompuServe before going to the trouble of using FTP. To look for a file in the many CompuServe libraries, click the Access CompuServe's File Finders option in the File Transfer Protocol window or click the Go icon on the toolbar and type **filefinder**.

To use FTP to download files to your computer, click the Internet button on the toolbar to display the Welcome to the Internet window, and then click the FTP button. Or click the Go icon, type **ftp**, and click Go. Or just click in the Page box in the upper left corner of the CompuServe window, type **ftp**, and press Enter.

Either way, CompuServe displays a serious-looking warning message, indicating that the CompuServe Information Service is not responsible for what's in the files you might or might not download and that it *doesn't* want to hear about it if you *don't* like what you find. Fair enough: FTP isn't a CompuServe service, after all. Click Proceed to continue.

You see the File Transfer Protocol window.

To download a file from the FTP archive that has the file you want, follow these steps:

1. **Click the Access a Specific Site button on the right side of the window.**

   You see the Access a Specific Site window.

2. **In the Site Name box, enter the Internet host name of the FTP archive in which the files you want are stored.**

   If you want to download a file from the Microsoft FTP server, for example, enter `ftp.microsoft.com`.

3. **If you know the directory on the FTP server in which the file is stored, enter it in the Directory box.**

   If you know that the file is in /pub/clip-art, for example, enter that.

4. **If you're using anonymous FTP (that is, you don't have your own account on the FTP server), leave the User Name as `anonymous`. If you have your own account, type it in the User Name box.**

   Publicly accessible FTP servers require you to log in as `anonymous`.

5. **If you're using anonymous FTP, leave the Password box set to your Internet address. If you have your own account, enter the password.**

   When you use anonymous FTP, you're supposed to enter your Internet e-mail address as the password. CompuServe fills it in for you.

6. **Click OK.**

   CompuServe contacts the FTP server and tries to log you in. The server may be busy, or down, in which case you see an error message — try again later.

   If you're able to log in to the FTP server, you see a message welcoming you to the server. You may also see information about the server.

7. **Click OK.**

CompuServe displays a directory listing of the current directory on the FTP server, as shown in Figure 15-8. The list on the left side of the window contains the subdirectories of the current directory, and the list on the right shows the files in the current directory.

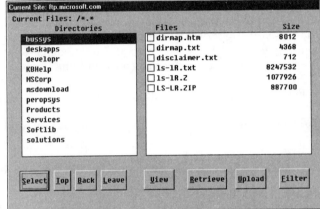

Figure 15-8: Here are the directories and files on an FTP server.

8. **Read the instructions.**

   The first directory you see may contain a list of the files on the FTP server, in a file with a name such as read.me or index.txt. If it does, take a look at it, by clicking the filename and the clicking the Yiew button.

9. **Move to the directory that contains the file (or files) you want.**

   To move to a subdirectory of the current directory, double-click the directory name in the list on the left. To move back to the preceding directory, click the Back button. To move back to the directory from which you started, click the Top button.

10. **When you see a file you want, click the filename so that an X appears in its little box. Then click the Retrieve button.**

    You can choose more than one file, if you want. CompuServe asks where you want to store the file (or files).

11. **Choose a directory in which to store the files and click OK.**

    CompuServe downloads the file from the FTP server to CompuServe to your own computer.

12. **When you finish, click Leave.**

    CompuServe logs you off the FTP server.

The CompuServe File Transfer Protocol window lets you log in to an FTP server, look around, and download some files. The Selected Popular Sites and List of Sites buttons in the window display lists of popular FTP servers — choose an FTP server from one of these lists, and you see the Access a Specific Site window with the host name of the FTP server filled in for you. The Site Descriptions button lets you see descriptions of some popular FTP servers, including the types of files stored on each server.

Using Other Programs with Your CompuServe Account

CompuServe provides a good e-mail program, an excellent Web browser, and a serviceable if clunky Usenet newsreader. What happens, however, if you would rather use your favorite Internet programs, such as Netscape Navigator and Eudora?

If you use WinCIM 2.5 or CompuServe 3.0 for Windows (or a later version), you can use almost any Winsock-compatible program you want. If you use CompuServe 3.0 for Macintosh, you can use MacTCP-compatible programs. (See Chapter 13 for more information about Winsock and MacTCP programs.)

What if CompuServe doesn't have a local number?

Although CompuServe has a pretty good phone network, it doesn't reach way out into the sticks. If you want access to the superb CompuServe technical information and you live in rural Vermont (as Margy does), you can connect to a local Internet provider and then connect to CompuServe over the Internet.

This method requires two accounts — one with a local Internet provider (with luck, at a flat rate) and one with CompuServe. The second account is an extra cost, but probably not as expensive as hours of long-distance charges!

First connect to your Internet provider. Then configure the CompuServe, WinCIM, or MacCIM program to connect to CompuServe. In CompuServe 3.0 for Windows (running under Windows 95), you choose Access➪Preferences from the CompuServe menu when you aren't connected. Click the Connection tab along the top of the window. Set the Connection Type Winsock setting to Dial-Up Networking. Set the Connect using setting to the dial-up connection you use to connect to the Internet. Then click OK. Now when you connect to CompuServe, rather than dial the phone, your CompuServe program communicates via your existing Internet connection.

Using another Web browser

You can use Netscape, Internet Explorer, or another Web browser with the CompuServe 3.0 for Windows program. To tell CompuServe which Web browser to fire up when you request a Web page:

1. **Choose Access⇨Preferences from the CompuServe program's menu.**

   You see the Preferences menu for the CompuServe program, with tabs along the top of the window.

2. **Click the General tab.**

   You see a bunch of options that include Internet Browser Options. Cool!

3. **Click the box labeled o Use external Internet browser and then click the Select button way over to the right of the window to find the path and filename of the browser program you want to use.**

   Hint: In Windows 95, the Navigator program is usually installed in the C:\Program Files\Netscape\Navigator\Program folder, with the filename netscape.exe.

4. **Click OK.**

Using another e-mail program

During the first half of 1997, CompuServe is scheduled to install a POP server, a program that can deliver your mail to popular mail programs, such as Eudora, Netscape Mail, and Microsoft Internet Mail. Check with CompuServe if you want to use one of these e-mail programs to read and send mail. You need to know the Internet host name of the computer on which CompuServe runs its POP server; it's probably something like pop.compuserve.com or mail.compuserve.com. Check with the CompuServe support folks for the correct name of its POP server, and then configure your e-mail program to use it.

Using another newsreader

The CompuServe newsreader has a few nice features, such as its capability to ignore people you don't want to hear from. There are lots of features it doesn't have, however, and its text-based windows look old-fashioned.

If these shortcomings bother you, you can use any Winsock or MacTCP-compatible newsreader to read your Usenet newsgroups, such as Netscape, Microsoft Internet News, or Free Agent. Just configure your newsreader to use news.compuserve.com as its NNTP server; that is, when your newsreader wants to retrieve articles, tell it to ask `news.compuserve.com` for them. Don't set a username or password in the news program; you have already logged in to CompuServe and don't need any additional ID.

Using other Internet programs

You can also use other Winsock or MacTCP-compatible programs with CompuServe 3.0 for Windows or Macintosh. For example, go ahead and use WS_FTP or Fetch for file transfer (see Chapter 12 for a description of FTP).

Although it's convenient to use your CompuServe account as a PPP account, it's not cheap — it can cost as much as $3 an hour, depending on how many hours you use. If you spend a great deal of time using CompuServe as a PPP account, it would be cheaper to get a real PPP account with an Internet provider.

For More Information

You can get lots of help with CompuServe from CompuServe itself:

- ✔ For help in using CompuServe and to find out about upgrades to the software, go to Member Services (service name HELP).

- ✔ To find out how much you're shelling out for CompuServe, go to service name BILLING. This is also the place to change the way to pay for the service, change your password, or cancel your account.

- ✔ For information about getting started with CompuServe, go to the New Member Welcome Center (service name WELCOME).

- ✔ For finding out someone's CompuServe ID, go to the Member Directory (service name DIRECTORY).

- ✔ For help with using the Internet, go to the INTERNET or INETNEW service.

- ✔ If you use WinCIM with Windows 3.1 (because the newer CompuServe Version 3.0 software doesn't run under Windows 3.1), go to the WINCIM service.

See Chapter 22 for other sources of information about CompuServe and the Internet.

Part IV
The Part of Tens

The 5th Wave   By Rich Tennant

"QUICK KIDS! YOUR MOTHER'S FLAMING SOMEONE ON THE INTERNET!"

In this part . . .

Because some things just don't fit anywhere else in the book, they're grouped into lists. By the strangest coincidence, exactly *ten* facts happen to be in each list. (*Note to the literal-minded:* You may have to cut off or glue on some fingers to make your version of ten match up with ours. Perhaps it would be easier just to take our word for it.)

Chapter 16

Ten Frequently Asked Questions

In This Chapter

▶ Answers to some general Internet questions

▶ Answers to some general e-mail questions

*W*e get lots of questions in our e-mail every day. We picked some common questions in the hope that the answers can help you.

It also means that now, whenever someone asks us one of these questions, rather than answer it, we can tell them to get a copy of this book and read the chapter. Heh, heh.

If you have more than ten remaining questions after you read this book, turn to Chapter 22, where we tell you where to find hundreds of answers.

Why Can't You Just Give Me Step-By-Step Instructions?

We get this question by e-mail all the time: Other ...*For Dummies* books include detailed step-by-step instructions, but this book can be frustratingly vague.

Two reasons spring to mind. One is that we don't know which type of computer you use (Windows 3.1, Windows 95, a Mac, or another kind), and we don't know which programs you use (America Online, Netscape, Eudora, or other software). We have tried to give you lots of general background so that you have a good idea about how the Internet works in addition to, wherever possible, specific instructions for the most commonly used systems. Chapter 22 lists books and Web sites with more specific instructions for many systems and programs.

The other reason is that programs change constantly. Since we started revising this edition of the book, for example, companies have released new versions of most of the programs we describe in it. By the time you read this chapter, even newer versions may appear and may work a little differently than we describe. We hope that the general understanding you gain from this book helps you negotiate the inconsistencies you're bound to run into as you learn to use the Net.

Are the Internet and the World Wide Web the Same Thing?

No, the Internet started out in 1969 and is a network of networks. The World Wide Web, born in 1989, is a system of interconnected information that lives on the Internet.

What's the Difference between a Browser and a Search Engine?

A *browser* is the software that lets your computer show you pages on the World Wide Web. A *search engine* (or directory or index) helps you find pages about specific topics of interest to you. Netscape Navigator and Internet Explorer are browsers. AltaVista, Yahoo!, Lycos, Excite, and a host of other search engines can help you find stuff on the Web.

Should I Buy WebTV?

Probably not this year, unless it gets much better. When Carol checked out WebTV in a local department store, she found the experience frustrating and could not recommend that anyone pay money for such a thing. John had somewhat better luck when he saw it demonstrated at a trade show, although not quite enough to recommend that you go out and buy one. The good thing about WebTV is that it does get you on the Net, for $300 plus $20 per month; if you use it much, however, you will soon pine for a real computer with a real screen.

If you do buy WebTV, you can use a cheapo $20 computer store keyboard rather than the more expensive wireless keyboard WebTV offers. Don't try to use it without a keyboard, unless you're the type of person who likes to watch grass grow.

Can I Change My E-Mail Address?

It depends. (Don't you hate it when we say that?)

On most systems, you can't just change your e-mail address. Your e-mail address is usually just your username on your provider's system. Most Internet providers let you choose any username you want, as long as it's not already taken. If you want to be called SnickerDoodles, your e-mail address will be something like snickerdoodles@furdle.net, and that's okay with them.

Later, when it occurs to you that you will have a great deal of explaining to do if you put SnickerDoodles on your business card, you may want to change your mail address. If you're using a small, local provider, you can probably call up and ask politely, and the company will grumble and change the name. If they don't, or if you like being SnickerDoodles to your friends, you can usually get a mail alias.

No law says that each address corresponds to exactly one mailbox, and it's common to have several mail addresses that put all the mail in one mailbox. Although John's true mailbox name is john1, for example, mail addressed to john, john1, jlevine, and a couple of other misspellings all are aliased to john1 so that the mail is delivered automatically. (Because he's the system manager, he can have all the aliases — nicknames — he wants.)

Ask your provider whether it will give you a mail alias. Most will — it's just a line in a file full of mailing addresses. After the provider does that, you can set your return address (in Eudora, for example) to the alias so that your address is, as far as anyone can tell, your new alias.

CompuServe and Prodigy Classic assign you an arbitrary username, which is, by default, your mail address. Both let you get a reasonable mail alias as well; call your provider and ask how you do it.

If your provider can't or won't give you a mail alias, you can check out some third-party e-mail alias services. One is PoBox, which likens itself to a post-office-box service. It gives you, for a modest fee, any addresses you want at pobox.com, which it then forwards to your true mail address. Contact PoBox at http://www.pobox.com, or you can send mail to info@pobox.com.

America Online (AOL) is a special case because it lets its users change their e-mail addresses with wild abandon at a moment's notice. When you sign up for AOL, you choose a screen name, which is your username and e-mail address. Each AOL user can choose as many as four extra screen names, ostensibly for other family members, and can change them at any time.

Although the good news is that AOL users can have any addresses they want (as long as they don't conflict with any of the five million AOL addresses already assigned), the bad news is that it's practically impossible to tell who's sending any particular piece of mail from AOL.

How Can I Get a File from My Word Processor into E-Mail?

It depends. (Oops, we said it again.) It depends in part on what you want to send — just the contents in plain text or in pretty formatted text, or what some people call *rich text*. It depends too on to whom you are sending the file and what they're able to receive.

Everyone can always read plain text, and if that's all that's required, that's pretty easy. Using simple copy and paste commands, either from the Edit menu in your word processor and e-mail programs or by pressing Ctrl+C (⌘+C on the Mac) and Ctrl+V (⌘+V), select and copy the text of the document in your word processor and paste it into your e-mail message.

If both your e-mail program and that of your recipient can handle attachments and your recipient uses the same word-processing software that you do, you can attach the word-processing file to your e-mail message (see Chapter 9 for details).

Is It Safe to Send My Credit Card Number through E-Mail?

Everyone's idea of what is safe is different. Some people say that using a credit card is a lousy idea — period. Others think that the Net is full of people trying to steal credit card numbers and in no case should you ever send your card number across the Net.

Wait a second. Do you ever order anything from a catalog and give your credit card number from your cordless or cellular phone? Have you ever thrown away a receipt from a credit card purchase without shredding it? Have you ever left a restaurant or store with only your receipt, leaving the carbon behind? Yes, although in theory it's possible for some ambitious and highly talented person to grab your account number off the Net, we don't consider credit card transactions on the Net to be any more dangerous than most other credit card transactions. If we were in a mood to steal credit card numbers, we wouldn't waste time on the Net. We would go Dumpster diving. (John notes that, as he writes this, he's wearing a pair of pants he ordered over the Net from a well-known vendor in Dodgeville, Wisconsin, including sending his plastic info over the Net, and lived to tell the tale.)

How Important Is This Internet Stuff?

Darned important. We're here rewriting this same book for the third time in less than four years. We're here to tell you that there's no ignoring it anymore. Yeah, you might get away with not knowing about it for another year; if you're in school, in business, or looking for a job, however, you're doing yourself a big disservice. Learn it now. It's really not that tough.

Who's the Best Internet Provider?

Who's asking the question? What do you mean by "best"? For many people, best means cheapest. Right now, what's cheap are shell accounts and freenets. For people who aren't computer savvy, these accounts might be a difficult place to begin.

What do you plan to do on the Internet? If all you want is e-mail and access to the World Wide Web, almost any account will do, but the price ranges vary widely, and how easy it is to get started may be the deciding factor for you. If you have never, ever used a computer in your life and think that you may get easily frustrated, we recommend choosing a service that's putting a great deal of effort into making your life easier. Depending on where you live, you might not have much of a choice. If you do have a choice, find out how much help is available from your provider. Talking to a service before you begin and asking your online friends how they like its services can give you valuable insight into which service is best for you. These days, the biggest difference between providers isn't technical — it's the level of service — so there's no reason to waste time with one that doesn't understand that.

How Can I Make Money on the Net?

We can't remember exactly how many trillions of dollars of business opportunity the Internet represents according to the people who claim to know about these things. We do see that businesses rely on communication. As a new medium of communication, the doors of the Internet are being flung open for new ways of doing business.

We recommend that, rather than try to figure out how to make money in the Internet business, you spend time getting to know the Net extensively — by checking out newsgroups and mailing lists in addition to exploring the World Wide Web. The more you see, the more you can think about organic ways in which your business can use the Net. Follow your loves: Find newsgroups and mailing lists that excite you. You will meet all kinds of interesting people and get new ideas. We think that what you can learn from the Net can help you find for yourself where your unique opportunities lie.

(We have found that the best way to make money on the Net is to write books about it! Then again, we were writing books when dirt was two days old and have been playing with the Internet for longer than that.)

What Type of Computer Should I Buy to Use the Net?

You can guess what we're going to say, right? We're going to say, "It depends." For many people, the Internet is the first good reason they have for buying a computer. Which type of computer you buy depends on who you are and how you expect to use it.

If you're purchasing a new computer primarily to surf the Net, buy a reasonably fast computer: a Pentium with a color monitor, which costs between $1,000 and $1,500. The World Wide Web is a colorful place; to get the real effect, you have to see it in color.

On the other hand, if you already have a computer, get a modem if you don't already have one (less than $100 in most places), and try it out with what you have. By the time you really get started on the Net, you will have a much better idea about which features are important to you. Not only that, but technology is also constantly changing, and prices tend to go down the longer something is on the market.

Pardon our limited vision, but we tend to talk about only two categories of computers: Macintoshes and IBM PC clones. Which one is for you? Our experience, which includes all the stories we hear from first-time computer users, leads us to conclude the following: Macintoshes are somewhat easier to use, and IBM clones are somewhat cheaper to buy, but either is okay, particularly if you have friends with a similar computer who can help you get started. Here's where you have to assess your own abilities and your own resources and those of people around you. Our advice: Buy what your friends have so that you can ask them for help.

When you're talking to other people and asking them what to buy, talk to people who do the same kinds of things you do, not just people who have computers. If you're a chimney sweep, find out what other sweeps use and like and why. Computers are not fair. They're more difficult to use than they should be. Some are easier to use than others. Life is not fair. Some people can afford to pay more for a machine than others can. Try as best as you can to determine which machine you will like using best — chances are that you can try them out in a computer store. When you evaluate price, try to factor in the value of your own time spent learning how to set up and use a computer and its software and your own nature when it comes to mechanical devices.

Incidentally, if you have some other type of computer, such as an Amiga or other "niche" machine (boy, are we going to hear from Amiga users about that), try to track down a local users' group and find out which type of Internet software is available for your machine. More likely than not, there will be something cheap or free you can use.

How Do I Send E-Mail to Usenet?

You don't. Usenet is one thing, and e-mail is another, even though they both pass messages around the Net. To add to the confusion, some programs (such as Agent and Netscape, which we mention in Chapters 5 and 11) can handle both mail and Usenet news, but underneath they're different. A few systems just provide mail without providing news; if you're on one of them, you're out of luck, news-wise.

Turn to Chapter 11 to read all about Usenet newsgroups, and then, if you're using a commercial provider, look at the chapter in Part III about your Internet provider for the nitty-gritty.

What's Your Favorite Web Page?

WHOOSH

It's `http://net.dummies.net`, of course. We never said we aren't vain. (If you visit there, you find links to some of our other favorite pages, of course.)

Chapter 17
Ten Ways to Find E-Mail Addresses

Where in Cyberspace Is Everyone?

As you probably have figured out, one teensy detail is keeping you from sending e-mail to all your friends: You don't know their addresses. In this chapter, you learn lots of different ways to look for addresses. We save you the trouble of reading the rest of the chapter by starting out with the easiest, most reliable way to find out people's e-mail addresses:

> Call them on the phone and ask them.

Pretty low-tech, huh? For some reason, this seems to be absolutely the last thing people want to do (see the sidebar "Top ten reasons not to call someone to get an e-mail address," later in this chapter). Try it first. If you know or can find out the phone number, it's much easier than any of the other methods.

Search for them on the Web

The world's changing. Perhaps your friend (?) has created a home page. Use your favorite directory or index to search using your friend's name in quotes (" ") as the keyword for your search. If your friend does have a home page, chances are that an e-mail address is somewhere on the page (see Chapter 7).

Whaddaya mean you don't know your own address?

It happens frequently — usually it's because a friend is using a private e-mail system which has a gateway to the outside world that provides instructions for how to send messages to the outside but no hint about how outsiders send stuff in. The solution is, fortunately, usually easy: Tell your friend to send you a message. All messages have return addresses, and all except the absolute cruddiest of mail gateways put on a usable return address. Don't be surprised if the address has a great deal of strange punctuation. After a few gateways, you always seem to end up with things like this:

```
"blurch::John.C.Calhoun"%farp@
slimemail.com
```

If you type the strange address back in, it usually works, so don't worry about it.

You can find out your own address this way by sending a message to our ever vigilant mail robot, at `internet4@dummies.net`, which sends you back a note telling you what the return address in your message was. (Because the human authors see those messages as well, feel free to add a few words telling us whether you like the book and which Internet software you use.)

Hey, Ms. Postmaster

Sometimes you have a pretty good idea what machine someone uses but you don't know the name. In that case, you can try writing to the postmaster. Every *domain,* the part of the address after the at-sign (@), that can receive Internet mail has the e-mail address `post-master`, which contacts someone responsible for that machine. If you're pretty sure that your friend uses `my.bluesuede.org`, you might try asking (politely, of course) `postmaster@my.bluesuede.org` what the address is. (We assume that, for some reason, you can't just call your friend and ask for the e-mail address.)

Most postmasters are overworked system administrators who don't mind an occasional polite question, but you shouldn't expect any big favors. Keep in mind that the larger the mail domain, the less likely it is that the postmaster knows all the users personally. Don't write to `postmaster@ibm.com` to try to find someone's e-mail address at IBM. (For people who want to find correspondents in the Blue Zone, IBM has, fortunately, an online directory — see the sidebar "Okay, how do I find people at big companies?" later in this chapter.)

Postmaster is also the appropriate place to write when you're having trouble with mail to or from a site. If your messages to someone are coming back with a cryptic error message which suggests that the mail system is fouled up or if you're receiving a flood of mechanically generated junk mail from a deranged automatic mail server (see Chapter 10), the postmaster at the relevant site is the one to write.

Top ten reasons not to call someone to get an e-mail address

1. You want to surprise a long-lost friend.

2. You want to surprise a long-lost *ex*-friend who owes you a large amount of money and thinks that he's given you the slip.

3. You or your friend don't speak English. (Actually happens because many Internauts are outside the United States.)

4. You or your friend don't speak at all. (Actually happens — networks offer a uniquely friendly place for most people with handicaps because nobody knows or cares about the handicaps.)

5. It's 3 A.M. and you need to send a message right now or else you will never get to sleep.

6. You don't know the phone number, and, because of an unfortunate childhood experience, you have a deathly fear of calling directory assistance.

7. The phone takes only quarters; nobody around can break your $100 bill.

8. The company installed a new phone system, no one has figured out how to use it, and no matter what you dial, you always end up with Dial-a-Prayer.

9. You inadvertently spilled an entire can of soda into the phone and can't wait for it to dry out to make the call.

10. You called yesterday, didn't write down the answer, and forgot it. Oops.

Search for them in newsgroups

If your friend participates in any newsgroups, you can use AltaVista to search Usenet or check out www.dejanews.com. Remember that although your friend may not use his full name or anything resembling his name, it's worth a try. Again, see Chapter 7 for some hints.

Online Directories

Wouldn't it be cool if some online directory listed everybody's e-mail address? Maybe, but there isn't one. For one thing, nothing says that somebody's e-mail address has any connection to her name. For another, not everybody wants everybody else to know his e-mail address. Although lots of directories in progress are attempting to accumulate e-mail addresses, none is complete, and many work only if people voluntarily list themselves with the service. This situation reiterates, of course, our point that the best way to find someone's e-mail address is to ask. When that's not an option, here are some other routes to try.

Some of the directories you can use to find people provide an e-mail address if it's known. Although we talked about these directories back in Chapter 7, it's worth pointing out which ones purport to find e-mail addresses.

Four11.com

Chapter 7 tells you all about the Four11 directory service. Go to `http://www.four11.com` and try the e-mail search. If you want other people to find you, it's a good place to list yourself.

WhoWhere?

Go to `http://www.whowhere.com`, enter the person's name, and press the WhoWhere search button. Look up yourself, and find your long-lost relatives.

InterNIC

Back in Chapter 7, where we tell you how to find people, we also tell you about InterNIC. The short version is to go to `http://www.internic.net/wp/whois.html`, enter the name in the search string, and press the search button. If you're looking for someone who runs an Internet computer, this is a good place to look.

Online services directories

Both America Online and CompuServe have member directories. If you don't have an account with them but you know someone who does, you might ask your acquaintance to look up someone's address for you.

Alumni directories

Colleges and universities are putting up Web sites to help promote themselves. Many are choosing to put up some sort of alumni directory. Check your alma mater and see whether it has a place for you to list yourself, your e-mail address, or your home page.

Okay, how do I find people at big companies?

We thought that you would never ask. IBM has a mail server that lets you look up people's names. Send to `nic@vnet.ibm.com` a message that contains a line like this:

`whois Watson, T`

It lists any users with e-mail addresses whose names match. Although nearly all IBM employees have internal e-mail addresses, only a fraction can receive mail from the outside, and you can see only those addresses. (Makes sense — no point in telling you about mail addresses you can't use.)

Many other companies have a straightforward addressing system that gives everyone at the company an alias, such as

`Firstname.Lastname`

This technique works at AT&T, so mailing to the following address finds someone reliably:

`Theodore.Vail@att.com`

This technique also works at Sun Microsystems (`sun.com`). It's always worth a try because the worst that can happen is that you get your message back as undeliverable. If several people have the same name, you usually get a mechanical response telling you how to figure out which of them you want and what the correct address is.

KIS

One more address-finding system worth trying is the *knowbot information system,* or *KIS.* It's on the Web at `http://info.cnri.reston.va.us/kis.html`. Type the person's name and as much of the rest of the information as you know. Select the directories you want it to check, and click the Submit Query button. Because knowbot has access to some directories not otherwise easily accessible, including the one for MCI Mail, it's worth checking.

Compatible Mail System — an Oxymoron?

A zillion different networks are spliced into the Internet in one way or another. With many of them, you can barely tell that it's a different network. Because most UNIX systems, for example, have arranged to register standard Internet addresses, you can send mail to them in the same way as you send mail to any other Internet mailbox.

Many other mail systems are also out there, and several of them are in fact connected to the Internet. Because most of the connections seem to have been assembled with spit and baling wire, however, you have to type something strange to get the mail through. In this section, we talk about how to send mail to the most popular systems.

X.400: Just as friendly as it sounds

A great deal of international mail uses this somewhat unpleasant addressing system. If you want to know how this happened, read the following sidebar about the government. Otherwise, we'll just cut to the chase.

We're from the government, and we're here to help you

After the Internet had been around for several years and some types of e-mail had been flowing for much longer than that, the international organization in charge of standards for telephones and stuff like that, known then as the *CCITT* (a French acronym for the International Telephone and Telegraph Consultative Committee), decided that it too was going to get into the e-mail business.

You might think that the obvious thing to do would be to adopt the existing Internet standards because they had been shown to be reliable and robust. (Silly you — that just goes to show that *you* will never get far as an international telecommunications bureaucrat.) The committee decided to come up with *X.400*, something all-new, all-singing, all-dancing, and much, much more complex — as befits the grandeur of the international telecommunications establishment. In all fairness, X.400 does handle a few things that Internet mail (known as *RFC822*, after the document that describes it) doesn't, or at least didn't until recently. X.400 is so complicated, however, that it has taken nearly ten years from the publication of the first version for it to become at all common. Only the most wildly enthusiastic bureaucrats think that X.400 and its ilk will ever replace its Internet equivalents.

Incidentally, because of rumors that non-bureaucrats had begun to figure out who the CCITT was, it was reconstituted as the Telecommunications Branch of the International Telecommunications Union, now known as ITU-T. It's still composed of the same well-paid international bureaucrats in Geneva, Switzerland, who have important meetings, often over an excellent (but rather expensive) lunch eaten at restaurants overlooking beautiful Lac Leman and washed down with excellent (but rather expensive) Swiss regional wine, paid for by the taxpayers of the 100 countries that constitute the ITU, which is in turn a branch of the United Nations. For a more detailed discussion of what life at the ITU is like, see the first few chapters of Carl Malamud's book *Exploring the Internet, a Technical Travelogue,* (Prentice-Hall, 1993), which, after you wade through the network geek parts, is screamingly funny. (True fact: Until recently, the headquarters of the ITU, which has 900 employees charged with coordinating the world's telecommunications and is entitled by treaty to free phone calls anywhere in the world, had only one fax machine.) But we digress.

An X.400 address isn't just a name and a domain: It's a bunch of attributes. Although the official specification goes on for dozens, if not hundreds, of pages, we spare you the detail (which would have been fascinating, you can be sure, if we had had the space) and report on the bare minimum. The attributes that are usually of interest and the codes used to represent them are shown in the following list:

Surname (S): Recipient's last name

Given name (G): Recipient's first name

Initials (I): First or middle initial (or initials)

Generational qualifier (GQ or Q): Jr., III, and so on (these folks think of everything)

Administration Domain Name (ADMD or A): More or less the name of the mail system

Private Domain Name (PRMD or P): More or less the name of a private system reached via a public ADMD

Organization (O): The organization with which the recipient is affiliated, which may or may not have anything to do with the ADMD or PRMD

Country (C): A two-letter country code (see the list at our Web site, at `http://net.dummies.net/countries`)

Domain-Defined Attribute (DD or DDA): Any magic code that identifies the recipient, such as username or account number

You encode these attributes in an address, using / (a slash) to separate them and writing each attribute as the code, an equal sign, and the value. Is that clear? (No? Can't imagine why.)

Here's a concrete example: Suppose that your friend uses the Sprint Sprintmail service (formerly known as Telemail, the ADMD), which has an X.400 connection to the Internet. Your friend's name is Samuel Tilden, he's in the United States, and he's with Tammany Hall. His attributes would be

G: Samuel

S: Tilden

O: TammanyHall

C: US

Because the Internet domain for the gateway is `sprint.com`, the address would be

```
/G=Samuel/S=Tilden/O=TammanyHall/C=US/ADMD=TELEMAIL/
          @sprint.com
```

We're not making up this syntax. Sorry. Notice that a slash appears at the beginning of the address and just before the @. The order of the slash-separated chunks doesn't matter.

Exactly which attributes you need for a particular address varies all over the place. Because some domains connect to only a single country and ADMD, you don't use those attributes with those domains. Others (such as Sprintmail) connect to many, so you need both. It's a mess. You have to find out for each X.400 system which attributes it needs. In theory, redundant attributes shouldn't hurt; in practice, however, who knows?

One minor simplification applies to the hopefully common case in which the only attribute necessary is the recipient's actual name. If the user's name is Rutherford B. Hayes, the full attribute form is

```
/G=Rutherford/I=B/S=Hayes/
```

Instead, you can write

```
Rutherford.B.Hayes
```

Pretty advanced, eh? You can leave out the given name or the initial if you want. Although you can hope that most X.400 addresses can be written this way, you're probably doomed to disappointment.

In most cases, the easiest way to figure out someone's X.400 address is to have your recipient send you a message and see what the From: line says. Failing that, you have to experiment.

X.500: We're from the government, and we're back

An official white pages directory-service model to look up people's e-mail addresses called *X.500* is brought to us by the same people who brought us X.400. Not surprisingly, considering who defined it, X.500 organizes its data like a shelf full of phone books (or, in a large X.500 system, like a library of shelves organized by country). For any particular person, you have to tell X.500 which book or books to look in.

Another true fact: If you're in one country, country A, and you want the phone number of someone in country B, the official ITU-T directory-assistance procedure is to connect you to someone in country A in a room full of old phone books from all over the world, in which they attempt to find the appropriate country B phone book and look up the person. If they can't find the number — because their country B phone books are all 15 years old and your friend moved 12 years ago, for example — tough. The scheme used in the United States in which they connect you to an actual directory operator in country B who is likely to have current phone numbers is in complete violation of standards. We feel that a moment of breathless admiration is appropriate for people who can invent standards like that.

Note: It looks like X.500 will be widely used, for two reasons: It is somewhat more usable than X.400, and no other competing candidates exist. (You get one guess about which is the more important reason.)

You can search a variety of X.500 directories via the World Wide Web. To get started, point your browser at `http://www.hq.nasa.gov/x.500.html`.

A Parade of Mail Systems

This section presents a short (well, *pretty* short) list of major mail and online systems connected to the Internet and instructions for how to send mail to people on that system.

America Online

An AOL user's mail address is the "screen name," usually his full name. To send mail to a user named Aaron Burr, you type

```
aaronburr@aol.com
```

If there are spaces in the screen name, leave them out.

Some AOL users prefer their "stage name," such as `dickhmr@aol.com`. If you can't find your friend on AOL after trying the obvious, call your friend and ask. AOL makes it extremely easy to change your screen name, and a single user can have several screen names, so AOL addresses change frequently.

For more information about using AOL, see Chapter 14.

AT&T Mail

AT&T Mail users have arbitrary usernames. To send mail to a user whose username is `blivet`, type

```
blivet@attmail.com
```

Note: AT&T Mail provides gateways to some companies' internal mail systems. In these cases, you may have an address like this:

```
argle!bargle!google@foocorp.attmail.com
```

BITNET

BITNET is a network of mostly IBM mainframes. Each system name is eight characters long or fewer. System names often contain the letters *VM,* the name of the operating system used on most BITNET sites. Although usernames are arbitrary, they're usually also eight characters or fewer. Because many BITNET sites also have Internet mail domain names, you can send mail to them in the regular Internet way.

If the mailer you use is well configured, it probably has a BITNET support setup to handle BITNET systems not directly on the Internet. You can send mail to `JSMITH` at `XYZVM3,` for example, by typing

```
jsmith@xyzvm3.bitnet
```

Failing that, you have to address mail directly to a BITNET gateway. Here are addresses using two gateways that tolerate outsiders' mail:

```
jsmith%xyzvm3.bitnet@mitvma.mit.edu
jsmith%xyzvm3.bitnet@cunyvm.cuny.edu
```

These two gateways are provided by MIT and the City University of New York (CUNY), respectively, as a courtesy to the Net community.

BIX

BIX is a commercial system formerly run by *Byte* magazine and now run by Delphi. Usernames are arbitrary short strings. To mail to user `xxxxx`, type

```
xxxxx@bix.com
```

CompuServe

CompuServe is a large online service. For ancient, historical reasons, CompuServe usernames are pairs of *octal* (base eight) numbers, usually beginning with the digit 7 for users in the United States and 10 for users overseas. If a user's number is 712345,6701, the address is

```
712345.6701@compuserve.com
```

Note: The address uses a *period,* not a comma, because Internet addresses cannot contain commas. Although some users now also have regular-looking addresses, such as johnsmith@compuserve.com, their old numeric addresses still work too.

Because CompuServe used to charge its users for *incoming* Internet mail, many users have set their accounts to refuse mail from the Net.

To find out how to use CompuServe to use Internet services, see Chapter 15.

Delphi

Delphi is an online service from the same people who run BIX, although the services are separate. (Rupert Murdoch, the media baron, bought both of them, and Delphi is being merged into the MCI Internet service.) Delphi usernames are arbitrary strings, most often the first initial and last name of the user. To send to user support, you type

```
support@delphi.com
```

Easylink

Easylink is a messaging service formerly run by Western Union and now run by AT&T. Users have seven-digit numbers beginning with 62. To mail to user 6231416, type

```
6231416@eln.attmail.com
```

FIDONET

FIDONET is a very large, worldwide BBS network. On FIDONET, people are identified by their names, and each individual BBS (called a *node*) has a three- or four-part number in the form 1:2/3 or 1:2/3.4. To send a message to Grover Cleveland at node 1:2/3.4, type

```
grover.cleveland@p4.f3.n2.z1.fidonet.org
```

If a node has a three-part name, such as 1:2/3, type

```
grover.cleveland@f3.n2.z1.fidonet.org
```

Note: Many FIDO systems no longer accept incoming Internet mail because of the recent glut of junk e-mail. Too bad.

GEnie

GEnie is an online service formerly run by General Electric, originally the consumer end of the GE commercial online service, which dates back to the 1960s. Each user has a username, which is an arbitrary and totally un-memorable string, and a mail name, which is usually related to the user's name. You have to know a user's mail name, something like J.SMITH7:

```
J.SMITH7@genie.geis.com
```

MCI Mail

MCI Mail is a large, commercial e-mail system. Each user has a seven-digit user number guaranteed to be unique and a username that may or may not be unique. You can send mail to the number or the username or the person's actual name, using underscores rather than spaces:

```
1234567@mcimail.com
jsmith@mcimail.com
john_smith@mcimail.com
```

If you send mail to a username or an actual name and the name turns out not to be unique, MCI Mail thoughtfully sends you a response listing the possible matches so that you can send your message again to the unique user number. Although MCI user numbers are sometimes written with a hyphen, like a phone number, you don't have to use the hyphen in your address.

Microsoft Network (MSN)

Microsoft Network is a commercial online service run by the software giant Microsoft. You have to use Windows 95 to connect to MSN. It's described briefly in Chapter 13.

If your account name is Bill Gates (for example), your Internet e-mail address is

```
BillGates@msn.com
```

Prodigy

Prodigy is a large online system that lost many millions of dollars while it was run by IBM and Sears. They sold it in 1996, so now it's losing someone else's money.

Prodigy is now two almost unrelated services. Prodigy Classic, which lives at `prodigy.com`, gives users arbitrary usernames like KS8GN3. Send mail to them at

```
KS8GN3@prodigy.com
```

Prodigy Internet, at `prodigy.net`, is a conventional Internet provider. If a user's name is `jqadams`, the address is

```
jqadams@prodigy.net
```

Sprintmail (Telemail)

The Sprintmail e-mail system is provided by Sprintnet. Sprintmail used to be called Telemail because Sprintnet used to be called Telenet before Sprint bought it. (It was a technological spinoff of the original ARPANET project that led to the Internet.) Sprintmail is the major X.400 mail system in the United States. As mentioned earlier, in the section that disparages X.400, to send a message to a user named Samuel Tilden who is with Tammany Hall in the United States, you type

```
/G=Samuel/S=Tilden/O=TammanyHall/C=US/ADMD=TELEMAIL/
              @sprint.com
```

Many corporate and government e-mail systems are attached to Sprintmail. Each has a distinct organization (O=) name and sometimes a private mail domain (PRMD=) name also that have to be entered in the address.

UUCP

UUCP is an old and cruddy mail system still used by many UNIX systems because (how did you guess?) it's free. UUCP addresses consist of a system name and a username, which are both short, arbitrary strings. The system here at Internet For Dummies Central, for example, for historical reasons has a UUCP address — `iecc` — in addition to its normal Internet address, so you could address mail to `iecc!idummies4`. (The ! is pronounced "bang," and this is called a *bang path address*.) Multihop UUCP addresses also exist: `world!iecc!idummies` says to send the message first to the machine called world, which can send it to iecc, where the address is dummies. (Think of it as e-mail's Whisper Down the Lane.) Most often, UUCP addresses are written relative to an Internet host that also talks UUCP, so you could address mail to this address:

```
world!iecc!idummies4@uunet.uu.net
```

(It gets here faster, though, if you send it to internet4@dummies.net because that avoids the UUCP nonsense.) This address means to send the message to uunet.uu.net by using regular Internet mail, and then by UUCP to world, and another UUCP hop to iecc, and from there to the mailbox called idummies. If you think that this is ugly and confusing, you're not alone.

Because UUNET Communications is a large outfit that, among other things, brings e-mail to the UUCP-speaking masses, it's the Internet system most often seen with UUCP addresses. Most UUNET customers also have regular Internet addresses that internally are turned into the ugly UUCP addresses. If you know the Internet address rather than the UUCP address, use it.

Chapter 18

Ten Types of Files and What to Do with Them

*N*ow that you know how to use the Web and FTP and you know how to download, you probably have already retrieved zillions of files (or maybe three or four). When you look at them with your text editor, however, you may notice that they're garbage. In this chapter, we consider the various types of files on the Net, how to tell what they are, and what to do with them.

How Many Kinds of Files Are There?

Hundreds, at least. Fortunately, they fall into five general categories:

- ✔ **Text files:** Files that contain text, believe it or not

- ✔ **Executable files:** Files you can execute, or run; in other words, programs

- ✔ **Compressed files:** Archives, ZIP files, SIT files, and other compressed files

- ✔ **Graphics and video files:** Pictures and moving pictures

- ✔ **Data files:** Any other type of file

Macs are different too

Macintosh files, regardless of what's in them, usually come in two or three chunks, one of which is the data file. You don't see the chunks on your own Macintosh, but you do see them if you try to upload them to a non-Mac server on the Net. In the Macintosh world, the three files are all pieces of one file and are referred to as *forks* — the data fork, the resource fork, and the information fork. When you upload what you think is one file from the Macintosh, it often appears as three separate files with the extensions .data, .resc, and .info appended to the filename. Various schemes exist to glue the forks back together for transportation over the Net, which we discuss later in this chapter.

Just Plain Text

Text files contain readable text. (What did you expect?) Sometimes the text is actually human-readable text, such as the manuscript for this book, which we typed into text files the first time we wrote it. Sometimes the text is source code for computer programs in languages such as *C* or *Pascal*. Occasionally the text is data for programs. PostScript printer data is a particular kind of text file discussed later in this chapter.

On PCs, text files usually have the file extension TXT. You can look at them using Notepad in Windows 3.1, WordPad in Windows 95, or any word-processing program. You can read Macintosh text files with SimpleText or any other word processor.

There isn't much to say about text files — you know them when you see them. As mentioned in Chapter 12, because the way text is stored varies from one system to another, you should FTP text files in ASCII mode to convert them to your local format automatically. That is, if you're using an FTP program, choose the ASCII rather than Binary option when you're downloading; if you're using a Web browser, never mind.

A few text documents are really archives or nontext files in drag. See the discussions of uuencoded files in Chapter 12.

TIP

It's a program that draws a picture

If you encounter a text file that starts out something like the following, you have a PostScript document:

```
%!PS-Adobe-2.0
%%Title: Some Random Document
%%CreationDate: Thu Jul 5 1996
/pl transform 0.1 sub round 0.1
   add exch

 0.1 sub round 0.1 add exch
   itransform bind def
```

A PostScript document is actually a program in the PostScript computer language that describes a document. Unless you're a world-class PostScript weenie, the only sensible thing to do with this type of document is to run the program and see the document. The normal way to do that is to send it to a PostScript printer. PostScript interpreter programs, such as *GNU Ghostscript,* are available that can turn PostScript into other screen and printer formats for users without PostScript printers.

Any Last Requests before We Execute You?

Executable files are actual programs you can run on a computer. Executable programs are particularly common in archives of stuff for PCs and Macs. Some executable programs are also available on the Net for other kinds of computers, such as various workstations. Any single executable file runs on only a particular type of computer: A Mac executable file is useless on a Windows machine and vice versa.

The most commonly found executable programs are for DOS and Windows. These files have filenames such as FOOG.EXE, FOOG.COM, or (sometimes in Windows) FOOG.DLL. You run them in the same way as you run any other DOS or Windows program: Double-click its filename in File Manager in Windows 3.1 or in My Computer or Windows Explorer in Windows 95.

WARNING!

Some chance always exists that any new PC or Mac program may be infected with a computer virus. (Because of the different ways in which the systems work, it's much less likely for UNIX programs to carry viruses.) Stuff from well-run software archives is unlikely to be infected; if you run a random program from a random place, however, you deserve whatever you get.

Executable programs for workstations don't have easily recognizable filenames, although any file whose filename contains a dot is unlikely to be an executable. Even though nearly every kind of workstation runs UNIX, the executables are not interchangeable. Code for a SPARC, for example, doesn't work on an IBM RS/6000 or vice versa. Several different versions of UNIX run on 386 PCs, with different executable formats. Generally, newer versions of PC UNIX run executables from older versions but not vice versa.

Packing It In

A particular software package often requires a bunch of related files. To make it easier to send the package around, the files can be glommed to-gether into a single file known as an *archive.* (Yes, the term archive also refers to a host from which you can FTP stuff. Sorry. In this chapter, at least, archive means *a multifile file.*) After you retrieve an archive, you use an *unarchiving program* to extract the original files.

Some files are also *compressed,* which means that they're encoded in a special way that takes up less space but that can be decoded only by the corresponding *uncompressor.* Most files you retrieve by anonymous FTP are compressed because compressed files use less disk space and take less time to transfer over the Net. In the PC world, archiving and compression usually happen together by using utilities such as WinZip, to create *ZIP files.* In the Mac world, the StuffIt program is very popular. In the workstation world, however, the two procedures — compression and archiving — are usually done separately: The programs *tar* and *cpio* do the archiving, and the programs *compress, pack,* and *gzip* do the compressing.

If you retrieve many files from the Net, you have to learn how to uncompress stuff. The four main compression schemes are

- ✔ ZIP
- ✔ compress
- ✔ gzip
- ✔ StuffIt

ZIPping it up

The most widely used compression and archiving programs for Windows and DOS are the shareware programs WinZip and PKZIP. Zipped files all end with the extension .ZIP.

Windows users all use the excellent shareware WinZip program, mentioned in Chapter 12 and included on the CD-ROM in the back of this book. It not only handles ZIP files but also knows how to extract the contents of most of the other types of compressed files you run into on the Net.

Non-Windows DOS users can use the original shareware PKZIP and PKUNZIP programs to create and extract ZIP files.

Compatible UNIX zipping and unzipping programs called *zip* and *unzip* (the authors are creative programmers but not creative namers) are available at `ftp.uu.net` and elsewhere. For situations in which the shareware nature of PKUNZIP is a problem, a DOS version of UNIX unzip is available, although it's only about half as fast as PKUNZIP.

Many ZIP files you encounter on the Net are *self-extracting,* which means that the ZIP file is packaged with an unzipping program; even if you don't already have an unzipper, you just run the archive and it extracts its contents. (PKZIP and WinZip themselves are distributed in this way.) Because self-extracting archives are programs, they have the extension EXE rather than ZIP. If you *do* have an unzipper already, use it to extract the files; tell it to open the archive in the same way as you would open any other archive. This process ensures that the archive contains what it says it does and also lets you use the WinZip installation-assist feature.

Compression classic

Back in 1975, a programmer named Terry Welch published a paper about a swell new compression scheme he had just invented. A couple of UNIX programmers implemented it as the program *compress,* and it quickly became the standard compression program on UNIX systems. Better compressors are available now, but compress is still the standard.

You can easily recognize a compressed program because its name ends with .Z. On PCs, compressed files often have names ending with Z, such as BLURFLE.TAZ. A UNIX-compatible version of compress is available in the SIMTEL archive (see Chapter 21), in the directory /msdos/compress as COMP430D.ZIP, but it's easier for Windows users to use WinZip.

It's patently obvious

Something that the people who wrote compress didn't realize is that Welch not only published the scheme that compress uses but also patented it. (Two other guys at IBM named Miller and Wegman independently invented the same scheme at the same time and also got a patent on it, something that's not supposed to happen because only the first person to invent something is allowed to patent it. But the patents are definitely there.) UNISYS, which employs Welch, has said from time to time that it might someday begin to collect royalties on compress. It has done so for other things that use the same compression scheme, notably CompuServe GIF files, but never compress itself.

So the Free Software Foundation, which runs the GNU free software project, wrote *gzip,* which uses 100 percent nonpatented algorithms. Files that are gzip-ped use the filename extension .gz and can also be decompressed by WinZip.

Just StuffIt!

The most popular Macintosh compression and archiving program is a shareware program, written by Raymond Lau and known as StuffIt. StuffIt comes in many flavors, including a commercially available version called StuffIt Deluxe. StuffIt files of all varieties generally use the filename extension SIT.

For decompression, you can use the freeware programs UnStuffIt, StuffIt Expander (included on the CD-ROM in the back of this book), or DropStuff with Expander Enhancer, widely available for Macs.

Other archivers

Dozens of other compressing archivers are out there, with names such as LHARC, ZOO, and ARC. DOS and Mac users can find unarchivers for all of them in the SIMTEL repository. The only other one that's widely used is the Japanese LHA because it compresses well and is free. Look for LHA213, the most recent version.

In the Archives

Two different UNIX archive programs are *tar* and *cpio.* They were written at about the same time by people at two different branches of Bell Laboratories in different parts of New Jersey. They both do about the same thing; they're just different.

An important difference between UNIX-type archives and ZIP files is that UNIX archives usually contain subdirectories; ZIP files rarely do. You should always look at a UNIX archive's table of contents (the list of files it contains) before extracting the files so that you know where the files will end up.

The name tar stands for *tape ar*chive. Although tar was designed to put archives of files on old reel-to-reel tapes, it writes to any medium. Files archived by tar usually have the filename extension .tar, and the frequent combination of tar archiving followed by compress compression creates the extension .tar.Z or TAZ. Windows users can, as usual, unscramble either with WinZip.

Cpio files are difficult to handle if you're not running on a UNIX system. If someone gives you one, give it back and ask him to rearchive it in a more tractable format.

For the Artistically Inclined

A large and growing fraction of all the bits flying around the Internet is made up of increasingly high-quality digitized pictures. About 99.44 percent of the pictures are purely for fun, games, and worse. We're sure that you're in the 0.56 percent of users who need the pictures for work, so here's a roundup of picture formats.

The most commonly used graphics formats on the Net are GIF, JPEG, and PNG. You almost never find GIF or JPEG image files compressed or archived. That's because these formats already do a pretty fair job of compression internally, so compress, zip, and the like don't help any.

I could GIF a. . . .

The most widely used format on the Internet is the CompuServe *GIF* (Graphics Interchange Format). The GIF format is well-matched to the capabilities of the typical PC computer screen — no more than 256 different colors in a picture and usually 640 x 480, 1024 x 768, or some other familiar PC screen resolution. Two versions of GIF exist: *GIF87* and *GIF89*. The differences are small enough that nearly every program that can read GIF can read either version equally well. Because GIF is well standardized, you never have problems with files written by one program being unreadable by another.

Dozens of commercial and shareware programs on PCs and Macs can read and write GIF files. The CD-ROM in this book includes Paint Shop Pro (Windows) and Graphic Converter (Mac).

PNG-a-ding

GIF files use the same patented compression as the UNIX compress program, and in 1995 UNISYS began collecting royalties from CompuServe and anyone else it could find who sells software that uses the patented technique. As a result, a group of Net graphics users came up with a patent-free replacement for GIF called PNG. We expect to see GIF fade away over the next year or two and PNG replace it. PNG handles the same kinds of images that GIF does, and most programs that can handle GIF are being updated for PNG.

The eyes have it

A few years back, a bunch of digital photography experts got together and decided that a.) it was time to have an official standard format for digitized photographs and b.) none of the existing formats was good enough. So they formed the Joint Photographic Experts Group (JPEG), and, after extended negotiation, the JPEG format was born. JPEG is designed specifically to store digitized, full-color or black-and-white photographs, not computer-generated cartoons or anything else. As a result, JPEG does a fantastic job of storing photos and a lousy job of storing anything else.

A JPEG version of a photo is about one-fourth the size of the corresponding GIF file. (JPEG files can be *any* size because the format allows a trade-off between size versus quality when the file is created.) The main disadvantage of JPEG is that it's considerably slower to decode than GIF, but the files are so much smaller that it's worth it. Most programs that can display GIF files now also handle JPEG. JPEG files usually have filenames with the extension .jpeg or .jpg.

The claim occasionally has been made that JPEG pictures don't look anywhere near as good as GIF pictures do. What is true is that if you take a full-color photograph and make a 256-color GIF file and then translate that GIF file into a JPEG file, it doesn't look good. So don't do that. For the finest in photographic quality, however, demand full-color JPEGs.

A trip to the movies

As networks get faster and disks get bigger, people are starting to store entire digitized movies (still rather *short* ones at this point). The standard movie format is called Motion Picture Experts Group (MPEG). MPEG was designed by a committee down the hall from the JPEG committee and — practically unprecedented in the history of standards efforts — was actually designed based on earlier work.

MPEG viewers are found in the same places as JPEG viewers. You need a reasonably fast workstation or a top-of-the-line power-user PC to display MPEG movies in anything like real time.

A few other competing movie formats are also used, notably Shockwave and Apple QuickTime, that appear on Web pages. You can get Web browser plug-ins that run the movies for you, as mentioned in Chapter 21.

Let a hundred formats blossom

Many other graphics-file formats are in use, although GIF and JPEG are by far the most popular ones on the Internet. Other formats you run into include the following:

✔ **PCX:** This DOS format is used by many paint programs — it's also okay for low-resolution photos.

✔ **TIFF:** This enormously complicated format has hundreds of options — so many that a TIFF file written by one program often can't be read by another.

✔ **TARGA:** (Called TGA on PCs.) This is the most common format for scanned, full-color photos. In Internet archives, TARGA is now supplanted by the much more compact JPEG.

✔ **PICT:** This format is common on Macintoshes because the Mac has built-in support for it.

✔ **BMP:** This Windows bitmap format is not used much on the Net because BMP files tend to be larger than they need to be.

A few words from the vice squad

We bet you're wondering whether any public online archives contain, er, exotic photography but you're too embarrassed to ask. Well, we'll tell you — they don't. Nothing in any public FTP archive is any raunchier than fashion photos from *Redbook* or *Sports Illustrated*.

That's for two reasons. One is political. The companies and universities that fund most of the sites on the Internet are not interested in being accused of being pornographers or in filling up their expensive disks with pictures that have nothing to do with any legitimate work. (At one university archive, when the *Playboy* pictures went away, they were replaced by a note which said that if you could explain why you needed them for your academic research, they would put them back.)

The other reason is practical. From time to time someone makes his (almost always *his,* by the way) private collection of R- or X-rated pictures available for anonymous FTP. Within five minutes, a thousand sweaty-palmed undergraduates try to FTP in, and that corner of the Internet grinds to a halt. After another five minutes, out of sheer self-preservation, the pictures go away. (If you don't believe us, see *Sex For Dummies* (published by IDG Books Worldwide, Inc.), in which Dr. Ruth Westheimer says the same thing.)

If someone you know is in desperate need of such works of art (not you, of course, but, er, someone down the hall needs it for sociology research — that's it), you might direct him to the Usenet group `alt.binaries.pictures.erotica`. The last time we looked there for *our* sociology research, however, we found that the pictures are largely gone and that what's there now are ads for paid-access WWW sites. He might also look at the free sites `www.playboy.com` and `www.penthousemag.com`, which usually contain a few of the milder pictures from the current issues of the magazines.

Plenty of sites on the Web *will* show you porn if you give them a credit card number to pay for it. We're cheap, so we have never looked to see what they offer.

None of the Above

Another type of information that files can contain is sound, such as clips from radio shows. Sound files tend to have the filename extensions WAV, AU, or AIF. MPLAYER, which comes with Windows 3.1, can play WAV files. You can download sound players from many online software archives, as mentioned in Chapter 21. The latest Web browsers have built-in sound players too.

You also occasionally find formatted word-processor files to be used with programs such as WordPerfect and Microsoft Word. If you encounter one of these files and don't have access to the matching word-processor program, you can usually load them into a text editor where you see the text in the file intermingled with nonprinting junk that represents formatting information. In a pinch, you can edit out the junk to recover the text. Before you resort to that method, however, try loading them with whatever word processor you have. A great deal of word-processing software can recognize a competitor's format and makes a valiant effort to convert it to something usable by you so that you aren't tempted to buy the other product. For the particular case of Microsoft Word, the company gives away a free program for Windows that displays and prints Word documents. It's at

```
http://www.microsoft.com/word/Internet/Viewer/
```

The most commonly used text-processing program on the Net remains the elderly but serviceable TeX. It takes as its input plain text files with formatting commands in text form, something like this:

```
\begin{quote}
Your mother wears army boots.
\end{quote}
```

If you want to know more about TeX, see the Usenet newsgroup `comp.text.tex`. Free versions of TeX are available for most computers, described in a monthly posting on the newsgroup. Another, even more elderly, text processor called troff (pronounced "tee-roff," and we used it to write the first edition of this book, so don't make too many smart-alecky comments) is also in moderately wide use, and free versions of troff are available as well. For details, read the FAQ posted to `comp.text.troff`.

Chapter 19

Ten Ways to Avoid Looking Like a Klutz

. . . .

In This Chapter

▶ Tips for suave, sophisticated Net usage

▶ Some bonehead moves not to make

. . . .

*G*osh, using the Internet is exciting. And gosh, it offers many ways to make a fool of yourself — heaven forbid that you should act like a *clueless newbie*. We round up the usual suspects of unfortunate moves so that you can be the coolest Web surfer on your block.

Read before You Write

The moment you get your new Internet account, you may have an overwhelming urge to begin sending out lots of messages right away. *Don't do it!*

Read Usenet newsgroups, mailing lists, Web pages, and other Net resources for a while before you send anything out. You will be able to figure out where best to send your messages, which makes it both more likely that you will contact people who are interested in what you say and less likely that you will annoy people by bothering them with irrelevancies because you sent something to an inappropriate place.

Particularly if you're going to ask a question, look for a Usenet newsgroup (see Chapter 11) related to your question and see whether it has a Frequently Asked Questions (FAQ) posting that answers it. Although you might think that this advice is obvious, we can report from experience that it's not: On the Usenet group that John moderates (a technoid one called `comp.compilers`), he gets at least two messages a day from clueless newbies asking the same old questions that have been in the FAQ for the past five years. Don't let yourself be one of them.

Netiquette Matters

On the Net, you are what you type. The messages you send are the only way that 99 percent of the people you meet on the Net will know you.

Speling counts

Many Net users feel that because Net messages are short and informal, spelling and grammar don't count. Some even think that strange spelling makes them K00L D00DZ. If you feel that wey, theirs' not much wee can do abowt it. We think that sending out a sloppy, misspelled message is similar to showing up at a party with big grease stains on your shirt — although your friends will know that it's you, people who don't know you will tend to conclude that you don't know how to dress yourself.

Many mail programs have spell checkers. Eudora Pro (the commercial version of Eudora) checks your spelling after you click the dictionary icon (the one with the letter *A*) on the toolbar; in Netscape 4.0, which also comes with a spell checker, you choose Tools➪Check Spelling from the menu. In Pine, you check your spelling by pressing Ctrl+T. Although spell checkers aren't perfect, at least they ensure that your messages consist of 100 percent genuine words.

DON'T SEND YOUR ENTIRE MESSAGE IN CAPITAL LETTERS. It comes across as shouting and is likely to get you some snappy comments suggesting that you do something about the stuck Shift key on your keyboard. Computer keyboards have handled lowercase since about 1970, so avail yourself of this modern technical marvel and aid to literate writing.

now and then we get mail from someone who says "i dont like to use capital letters or punctuation its too much work." Uh-huh.

If you don't have anything to say, don't say it

Avoid trying to sound smart. When you do, the result is usually its opposite. One of the stupidest things we have seen was on the mailing list TRAVEL-L. Someone posted a legitimate request for information about some travel destination. Then came the edifying comment "Sorry, Bud, Can't Help You." We would have thought that people who don't know anything could keep their mouth shut, but apparently we were wrong. Each message you post to a list goes to the entire list. Each list member is there on a voluntary basis. If other members are like us, they often have conflicts about mailing-list subscriptions. Does the good content of the list outweigh the noise and inanity? The more inanity flourishes, the more sensible subscribers will unsubscribe and the list itself will deteriorate. This entire issue is of major concern to the Usenet community, which has been opened to millions and millions of new users. If you're going to participate, find a constructive way to do so.

Keep your hands to yourself

Another stupidity we witnessed involved someone subscribing his arch-enemy to a list against his wishes. Okay, folks. This is not kindergarten. When you start to abuse public lists, they go private. Lists that are unmoderated turn moderated. Moderated lists become "by invitation only." Look around; although some lists thrive on juvenile behavior, it's not the norm, and it's not welcome on most lists.

Subscription inscription (and defection)

Signing up for a mailing list is a cool thing. We tell you all about how to do it in Chapter 10. Still, however, or maybe this is just for people who aren't reading our book, one of the most common ways of looking like a klutz is to send to the list itself a message asking to be added to or taken off a list, where all the people on the list can read it but it doesn't actually get the sender subscribed or taken off. Subscribe and unsubscribe requests go to the list server program in a particular format or, in the case of lists that are not automated, to the list owner. Read Chapter 10 carefully please, lest you be the next person impressing every list member with your newbieness.

Read the rules

When you first subscribe to a mailing list, you usually get back a long message about how this particular list operates and how to unsubscribe if you want. Read this message. Save this message. Before you go telling other people on the list how to behave, read the rules again. Some officious newbie, newly subscribed to JAZZ-L, began flaming the list about the off-topic threads. JAZZ-L encourages this kind of discussion — it says so right in the introduction to the list. Can't say as how she made herself real welcome with that move.

Edit yourself

When you're posting to a Usenet group or mailing list, remember that your audience is the entire world, made up of people of all races, speaking different languages and representing different cultures. Work hard to represent yourself and your culture well. Avoid name-calling and disparaging comments about other peoples and places. It's all too easy to be misunderstood. Read several times through whatever you intend to post before you send it. We have seen inadvertent typos change the intended meaning of a message to its complete opposite.

Discretion is the better part

Sooner or later you will see something that cries out for a cheap shot. Sooner or later someone will send you something you shouldn't have seen and you're going to want to pass it on. Don't do it. Resist cheap shots and proliferating malice. The Net has plenty of jerks — don't be another one. (See the suggestion later in this chapter about what to do when you're tempted to flame.)

Keep it private

Okay, someone makes a mistake, such as sending to the entire mailing list a message that says "subscribe" or posting a message that says "Gee, I don't know!" in response to a request for help on a newsgroup. Yes, it's true, someone made a dumb move, but don't compound it by posting additional messages complaining about it. Either a.) delete the message and forget about it or b.) respond privately, by e-mail addressed to the person only, not to the mailing list. The entire mailing list or newsgroup probably doesn't want to hear your advice to the person who blew it.

For example, you could send a private e-mail message saying, "In the future, send subscription and unsubscription messages to `eggplants-request`, not to `eggplants`, okay?" or "This is a list for discussing domestic laying hens, so could you post your message about cats somewhere else?"

Signing off

All mail programs let you have a *signature,* a file that gets added to the end of each mail or news message you send. It's supposed to contain something to identify you. It quickly became common to put in a snappy quote, to add that personal touch. Here's John's signature, for example:

```
Regards,
John R. Levine, Trumansburg NY, http://net.dummies.net
Primary perpetrator of "The Internet for Dummies"
and Information Superhighwayman wanna-be
```

Some people's signatures get way out of hand, going on for 100 lines of "ASCII art," long quotations, extensive disclaimers, and other allegedly interesting stuff. Although this type of signature may seem cute the first time or two, it quickly gets tedious and marks you as a total newbie.

Keep your signature to four lines or fewer. All the experienced Net users do. If you want to see some examples of truly absurd signatures, visit the Usenet newsgroup alt.fan.warlord, named after the Warlord of the West, possessor of one of the most excessive signatures of all time.

Flame Off!

For some reason, it's easy to get VERY, VERY UPSET ABOUT SOMETHING SOMEONE SAYS ON THE NET. (See, it even happens to us.) Sometimes it's a Usenet posting with which you strongly disagree, sometimes it's something you find on the Web, and sometimes it's personal e-mail. You will be tempted to shoot a message right back telling that person what a doofus he is. Guess what? He will almost certainly shoot back. This type of overstated outrage is so common that it has its own name: *flaming.* Although now and then it's fun (if you're certain that the recipient will take it in good humor), it's always unnecessary. For one thing, e-mail messages always come across as crabbier than the author intended, and for another, crabbing back is hardly going to make the person more reasonable.

A technique we often find helpful is to write the strongest, crabbiest response possible, full of biting wit and skewering each point in turn. Then we throw it away rather than send it.

Spam, Chain Letters, and Other Antisocial Mail

Although we mention this in Chapters 8 and 10, it's worth mentioning again: There are a few kinds of messages you should never, ever, send. Most are not illegal (at least not in most places), but you will quickly find your mailbox filled with displeased responses, and your provider will soon cancel your account.

The chain gang

It's easy to send a chain letter on the Net: Just hit the Forward button, type a few names, and send it off. It's a lousy idea. We have never, ever, gotten a chain letter that was worth passing along. A bunch of classic chain letters have been circulating around the Net for a decade (Chapter 9 has details about the boy who doesn't want cards, the phantom good-times virus, the nonexistent modem tax, the overpriced recipe that isn't, and a way that you won't make money fast). Regardless of where they come from, please just throw them away.

Some of the online chain letters started as paper letters. We once got a paper version of the "Make Money Fast" chain letter from, of all places, Guam. We did the same thing with it that we do with computer chain letters — into the trash.

Spammity-spam, horrible spam

One of the least pleasant Usenet innovations in recent years is *spamming,* or sending lots and lots of copies of a message — usually selling something that was pretty dubious in the first place — to as many e-mail addresses or Usenet groups as possible. It's annoying, and in many cases the spammer is liable for her provider's expenses in cleaning it up. It's also ineffective because automatic systems identify and cancel most spams within minutes after they occur. For more about this topic, see the sidebar "Spam wars" in Chapter 11.

Don't Be a Pig

Unbelievable amounts of material are on the Net: programs, documents, pictures, megabyte after megabyte of swell stuff — all free for the taking. You could download it all. Don't. Go ahead and take whatever you're likely to use — just don't download entire directories full of stuff "just in case."

Your Internet provider sets its charges based on the resources a typical user will use. A single user can use a substantial fraction of the provider's Net connection by sucking down files continuously for hours at a time. Providers typically "overcommit" their Net connection by a factor of three or so. That is, if every user tried to transfer data at full speed at the same time, it would require three times as fast a connection as the provider actually has. Because real users transfer for a while and then read what's on their screen for a while, it works out okay to share the connection among all the users.

(The provider is not cheating you when it does this; it's a sensible way to provide access at a reasonable cost. Although you can get guaranteed connection performance if you want it, you will be horrified at the price.) If users begin using several more connections than the provider budgeted for, the prices will go up.

Hang up, already!

This advice applies particularly to providers who offer unlimited connect-time per month. Don't leave your computer connected if you're not using it. Most Net software packages have a time-out feature that hangs up if no data is transferred to or from the Net for a given period. We leave ours set to 15 minutes on our dial-up connections. Otherwise, other users get a busy signal when they try to connect.

Audio and video pigs

Internet Phone and the like present a particular problem on the Net because they put a much, much heavier load on both the local provider and the Net in general than do other Internet services. When you're transferring voice information over the Net, you're pumping data through as fast as your connection will let you. Video connections are even worse: When sites with fast Net connections begin sending video programs around to each other, the entire Net slows down.

For the moment, few enough people are using Internet Phone that it hasn't become a big problem. If it becomes popular enough, providers will have to provide "no phone" and "phone" accounts, with the latter costing much more, to keep reasonable access for all their users.

Cybercafé Etiquette

Cybercafés are new, and our parents never had the opportunity to teach us the ins and outs. As experienced Internet users, however, we have a few tips to help you ease your way into the scene and not embarrass yourself completely.

No gawking over other people's shoulders

Okay, we understand that you're curious — that's why you're here, to find out about this stuff. Great. Cool. Rent some time, and get some help. Don't stand over other people's shoulders reading their screen. It's rude.

Clean up after yourself

Not just the trash around your computer but also the trash you probably left on the computer. It seems that a number of folks aren't aware that most mailer programs keep copies of the messages you send. If you don't want someone to read your mail, make sure that you find the sent-message folder and delete your mail. Then take the next step and empty the trash. We have found all kinds of interesting goodies that we're sure the sender wouldn't have wanted to share.

Some Web Wisdom

Most Internet providers let you put your own private pages up on the World Wide Web. Again, what you put on your Web page is all that most people will know about you, so this section provides a few suggestions.

Small is beautiful, Part I

Most people who look at your Web page are connected by using a dial-up line and a modem, which means that great big pictures take a long time to load. If your home page contains a full-page picture that takes 12 1/2 minutes to load, you might as well have hung out a Keep Out sign. Keep the pictures small enough that the page loads in a reasonable amount of time. If you have a huge picture that you think is wonderful, put a small "thumbnail" version of it on your home page and make it a link to the full picture for people with the time and interest to look at the big version.

Small is beautiful, Part II

Small pages that fit on a screen or two work better than large pages. They're easier to read, and they load faster. If you have 12 screens full of stuff to put on your Web page, break it up into five or six separate pages with links among them. A well-designed set of small pages makes it easier to find stuff than does one big page because the links can direct the readers to what they want to find.

If we want the White House, we know where to find it

No Web page (or set of Web pages, as we just suggested) is complete without some links to the author's other favorite pages. For some reason we can't explain, every new user's Web page seems to have a link to `http://www.whitehouse.gov` and maybe to Yahoo!, Netscape, and a few other sites that every Net user already knows about. Cool Web sites give us links to interesting pages we *don't* already know about.

Let a hundred viewers blossom

Whenever you create a new Web page, look at it with as many Web browsers as possible. Sure, most people use some version of Netscape Navigator or Internet Explorer, but Prodigy and AOL users (close to 10 million possible visitors to your site) use the browsers that come with those services, and users with dial-up shell connections use the text-only browser Lynx. Take a look at your pages to make sure that they're at least legible regardless of which browser people are using.

Don't be dumb

Don't put information on your Web page that you don't want everyone in the world to know. In particular, you might not want to include your home address and phone number. We know at least one person who received an unexpected phone call from someone she met on the Net and wasn't too pleased about it. Why would Net users need this information, anyway? They can send you e-mail!

Part V
Resource Reference

The 5th Wave   By Rich Tennant

"IT'S JUST UNTIL WE GET BACK UP ON THE INTERNET."

In this part . . .

*N*ow that you're an Internet expert, only one tiny detail remains: How do you get on in the first place? These last three chapters list places that provide access, places that provide software you need to use that access, and, finally, some points of departure for continuing on your Internet journey.

Chapter 20

Finding an Internet Service Provider

. . . .

In This Chapter

▶ How to find a provider

▶ A bunch of places that can provide Internet access

▶ Some places that can even provide access for free

. . . .

Gimme Gimme

All this talk about the Internet is well and good, but it's sort of like sitting by the edge of the pool and thinking, "Wouldn't it be nice to know how to swim?" To learn about the Internet, you have to dive in.

Consider (as best you can, given what we have told you so far) whether you want to connect to the Internet through a commercial online service, such as America Online or CompuServe, or whether you want a simple Internet service provider. If you have chosen "simple Internet service provider," read on. If you have chosen a commercial online service, turn back to your provider's chapter in Part III and follow the instructions there. One thing in favor of using a commercial online service is that most of them give you some free time to start with so that you can try before you buy. On the downside, depending on your geography, the closest commercial provider's access number might be a toll call away. If you can find a local Internet provider, you're probably better off, at least costwise.

How to Find a Local Service Provider

An important topic to consider in choosing your provider is the cost of the phone call because calls to online systems tend to be long ones. You want to find, ideally, a provider that has a phone number that's a local call for you — either a direct number or by way of a network such as Tymnet or Sprintnet or the CompuServe network.

A few providers have 800 numbers, but their hourly rates have to be high enough to cover the cost of the 800 call. It's almost invariably cheaper to dial direct and pay for the call yourself than to use an 800 access number; someone has to pay for the 800 call, and that someone is you. Access to an 800 number is attractive to people who travel frequently. (Many local providers have local numbers for day-to-day use and a more expensive 800 number to use while traveling, which is what we use.)

Here are the best ways we know to find a provider close to home:

- ✔ Check the business pages of your local newspaper for advertisements from local-access providers.

- ✔ Ask your public library's research librarian or online services staff.

- ✔ Look in your local yellow pages under "Online service providers."

- ✔ Use a friend's Internet account or a trial account from a commercial provider to access the World Wide Web. Search for "Internet service providers." You will find numerous lists of them that you can then search for something close to home. For an excellent list of providers, grouped by area code, go to `http://thelist.com`.

- ✔ Ask anyone you know who already has access what she's using.

Signing Up

Many dial-in services list two numbers: a voice number and a modem number. If you're new at this (some of us are new at this for *years* — don't take it personally), we think that it's useful to call and talk to the human beings on the other end of the voice line to get their helpful guidance. Talking to a person enables you to ask the questions you have and in many cases goes a long way toward calming the trepidation that often accompanies this step. If you're signing up for a PPP or SLIP account (which the vast majority of new folks should sign up for), talk to your provider about which software you plan to use, or ask what software they can provide you with. If you don't get understandable answers or the person you're talking to sounds like he has better things to do than answer customer questions, look for a different provider.

If you're an old pro or would rather talk to a machine, set up your communications software to dial the modem number and follow the instructions that appear on-screen. If your modem is dialing the correct number but you're not getting anything usable on your screen, try calling the voice line to verify the modem settings and to get any other useful advice from this service you're about to begin paying for. If you *really* don't want to talk to a person, turn to Chapter 22 for hints on where you can find more info about modems.

Sign-up generally involves providing your name, address, and telephone number along with billing information, almost invariably including a credit card number. Access is often granted immediately, or the service may call you on the phone to verify that you are who you said you were.

National Providers

Because we don't have space to list the thousands of Internet providers you can choose from, in this section we focus on national providers in English-speaking countries.

Most providers have software available that includes dial-up software and a Web browser, usually Netscape or Internet Explorer, which they provide for free or as part of a sign-up package.

U.S. providers

AT&T WorldNet Service

Phone:	800-WORLDNE
E-mail:	worldnet@attmail.com
URL:	http://www.att.com/worldnet

Note: Software package included on the CD-ROM in this book.

Concentric Network

Phone:	800-939-4262
URL:	http://www.concentric.net

DELPHI

Phone:	800-695-4005
Modem:	800-695-4002 (for sign-up only, log in as JOINDELPHI; password DUMMIES)
E-mail:	info@delphi.com (automatic response) service@delphi.com (personal response)
URL:	http://www.delphi.com

Note: A free, ten-hour test drive usually is available when you sign up.

IBM Internet Connection

Phone: United States: 800-821-4612   Ireland: 1-800-553175
Canada: 800-821-4612   New Zealand: 0800-801-800
Australia: 1300-307005   South Africa: 011-7001370
Hong Kong: 2515-4511   or 0800-117888
United Kingdom: 0800-963949

URL:	http://www.ibm.net

If you travel internationally, IBM has the most complete set of Internet dial-ins around the world. At the time this chapter was written, U.S.-based customers could call in from cities around the world and pay a monthly fee of less than $20 and no per-hour charge.

MCI Internet Access

Phone:	800-550-0927
URL:	http://www.mci.com/resources/forhome

NETCOM Online Communication Services

Phone:	800-NETCOM1
E-mail:	info@netcom.com
Modem:	Many modem numbers are available. Call for the number nearest you. Free Netcruiser and Netcomplete software are available.

Sprint Internet Passport

Phone:	800-359-3900
URL:	http://www.sprint.com/sip

Canadian providers

IBM Internet Connection

See the "U.S. providers" section, earlier in this chapter.

Internex Online Toronto

Phone:	416-363-8676
E-mail:	vid@io.org
Modem:	416-363-3783 (log in as new)
URL:	http://www.io.org

Sympatico (Bell Canada)

Phone:	800-773-2121
E-mail:	assistance@sympatico.ca
URL:	http://www.sympatico.ca/

Australian providers

access one

Phone:	1800-672-395
E-mail:	info@aone.net.au
URL:	http://www.aone.net.au/

APANA (Australian Public Access Network Association)
Regional contacts for each state and territory.

Phone:	06 282 4328
	08 278 4742 (fax)
	02 9267 0151
	07 3399 9418
	03 6234 3913
	070 51 4110
	09 483 3934 (pager)
	089 72 3030
	03 9650 7862
E-mail:	sydney@apana.org.au
	act@apana.org.au
	adelaide@apana.org.au
	brisbane@apana.org.au
	cairns@apana.org.au
	hobart@apana.org.au
	melbourne@apana.org.au
	nt@apana.org.au
	perth@apana.org.au
	sydney@apana.org.au
URL:	http://www.apana.org.au/

Enternet by connect.com.au

Phone:	1800 681 113
E-mail:	sales@enternet.com.au
URL:	http://www.enternet.com.au

IBM Internet Connection
See the "U.S. providers" section, earlier in this chapter.

OZ e-mail

Phone:	1800 805 874
E-mail:	INFO@ozemail.com.au
URL:	http://www.ozemail.com.au

Irish providers

Cork Internet Services, Ltd.

Phone:	021 277124
E-mail:	info@cis.ie
URL:	http://www.cis.ie/

HomeNet

Phone:	01-6707355
E-mail:	info@Homenet.ie
URL:	http://www.HomeNet.ie/

IBM Internet Connection

See the "U.S. providers" section, earlier in this chapter.

New Zealand providers

IBM Internet Connection

See the "U.S. providers" section, earlier in this chapter.

Internet Company of New Zealand

Phone:	0800 843 638
E-mail:	info@iconz.co.nz
URL:	http://www.iconz.co.nz

Singapore providers

Pacific Internet

Phone:	1800-872-1455
E-mail:	info@pacific.net.sg
URL:	http://www.pacific.net.sg

Singapore Telecom

Phone:	166 (It's the phone company, so it gets to give itself a cool number.)
Fax:	535 8191
E-mail:	sales@singnet.com.sg
URL:	http://www.singnet.com.sg/

South African providers

Commercial Internet Services / Worldnet Africa

Phone:	0800 03 20 00
E-mail:	info@cis.co.za
URL:	http://africa.cis.co.za

IBM Internet Connection

See the "U.S. providers" section, earlier in this chapter.

Internet Africa

Phone:	0800-020-003
E-mail:	info@iafrica.com
URL:	http://www.iafrica.com/iafrica/home.html

U.K. providers

CityScape Internet Services Ltd.

Phone:	01223 566950
E-mail:	sales@cityscape.co.uk
URL:	http://www.cityscape.co.uk

Demon Internet Systems

Phone:	0181-371-1234
E-mail:	sales@demon.net
Modem:	0181-343-4848
URL:	http://www.demon.net

Direct Connection

Phone:	0181-297-2200
E-mail:	sales@dircon.co.uk
URL:	http://www.dircon.co.uk/

IBM Internet Connection

See the "U.S. providers" section, earlier in this chapter.

Total Connectivity Providers Ltd.

Phone:	01703 571300
E-mail:	sales@tcp.co.uk
URL:	http://www.tcp.co.uk

UUNET Pipex

Phone:	0500-474739
E-mail:	sales@dial.pipex.com
URL:	http://worldserver.pipex.com

Win Net

Phone:	0181-930 6688
E-mail:	info@win-uk.net
URL:	http://www.win-uk.net

It's free, but just for e-mail

We know of one free e-mail service in the United States — Juno Online. The service really is free, supported by advertisements that play on-screen while it's uploading and downloading your mail. The mail works, and the ads are not unduly intrusive. The company has local dial-up numbers in most large cities and an 800 number you can use if none of its other numbers is a local call for you.

To get your own copy of the software, call 1-800-654-5866, or, if you already have e-mail access somewhere else, drop these folks a note at `signup@juno.com` with your postal mailing address so that they can send you a sign-up kit.

It's Free!

Four years or so ago, a bunch of civic-minded people at a university in Cleveland got together and created what they called a *freenet*. People in the community use this free system to share information and to take advantage of the Internet. It was quite successful (the Cleveland Freenet now consists of three machines, each supporting many users), and freenets (also called *community networks*) have appeared all over the United States and Canada.

Freenets provide lots of local community information and offer limited Telnet and FTP, which allows general access to libraries and other public-interest kinds of hosts. It's not full Internet access by any means, but it's interesting in its own right. And, after all, it's *free*. Because you can Telnet from one freenet to another, if you can get to one of them, you can get to all of them.

Freenets really are free (except in Los Angeles); to get full access, however, you have to register so that they have some idea of who's using the system. They all allow online registration. Because freenets generally allow incoming Telnet access, if you have Internet access elsewhere, drop into a freenet and look around.

How can freenets really be free?

Most freenets are run by unpaid volunteers who borrow facilities from a local college or university. Many of them have managed to acquire charitable-foundation money too because they're community-based and educational.

Most of them welcome contributions from users, although they aren't pushy about it.

There used to be a coordinating organization for freenets, called NPTN, in Cleveland, home of the first freenet. Unfortunately, it ran out of money and went bust, a chronic problem of freenets. (**Hint:** If you use your freenet and don't make at least a small contribution, you're the reason that they have this problem.)

This small organization coordinates freenets in the United States and has a frequently updated list of freenets on its Web page:

Organization For Community Networks, P.O. Box 32175, Euclid, OH 44132; phone 216-731-9801, fax 216-731-9802; Web site http://www.ofcn.org.

Chapter 21

Sources of Internet Software

● ●

In This Chapter

▶ Software on the CD-ROM in the back of this book

▶ Software to use with commercial online services

▶ Software to connect to PPP and SLIP accounts

▶ Winsock and MacTCP programs you can use with PPP and SLIP accounts and with America Online and CompuServe

▶ Software for UNIX shell accounts

▶ Other useful software

● ●

*W*hen it comes to installing software, there are two kinds of people: those who dislike doing it and those who just plain won't. If you're in the former category, this chapter tells you how to get Internet software to use on your computer, much of it for free.

Much of the software we recommend is already in your hands, on the CD-ROM in the back of this book (this icon tells you which ones). The appendix explains how to install each of these programs from the CD-ROM.

Software for Commercial Online Services

Good news! If you use America Online (AOL) or CompuServe, you get all the software you need for free. If you're like us, you get another disk for your AOL Disk Coaster Set every day or so in the mail.

To install the software, follow the instructions on the label or packaging. To see how to use the AOL and CompuServe software after you have it installed, turn to Chapters 14 and 15.

You can use Winsock or MacTCP programs with America Online and CompuServe; see the sections later in this chapter about Winsock and MacTCP programs.

Connecting to PPP and SLIP Accounts

Although more than a dozen Internet software packages are available, only a few are widely used by individuals. These packages include the TCP/IP stack that lets your computer connect to the Net, an e-mail program, a Usenet newsreader, a Web browser, an FTP program, and maybe some other useful Net programs.

Windows users can mix and match their Internet software packages. Because everyone supports Winsock, you can use any Winsock application with any underlying TCP/IP package and expect it to work. (You may occasionally be disappointed, but our experience has been good.) If you use a Winsock-compatible Internet package, for example, you can run Netscape Navigator rather than the Web browser that comes with the package. Mac users can too — almost all Mac Internet software is compatible with MacTCP. Because no such standard for DOS exists, whatever comes with a particular package is all you can use.

Many Internet applications, such as Eudora and Netscape, have commercial versions that come bundled with a TCP/IP package. Even when you can get the applications for free over the Net, for the modest price they cost it can be worth it to get the whole thing on a few floppies that you can just install and that usually have extra features not in the free version.

This section discusses some programs you need to get your computer connected to your PPP or SLIP account. After you're connected, for software you can use with your PPP or SLIP account, see the sections later in this chapter about Winsock and MacTCP programs.

Trumpet Winsock for Windows 3.1 users

Trumpet Winsock is a Winsock-compatible TCP/IP package for Windows 3.1. Although it comes with a few simple applications, most people just use the basic TCP/IP package to connect to their PPP or SLIP account and add other applications, such as Netscape. Many Internet providers hand out a disk with Trumpet Winsock to their new customers. Remember to send in your fee if you use it because in most cases your provider hasn't paid for the software. The latest version comes with a 30-day evaluation period.

Trumpet Winsock Version 3.0 is on the CD-ROM in the back of this book. To install it, see the appendix.

Microsoft TCP/IP-32 for Windows for Workgroups 3.11

Microsoft gives away a Winsock software package for Windows for Workgroups 3.11 (but *not* for Windows 3.1). You can FTP it from ftp.microsoft.com, in the directory /peropsys/windows/Public/tcpip. For more information, take a look at the index.txt file in the same directory.

Dial-up networking for Windows 95 users

Windows 95 comes with built-in Internet support. You can use the Windows 95 Internet Setup Wizard by clicking the Start button and choosing Programs Accessories Internet Tools Internet Setup Wizard.

MacTCP for Mac users

Nearly every Mac Internet application requires MacTCP, which is included in Mac System 7.5. If you're still running an older version of Mac software, you're best off upgrading to System 7.5 because it offers many other features you might want. If you feel compelled to stick to your current operating system, you can get a copy from the Apple Developer's Catalog (phone 800-282-2732 or 716-871-6555). The TCP/IP Connection for Macintosh is available for $59.

If you already have System 7.5, Apple offers an Internet Connection Kit featuring a great deal of Internet software, including Netscape and Real Audio. It sells for $44.99.

Many universities and large corporations have inexpensive site licenses; check before you shell out the bucks for your own copy. Send e-mail to apda@applelink.apple.com.

Although MacTCP provides the guts of the Internet software, you need an add-on package to handle dial-up PPP or SLIP. Some good programs are shown in this list:

- ✔ **FreePPP:** A great freeware program on the CD-ROM in the back of this book. The appendix explains how to install it.

- ✔ **tcpCONECT4PPP:** Commercial software available from InterCon Systems, at 800-468-7266 or 703-709-5500.

- ✔ **MacPPP:** Commercial software available as part of the Apple Internet Connection Kit.

Winsock Programs for E-Mail, Web Browsing, and More

After you're connected to the Net using a SLIP or PPP account (or CompuServe or America Online), you can use lots of cool Winsock and MacTCP programs. This section lists free, shareware, and commercial packages for DOS, Windows, and the Mac.

Where to get these programs

Many of the programs in this section are on the CD-ROM in the back of this book. All the programs are available for downloading from these Web sites:

- **Forrest Stroud's Consummate Winsock Applications:** This page, at `http://www.stroud.com`, is a large, well-organized set of reviews of Winsock software available over the Net. It has links to all the archives, so you can download with a click or two anything that looks interesting. (Expect a somewhat long wait because some of those suckers are *big.*)

- **The Ultimate Collection Of Windows Software** (TUCOWS, for short): Despite its name, TUCOWS offers Mac programs too. Because TUCOWS, at `http://www.tucows.com`, maintains its own libraries of programs, you're less likely to encounter the Web equivalent of a busy signal.

- **Jumbo!** At `http://www.jumbo.com`, this site includes all types of freeware and shareware programs, not just Internet software. You can download spreadsheet programs, games, programming tools, and other neat stuff. Jumbo! is fun to look around because you can browse through categories of programs.

- **Shareware.com:** This site, at `http://www.shareware.com`, is run by CNET: The Computer Network and features programs from the Virtual Software Library (VSL), a database of more than 160,000 programs. Shareware.com includes all types of programs, including programs for UNIX, the Amiga, and other operating systems. Unlike Jumbo!, you can't browse through the selections; instead, you search for the specific program you want.

Eudora Light and Eudora Pro

Eudora, the most widely used e-mail program, comes in two flavors: Eudora Light (the freeware version) and Eudora Pro (the more powerful commercial version). Both run on Windows 3.1, Windows 95, and the Mac. To find out how to install Eudora Light from the CD-ROM, see the appendix. For more information about using Eudora, see Chapter 8.

You can buy Eudora Pro at most software stores or download it after paying online from the Web sites listed in the section "Where to get these programs," earlier in this chapter. The Eudora home page on the Web is at `http://www.eudora.com`, or call Qualcomm, the company that makes Eudora, at 619-587-1121.

Pegasus Mail

Pegasus Mail is another excellent free e-mail program from New Zealand. You can download it from the Web sites listed in the section "Where to get these programs," earlier in this chapter, or from its main Web site, at `http://www.pegasus.usa.com`.

Internet Mail

Internet Mail is a free e-mail program from Microsoft. It's not so excellent, but it does work. You can download it from the Web sites listed in the section "Where to get these programs," earlier in this chapter, or from the Microsoft home page, at `http://www.microsoft.com`. Chapter 8 tells you how to use it.

Netscape Navigator

Netscape is the most widely used Web browser in existence, and Chapter 5 explains how to use it. If you install the AT&T WorldNet Service software from the CD-ROM, you get a licensed copy of Netscape (unless you choose the Internet Explorer version of the software). You can buy a licensed copy of Netscape, along with a TCP/IP program to connect to the Net, at most software stores. Or you can download it from the Web sites listed in the section "Where to get these programs," earlier in this chapter, or from the Netscape home page, at `http://home.netscape.com`.

Microsoft Internet Explorer

Microsoft wants to knock Netscape out of the Web browser game so as to continue its march toward World Domination. (Who? Us? Opinionated?) Microsoft Internet Explorer is the Web browser it has written to challenge Netscape. If you install the Windows 95 version of the AT&T WorldNet Service software from the CD-ROM, you get a licensed copy of Internet Explorer (unless you choose the Netscape version of the software). You can download it from the Web sites listed in the section "Where to get these programs," earlier in this chapter, or from the Microsoft home page, at `http://www.microsoft.com`. Check out Chapter 5 to see how to use it.

Free Agent

Although Netscape comes with a built-in newsreader and Microsoft gives away the Internet News program, they aren't as powerful as Free Agent, from Forté, Inc. Free Agent, a freeware newsreader, has lots of convenient features, such as kill files that let you ignore articles by jerks or on topics that bore you. Free Agent is on the CD-ROM in the back of this book. The appendix tells you how to install it, and Chapter 11 tells you how to use it.

Internet News

The free Microsoft newsreader is called Internet News, and it's not bad. You can download it from the Web sites listed in the section "Where to get these programs," earlier in this chapter, or from `http://www.microsoft.com`. See Chapter 11 to find out how to use it.

WS_FTP

If you want to upload or download files using FTP, WS_FTP is an excellent choice. WS_FTP LE (Limited Edition) is free, and it's on the CD-ROM in the back of this book. WS_FTP lets you move, rename, delete, and view files on an FTP server too, assuming that you have permission to do so. The appendix tells you how to install WS-FTP; Chapter 12 tells you how to use it.

Netscape plug-ins

Netscape, the world-famous Web browser, lets you extend its capabilities by adding plug-in programs, as described in Chapter 6. You can download Netscape plug-ins from TUCOWS (at `http://www.tucows.com`) or from the Netscape home page (at `http://home.netscape.com`), among other places.

mIRC

If you have an excess of free time and are interested in joining an Internet Relay Chat channel, install mIRC from the CD-ROM in the back of this book. We couldn't fit a chapter about IRC in this book, but you can read about it at our Web site:

```
http://net.dummies.net/irc
```

MacTCP Programs for E-Mail, Web Browsing, and More

MacTCP provides only low-level support and a control panel. If you want to do something, you have to have application programs. Many are freeware or shareware and can be downloaded from the Web or by FTP. Our favorites are on the CD-ROM in the back of this book.

Where to get these programs, Part II

The Web-based software archives at TUCOWS (at http://www.tucows.com) and Shareware.com (at http://www.shareware.com) include Mac software — see the section "Winsock Programs for E-Mail, Web Browsing, and More," earlier in this chapter.

Here are some FTP servers that can provide lots of Mac software if you have access to an FTP program:

- **The Apple Archive:** This is the official Apple archive for free Apple-provided software. Connect to ftp.apple.com.

- **The SUMEX Archive:** Connect to sumex-aim.stanford.edu. Because it's the best-known archive, it's badly overloaded — try others first.

- **The University of Michigan Macintosh Archive:** Connect to mac.archive.umich.edu outside business hours and go to the pub directory. Or connect to the mirrors.aol.com FTP server and go to the pub/mac directory. If you're in Eudora, connect to the ftp.sunet.se FTP server and go to the pub/mac/umich directory. If you're in Asia, connect to the archie.au FTP server and go to the micros/mac/umich directory.

- **The Washington University Archive:** Connect to the FTP server at wuarchive.wustl.edu and move to the mirrors/infomac or mirrors/archive.umich.edu directory.

Eudora Light and Eudora Pro

Mac Eudora is the most widely used mail package, and the Mac version, because it's the original, is even better than the Windows version. Eudora Light is on the CD-ROM in the back of this book. The appendix tells you how to install it; Chapter 8 tells you how to use it. You can buy Eudora Pro at most software stores.

Pegasus Mail

Pegasus Mail is a good e-mail program too, and it's free. Download it from the TUCOWS or Shareware.com Web sites or from `http://www.pegasus.usa.com`.

Internet Mail

Internet Mail is a free e-mail program from Microsoft. You can download it from the TUCOWS or Shareware.com Web sites or from the Microsoft home page, at `http://www.microsoft.com`. See Chapter 8 to find out how to use it.

InterNews

The InterNews shareware program lets you participate in Usenet newsgroups. It's on the CD-ROM in the back of this book; see the appendix to find out how to install it. You can get updated versions from TUCOWS and other sites.

NewsWatcher

NewsWatcher is a freeware Usenet newsreader program, available from the Mac software archives on the Web or by FTP.

Nuntius

Nuntius is another popular Usenet newsreader. You can download it from the TUCOWS or Shareware.com Web sites or download it from most Mac FTP servers.

Internet News

Microsoft Internet News is not bad. You can download it from the TUCOWS or Shareware.com Web sites or from `http://www.microsoft.com`. To find out how to use it, see Chapter 11.

Anarchie

The Anarchie program uploads and downloads files using FTP (see Chapter 12). It's on the CD-ROM in the back of this book; the appendix explains how to install it.

Ircle

If you want to join an Internet Relay Chat channel, install Ircle from the CD-ROM in the back of this book. We couldn't fit a chapter about IRC in this book, but you can read about it at our Web site:

```
http://net.dummies.net/irc.
```

NCSA Telnet

Telnet is a system that lets you log in to computers over the Internet, and the NCSA Telnet program lets you use it. It used to be a popular Internet service, but the Web has largely supplanted it. NCSA Telnet is on the CD-ROM in the back of this book (see the appendix to find out how to install it). For information about using telnet, see our Web page:

```
net.dummies.net/telnet
```

Software for UNIX Shell Accounts

To use a UNIX shell account, all you need is a terminal program. Windows 3.1 comes with Windows Terminal, and we also like ProComm, a commercial terminal program. Windows 95 comes with HyperTerminal. Mac users can get Mac Terminal, Microphone, or something like it. Most modems come with a disk containing a terminal program.

Make sure that your terminal program can do the following:

- Upload and download files by using Xmodem, Zmodem, or Kermit.
- Pretend to be (*emulate*) a VT100 terminal. Lots of UNIX systems like to talk to VT100 terminals. It doesn't matter that none of us has seen an actual VT100 in decades.
- Store the phone number and communications settings of your provider so that you don't have to set them every time.

Other Programs You'll Like

The CD-ROM in the back of this book includes some other programs that are useful for internauts such as yourself.

HotDog and BBEdit Lite

The two programs Hot Dog Web Editor (for Windows) and BBEdit (for the Mac) help you create your own Web pages. The appendix explains how to install these programs, and Chapter 7 tells you how to make Web pages.

WinZip and StuffIt Expander

Chapter 18 describes what to do when you download compressed files. WinZip (for Windows) is our favorite unzipping program. The CD-ROM in the back of this book includes both Windows 95 and Windows 3.1 versions of WinZip, which works beautifully with both the Windows 3.1 Program Manager and Windows 95 Explorer.

For Mac users, we have included StuffIt Expander and DropStuff with Expander Enhancer on the CD-ROM. The appendix tells you how to install them.

Paint Shop Pro and Graphic Converter

If you want to create Web pages, you have to make some graphics to spice them up. If you download pictures from the Web or Usenet newsgroups or receive pictures by e-mail, you will want to look at them. Windows users can install Paint Shop Pro, an excellent shareware graphics program that is on the CD-ROM. Mac users can install Graphic Converter, which also displays graphics. The appendix gives you installation instructions.

ThunderByte Anti-Virus and Disinfectant

If you plan to download software from the Internet, you had better get an antivirus program. Chapter 12 describes viruses, and the CD-ROM in the back of this book contains two programs you can use to protect your computer from them. ThunderByte Anti-Virus runs on both Windows 95 and Windows 3.1. Disinfectant runs on the Mac. The appendix explains how to install them.

Adobe Acrobat Reader

Many programs come with documentation in the form of Acrobat PDF files. To see the document, you need the Acrobat Reader program. Luckily, we include the program for Windows 95, Windows 3.1, and the Mac right on the CD-ROM. The appendix tells you how to install the Acrobat Reader and use it to look at PDF files.

Chapter 22

I Want to Learn More

*T*he Internet is growing so fast that no single human can keep up with it all. This chapter suggests some resources to help keep abreast of what's new.

Our Very Own Web Site and E-Mail Address

One of the hardest parts of this book to keep up-to-date is information about addresses, particularly e-mail addresses and Web sites. Because almost all the information about the Internet is somewhat transitory, we have stuck the more labile information on the Web, where we can change it quickly and where you can continue to find the most up-to-date information we have available.

Here's what we have put up on the site so far:

net.dummies.net/search	Web searching
net.dummies.net/irc	IRC stuff
net.dummies.net/kids	Kids' resources
net.dummies.net/mac	Macintosh info
net.dummies.net/shell	Shell account info
net.dummies.net/countries	Internet access info by country (can you send e-mail to Papua New Guinea?)

`net.dummies.net/lists`	Mailing lists
`net.dummies.net/newsletters`	Electronic newsletters
`net.dummies.net/software`	Internet software

Please send us your suggestions for any great resources you come across in your surfing. Send your ideas to `suggestions@dummies.net`. To comment about this book and verify your e-mail address, send us mail at `internet4@dummies.net`. For a list of our favorite mailing lists, send mail to `lists@dummies.net`.

Books

Lots and lots of great books have been written about specific aspects of the Internet. We even wrote a slew of them ourselves. Rather than plague you throughout the book with constant references to this repertoire, we have listed all the important ones, by topic, for your convenience (all the books in this list are published by IDG Books Worldwide, Inc.):

More about the Internet

MORE Internet For Dummies, 3rd Edition, by John R. Levine and Margaret Levine Young

Internet Secrets, by John R. Levine and Carol Baroudi

Internet FAQs: Answers to the Most Frequently Asked Questions, by Margaret Levine Young and John R. Levine

Dummies 101: The Internet for Windows 95, by Margaret Levine Young and Hy Bender (comes with AT&T WorldNet software and step-by-step instructions for installing the software, signing up for an account, and using the included version of Netscape Navigator)

Creating Web pages and HTML, the Web programming language

HTML For Dummies, 2nd Edition, by Ed Tittel and Steve James

Creating Web Pages For Dummies, by Bud Smith and Arthur Bebak

MORE Internet For Dummies, 2nd Edition, by John R. Levine and Margaret Levine Young

Privacy and security

Internet Secrets, by John R. Levine and Carol Baroudi

E-mail

Internet E-Mail For Dummies, by John R. Levine, Carol Baroudi, Margaret Levine Young, and Arnold Reinhold

Internet Secrets, by John R. Levine and Carol Baroudi

Modems

Modems For Dummies, 2nd Edition, by Tina Rathbone

Help for teachers

The Internet For Teachers, by Bard Williams

UNIX

UNIX For Dummies, 2nd Edition, by John R. Levine and Margaret Levine Young

MORE UNIX For Dummies, by John R. Levine and Margaret Levine Young

Online Services

America Online For Dummies, 2nd Edition, by John Kaufeld

CompuServe For Dummies, by Wallace Wang

Microsoft Network For Dummies, by Doug Lowe

Netscape Navigator

Dummies 101: Netscape Navigator, by Margaret Levine Young and Hy Bender (describes how to browse the Web with Netscape plug-ins and create Web pages with Netscape Navigator Gold)

Publications

Magazines and newsletters abound to track the growth and use of the Net. Two of these publications are available either on paper or in electronic versions over the Net.

*I*way*

I*way is a new, glossy bimonthly aimed at nontechnical Internet users. Look for it on your newsstand, or contact:

I*Way   **Phone:** 800-349-7327
Business Computer Publishing

86 Elm Street
Peterborough, NH 03458

WWW: Connect to http://www.cciweb.com/iway.html.

Internet World

This bimonthly, glossy magazine is for Internet users. Articles include tips, case histories, interviews with notable internauts, and product and service reviews. Contact:

Internet World   **Phone:** 800-573-3062
P.O. Box 713   (United States and Canada)
Mt. Morris, IL 61054   **E-mail:** wsubs@kable.com

WWW: Connect to http://www.mecklerweb.com/mags/iw/iwhome.html.

Matrix News

Matrix News, a monthly newsletter about networks, including but not limited to the Internet, is available on paper or by e-mail. The price is $25 per year delivered online, $30 per year on paper, and $10 less for students. Contact:

Matrix Information   **Phone:** 512-451-7602
  and Directory Services   **E-mail:** mids@tic.com
1106 Clayton Lane
Suite 500W
Austin, TX 78723

Internet Business Report

This newsletter tracks business use of and opportunities on the Internet. It's well focused but expensive. Contact:

Internet Business Report   **Phone:** 800-488-4345
Jupiter Communications   **Fax:** 212-780-6075
627 Broadway
New York, NY 10012

WWW: Connect to http://www.jup.com.

Internet Business Journal

The *Journal* covers business issues on nascent commercial Internet, with case histories, studies, and the like. It's available both online and on paper. Contact:

Michael Strangelove, Publisher **Phone:** 613-747-0642
The Internet/NREN Business Journal **Fax:** 613-564-6641
1-60 Springfield Road **E-mail:** 441495@acadvm1.
Ottawa, Ontario, CANADA, K1M 1C7 uottawa.ca

WWW: Connect to http://www.strangelove.com/ibj/

Inside the Internet

A monthly newsletter with Internet tips and tricks. The price is $69 per year in the United States and $89 per year elsewhere. Contact:

Inside the Internet **Phone:** 800-223-8720
The Cobb Group, Customer Relations or 502-493-3300
9420 Bunsen Parkway, Suite 300 **E-mail:** ineteditor@merlin.
Louisville, KY 40220 cobb.ziff.com

The COOK Report

The COOK Report online newsletter looks at developments on the Internet, particularly political and infrastructure issues and considerable investigative reporting. Individual subscriptions cost $85. Contact:

The COOK Report on Internet **Phone:** 609-882-2572
431 Greenway Avenue **E-mail:** cook@
Ewing, NJ 08618 cookreport.com

WWW: Connect to http://www.netaxs.com/~cook.

Wired

Wired is the trendy, glossy, magazine of the cybergeneration. If you can claw your way though the stupendously ugly graphics at the front, some of the articles are actually interesting. There's also an online version called *HotWired,* which you have to sign up for but is free.

WWW: Connect to http://www.hotwired.com.

Organizations

Each of the organizations in this section also publishes a magazine.

The Internet Society

The Internet Society is dedicated to supporting the growth and evolution of the Internet. It supports the development and evolution of Internet standards to keep the Net working as it grows. The society publishes an interesting glossy magazine and holds conferences, and it has many online resources. Both individual and organizational memberships are available. Contact:

Internet Society
1895 Preston White Drive
Suite 100
Reston, VA 22091

Fax: 703-620-0913
E-mail: membership@isoc.org

WWW: Connect to http://www.isoc.org.

The Electronic Frontier Foundation (EFF)

The EFF works on the electronic frontier with issues of free speech, equitable access, and education in a networked context. It offers legal services in cases in which users' online civil liberties have been violated. It publishes a magazine, has a Usenet group, keeps online files, and maintains human resources. Contact:

Electronic Frontier Foundation
P.O. Box 17
San Francisco, CA 94117

Phone: 415-668-7171
Fax: 415-668-7007
E-mail: ask@eff.org

Usenet: Contact comp.org.eff.news and comp.org.eff.talk.

WWW: Connect to http://www.eff.org.

Appendix

Installing the Programs on the CD-ROM

*I*n this appendix, we tell you how to install and learn about using the programs on the *Internet For Dummies,* Starter Kit Edition, CD-ROM.

We first provide a brief description of each program and then explain how to use the CD-ROM's Installer to copy each program to your hard disk. We also provide details about each program, such as installation and usage tips and pointers for where to get more information.

The program descriptions are organized into two groups: one for Windows 95 and Windows 3.1 software and one for Macintosh software. Within each group, the programs are listed alphabetically.

Here are the Windows 95 and Windows 3.1 programs on the CD-ROM:

- ✔ **Adobe Acrobat Reader:** A free program you can use to view and print Portable Document Format, or *PDF,* files.

- ✔ **AT&T WorldNet Service:** Software that helps you sign up for an Internet account with AT&T WorldNet Service; it includes a free version of Netscape Navigator or Microsoft Internet Explorer.

- ✔ **Eudora Light:** An excellent, free electronic mail program you can use to send and receive e-mail messages over the Internet.

- ✔ **Free Agent:** An excellent, free newsgroup reader (or *newsreader*) program you can use to participate in thousands of online discussions over the Internet.

- ✔ **HotDog:** A shareware program that enables you to create your own World Wide Web pages without requiring you to be an HTML programming whiz.

- ✔ **mIRC:** A shareware Internet Relay Chat, or *IRC,* program you can use to interact live, via your keyboard, with a group of people on the Internet.

- ✔ **NetTerm:** A shareware program that lets you log on to other computers as a terminal via a slightly old-fashioned method called Telnet.

- ✔ **Paint Shop Pro:** A shareware graphics program you can use to view virtually any image you're likely to encounter on the Web. Using this program, you can create and edit images and convert them into different file formats, which is useful if you want to make your own Web pages.

- ✔ **ThunderBYTE Anti-Virus:** A shareware virus-detection tool that helps you safeguard your data from destructive programs.

- ✔ **Trumpet Winsock:** A shareware TCP/IP program that provides the foundation a Windows 3.1 PC needs in order to connect to the Internet. (Windows 95 has built-in TCP/IP software.)

- ✔ **WinZip:** An invaluable shareware decompression utility you can use to make compressed files usable again.

- ✔ **WS_FTP LE:** A free (for noncommercial use) File Transfer Protocol, or *FTP,* program you can use to copy files between your PC and a computer on the Internet.

The Macintosh programs on the CD-ROM are shown in this list:

- ✔ **Adobe Acrobat Reader:** A free program you can use to view and print Portable Document Format, or *PDF,* files.

- ✔ **Anarchie:** A shareware File Transfer Protocol, or *FTP,* program you can use to copy files between your Macintosh and a computer on the Internet.

- ✔ **AT&T WorldNet Service:** Software that helps you sign up for an Internet account with AT&T WorldNet Service; it includes a free version of Netscape Navigator.

- ✔ **BBEdit Lite:** A freeware text editor that enables you to create your own World Wide Web pages using HTML programming.

- ✔ **Disinfectant:** A freeware virus-detection tool that helps you safeguard your data from destructive programs.

- ✔ **DropStuff with Expander Enhancer:** An invaluable shareware decompression utility that allows you to create a StuffIt archive just by dragging and dropping files on its icon. DropStuff also gives the freeware program StuffIt Expander the ability to decompress PC ZIP archives and much more.

- ✔ **Eudora Light:** An excellent free, electronic-mail program you can use to send and receive e-mail messages over the Internet.

- ✔ **FreePPP:** A shareware TCP/IP program that provides the foundation software a Macintosh needs in order to get connected to the Internet.

- ✔ **GraphicConverter:** A shareware graphics program you can use to view virtually any image you're likely to encounter on the Web. Using this program, you can transform images from one file format to another, which is useful if you want to make your own Web pages.

✔ **InterNews:** A shareware newsgroup reader (or *newsreader*) program you can use to participate in thousands of online discussions over the Internet.

✔ **Ircle:** A shareware Internet Relay Chat, or *IRC,* program you can use to interact live, via your keyboard, with a group of people on the Internet.

✔ **NCSA Telnet:** A shareware program that lets you log on to other computers as a terminal via a slightly old-fashioned method called Telnet.

✔ **StuffIt Expander:** A freeware program which opens files that have been compressed in StuffIt archives. It can also decode files sent as BinHex, the Internet file encoding scheme for Macs.

A few words about shareware and freeware: Shareware programs are available to you for an evaluation period (typically anywhere from 30 to 90 days). If you decide that you like a shareware program and want to keep using it, you're expected to send to its author or publisher a registration fee that entitles you to technical support and notifications about new versions. (It also makes you feel good.) Freeware is, well, free for you to use with no obligation.

Because most shareware operates on an honor system, the programs continue working even if you don't register them. It's a good idea, however, to support the shareware concept and encourage the continued production of quality, low-cost software by sending in your payment for the programs you use.

If you don't know the letter of your computer's CD-ROM drive: Most PCs assign the letter D to a CD-ROM drive. Here's how to find out which letter your CD-ROM drive uses:

✔ If you use Windows 95, double-click the My Computer icon on your Windows 95 desktop. A window appears that lists all your drives, including your CD-ROM drive (which is usually represented by a shiny disc icon), and shows you the letter of each drive. When you're done examining the My Computer display, exit by clicking the window's Close button in its upper right corner.

✔ If you use Windows 3.1, double-click the File Manager icon in Program Manager. In the File Manager window, you see a row of disk icons. The CD-ROM drive is the one with the little CD-ROM sticking out of it.

✔ If you use a Macintosh, you don't have to worry: After you place a disc in your CD-ROM drive and close the drive door, an icon representing the disc soon appears on the desktop. Simply double-click the icon named *Internet FD Starter Kit* on your desktop.

Installing the Programs

To install any of the programs from the CD-ROM, follow these steps:

1. **Insert the CD-ROM into your CD-ROM drive. Be careful to touch only the edges of the CD-ROM.**

   If your CD-ROM drive requires a *caddy* (a protective plastic holder), insert the CD-ROM into an empty caddy and then place the caddy in your drive. Otherwise, simply insert the CD-ROM directly into the holder provided by your drive. In either case, be sure to insert the CD-ROM with its printed side up.

2. **If you're using a Macintosh, , an icon representing your CD-ROM drive (most of you will see a CD-shaped icon) appears on the desktop within a minute of inserting the CD-ROM into the drive. Double-click the icon (if necessary) to open a window containing the Installer icon. Double-click on the icon named Internet FD Starter Kit in the window, and then skip to Step 6.**

   If you're using Windows 95, within a minute of inserting the CD-ROM into the drive, the CD-ROM's Installer program should start running automatically and display a license agreement. If this occurs, skip to Step 6.

   If you're using Windows 3.1, click the File menu from the Program Manager and choose the Run option. Similarly, if you're using Windows 95 but the Installer program didn't run automatically, click the Start button (located in the bottom left corner of your screen) and choose the Run option.

3. **In the Run dialog box that appears, type** d:\install **— that is, the letter** *d,* **a colon (:), a backslash (\\), and the letters** *install.* **If your CD-ROM isn't drive D, type the appropriate letter for your drive.**

   If you're not sure which letter to type, see the end of the preceding section.

4. **Press Enter or click OK.**

   A tiny program on the CD kindly creates a program group named IDG Books Worldwide in your Program Manager or Start button, depending on the version of Windows you're using.

5. **Windows 95 users: Click the Start button, and choose Programs⇨IDG Books Worldwide⇨The Internet For Dummies Starter Kit CD to start the Installer program. If you use Windows 3.1, double-click the IDG Books Worldwide icon in Program Manager, and double-click The Internet For Dummies Starter Kit CD icon to start the Installer program.**

The Installer program runs and, within a minute, displays a license agreement.

6. **You should see an IDG Books Worldwide, Inc. license agreement. Read (or at least skim) the agreement to make sure that you're comfortable with its terms. When you're ready, click the Accept button.**

If you don't click Accept, you can't use the Installer program. After you click, an opening screen appears.

7. **Admire the attractive screen (a representation of the cover of this book), and then click anywhere to continue.**

A menu displays three software categories: Connecting, for programs that get you connected to the Net; Communicating, for programs that let you interact on the Net; and Working Offline, for programs that help you deal with files you have downloaded from the Net. This menu, the Installer's *main menu,* is so named because all your other selections stem from this initial menu.

8. **Click a category in which you're interested.**

A submenu displays the particular programs grouped under the category you selected.

9. **Click a program in which you're interested.**

A description of the program appears.

10. **If you want the program copied to your hard disk, click the appropriate Install button at the bottom of the screen. Depending on the program, there may be more than one kind of Install button. (Otherwise, skip to Step 11.)**

After you click Install, installation for the program you selected begins.

11. **To complete the installation of the program, follow the prompts that appear on-screen.**

When the installation is finished, you return to the program's information screen.

Notice that the screen displays, in addition to the Install button, Go Back and Exit buttons.

12. **Click the Go Back button in the bottom left corner to return to previous menus and explore the other contents of the CD-ROM.**

The Go Back button is available on every screen (except the first one), so you can always use it to retrace your steps to the main menu.

13. **When you're done examining all the options you're interested in and installing all the programs you want, click the Exit button.**

The Installer program closes. You can now start using the new software you have installed on your hard disk!

To run the Installer program again in Windows 3.1: If you have exited the Installer program and then want to run it again while the CD-ROM is still in your drive, simply return to Step 6 (assuming that you followed Steps 1 through 5). If you installed icons to your Start menu in Windows 95, you should also follow Step 6.

Alternatively, if you're using Windows 95 and the Installer started up automatically moments after you placed the CD in your CD-ROM drive, you can double-click the My Computer icon on your desktop and then double-click the icon that looks like a shiny CD; or you can just eject the CD-ROM and reinsert it in your CD-ROM drive to make Installer run automatically again.

To examine the contents of the CD-ROM: You can use the *Internet For Dummies* Installer program to install all the software on your CD-ROM. If you're simply curious about the CD-ROM, however, you can examine its contents after you exit the Installer. If you're using Windows 95, open a Windows Explorer window (as opposed to a My Computer window) and double-click the CD-ROM's icon. If you're using Windows 3.1, double-click the CD-ROM icon in File Manager. If you're using a Macintosh, just double-click the CD-ROM icon on the desktop to open a window to show the contents.

Windows 95 and Windows 3.1 Programs

This section describes the programs on the CD-ROM that you can use with Windows 95 and Windows 3.1.

Acrobat Reader for the PC

By using the free program Acrobat Reader 3.0, from Adobe Systems, you can view and print Portable Document Format, or *PDF,* files. The PDF format is used by many programs on the Internet for storing documentation because it supports the use of such stylish elements as assorted fonts and colorful graphics, in contrast to the standard plain-text format that doesn't allow for any special effects in a document.

For example, a manual for the e-mail program Eudora Light is included on the CD-ROM in the EUDLT154 folder. This document is a PDF file and requires you to use the Acrobat Reader program to view or print it.

Installing Acrobat Reader

To install Acrobat Reader, follow these steps:

1. **Follow Steps 1 through 7 in the "Installing the Programs" section, earlier in this appendix.**

   The main menu is displayed.

2. **Click the Working Offline category, click the Acrobat Reader option, and then click the appropriate Install button for your version of Windows.**

   The Acrobat Reader installation program is launched.

3. **Click the Yes button to confirm installation.**

   After some initial data copying, the Adobe Acrobat 3.0 Setup screen appears.

4. **Click the Next button.**

   A license agreement appears.

5. **Read or skim the agreement, and then click the Yes button to accept it.**

   You're told that the software will be installed in a folder named C:\Acrobat3\Reader. If you're comfortable with this folder name and location, skip to Step 7.

6. **To select a different drive or folder name in which to store the software, click the Browse button and use the Choose Directory dialog box that appears. When you're done, click the OK button.**

   The name of the folder you selected is displayed in the dialog box.

7. **Click the Next button.**

   The software is copied to your hard disk. When the installation is completed, a dialog box appears.

8. **Click the Finish button.**

   A text file shows you last-minute technical notes about the program.

9. **Skim the document for anything that might apply to your particular PC system, and then exit the Notepad file and click the OK button that appears.**

   After the installation is complete, you return to the Installer program.

You can now run Acrobat Reader at any time by opening your Windows 95 Acrobat Reader folder (which, if you accepted the Installer's suggestion, is named Acrobat3\Reader) or by opening your Windows 3.1 Acrobat Reader Program Group and double-clicking a program icon named AcroRd32 or Acroread. Alternatively, if you use Windows 95, click the Start button and then choose Programs⇨Adobe Acrobat⇨Adobe Acrobat 3.0.

Reading documents with Acrobat Reader

After you run Acrobat Reader, follow these steps to use it:

1. **Choose File⇨Open from the menu.**

   A dialog box prompts you to choose the PDF file you want to view.

2. **Use the dialog box to select the drive and folder that contain the file you want.**

3. **Scroll through the list of PDF files until the one you want is listed, and then double-click the file's name.**

   For example, if you want to view the manual for Eudora Light, just switch drives in the Open dialog box to your CD-ROM drive, open the EUDLT154 folder, and open the PDF file that appears.

   After you double-click the name of the file you want to view, the document appears in the Acrobat Reader window. Use the VCR-like Forward and Backward buttons on the toolbar near the top of the window to move to the next or preceding page or to the end or beginning of the document.

4. **If you want to print the document you're viewing (which we recommend for long documents), make sure that your printer is turned on and has paper in its paper tray, choose File⇨Print from the menu, and then click OK.**

   The document is printed, making it easier to read.

5. **If you want to open additional documents, repeat Steps 1 through 3.**

   Each document opens in its own window. You can switch to any document by clicking the window it's in or by clicking the Window menu and then clicking the name of the file you want (which is listed near the bottom of the menu).

6. **When you're done using Acrobat Reader, choose File⇨Exit from the menu.**

   All your PDF documents close, and then the Acrobat Reader program exits.

Getting more information about Acrobat Reader

To learn more about using Acrobat Reader, click the Help menu and then the Reader Online Guide option. You can also get more information by visiting the Adobe Systems Web site, at http://www.adobe.com.

AT&T WorldNet ℠ Service

For a monthly charge, the world-class Internet provider AT&T WorldNet Service supplies you with an Internet e-mail account and full access to all Internet features. AT&T WorldNet Service also provides such fine services as free technical support via an 800 number that's available 24 hours a day, seven days a week.

The CD-ROM contains four AT&T WorldNet Service sign-up kits. Three of them — for Windows 95, Windows 3.1, and the Macintosh — include a free, fully registered copy of Netscape Navigator, a powerful program you can use to send and receive e-mail, cruise the World Wide Web, and participate in online discussions via Usenet newsgroups. The fourth kit, also for Windows 95, contains instead a free copy of Microsoft Internet Explorer.

To launch an AT&T WorldNet Service sign-up kit, follow Steps 1 through 7 in the "Installing the Programs" section, earlier in this appendix. When you see the main menu, click the Connecting category, then the AT&T WorldNet Service option, and then the appropriate Install button for both your version of Windows and the program you want to use with it (Netscape Navigator or Internet Explorer). To complete the installation, follow the prompts that appear on-screen.

To use AT&T WorldNet Service, your computer needs a high-speed modem (14,400 bps is the slowest you should use) that can access a local phone line (like the one in your home). AT&T wants you to pay for the use of its services, so have your credit card handy during the installation process.

Near the end of the installation process, you're asked for a registration number. If you use AT&T long distance service in your home, carefully enter this registration code: **L5SQIM631**. If you don't use AT&T for your long-distance calls, please use this registration code: **L5SQIM632**.

Eudora Light

Eudora Light 1.5.4, from Qualcomm, Inc., is a free but powerful electronic-mail program. If you have an Internet e-mail account, you can use Eudora Light to send e-mail to and receive it from any of the tens of millions of other people around the world who are connected to the Net. Because Eudora Light also lets you attach files to e-mail, you can use the program to transmit electronic pictures, sound clips, or any other type of data stored in files.

To install Eudora Light, follow Steps 1 through 7 in the "Installing the Programs" section, earlier in this appendix. When you see the main menu, click the Communicating category, then the Eudora Light option, and then the appropriate Install button for your version of Windows. To complete the installation, follow the prompts that appear on-screen.

To run the program, double-click the Eudora Light icon from its folder or program group. Alternatively, if you use Windows 95, click the Start button and then choose Programs➪Eudora Light.

For information about how to use Eudora Light (and its even more capable commercial version, Eudora Pro), see Chapters 8 and 9 in this book. You can also learn more about Eudora Light by selecting options from its Help menu and by visiting its Web site, at http://www.eudora.com.

Free Agent

When you use the free Windows program Free Agent 1.1 (from Forté, Inc.), you can read and participate in ongoing group discussions that take place over the Internet via Usenet newsgroups. Tens of thousands of newsgroups exist, devoted to virtually every topic under the sun, ranging from knitting to high finance and from decoding DNA to dating, and Free Agent is one of the best programs available for accessing them. Among the great Free Agent features is its capability to let you read newsgroup articles offline, which can save you Internet connection charges and phone charges.

To install Free Agent, follow Steps 1 through 7 in the "Installing the Programs" section, earlier in this appendix. When you see the main menu, click the Communicating category, then the Free Agent option, and then the appropriate Install button for your version of Windows. To complete the installation, follow the prompts that appear on-screen.

To run Free Agent, double-click the Agent icon from its folder or program group. Alternatively, if you use Windows 95, click the Start button and then choose Programs and one of the Agent options that appear.

For information about how to use Free Agent (and its even better commercial version, Agent), see Chapter 11 in this book. You can also learn more about Free Agent by clicking its Help menu and then choosing Contents to launch its online manual and by visiting the Free Agent Web site, at http:// www.forteinc.com.

HotDog

HotDog, from Sausage Software, is a powerful but easy-to-use Windows shareware program that helps you to create Web pages. The Windows 3.1 edition of the program is HotDog 16 Version 2.54; the Windows 95 edition is HotDog Professional Version 3.0.19.

The only way you have interacted with the World Wide Web so far is probably by surfing Web pages other people have created. The Web also offers you the option of publishing your _own_ Web pages, however. Doing so enables you to reach out and communicate with the tens of millions of people on the Net.

If the prospect of publishing your own material on the Web sounds appealing — and if you're willing to teach yourself some technical stuff involving the way Web pages are put together — you may enjoy using a program such as HotDog to compose your pages. HotDog enables you to create pages visually, instead of requiring you to become a whiz in the use of Hypertext Markup Language, or _HTML,_ which is the programming language in which Web pages are built.

To install HotDog, follow Steps 1 through 7 in the "Installing the Programs" section, earlier in this appendix. When you see the main menu, click the Communicating category, then the HotDog option, and then the appropriate Install button for your version of Windows. To complete the installation, follow the prompts that appear on-screen.

To run the program, double-click its icon from its folder or program group. Alternatively, if you're using Windows 95, click the Start button, choose Programs, and then click the HotDog icon. You initially see several areas of the screen that offer help, including a HotDog Handy Hints dialog box (only in the Windows 95 version); a Welcome to HotDog! box with big, friendly picture buttons; and a Help menu with several useful options.

mIRC

mIRC 4.72 is an excellent Windows program from the shareware author Khaled Mardam-Bey. Using mIRC, you can participate in Internet Relay Chat (*IRC*), a worldwide system in which you receive messages over the Internet within seconds of when other people type them and vice versa.

Because thousands of folks at a time use this Internet feature, to prevent total chaos, IRC is divided into groups of people, or *channels*. When you participate in a discussion, you see the messages from everyone in your channel, and they all see your messages. It's similar to having a global party line on your computer screen.

To install mIRC, follow Steps 1 through 7 in the "Installing the Programs" section, earlier in this appendix. When you see the main menu, click the Communicating category, then the mIRC option, and then the appropriate Install button for your version of Windows. To complete the installation, follow the prompts that appear on-screen.

To run mIRC, double-click the mIRC icon from its folder or program group. Alternatively, if you use Windows 95, click the Start button, and then choose Programs⇨mIRC 4.72⇨mIRC.

To learn how to use mIRC, click the program's More Info button in the first window that appears. After you're past the opening window, you can get more information by pressing F1, clicking a Help button that looks like a life preserver, or choosing Help⇨Contents from the menu.

For more facts about IRC, visit our IRC information Web page, at http://net.dummies.net/irc. The mIRC Web page, at http://www.mirc.co.uk, is a good source of information too.

NetTerm

NetTerm 4.0.2, from InterSoft International, Inc., is a Telnet shareware program for Windows. You can use this program to connect to other computers over the Internet when more modern routes (such as the World Wide Web) aren't feasible or available.

Telnet lets you log on to another computer as though your PC were a terminal attached to that computer. In the old days (way back in 1992), Telnet was the way to get lots of information; for example, libraries let you Telnet into their card catalogs.

To install NetTerm, follow Steps 1 through 7 in the "Installing the Programs" section, near the beginning of this appendix. When you see the main menu, click the Communicating category, then the NetTerm option, and then the appropriate Install button for your version of Windows. To complete the installation, follow the prompts that appear on-screen.

To run the program, make sure that your modem is turned on and your phone line is hooked in, and then double-click the NetTerm icon in your folder or program group.

To learn more, visit our Telnet information Web page, at `http://net.dummies.net/telnet`, and visit the NetTerm Web site, at `http://starbase.neosoft.com/~zkrr01`.

Paint Shop Pro

Paint Shop Pro, from JASC, Inc., is a multipurpose graphics tool for Windows. Using this superb shareware program, you can view images in virtually any graphics format you're likely to encounter on the Internet. In addition, you can edit and crop images, convert images from one file format to another, and even create pictures from scratch, all of which can be useful in creating your own World Wide Web pages. The CD-ROM in the back of this book installs Paint Shop Pro Version 4.12 for Windows 95 and Version 3.11 for Windows 3.1.

To install Paint Shop Pro, follow Steps 1 through 7 in the "Installing the Programs" section, near the beginning of this appendix. When you see the main menu, click the Working Offline category, then the Paint Shop Pro option, and then the appropriate Install button for your version of Windows. To complete the installation, follow the prompts that appear on-screen.

To run Paint Shop Pro, double-click the program's icon in its folder or program group. Alternatively, if you use Windows 95, click the Start button, and then choose Programs⇨Paint Shop Pro⇨Paint Shop Pro 4.

For more information about Paint Shop Pro, click the floating question-mark icon on the program's toolbar, or choose Help⇔Help Topics from the menu. Also, visit the program's Web site, at `http://www.jasc.com/psp.html`.

ThunderBYTE Anti-Virus

The Windows shareware utility ThunderBYTE Anti-Virus 7.07, from TCT-ThunderBYTE, Inc., detects a nasty type of program known as a virus. Broadly defined, a *virus* is a program (typically hidden inside another, benign program) that's created to deliberately wreak havoc with computers by destroying their data.

Although the odds of encountering a virus are relatively low, it's a good idea to play it safe by scanning each new program you're about to run for the first time using a tool such as ThunderBYTE to make sure that your new software isn't housing a virus. We also recommend that you at least occasionally scan your entire hard disk for viruses. If one is detected, you can also use ThunderBYTE to eliminate the virus.

For more information about ThunderBYTE Anti-Virus, visit the program's Web site, at `http://www.thunderbyte.com`.

Trumpet Winsock

Trumpet Winsock 3.0d, from Trumpet Software International, is Windows shareware that provides the foundation TCP/IP software your PC needs to get connected to the Internet. Windows 95 comes with TCP/IP software built-in, and this type of software is usually provided automatically when you sign up with an Internet provider. If you're using Windows 3.1 and need to get a TCP/IP program on your own, though, or if you're not satisfied with the TCP/IP software you already have, you can use the excellent Trumpet Winsock program.

For more information about TCP/IP software and Trumpet Winsock, see Chapters 2, 13, and 21 in this book; you can also visit the program's Web site, at `http://www.trumpet.com.au`.

WinZip

WinZip 6.2, from Nico Mak Computing, is an invaluable Windows file-compression and -decompression shareware utility. Many files you find on the Internet are compressed (shrunken in size via special programming tricks) both to save disk storage space and to cut down on the amount of time it takes to download them. You may also occasionally receive compressed files as e-mail attachments. After you have a compressed file on your hard disk, you can use WinZip to decompress it and make it useable again.

To install WinZip, follow Steps 1 through 7 in the "Installing the Programs" section, near the beginning of this appendix. When you see the main menu, click the Working Offline category, then the WinZip option, and then the appropriate Install button for your version of Windows. To complete the installation, follow the prompts that appear on-screen.

To run WinZip, double-click the WinZip icon from its folder or program group. Alternatively, if you use Windows 95, click the Start button, and then choose Programs➪WinZip➪WinZip 6.2 32-bit.

The first time you launch WinZip, it displays a bunch of messages and configuration questions. When asked whether you want the program to operate in WinZip Wizard or WinZip Classic mode, we recommend that you choose WinZip Classic, which we consider easier to use. After you have answered all the questions, WinZip is ready to go.

For information about using WinZip, see Chapters 12 and 18 in this book, or click the program's Help menu and choose the Contents option, or double-click the program's Online Manual icon from its folder. To learn even more about WinZip, visit the program's Web site, at `http://www.winzip.com`.

WS_FTP LE

WS_FTP LE 4.04, from Ipswitch, Inc., is a free (for noncommercial use) Windows File Transfer Protocol, or *FTP,* program you can use to find files on the Net and to copy files between your PC and a computer on the Net. FTP programs were more useful before the World Wide Web took hold and made finding and downloading files a snap. FTP programs are still handy for activities not supported by the Web, however, such as uploading files and your own Web pages.

To install WS_FTP LE, follow Steps 1 through 7 in the "Installing the Programs" section, near the beginning of this appendix. When you see the main menu, click the Communicating category, then the WS_FTP LE option, and then the appropriate Install button for your version of Windows. To complete the installation, follow the prompts that appear on-screen.

To run the program, double-click the WS_FTP icon from its folder or program group. Alternatively, if you use Windows 95, click the Start button, and then choose Programs➪Ws_ftp➪WS_FTP95 LE.

For information about using WS_FTP LE, see Chapter 12. You can also learn more by clicking the Help button from the program's main window or Session Profile dialog box or by double-clicking the WS_FTP Help icon from the WS_FTP folder; you can also visit the WS_FTP LE Web site, at `http://www.ipswitch.com`.

Macintosh CD-ROM Programs

This section describes the programs on the CD-ROM that you can use with the Macintosh.

Acrobat Reader for the Macintosh

Acrobat Reader 3.0, from Adobe Systems, is a free program that enables you to view and print Portable Document Format, or *PDF,* files. The PDF format is used by many programs on the Internet for storing documentation because it supports the use of such stylish elements as assorted fonts and colorful graphics, in contrast to the standard plain-text format that doesn't allow for any special effects in a document.

Installing Acrobat Reader

To install Acrobat Reader, follow these steps:

1. **Follow Steps 1 through 7 in the "Installing the Programs" section, near the beginning of this appendix.**

   You see the main menu.

2. **Click the Working Offline category, then the Acrobat Reader option, and then the Install button.**

   The Acrobat Reader installation program is launched.

3. **Click the Continue button, and then click Accept to accept the license agreement.**

   If you're comfortable installing the program into the suggested folder name and location (which is Adobe Acrobat 3.0 on your desktop), skip to Step 5.

4. **Use the Switch Disk and Select Folder buttons to select the location and name of the folder in which you want to store the Acrobat software.**

   The name of the folder you have selected appears in the dialog box.

5. **Click the Install button.**

   A message notes that you have to restart your Macintosh after installing the software.

6. **Click the Continue button.**

   The software is copied to your hard disk. When the installation is
   completed, a dialog box instructs you to restart your Mac.

7. **Click the Restart button.**

   Your computer shuts down and then restarts. You should now see on
   your desktop an open folder that contains the Acrobat Reader files. To
   run the program, double-click the Acrobat Reader 3.0 icon from the
   folder.

You can now run Acrobat Reader at any time by opening the Acrobat Reader
folder (which, if you accepted the Installer's suggestion, is named Adobe
Acrobat 3.0) and double-clicking the Acrobat Reader 3.0 icon.

Reading documents with Acrobat Reader

After you run Acrobat Reader, follow these steps to use it:

1. **Choose File⇨Open from the menu.**

   A dialog box prompts you to select the PDF file you want to view.

2. **Use the dialog box to choose the drive and folder that contain the file
   you want.**

3. **Scroll through the list of PDF files until the one you want is listed,
   and then double-click the file's name.**

   The document appears in the Acrobat Reader window. You can now
   read it at your leisure. Use the VCR-like Forward and Backward buttons
   on the toolbar near the top of the window to move to the next or
   preceding page or to the end or beginning of the document.

4. **If you want to print the document you're viewing (which we recommend for long documents), make sure that your printer is turned on
   and has paper in its paper tray, and then choose File⇨Print from the
   menu and click OK.**

5. **If you want to open additional documents, repeat Steps 1 through 3.**

   Each document opens in its own window. You can switch to any document by clicking the window it's in or by clicking the Window menu and
   then clicking the name of the file you want (which is listed near the
   bottom of the menu).

6. **When you're done using Acrobat Reader, choose File⇨Quit from the
   menu or click the Close box in the window's upper-left corner.**

   All your PDF documents close, and the Acrobat Reader program exits.

Getting more information about Acrobat Reader

To learn more about using Acrobat Reader, view the Acrobat.pdf file that was installed in the same folder as the program. You can also get more information by visiting the Adobe Systems Web site, at `http://www.adobe.com`.

Anarchie

Anarchie 2.0, from Stairways Shareware, is a Macintosh shareware File Transfer Protocol, or *FTP,* program you can use to find files on the Net and to copy files between your Mac and a computer on the Net. FTP programs were more useful before the World Wide Web took hold and made finding and downloading files a snap. FTP programs are still handy for activities not supported by the Web, such as uploading files and your own Web pages.

To install Anarchie, follow Steps 1 through 7 in the "Installing the Programs" section, near the beginning of this appendix. When you see the main menu, click the Communicating category, then the Anarchie option, and then the Install button. To complete the installation, follow the prompts that appear on-screen. After the installation is finished, you can run the program by double-clicking the Anarchie icon from its folder.

To use Anarchie to find a file on the Internet, first click the File menu and then either the MacSearch option (for a Macintosh file) or the Archie option (for any other type of file). Type part of the name of the file you want and click the Find It button. If a matching list of files is displayed, double-click the one you're after; the file is then downloaded to your hard disk. After the file is saved, if it turns out that it's compressed, use StuffIt Expander (which is also on the CD-ROM) to decompress the file and make it usable.

For more information about downloading and uploading files, see Chapter 12 in this book; for more information about Anarchie, see its Web site, at `http://www.share.com/peterlewis/anarchie`.

AT&T WorldNet ᔆᴹ Service

For a monthly charge, the world-class Internet provider AT&T WorldNet Service supplies you with an Internet e-mail account and full access to all Internet features. AT&T WorldNet Service also provides such fine services as free technical support via an 800 number that's available 24 hours a day, seven days a week.

The CD-ROM contains four AT&T WorldNet Service sign-up kits. Three of them — for Windows 95, Windows 3.1, and the Macintosh — include a free, fully registered copy of Netscape Navigator, a powerful program you can use to send and receive e-mail, cruise the World Wide Web, and participate in online discussions via Usenet newsgroups. The fourth kit, also for Windows 95, contains instead a free copy of Microsoft Internet Explorer.

To launch an AT&T WorldNet Service sign-up kit, follow Steps 1 through 7 in the "Installing the Programs" section, earlier in this appendix. When you see the main menu, click the Connecting category, then the AT&T WorldNet Service option, and then the appropriate Install button for both your version of Windows and the program you want to use with it (Netscape Navigator or Internet Explorer). To complete the installation, follow the prompts that appear on-screen.

To use AT&T WorldNet Service, your computer needs a high-speed modem (14,400 bps is the slowest you should use) that can access a local phone line (like the one in your home). AT&T wants you to pay for the use of its services, so have your credit card handy during the installation process.

Near the end of the installation process, you're asked for a registration number. If you use AT&T long-distance service in your home, carefully enter this registration code: **L5SQIM631**. If you don't use AT&T for your long-distance calls, please use this registration code: **L5SQIM632**.

BBEdit Lite

BBEdit Lite 4.0, from Bare Bones Software, Inc., is a Macintosh freeware program that can help you to create Web pages.

The only way you have interacted with the World Wide Web so far is probably by surfing Web pages other people have created. The Web also offers you the option of publishing your *own* Web pages, however. Doing so enables you to reach out and communicate with the tens of millions of people on the Net.

If the prospect of publishing your own material on the Web sounds appealing — and if you're willing to teach yourself some technical stuff involving how Web pages are put together — you may enjoy using a program such as BBEdit Lite to compose your pages. BBEdit Lite is a text editor (that's a fancy name for a word processor without all the fancy formatting abilities) that lets punch in the content of your Web page using Hypertext Markup Language, or *HTML*, which is the programming language in which Web pages are built.

Although BBEdit Lite doesn't have many built-in tools to help you directly with HTML programming codes, some industrious people have created a few tools that can make your HTML programming much easier. Drop by the Bare Bones Web site, at `http://www.barebones.com/freeware.html` and search the page for HTML extensions you can download.

To install BBEdit Lite, follow Steps 1 through 7 in the "Installing the Programs" section, near the beginning of this appendix. When you see the main menu, click the Communicating category, then the BBEdit Lite option, and then the Install button. To complete the installation, follow the prompts that appear on-screen. You can then run the program by double-clicking the BBEdit Lite 4.0 icon from its folder.

Disinfectant

The free Macintosh utility Disinfectant 3.6, from the shareware author John Norstad, detects a nasty type of program known as a virus. Broadly defined, a *virus* is a program (typically hidden inside another, benign program) that's created to deliberately wreak havoc with computers by destroying their data.

Although the odds of encountering a virus are relatively low, it's a good idea to play it safe by scanning each new program you're about to run for the first time using a tool such as Disinfectant to make sure that your new software isn't housing a virus. We also recommended that you at least occasionally scan your entire hard disk for viruses. If one is detected, you can also use Disinfectant to eliminate the virus. Disinfectant can't detect the recent macro viruses in Word documents or viruses created with Apple HyperCard.

For more information about Disinfectant, visit the program's Web site, at `http://charlotte.acns.nwu.edu/jln/jln`.

DropStuff with Expander Enhancer

DropStuff with Expander Enhancer 4.0 (from Aladdin Systems, Inc.) is a Macintosh shareware utility that boosts the capabilities of StuffIt Expander (see the section "StuffIt Expander," near the end of this appendix) in four ways:

- ✔ It enables StuffIt Expander to deal with a much wider ranger of compressed file formats. After you have installed both programs, you're all set to handle virtually any compressed file you encounter.

- ✔ It makes StuffIt Expander decompress files as much as five times faster on the Power Macintosh.

✔ It enables you to compress and decompress files directly from any program you're using that's written to support StuffIt Expander.

✔ It lets you easily compress files and folders. Specifically, if you use your mouse to drag and drop a file or folder on the DropStuff with Expander Enhancer icon, the program automatically creates a compressed version of the file or folder in the same window from which you dragged.

To install DropStuff with Expander Enhancer, follow Steps 1 through 7 in the "Installing the Programs" section, near the beginning of this appendix. When you see the main menu, click the Working Offline category, then the DropStuff with Expander Enhancer option, and then the Install button. To complete the installation, follow the prompts that appear on-screen. DropStuff with Expander Enhancer then runs automatically whenever StuffIt Expander is activated.

For more information about decompressing files, see Chapters 12 and 18 in this book. For more information about both StuffIt Expander and DropStuff with Expander Enhancer, visit the Web site of these two programs, at `http://www.aladdinsys.com`.

Eudora Light

Eudora Light 3.0.1, from Qualcomm, Inc., is a free but powerful electronic mail program. If you have an Internet e-mail account, you can use Eudora Light to send e-mail to and receive it from any of the tens of millions of other people around the world who are connected to the Net. Because Eudora Light also lets you attach files to e-mail, you can use the program to transmit electronic pictures, sound clips, or any other type of data stored in files.

To install Eudora Light, follow Steps 1 through 7 in the "Installing the Programs" section, near the beginning of this appendix. When you see the main menu, click the Communicating category, then the Eudora Light option, and then the Install button. To complete the installation, follow the prompts that appear on-screen.

To run the program, double-click the Eudora Light 3.0.1 icon from its folder. For information about how to use Eudora Light (and its even more capable commercial version, Eudora Pro), see Chapters 8 and 9. You can also choose options from its Help menu and visit its Web site, at `http://www.eudora.com`.

FreePPP

FreePPP 2.5, from Rockstar Studios, is Macintosh shareware that provides the foundation TCP/IP software your computer needs to get connected to the Internet. This type of software is usually provided automatically when you sign up with an Internet provider. (For example, FreePPP is bundled with the AT&T WorldNet Service sign-up kit for the Macintosh included on the CD-ROM.) If you lack TCP/IP software, however, or if you're not satisfied with the software you have, try using the excellent FreePPP program instead.

For more information about TCP/IP software and FreePPP, see Chapters 2, 13, and 21 in this book; you can also visit the program's Web site, at `http://www.rockstar.com/ppp.shtml`.

GraphicConverter

The Macintosh program GraphicConverter 2.6, by the shareware author Thorsten Lemke, enables you to view images in virtually any graphics format you're likely to encounter on the Net. In addition, it can convert the most common Windows, DOS, Amiga, and Atari computer images to Macintosh formats and vice versa, and it provides a rich set of image-editing options. The latter two features are especially useful if you're interested in creating your own Web pages.

To install GraphicConverter, follow Steps 1 through 7 in the "Installing the Programs" section, near the beginning of this appendix. When you see the main menu, click the Working Offline category, then the GraphicConverter option, and then the Install button. To complete the installation, follow the prompts that appear on-screen. To run the program, click the GraphicConverter icon in its folder.

For more information about GraphicConverter, double-click the Documentation icon in the program's folder.

InterNews

InterNews 2.0.2, from Moonrise Software, is a Macintosh shareware program you can use to read and participate in ongoing discussions that take place over the Internet via Usenet newsgroups. Tens of thousands of newsgroups exist, devoted to virtually every topic under the sun, ranging from knitting to high finance and from decoding DNA to dating, and InterNews is one of the best Mac programs available for accessing them. Part of this program's charm is that it's trim and quick — to operate effectively, it doesn't require a large amount of memory or a superfast Mac. In addition, because it's highly customizable, you can tailor it to your tastes.

To install InterNews, follow Steps 1 through 7 in the "Installing the Programs" section, near the beginning of this appendix. When you see the main menu, click the Communicating category, then the InterNews option, and the Install button. To complete the installation, follow the prompts that appear on-screen. To run InterNews, double-click the program's icon from its folder.

To learn more about newsgroups, see Chapter 11 in this book; for more information about InterNews, visit the program's Web site, at `http:// www.dartmouth.edu/~moonrise`.

Ircle

Ircle 2.5 is a Macintosh shareware program from MacResponse. Using Ircle, you can participate in Internet Relay Chat (*IRC*), a worldwide system that enables you to receive messages over the Internet within seconds of when other people type them and vice versa.

Because thousands of folks at a time use this Internet feature, to prevent total chaos, IRC is divided into groups of people, or *channels.* When you participate in a discussion, you see the messages from everyone in your channel, and they all see your messages. It's similar to having a global party line on-screen.

To install Ircle, follow Steps 1 through 7 in the "Installing the Programs" section, near the beginning of this appendix. When you see the main menu, click the Communicating category, then the Ircle option, and then the Install button. To complete the installation, follow the prompts that appear on-screen. To run Ircle, double-click its icon.

For more facts about IRC, visit our IRC information Web page, at `http:// net.dummies.net/irc`. For more information about Ircle, click the program's Apple menu and choose the Help option; you can also visit the Ircle Web site, at `http://www.xs4all.nl/~ircle`.

NCSA Telnet

The shareware program NCSA Telnet 2.7, from NCSA Software Development, helps you connect your Macintosh to other computers over the Internet when more modern routes (such as the World Wide Web) aren't feasible or available.

Telnet lets you log on to another computer as though your PC were a terminal attached to that computer. In the old days (way back in 1992), Telnet was the way to get lots of information; for example, libraries let you Telnet into their card catalogs.

To install NCSA Telnet, follow Steps 1 through 7 in the "Installing the Programs" section, near the beginning of this appendix. When you see the main menu, click the Communicating category, then the NCSA Telnet option, and then the Install button. To complete the installation, follow the prompts that appear on-screen.

To run the program, make sure that your modem is turned on and your phone line is hooked in, and then double-click the NCSA Telnet icon from the Telnet2.7 folder.

For even more facts, visit our Telnet information Web page, at `http://net.dummies.net/telnet`; also visit the NCSA Telnet Web site, at `http://www.ncsa.uiuc.edu/SDG/Software/ Brochure/Overview/MacTelnet.overview.html`.

StuffIt Expander

StuffIt Expander 4.0.1, from Aladdin Systems, Inc., is an invaluable file-decompression shareware utility for the Macintosh. Many files you find on the Internet are compressed — shrunken in size via special programming tricks — both to save disk storage space and to cut down on the amount of time it takes to download them. You may also occasionally receive compressed files as e-mail attachments. After you have a compressed file on your hard disk, you should use StuffIt Expander to decompress it and make it useable again.

To install the program, follow Steps 1 through 7 in the "Installing the Programs" section, near the beginning of this appendix. When you see the main menu, click the Working Offline category, then the StuffIt Expander option, and then the Install button. To complete the installation, follow the prompts that appear on-screen.

You typically run StuffIt Expander indirectly because it activates automatically when you download a compressed file or double-click a compressed file. When StuffIt has finished its work, you can toss the compressed file in the trashcan and use the normal files it generates.

Although StuffIt Expander can operate on its own, we recommend that you improve both its capabilities and its performance by also installing the complementary program DropStuff with Expander Enhancer, described in the section "DropStuff with Expander Enhancer," a little earlier in this appendix.

For more information about decompressing files, see Chapters 12 and 18 in this book. For more information about StuffIt Expander and DropStuff with Expander Enhancer, visit the Web site of these two programs, at `http://www.aladdinsys.com`.

*A **final note:*** Although some of the programs on the CD-ROM are free, most of them are shareware. As mentioned near the beginning of this appendix, shareware programs are available to you for an evaluation period, after which you're expected to either stop using them or pay for them. Sending a registration fee to a shareware publisher typically entitles you to technical support and notifications about new versions — and it also makes you feel good. Most shareware operates on the honor system, but it's just plain sensible to support the shareware concept and encourage the continued production of quality low-cost software by sending in your payment for the programs you use. You can typically get information about where to send your payment for a shareware program by checking its online help system or by visiting its Web site. When you do, tell them that John, Carol, Margy, and Hy sent you!

Glossary

ActiveX   A Microsoft standard for computer program building blocks, known as *objects*.

ADSL (Asymmetric Digital Subscriber Line)   A technology that lets you transmit data over phone lines faster — as much as 7 million bps — in one direction than in the other.

alt   Allternative hierarchy of Usenet newsgroups

AltaVista   A search engine used for finding things on the World Wide Web (see Chapter 7).

America Online (AOL)   A value-added online service that provides many services in addition to Internet access, including making airline reservations, shopping, and access to popular chat groups.

anonymous FTP   A way of using the FTP program to log on to another computer to copy files, even though you don't have an account on the other computer. When you log on, you enter `anonymous` as the username and your e-mail address as the password.

applet   A small computer program written in the Java programming language. You can download applets by using a Web browser. Applets must obey special rules that make it difficult for the programs to do damage to your computer.

archive   A single file containing a group of files that have been compressed and glommed together for efficient storage. You have to use a program such as PKZIP, tar, or StuffIt to get the original files back out.

ARPANET   The original ancestor of the Internet, funded by the U.S. Department of Defense.

article   A message someone sends to a newsgroup to be available to everyone who enters the newsgroup.

attachment   A computer file electronically stapled to an e-mail message and sent along with it.

baud   The number of electrical symbols per second that a modem sends down a phone line. Often used as a synonym for bps (bits per second). Although this term is incorrect, only 43 people on the entire planet know why or care. Named after J. M. E. Baudot, inventor of the teletype.

BBS (bulletin board system)   An electronic message system you dial up directly to read and post messages.

BCC   *B*lind *c*arbon *c*opy. BCC addressees get a copy of your e-mail without other recipients knowing about it. Considered sneaky, but okay for long mailing lists. *See also* CC.

binary file   A file that contains information that does not consist only of text. For example, a binary file might contain an archive, a picture, sounds, a spreadsheet, or a word-processing document that includes formatting codes in addition to characters.

BinHex   A file-encoding system popular among Macintosh users.

bit   The smallest unit of measure for computer data. Bits can be *on* or *off* (symbolized by 1 or 0) and are used in various combinations to represent different types of information.

bitmap   Little dots put together to make a black-and-white or color picture.

BITNET   An older network of large computers that connects to the Internet.

bounce   To return as undeliverable. If you mail a message to a bad address, it bounces back to your mailbox.

bps (bits per second)   A measure of how fast data is transmitted. Often used to describe modem speed.

browser   A super-duper, all-singing, all-dancing program that lets you read information on the World Wide Web.

byte   A group of eight bits. Computer memory is usually measured in bytes.

CC   *C*arbon *c*opy. CC addressees get a copy of your e-mail, and other recipients are informed of this if they bother to read the message header. *See also* BCC.

CCITT   The old name for *ITU-T,* the committee that sets worldwide communication standards.

channel   In IRC, a group of people chatting together. Value-added providers use channel to mean a major interest area you can get to easily, like a TV channel.

chanop   In IRC, the *chan*nel *op*erator is in charge of keeping order in a channel. The chanop can throw out unruly visitors.

chat   To talk (or type) live to other network users from any and all parts of the world. To do this on the Internet, you use Internet Relay Chat (IRC). America Online, CompuServe, and Delphi have similar services.

client   A computer that uses the services of another computer, or *server* (such as Usenet, Gopher, FTP, or the Web). If you dial in to another system, your computer becomes a client of the system you dial in to (unless you're using X Windows—don't ask.)

client/server model   A division of labor between computers. Computers that provide a service other computers can use are known as *servers*. The users are *clients*.

communications program   A program you run on your personal computer that enables you to call up and communicate with other computers. These types of programs make your computer pretend to be a terminal (that's why they're also known as *terminal programs* or *terminal emulators*).

CompuServe (CIS)   A value-added online service that provides many services in addition to Internet access, including making airline reservations, shopping, and gaining access to popular chat groups.

cookie   A small chunk of information, stored on your computer by a Web site you have visited, that's used to remind that site about you the next time you visit it.

country code   The last part of a geographic address, which indicates in which country the host computer is located, such as us for the United States.

DB-25   The style of data plug on most modems and serial ports. DB-25s are shaped like a two-inch-high, skinny letter *D* with 25 pins. Macs use a smaller, round plug.

Delphi   A value-added online service that also supports text-oriented Internet tools. Especially good for users of older computers and for the visually impaired.

dial-up networking   The Windows 95 built-in TCP/IP program for connecting to PPP or SLIP accounts (see Chapter 13).

digest   A compilation of the messages that have been posted to a mailing list during the past few days.

domain   Part of the official name of a computer on the Net — for example, dummies.net. To register a domain name, point your browser to http://www.internic.net/.

domain name server (DNS)   A computer on the Internet that translates between Internet domain names, such as `xuxa.iecc.com`, and Internet numerical addresses, such as `140.186.81.2`. Sometimes just called *name server.*

download   To copy a file from a remote computer "down" to your computer.

dummies   People who don't know everything but are smart enough to seek help. Used ironically.

duplex   The ability to send information in both directions. Just say *full* when setting up a communications program.

Elm   A full-screen UNIX mail reader. Another good one is Pine.

Eudora   A popular mail-handling program that runs on the Macintosh and under Windows.

FAQ (Frequently Asked Questions)   An article that answers questions that come up. Many newsgroups have FAQs that are posted regularly. To read the FAQs for all newsgroups, FTP to `rtfm.mit.edu`.

FIDONET   A worldwide network of bulletin-board systems (BBSs) with Internet e-mail access.

finger   A program that displays information about someone on the Net. Used as a verb, finger means the act of getting info about someone on the Net by using the finger program.

flame   To post angry, inflammatory, or insulting messages. Don't do it!

flame war   Two or more individuals engaged in a great deal of flaming.

firewall   A specially programmed computer that connects a local network to the Internet and, for security reasons, lets only certain kinds of messages in and out.

freenet   A free online system offering local communities information and limited access to the Internet.

FTP (File Transfer Protocol)   A method of transferring files from one computer to the other over the Net.

FTP server   A computer on the Internet that stores files for transmission by FTP.

gateway   A computer that connects one network with another, where the two networks use different protocols.

GIF (Graphics Interchange Format)   A patented type of graphics file originally defined by CompuServe and now found all over the Net. Files in this format end in .gif and are called GIF files or just GIFs.

gigabyte   One billion bytes or characters of data.

GKA (government key access)   A U.S. government proposal to require that encryption software include a way for the government to break the code.

Gopher   An Internet system that lets you find information by using menus.

Gopherspace   The world of Gopher menus. As you move from menu to menu in Gopher, you are said to be sailing through Gopherspace.

gov   When these letters appear as the last part of an address (in cu.nih.gov, for example), it indicates that the host computer is run by some government body, probably the U.S. federal government.

handle   A user's nickname or screen name.

header   The beginning of an e-mail message containing To and From addresses, subject, date, and other gobbledygook important to the programs that handle your mail.

hierarchy   In Usenet, the major group to which a newsgroup belongs. The seven major hierarchies are comp, rec, soc, sci, news, misc, and talk. (See Chapter 11 for more information.)

home page   A Web page about a person or organization (see Chapters 5 and 6).

host   A computer on the Internet.

hostname   The name of a computer on the Internet (chico.iecc.com, for example).

HTML (Hypertext Markup Language)   The language used to write pages for the World Wide Web. This language lets the text include codes that define fonts, layout, embedded graphics, and hypertext links. Don't worry — you don't have to know anything about it to use the World Wide Web.

HTTP (Hypertext Transfer Protocol)   The way in which World Wide Web pages are transferred over the Net.

HTTPS   A variant of HTTP that encrypts messages for security.

hypermedia   *See* hypertext, but think about all types of information, such as pictures, sound, and video, not just text.

hypertext   A system of writing and displaying text that enables the text to be linked in multiple ways, be available at several levels of detail, and contain links to related documents. The World Wide Web uses both hypertext and hypermedia.

IETF (Internet Engineering Task Force)   The group that develops new technical standards for the Internet.

Internet   A system by which all the computers in the world talk to each other.

Internet Explorer   A popular Web browser from Microsoft that comes in Windows and Mac flavors.

Internet Phone   A program that enables you to use the Internet to talk to other people by using a microphone and speakers, thereby replacing long-distance phone calls.

Internet Relay Chat (IRC)   A system that enables Internet folks to talk to each other in real time (rather than after a delay, as with e-mail messages). (See Chapter 22.)

Internet Society   An organization dedicated to supporting the growth and evolution of the Internet. You can contact it at www.isoc.org.

InterNIC   The Internet Network Information Center, a central repository of information about the Internet. To register a domain name, point your browser to http://www.internic.net/.

interrupt character   A key or combination of keys you can press to stop whatever's happening on your computer. Common interrupt characters and keystrokes are Esc, Ctrl+C, and Ctrl+D. The usual Telnet interrupt character is Ctrl+]. Macs use ⌘+period.

intranet   A private version of the Internet that lets people within an organization exchange data using popular Internet tools, such as browsers.

ISDN (Integrated Services Digital Network)   A faster, digital phone service that operates at speeds as high as 128 kilobits per second.

ITU-T   The International Telecommunications Union committee that sets worldwide communication standards. Check out http://www.itu.int.

Java   A computer language invented by Sun Microsystems. Because Java programs can run on any modern computer, Java is ideal for delivering application programs over the Internet.

JPEG   A type of still-image file found all over the Net. Files in this format end in .jpg or .jpeg and are called JPEG (pronounced "JAY-peg") files. Stands for Joint Photographic Experts Group.

kill file   A file that tells your newsreader which newsgroup articles you always want to skip.

kilobyte   One thousand bytes or characters of data.

link   A *hypertext* connection that can take you to another document or another part of the same document. On the *World Wide Web,* links appear as text or pictures that are highlighted. To follow a link, you click the highlighted material.

Listproc   Like LISTSERV, a program that handles mailing lists (see Chapter 10).

LISTSERV   A family of programs that automatically manages mailing lists, distributing messages posted to the list, adding and deleting members, and so on, which spares the list owner the tedium of having to do it manually. The names of mailing lists maintained by LISTSERV often end with -L.

lurk   To read a Usenet newsgroup, mailing list, or chat group without posting any messages. Someone who lurks is a *lurker.* Lurking is okay, and it's much better than flaming.

Linux   A public-domain version of the UNIX operating system that runs on personal computers and is supported by a dedicated band of enthusiasts on the Internet. *See* the comp.os.linux.announce newsgroup.

Lynx   A character-based World Wide Web browser. No pictures, but it's fast.

MBone   The multicast backbone. A special Internet subnetwork that supports live video and other multimedia.

MacBinary   A file-encoding system that's popular among Macintosh users.

MacTCP   TCP/IP for the Macintosh. You can't put your Mac on the Internet without it or a newer product called Open Transport. Comes with System 7.5.

mail server   A computer on the Internet that provides mail services.

mailing list   A special type of e-mail address that remails all incoming mail to a list of *subscribers* to the mailing list. Each mailing list has a specific topic, so you subscribe to the ones that interest you (see Chapter 10).

Majordomo   Like LISTSERV, a program that handles mailing lists. (see Chapter 10).

megabyte   One million bytes or characters of data.

Microsoft Network, The (MSN)   A commercial online service that provides many Internet services, including e-mail, Usenet newsgroups, and access to the World Wide Web.

MIDI   A way to transmit music as actual notes rather than as digitized sounds. Many electronic instruments have a MIDI output.

mil   When these letters appear as the last part of an address (the zone), it indicates that the host computer is run by some part of the U.S. military.

MIME   Multipurpose Internet Mail Extensions. Used to send pictures, word-processing files, and other nontext information through e-mail.

mirror   An FTP or Web server that provides copies of the same files as another server. Mirrors spread out the load for more popular FTP and Web sites.

modem   A gizmo that lets your computer talk on the phone or cable TV. Short for *mo*dulator/*dem*odulator.

moderated mailing list   A mailing list run by a moderator.

moderated newsgroup   A newsgroup run by a moderator.

moderator   Someone who looks at the messages posted to a mailing list or newsgroup before releasing them to the public. The moderator can nix messages that are stupid, redundant, wildly off the topic, or offensive, in his or her opinion.

Mosaic   An older Web browser, now supplanted by Netscape Navigator, Microsoft Internet Explorer, and other browsers.

MPEG   A type of video file found on the Net. Files in this format end in .mpg. Stands for Motion Picture Experts Group.

MUD (Multi-User Dungeon)   Started as a Dungeons and Dragons type of game that many people can play at one time; now it's an Internet subculture. For information about joining a MUD, consult the newsgroup `rec.games.mud.announce`. (See Chapter 11.)

Netscape Navigator   A popular Web browser that comes in Windows, Mac, and UNIX flavors.

network   Computers that are connected together. Those in the same or nearby buildings are called *local area networks,* those that are farther away are called *wide area networks,* and when you interconnect networks all over the world, you get the Internet!

network computer   A computer that lacks a hard disk and gets all its data instead over a computer network, like the Internet.

newbie   A newcomer to the Internet (variant: *clueless newbie*). Now that you have read this book, of course, you're not a clueless newbie anymore!

news   A type of Usenet newsgroup that contains discussions about newsgroups themselves. Also used to refer to Usenet.

news server   A computer on the Net that receives Usenet newsgroups and holds them so that you can read them.

newsgroup   A topic area in the Usenet news system.

newsreader   A program that lets you read and respond to the messages in Usenet newsgroups.

NIC (Network Information Center)   Responsible for coordinating a set of networks so that the names, network numbers, and other technical details are consistent from one network to another. The address of the one for the United States part of the Internet is rs.internic.net.

nickname   In IRC, the name by which you identify yourself when you're chatting (see Chapter 22).

node   A computer on the Internet, also called a *host.*

objects   Data and the computer programs that work with the data, all tied up with a ribbon so that other programs can use the object without knowing what goes on inside.

packet   A chunk of information sent over a network. Each packet contains the address that it's going to and the address from which it came.

page   A document, or hunk of information, available by way of the World Wide Web. Each page can contain text, graphics files, sound files, video clips — you name it.

parity   A simple system for checking for errors when data is transmitted from one computer to another. Just say *none* when you're setting up a communications program.

password   A secret code used to keep things private. Be sure to pick one that's not crackable, preferably two randomly chosen words separated by a number or special character. Never use a single word that is in a dictionary or any proper name.

PCMCIA or PC cards   Little computer accessories, like modems, that look like fat credit cards. Used mostly in laptops.

PDF file   A method for distributing formatted documents over the Net. You need a special reader program called Acrobat, and you can get it at `http://www.adobe.com/acrobat`.

PGP (Phil's Pretty Good Privacy)   A program that lets you encrypt and sign your e-mail. Check in on `comp.security.pgp.discuss` for more information or point your Web browser to `http://web.mit.edu/network/pgp.html`.

PICS (Platform for Internet Content Selection)   A way of marking pages with ratings about what is inside. Designed to keep kids from getting at the racy stuff, but it has other applications as well.

Pine   A popular UNIX-based mail program. Pine is easy to use (for a UNIX program).

ping   A program that checks to see whether you can communicate with another computer on the Internet. It sends a short message to which the other computer automatically responds. If you can't ping another computer, you probably can't talk to it any other way either.

PKZIP   A file-compression program that runs on PCs. PKZIP creates a *ZIP file* that contains compressed versions of one or more files. To restore these files to their former size and shape, you use PKUNZIP or WinZip.

plug-in   A computer program you add to your browser to help it handle a special type of file.

POP (Post Office Protocol)   A system by which a mail server on the Net lets you pick up your mail and download it to your PC or Mac.

port number   On a networked computer, an identifying number assigned to each program that is chatting on the Net. You hardly ever have to know these numbers — the Internet programs work this stuff out among themselves.

posting   An article published on or submitted to a Usenet newsgroup or mailing list.

PPP (Point-to-Point Protocol)   A scheme for connecting your computer to the Internet over a phone line. Like *SLIP*, only better.

protocol   The agreed-on rules that computers rely on to talk among themselves. A set of signals that mean "go ahead," "got it," "didn't get it, please resend," "all done," and so on.

public key cryptography   A method for sending secret messages whereby you get two keys: a *public key* you give out freely so that people can send you coded messages and a second, *private key* that decodes them.

QuickTime   A video file format invented by Apple Computer and widely used on the Net.

RealAudio   A popular *streaming audio* file format that lets you listen to programs over the Net. You can get your very own player plug-in at `http://www.realaudio.com`.

RFC (Request for Comment)   A numbered series of documents that specify how the different parts of the Internet work. For example, RFC-822 describes the Internet e-mail message format.

router   A computer that connects two or more networks.

RSA   A popular, patented, *public key* encryption system (see Chapter 22).

RTFM (Read The Manual)   A suggestion made by people who feel that you have wasted their time by asking a question you could have found the answer to by looking it up in an obvious place. A well-known and much-used FTP site named `rtfm.mit.edu` contains FAQs for all Usenet newsgroups.

serial port   The place on the back of your computer where you plug in your modem. Also called a *communications port* or *comm port*.

server   A computer that provides a service to other computers (known as *clients*) on a network.

shareware   Computer programs that are easily available for you to try with the understanding that, if you decide to keep the program, you will send the requested payment to the shareware provider specified in the program. This is an honor system. A great deal of good stuff is available, and people's voluntary compliance makes it viable.

Shockwave   A standard for viewing interactive multimedia on the Web. For more information about Shockwave and for a copy of the program's plug-in for your browser, go to `http://www.macromedia.com/shockwave/`.

SLIP (Serial Line Internet Protocol)   A software scheme for connecting your computer to the Internet over a serial line. *See also* PPP.

smiley   A combination of special characters that portray emotions, such as :-) or :-(. Although hundreds have been invented, only a few are in active use (see Chapter 8).

SMTP (Simple Mail Transfer Protocol)   The misnamed method by which Internet mail is delivered from one computer to another.

soc   A type of newsgroup that discusses social topics, covering subjects from `soc.men` to `soc.religion.buddhist` to `soc.culture.canada`.

socket   A logical "port" a program uses to connect to another program running on another computer on the Internet. You may have an FTP program using sockets for its FTP session, for example, and have Eudora connect by way of another socket to get your mail.

spam   The act of posting inappropriate commercial messages to a large number of unrelated, uninterested Usenet newsgroups or mailing lists. It's antisocial and ineffective.

SSL (Secure Socket Layer)   A Web-based technology that lets one computer verify another's identity and allow secure connections.

stop bits   Just say *1* when you're setting up your communications software.

streaming audio   A system for sending sound files over the Net that begins playing the sound before the sound file finishes downloading, letting you listen with minimal delay. RealAudio is the most popular.

StuffIt   A file-compression program that runs on Macs. StuffIt creates an SIT file that contains compressed versions of one or more files. To restore one of those files to its former size and shape, you use UnStuffIt.

surf   To wander around the World Wide Web, looking for interesting stuff.

T1   A telecommunications standard that carries 24 voice calls or data at 1.44 million bps over a pair of telephone lines.

TCP/IP   The system networks use to communicate with each other on the Net. It stands for Transmission Control Protocol/Internet Protocol.

Telnet   A program that lets you log in to some other computers on the Net (see Chapter 22).

terminal In the olden days, a terminal consisted of a screen, a keyboard, and a cable that connected it to a computer. If you have a personal computer and you want to connect to a big computer somewhere, you can run a program that makes it *pretend* to be a brainless screen and keyboard — the program is called a *terminal emulator, terminal program,* or *communications program.*

text file A file that contains only textual characters, with no special formatting, graphical information, sound clips, video, or what-have-you. Because most computers, other than some IBM mainframes, store their text by using a system of codes named ASCII, these files are also known as *ASCII text files. See also* Unicode.

thread An article posted to a Usenet newsgroup, together with all the follow-up articles, the follow-ups to follow-ups, and so on.

Trumpet A widely used newsreader program that runs on Windows.

UDP (User Datagram Protocol) A system used for applications to send quick, one-shot messages to each other.

Unicode An up-and-coming extension of ASCII that attempts to include the characters of all active written languages.

UNIX An operating system developed by AT&T.

upload To put your stuff on somebody else's computer.

URL (Uniform Resource Locator) A standardized way of naming network resources, used for linking pages together on the World Wide Web.

URN (Uniform Resource Name) A Web page name that doesn't change when the page is moved to a different computer, proposed as a solution to the broken-link problem.

Usenet A system of thousands of newsgroups. You read the messages by using a *newsreader.*

uucp An elderly and creaky mail system still used by a few UNIX systems. Uucp stands for *UNIX-to-UNIX copy.*

uuencode/uudecode A method of encoding files to make them suitable for sending as e-mail. When the message arrives, the recipient can run *uudecode* to turn it back into the original file. Older and cruddier than MIME.

viewer A program used by Internet client programs to show you files that contain stuff other than text.

virtual reality A 3-D visual computer simulation that responds to your inputs so realistically that you feel you are inside another world.

VRML   A language used for building *virtual reality* pages on the Web.

VT100   The model number of a terminal made in the early 1980s by Digital Equipment Corporation. Many computers on the Internet expect to talk to VT-100-type terminals, and many communication programs can pretend to be (emulate) VT-100 terminals.

WAV file   A popular Windows format for sound files (.wav files) found on the Net.

Web page   A document available on the World Wide Web.

Winsock   A standard way for Windows programs to work with TCP/IP. You use it if you directly connect your Windows PC to the Internet, either with a permanent connection or with a modem by using PPP or SLIP.

WinZip   A file-compression program that runs under Windows. It reads and creates a ZIP file that contains compressed versions of one or more files.

World Wide Web (WWW)   A hypermedia system that lets you browse through lots of interesting information. The Web is the central repository of humanity's information in the 21st century.

X.400   A cumbersome, *ITU*-blessed mail standard that competes with the Internet SMTP mail standard.

X.500   A standard for white-pages e-mail directory services. It isn't quite as broken as X.400, and Internet people are trying to use it.

XON/XOFF   One way for your computer to say "Wait a sec!" when data is coming in too fast; the other way is usually called *hardware flow control.*

Xmodem   A protocol for sending files between computers; second choice after Zmodem.

Yahoo!   A set of Web pages that provide a subject-oriented guide to the World Wide Web. Go to the URL http://www.yahoo.com/.

ZIP file   A file that has been compressed using PKZIP, WinZip, or a compatible program. To get at the files in a ZIP file, you usually need WinZip, PKUNZIP, or a compatible program.

Zmodem   A protocol for sending files between computers; one of the best to use, if it's available.

zone   The last part of an Internet host name. If the zone is two letters long, it's the country code in which the organization that owns the computer is located. If the zone is three letters long, it's a code indicating the type of organization that owns the computer. (See Chapter 2.)

Index

Introducing
AT&T WorldNet^{SM} Service

A World of Possibilities...

With AT&T WorldNet^{SM} Service, a world of possibilities awaits you. Discover new ways to stay in touch with the people, ideas, and information that are important to you at home and at work.

Make travel reservations at any time of the day or night. Access the facts you need to make key decisions. Pursue business opportunities on the AT&T Business Network. Explore new investment options. Play games. Research academic subjects. Stay abreast of current events. Participate in online newsgroups. Purchase merchandise from leading retailers. Send e-mail.

All you need are a computer with a mouse, a modem, a phone line, and the software enclosed with this mailing. We've taken care of the rest.

If You Can Point and Click, You're There

Finding the information you want on the Internet with AT&T WorldNet Service is easier than you ever imagined it could be. That's because AT&T WorldNet Service integrates a specially customized version of popular Web browser software with advanced Internet directories and search engines. The result is an Internet service that sets a new standard for ease of use — virtually everywhere you want to go is a point and click away.

We're with You Every Step of the Way,
24 Hours a Day, 7 Days a Week.

Nothing is more important to us than making sure that your Internet experience is a truly enriching and satisfying one. That's why our highly trained customer service representatives are available to answer your questions and offer assistance whenever you need it — 24 hours a day, 7 days a week. To reach AT&T WorldNet Customer Care, call **1-800-400-1447**.

Safeguard Your Online Purchases

By registering and continuing to charge your AT&T WorldNet Service to your AT&T Universal Card, you'll enjoy peace of mind whenever you shop the Internet. Should your account number be compromised on the Net, you won't be liable for any online transactions charged to your AT&T Universal Card by a person who is not an authorized user.*

*Today cardmembers may be liable for the first $50 of charges made by a person who is not an authorized user, which will not be imposed under this program as long as the cardmember notifies AT&T Universal Card of the loss within 24 hours and otherwise complies with the Cardmember Agreement. Refer to Cardmember Agreement for definition of authorized user.

Minimum System Requirements

To run AT&T WorldNet Service on an IBM-compatible personal computer, you need

- An IBM-compatible personal computer with a 386 processor or better
- Microsoft Windows 3.1*x* or Windows 95
- 8MB RAM (16MB or more recommended)
- 11MB of free hard disk space
- 14.4 Kbps (or faster) modem (28.8 Kbps is recommended)
- A standard phone line

Macintosh users with 68030 processors or higher, and non-PCI-equipped Power Macs need

- System software version 7.1 or higher (System 7.5 recommended for Power Mac users)
- 8MB of RAM
- 12MB of free hard disk space
- 14.4 Kpbs (or faster) modem (28.8 Kbps is recommended)
- A standard phone line

Users of PCI-equipped Power Macintosh and compatibles, users of PowerBook 5300 models, and users of DOS-compatibility software or Connectix Ram Doubler need

- System 7.5.5 or higher
- Open Transport 1.1 or higher
- 8MB of RAM (16MB recommended for better performance)
- 12MB of free hard disk space
- 14.4 Kbps (or faster) modem (28.8 Kbps is recommended)
- A standard phone line

To upgrade to System 7.5.5, obtain System 7.5 Update 2.0 package and System 7.5.5 Update package, both from Apple Computer. You need to install System 7.5 Update 2.0 before installing System 7.5.5 Update.

System software updates can be obtained from Apple Computer by phone at 1-800-294-6617 (Canada 1-800-361-6075) or via Apple's download FTP site at: ftp://ftp.support.apple.com/pub/apple_sw_updates/US/Macintosh/System.

Installation Tips and Instructions

- If you have other Web browsers or online software, please consider uninstalling them according to the vendor's instructions.
- At the end of installation, you may be asked to restart your computer. Don't attempt the registration process until you have done so.
- If you are experiencing modem problems trying to dial out, try different modem selections, such as Hayes Compatible. If you still have problems, please call Customer Care at **1-800-400-1447**.
- If you are installing AT&T WorldNet Service on a computer with local area networking, please contact your LAN administrator for setup instructions.
- Follow the initial start-up instructions given to you by the vendor product you purchased. (See the appendix of *The Internet For Dummies,* Starter Kit Edition.) These instructions will tell you how to start the installation of AT&T WorldNet Service Software.
- Follow the on-screen instructions to install AT&T WorldNet Service Software on your computer.

When you have finished installing the software, you may be prompted to restart your computer. Do so when prompted.

Setting Up Your WorldNet Account

The AT&T WorldNet Service Program group/folder will appear on your Windows desktop or Mac's hard disk.

- Double-click on the WorldNet Registration icon. (Mac users, double-click the Account Setup icon.)
- Follow the on-screen instructions and complete all the stages of registration.

After all the stages have been completed, you'll be prompted to dial into the network to complete the registration process. Make sure your modem and phone line are not in use.

Registering with AT&T WorldNet Service

Once you have connected with AT&T WorldNet online registration service, you will be presented with a series of screens that confirm billing information and prompt you for additional account set-up data.

The following is a list of registration tips and comments that will help you during the registration process.

I.   Use one of the following registration codes, which can also be found in the appendix of *The Internet For Dummies,* Starter Kit Edition: L5SQIM631 if you are an AT&T Long-Distance residential customer or L5SQIM632 if you use another long-distance phone company.
II. We advise that you use all lowercase letters when assigning an e-mail ID and security code, since they are easier to remember.
III. Choose a special "security code" that you will use to verify who you are when you call Customer Care.
IV. If you make a mistake and exit the registration process prematurely, all you need to do is click on "Create New Account." Do not click on "Edit Existing Account."
V.   When choosing your local access telephone number, you will be given several options. Please choose the one nearest to you. Please note that calling a number within your area does not guarantee that the call is free.

Connecting to AT&T WorldNet Service

When you have finished registering with AT&T WorldNet Service, you are ready to make online connections.

- Make sure your modem and phone line are available.
- Double-click on the AT&T WorldNet Service icon.

Follow these steps whenever you wish to connect to AT&T WorldNet Service.

Choose the Plan That's Right for You

If you're an AT&T Long Distance residential customer signing up until March 31, 1997, you can experience this exciting new service for 5 free hours a month for one full year. Beyond your 5 free hours, you'll be charged only $2.50 for each additional hour. Just use the service for a minimum of one hour per month. If you intend to use AT&T WorldNet Service for more than 5 hours a month, consider choosing the plan with unlimited hours for $19.95 per month.* After March 31, 1997, please call 1-800-400-1447 for the current plan.

If you're not an AT&T Long Distance residential customer, you can still benefit from AT&T quality and reliability by starting with the plan that offers 3 hours each month and a low monthly fee of $4.95. Under this plan, you'll be charged $2.50 for each additional hour, or AT&T WorldNet Service can provide you with unlimited online access for $19.95 per month. It's entirely up to you.

AT&T

Explore our AT&T WorldNet Service Web site at http://www.att.com/worldnet
Over 200 local access telephone numbers throughout the U.S.

IDG BOOKS WORLDWIDE LICENSE AGREEMENT

Important — read carefully before opening the software packet. This is a legal agreement between you (either an individual or an entity) and IDG Books Worldwide, Inc. (IDG). By opening the accompanying sealed packet containing the software disc, you acknowledge that you have read and accept the following IDG License Agreement. If you do not agree and do not want to be bound by the terms of this Agreement, promptly return the book and the unopened software packet(s) to the place you obtained them for a full refund.

1. <u>License</u>. This License Agreement (Agreement) permits you to use one copy of the enclosed Software program(s) on a single computer. The Software is in "use" on a computer when it is loaded into temporary memory (i.e., RAM) or installed into permanent memory (e.g., hard disk, CD-ROM, or other storage device) of that computer.

2. <u>Copyright</u>. The entire contents of this disc and the compilation of the Software are copyrighted and protected by both United States copyright laws and international treaty provisions. You may only (a) make one copy of the Software for backup or archival purposes or (b) transfer the Software to a single hard disk, provided that you keep the original for backup or archival purposes. The individual programs on the disc are copyrighted by the authors of each program respectively. Each program has its own use permissions and limitations. To use each program, you must follow the individual requirements and restrictions detailed for each in the appendix in this Book. Do not use a program if you do not want to follow its Licensing Agreement. None of the material on this disc or listed in this Book may ever be distributed, in original or modified form, for commercial purposes.

3. <u>Other Restrictions</u>. You may not rent or lease the Software. You may transfer the Software and user documentation on a permanent basis provided you retain no copies and the recipient agrees to the terms of this Agreement. You may not reverse engineer, decompile, or disassemble the Software except to the extent that the foregoing restriction is expressly prohibited by applicable law. If the Software is an update or has been updated, any transfer must include the most recent update and all prior versions. Each shareware program has its own use permissions and limitations. These limitations are contained in the individual license agreements that are on the software disc. The restrictions include a requirement that after using the program for a period of time specified in its text, the user must pay a registration fee or discontinue use. By opening the package which contains the software disc, you will be agreeing to abide by the licenses and restrictions for these programs. Do not open the software package unless you agree to be bound by the license agreements.

Installing the CD

To get started with the *Internet For Dummies,* Starter Kit Edition, CD-ROM, follow these steps:

1. **Insert the CD-ROM into your CD-ROM drive. Be careful to touch only the edges of the CD-ROM.**

   If you're using Windows 95, the CD-ROM's Installer program should start running automatically in a moment and display a license agreement. If this occurs, skip to Step 6.

2. **If you're using a Macintosh, double-click the CD icon on the desktop (if necessary). Next, double-click the icon called Internet FD Starter Kit in the window and then skip to Step 6.**

   If you're using Windows 3.1, from Program Manager, choose File⇨Run.

   If you're using Windows 95 but the Installer program didn't run automatically, click the Start button and choose Run.

3. **In the Run dialog box, type** d:\INSTALL. **If your CD-ROM isn't drive D, type the appropriate letter for your drive.**

4. **Press Enter or click OK.**

   A tiny program on the CD creates a program group called IDG Books Worldwide in your Program Manager or Start button, depending on your version of Windows.

5. **Windows 95 users: Click the Start button and choose Programs⇨IDG Books Worldwide⇨The Internet For Dummies Starter Kit CD to start the Installer program.**

   Windows 3.1 users: Double-click the IDG Books Worldwide icon in Program Manager and double-click The Internet For Dummies Starter Kit CD icon to start the Installer program.

6. **Read the license agreement. When you're ready, click the Accept button.**

For details on using the software included with this CD, see the "Installing the Programs on the CD-ROM" appendix in the book.